Dux via

Coronata fides

prudens simplicitas

The golden grove

GOLDEN GROVE

The Seat of the Earl of Carbery in Carmarthenshire

The
Golden Grove

The
GOLDEN GROVE

SELECTED PASSAGES FROM THE
SERMONS AND WRITINGS OF

Jeremy Taylor

Edited by

Logan Pearsall Smith

With a Bibliography of the Works
of Jeremy Taylor by

ROBERT GATHORNE-HARDY

OXFORD
At the Clarendon Press
M CM XXX

OXFORD UNIVERSITY PRESS
AMEN HOUSE, E.C. 4
LONDON EDINBURGH GLASGOW
LEIPZIG NEW YORK TORONTO
MELBOURNE CAPETOWN BOMBAY
CALCUTTA MADRAS SHANGHAI
HUMPHREY MILFORD
PUBLISHER TO THE
UNIVERSITY

Printed in Great Britain

31 — 3379

CONTENTS

Contents.

Contents.   vii

viii   **Contents.**

Contents.

LIST OF ILLUSTRATIONS

NOTE

THE text of the passages in this volume is taken from the first editions of the works in which they appear. There is, however, one exception, the *Sermon at the Funeral of the Archbishop of Armagh*, where the third edition has been made use of, as the earlier editions are imperfect. A few obvious misprints in the text have been corrected.

In editing Jeremy Taylor's works Bishop Heber identified a very large number of Taylor's quotations from the classics and the Church Fathers. These references were revised and corrected and added to by the Rev. Charles Eden in subsequent editions, and I have availed myself of many of their notes, marking them [H] to show their derivation. Mr. Edward Bensly—the greatest of living authorities on these matters—has very kindly traced for me to their sources a number of other quotations.

I am greatly obliged to Mr. Robert Gathorne-Hardy for allowing me to print in this volume his very full bibliography of Jeremy Taylor's works.

The frontispiece is from the first edition of *The Golden Grove* (1655), the name, however, of that residence being added from the reproduction of this print of Hollar's on the half-title in the *Polemical and Moral Discourses* (1657). The portrait of Jeremy Taylor (facing p. xviii) is from the frontispiece of that volume.

L. P. S.

INTRODUCTION

OUR Romantic critics, Coleridge and Lamb and Hazlitt, rendered an important service to English letters by their re-discovery of many old English writers who had fallen out of fashion. They saw, however, these favourites of theirs, these old divines and dramatists, looming somewhat larger than life in the misty past, and often praised them with more zeal than cool discrimination. There is no one perhaps whose fame has been more affected by this splendid injustice than that seventeenth-century prelate and controversial writer, Jeremy Taylor. Coleridge, to whom he was an object of almost unbounded admiration, extolled his 'great and lovely mind'; and comparing him more than once with Shakespeare, placed him with Shakespeare and Milton and Bacon among the four great geniuses of our older literature.[1]

Coleridge inspired Charles Lamb, as Lamb tells us in one of his letters, with this 'LOVE of Jeremy Taylor', which led him to declare that Taylor 'has more and more beautiful imagery, . . . more knowledge and description of human life and manners than any prose book in the language: he has more delicacy and sweetness than any mortal, the "gentle" Shakespeare hardly excepted'.[2] Hazlitt equalled

---

[1] Coleridge's *Table Talk* (Oxford, 1917), p. 110. Elsewhere Coleridge writes: 'Learning, fancy, discursive intellect, *tria juncta in uno*, and of each enough to have alone immortalized a man he had. . . . Images, conceptions, notions, such as leave him but one rival, Shakespeare, there were' (*Literary Remains*, 1838, vol. iii, p. 333). In one of his letters Coleridge describes Jeremy Taylor as 'a miraculous combination of erudition, broad, deep and omnigenous; of logic subtle as well as acute, and as robust as agile, of psychological insight, so fine and yet so secure!' 'I believe', he adds, 'such a complete man hardly shall we meet again' (*Letters*, 1895, p. 640).

[2] Letter to Robert Lloyd, 6 Apr. 1801.

Coleridge and Lamb in his enthusiasm; 'when the name of
Jeremy Taylor is no longer remembered with reverence',
he declared, 'genius will have become a mockery, and
virtue an empty shade'.[1] These are indeed high praises,
and they come to us from sources which we cannot disregard. Any one however who, inspired by them, might
undertake to read the massive tomes of this 'Shakespeare
of divines',[2] as he has been often called, is likely to
meet with no small disappointment. Jeremy Taylor's
works, which, in their modern reprint, fill nine closely-
printed volumes, belong almost altogether to that class of
theological, hortatory, and devotional writing which has
now but little interest, save for special students of religious
history. He wrote for his own age, but the concerns of
that age are no longer ours; the controversies in which he
engaged have been almost forgotten; the doctrines he expounded, the ideals of piety and religion he upheld, have
changed their aspect, and have been stated in other terms;
his exhortations and denunciations fall but faintly upon
our ears. A few fine passages in prose anthologies, a few
sentences in his praise from Coleridge and Lamb and
Hazlitt, preserve his fame, but it is a fame at second hand,
a borrowed glory, and one that seems to be waning with
the years.

It is no superfluous task for a modern student to fix his
attention now and then on the fading splendours of these
ancient reputations. Although he may hardly hope to restore their pristine lustre to such writers, he may yet find

---

[1] *Lectures Chiefly on the Dramatic Literature of the Age of Elizabeth* (1820),
p. 314.
[2] The phrase is William Mason's, though it has been attributed to Gray.
See Mason's letter to Gray, of 8 Jan. 1761. Gray's *Letters*, ed. Tovey,
vol. ii, p. 191.

elements in their work which are of enduring value; and by disengaging these from the dead matter which surrounds them, and calling attention to their quality and interest, he may help to keep alive the renown of these 'ever-memorable' authors, whose names are famous, but whose works are no longer read. Literature, moreover, has its outskirts, its environing regions, where many of the streams arise which enrich its soil; there are orators like Burke, who, though not primarily men of letters, must be counted among them, and especially do the contributions to English literature of the great divines of the golden age of the English Church deserve all the attention—if not quite all the praise—which has been given to them by our great English critics.

Jeremy Taylor has been fortunate, not only in his critics, but in his biographers as well. The account of his life which Reginald Heber, afterwards Bishop of Calcutta, wrote as a preface to the modern reprint of Taylor's works, is full of information and acute criticism, and in 1847 the Rev. Robert Willmott published a charming and sympathetic study of his life and writings. These volumes are mainly concerned with Jeremy Taylor as a theologian and Anglican divine; Sir Edmund Gosse, his latest biographer, in his volume in the English Men of Letters Series, has not only made considerable additions to our knowledge of Jeremy Taylor's life, but, treating him as a man of letters as well as a theologian, has attempted for the first time to define his place in our literary history.

Jeremy Taylor was born at Cambridge in 1613. His father, although a barber, seems to have been a man of education, and indeed barbers then occupied a position in society somewhat above that of their modern successors.

The boy was sent to the Perse School, and in 1626 entered
Gonville and Caius College as a sizar, and was elected to
a fellowship there, which he held until 1636. In 1633 he
took holy orders, and in the following year he was given
the opportunity of preaching in London at St. Paul's,
being asked to replace an older friend who was temporarily
disabled from performing his lecturer's duty there. The
sermons of this Cambridge youth aroused considerable
enthusiasm, and, attracting the attention of Archbishop
Laud, he was taken under the protection of that prelate
and joined to the group of young ecclesiastics who were
being prepared to carry out Laud's policy in the Church.[1]
By Laud's means Jeremy Taylor was given a fellowship at
All Souls College, Oxford, in 1635. Three years later he
received a country living at Uppingham in Rutlandshire,
where he resided with his wife, for he was now married,
till the outbreak of the Civil War in 1642. As Chaplain-
in-Ordinary to Charles I, he followed for two years the
King in his campaigns; but in the beginning of 1645 he
appears in South Wales, whither he seems to have retired
with the plan of settling down to clerical work, but
where he was followed by the storm of war and was again
involved in its vortex. In the defeat of a royalist force
before Cardigan Castle he was captured by the Parliamentarians and imprisoned in that Castle, but was soon
afterwards released. His release may have been due to the
intervention of an important magnate of that region, the
Earl of Carbery, a nobleman of moderate views, who con-

---

[1] George Rust, in his sermon at Jeremy Taylor's funeral, tells us that
Laud asked the young divine to preach before him. 'His discourse', Rust
says, 'was beyond exception, and beyond imitation: yet the wise Prelate
thought him too young; but the great Youth humbly begg'd his Grace
to pardon that fault, and promis'd *if he liv'd, he would mend it.*'

trived to keep on good terms with both the warring factions. At any rate we soon find Jeremy Taylor settled close
to Golden Grove, Lord Carbery's residence in Carmarthenshire, where he joined with two other clergymen in
conducting a school, and acted also as his patron's private
chaplain. Lord Carbery, and still more Lord Carbery's
young and saintly wife, played parts of great importance
in the life of this famous clergyman; the earl gave him
protection and peace and a means of living in those times
of trouble, while in Lady Carbery he found his Muse
and directing genius. It was for her that he wrote his
devotional works, the *Holy Living* and the *Holy Dying*;
she was a devout listener to his sermons, and it was at
her suggestion that he collected them for publication.

After Lady Carbery's death, and the death of his own
wife, which occurred at about the same time, Jeremy
Taylor remained for a few years more in his Welsh retirement. He visited London, however, now and then, to
attend to the publication of his books, and made the
acquaintance there of John Evelyn, in whom he found a
devoted friend and generous patron. He preached in secret
to little congregations of the anglicans and loyalists who
were now more or less persecuted and in danger; he
married again—an illegitimate daughter, it was said, of
Charles I; he was often in financial difficulties and was
more than once imprisoned, but he seems to have retained
some sort of refuge in South Wales until the death there
of two of his children, when he finally left that remote
region for the metropolis. This was in 1657, and in the
following year he accepted, though with some reluctance,
a modest position offered him by another noble patron,
Lord Conway. This position was that of assistant lecturer

at Lisburn in Ulster; and thither Jeremy Taylor took his family to reside at Portmore, Lord Conway's residence in Ireland. But he found anything but peace among the Ulster Presbyterians; he was persecuted and again imprisoned, but managed to escape to England in 1660. The Restoration made a great change in his fortunes, and it seemed as if he were now to enjoy the legitimate reward of his devotion to the Church and Throne. Charles II appointed him Bishop of Down and Connor; he was rich and honoured, but his prosperity brought with it little besides disillusion. His see proved to be to him, as he said himself, a place of torment; the implacable Presbyterians over whom he was set in authority threatened and attacked him; a committee of Scotch spiders, he said, examined his works to find poison in them; they denounced him as an Arminian, a Socinian, a Papist, and finally forced this kindly-hearted prelate to abandon the principles of toleration he had formerly advocated. Appealing to the force of the law, Jeremy Taylor dispossessed his opponents of their livings and drove them into prison and banishment or hiding. He did not, however, long survive his triumph over his enemies, dying in 1667 at the age of fifty-four.

Our most intimate glimpses of Jeremy Taylor as a man are derived from his funeral sermon preached by his friend and faithful companion, George Rust. He was a wonder in his youth, Rust rhetorically tells us, 'and had he lived amongst the ancient Pagans, he had been usher'd into the world with a Miracle, and Swans must have daunc'd and sung at his Birth'. When at the age of twenty-one or twenty-two he appeared in the pulpit of St. Paul's, he preached, we are told, 'to the admiration and astonishment

NON MAGNA LOQ   VIMVR, SED VIVIMVS.
NIHIL OPINIONIS   GRATIA, OMNIA
CONSENTIAE   FACIAM. *Sen. de Vit.B.f.20.*

P. Lombart. Sculpsit

JEREMY TAYLOR

of his Auditory; and by his florid and youthful beauty, and sweet and pleasant air, and sublime and rais'd discourses, he made his hearers take him for some young Angel, newly descended from the Visions of Glory'.

Jeremy Taylor seems to have preserved all his life this comeliness of personal appearance, and was apparently not unaware of his good looks himself. As Bishop Heber remarks, 'few authors have so frequently introduced their own portraits, in different characters and attitudes, as ornaments to their printed works. So far as we may judge from these, he appears to have been above the middle size, strongly and handsomely proportioned, with his hair long and gracefully curling on his cheeks, large dark eyes, full of sweetness, an aquiline nose, and an open and intelligent countenance.' [1]

Such, then, is the figure of this long-afflicted clergyman which, with a touch of not unamiable vanity, gazes out at us from the frontispieces of his various volumes. He was a person, Rust tells us, 'of a most sweet and obliging Humour, of great Candour and Ingenuity', whose 'Soul was made up of Harmony, and he never spake, but he charm'd his Hearer, not only with the clearness of his Reason; but all his Words, and his very Tone, and Cadencies were strangely Musical'.

This divine of 'golden voice and angelic aspect' has left behind him a large body of theological writings, many sermons and many volumes of religious edification and controversy. His first publication was a sermon preached at Oxford in 1638 on the anniversary of the Gunpowder Plot, and dedicated to Archbishop Laud. Four years later he published a controversial defence of

[1] Life of Jeremy Taylor, in *Works* (1861), vol. i, p. cxxii.

episcopacy, *Of the Sacred Order and Offices of Episco-pacie . . . Asserted against the Aërians, and Acephali, New and Old*. In 1647 he brought out the best known of his controversial works, *A Discourse of the Liberty of Prophesying*. The book, written to show, as it states on the title-page, 'the unreasonablenes of prescribing to other mens Faith, and the Iniquity of persecuting differing opinions', is important in English religious history as being one of the first—if not the first—deliberate appeal for religious toleration. The advantages of tolera-tion were no doubt more apparent to Jeremy Taylor when he and his fellow-Anglicans were being persecuted, and when this book was written, than they appeared after-wards, when his own Church had regained power, and he himself, as one of its prelates, felt himself compelled to fall back on the secular arm to silence his opponents. But his defence of toleration was, when it was written, both sin-cere and courageous, and caused some scandal even in his own party.

His next controversial work, *Clerus Domini* (1651), was a defence of the ministerial office directed against the Puritans; in the *Real Presence* (1654) he attacked the Roman Catholic doctrine of Transubstantiation, while in the following year he managed to involve himself by his *Unum Necessarium* in controversy, not only with Puritans and Catholics, but with the orthodox divines of his own Church; for in this volume, while he scandalized the Puri-tans by his denial of the damnation of unbaptized infants, and what he called 'the horrible doctrine of absolute Reprobation', and offended the Catholics by questioning the efficacy of death-bed repentance, he also, by his views regarding Original Sin and the consequences of Adam's transgression, fell under the suspicion of Pelagianism, and was bitterly attacked by several Anglican writers. He obstinately defended his unorthodox views, however, in his next publication, *Deus Justificatus* (1656), and also in certain letters which were published in the same year. His last two important controversial works were written after he had become an Irish bishop, and were directed against the Roman Catholics. The first of these, the *Dissuasive from Popery*, was published in 1664, and was followed in 1667 by a Second Part, more than three times the length of the original volume.

With these books of controversy may be placed Jeremy Taylor's *Ductor Dubitantium*, his longest production, which was published in two immense folios in 1660. Though they contain much controversy, the main subject-matter of these volumes is what is called casuistry—that is to say, cases of conscience which are discussed and decided in accordance with certain general religious and moral considerations. Many of these questions are more curious than edifying, and concern subjects which it is not usual to discuss in print; while there are other points which it hardly seems necessary to raise, as when, for example, he discusses whether, in menacing the wicked with punishments and terrors, it would be wise for an English clergyman to warn a sinner that if he profanes the holy sacrament a tiger will meet and tear him in the churchyard; such a threat, he wisely decides, would be more likely to make the clergyman ridiculous than the sinner apprehensive. Jeremy Taylor spent many years in composing the *Ductor Dubitantium*; he regarded it as his masterpiece, and believed that it would secure his fame to succeeding ages. But succeeding ages have been otherwise preoccupied, and this 'most ele-

phantine of all theological works', as it has been called,
is completely forgotten now. This is indeed true of
all Jeremy Taylor's controversial works; those who supported his views, as well as those who opposed them, have
all vanished into oblivion; 'the Aërians and the Acephali,
new and old', have long since ceased from troubling, and
his learned expositions are left to gather dust undisturbed
on the shelves of old libraries.

Almost equal in bulk and in unreadableness are the
various devotional writings which Jeremy Taylor has left
behind him. The first and the longest of these is *The Great
Exemplar*, which was published in 1649—a life of Christ, or
rather a series of disquisitions and devout meditations on
the principal events of Christ's life as recorded in the
Gospels and the better-known traditions of the Church.
The work is entirely uncritical; it pays no regard to facts
and dates and the various narratives of the synoptists, but
is didactic, devotional, and practical in its purpose. Still
more practical are two manuals of prayers and litanies, *The
Golden Grove* (1655) and the *Collection of Offices* (1658),
which Jeremy Taylor composed as substitutes for the
Church of England Liturgy, whose use was then forbidden.

Jeremy Taylor published three other devotional works,
the *Holy Living* (1650), the *Holy Dying* (1651), and *The
Worthy Communicant* (1660). The last of these is a discourse on the nature and uses of the Lord's Supper, and
a manual of prayers and devotions preparatory to the Communion; while in the *Holy Living* and *Holy Dying*, Jeremy
Taylor covers the whole ground of the Christian religious
life as he understood it—of sin and repentance, of health
and illness, of the duties and devotions and diet of the true
Christian, and his preparation for the great and final act

of death. The title of the first of these volumes well describes its contents, 'The Rule and Exercises of Holy Living. *In which are described* the *Means* and *Instruments* of obtaining every Virtue, and the *Remedies* against every Vice, and *Considerations* serving to the resisting all Temptations'. Most of the practical as well as the controversial questions with which he was concerned Jeremy Taylor treats also in his sermons, of which sixty-four have been preserved, in addition to long passages in *The Great Exemplar*, which are plainly passages from sermons preached at various times. Such, then, in outline is the bulk of Jeremy Taylor's work; all of it is religious writing, the only partial exception being a little *Discourse of Friendship*, though this, too, was written to discuss 'how far a dear and private friendship was authorized by the principles of Christianity'. This inquiry came to him from a neighbour in South Wales, Mrs. Katherine Philips of Cardigan Priory, who, as 'The Matchless Orinda', was a famous figure in the seventeenth century, and indeed the first English poetess whose name is known to fame. Sir Edmund Gosse gives an account of this lady, who was the unquestioned Muse of South Wales, into which remote region she was the first to introduce, he tells us, 'a new sort of sentimentality, an effusive celebration of friendship between persons of the same sex, which was quite fresh in England, and which attracted a great deal of attention'.[1] She formed about her a group of *précieuses*, a society for the cultivation of 'brave friendships', to which a few men were admitted. To each member she gave a romantic name, such as Rosania, Polycrite, Poliarchus, and Regina. Is was for this sibyl of South Wales and her sisters

[1] Edmund Gosse, *Jeremy Taylor*, 1904, p. 139.

that Jeremy Taylor, or 'The noble Palaemon', as they called him, wrote this pious and eloquent justification of their cult. With the 'Matchless Orinda' and the lettered ladies of her court, with the poet Vaughan in the neighbourhood, and with Jeremy Taylor not far off, a lustre of literary distinction falls for a brief period of the seventeenth century on the south of Wales, and then fades away again from the mountains and valleys of that remote region.

Jeremy Taylor's object in writing his books of devotion was to provide Anglicans with those manuals of prayer and piety which serve so useful a purpose in the Roman Catholic communion. He seems to have followed the example and to have imitated the style of that devout soul and exquisite writer, St. François de Sales, whose volumes, although he does not mention them, must have been familiar to him. Both writers employ the same images of bees and birds, of the morning mushroom and the trembling needle; and the correspondence in method and form of Taylor's *Holy Living* and St. François's *Introduction à la vie dévote* is too close to be due to chance.

In writing of St. François de Sales, Sainte-Beuve distinguishes in the history of Christianity between two types of its divines and spiritual fathers; there are the stern, masculine teachers, like St. Peter, Athanasius, St. Dominic, Bossuet, Luther, and Calvin; and contrasted with these combative doctrinal masters, there are gentler spirits like the author of the Fourth Gospel, like St. Francis of Assisi, like Melanchthon, St. François de Sales, and Fénelon— spirits whose zeal takes the form of charity and love. As contrasted with Hooker and Andrewes, Jeremy Taylor

would represent in the English Church this class of gentle
spirits. The writing of his controversial works was for him
a painful duty; he was 'weary and toiled', he said, 'with
rowing up and down in this sea of questions'; and indeed
the angry altercations of old theologians, exuding what
Jeremy Taylor called 'the spit-venom of their poisoned
hearts', do not present an attractive or edifying spectacle.
His devotional works, however, breathe the spirit of holy
charity and joy, 'the sweetness of that fragrant piety',
which Emerson found in his writings and which, indeed,
as he said, is almost departed out of the world.[1] Such a
religion as 'leads us to a huge felicity through pleasant
ways' was Jeremy Taylor's ideal of the Christian faith;
Christianity was not so much a divine institution as 'a
divine frame and temper of spirit', 'rather a divine life
than a divine knowledge'.[2] Faith was the daughter of the
affections and the will; 'the will', he said, 'must open the
windowes, or the light of faith would not shine into
the chamber of the soule'.[3] In heaven we shall first see
and then love, but on earth we must first love, and then
the divine knowledge will be bestowed upon us. This love,
or 'Charity' in the theological sense of the word—a sense
for which we have, most unfortunately, no name in English
since 'Charity' has become so narrowed in significance—
this 'divine frame and temper of spirit', which is so much
more than benevolence, and without which, as St. Paul
said, all faith and all knowledge could profit nothing, and
the tongues of men and angels were but a tinkling cymbal—
it was this Christ-like temper of the soul which was for
Jeremy Taylor the crown of all religion, the essence of the

[1] Emerson's *Journals*, vol. iv, p. 31.   [2] No. 135.
[3] *Great Exemplar*, Part II, p. 50.

Christian faith. It was, he said, a rejoicing in God, a gladness in our neighbour's good, a pleasure in doing him good —a union, in fact, of 'joys concentred in the heart', a 'festival spirit', that filled the soul with holy joy.[1]

Like St. François de Sales and other devotional writers of his kind, Jeremy Taylor was a director of souls and a spiritual guide, especially for holy women; and just as de Sales wrote his *Introduction* for the edification of Madame de Charmoisy, Jeremy Taylor wrote his *Holy Living* and his *Holy Dying* for Lady Carbery; and these, and his other devotional works, became the favourite reading for generations of pious English gentlewomen.[2]

If Jeremy Taylor's controversial works have lost their interest for modern readers, his devotional writings stand in almost equal danger of oblivion. Pious writing of this kind soon falls out of fashion; and even the *Holy Dying*, which is considered Jeremy Taylor's masterpiece, and which has been described as one of the most beautiful prose compositions of the seventeenth century, will, I am afraid, in spite of a few splendid chapters, prove a disappointment to any one who attempts to read it through. Its lack of lucid arrangement, its wearisome reiterations of pious platitudes, its elaborate rules and tabulated exercises and lists of prayers and 'ejaculations', make it a manual of practical devotion rather than a book for general reading.

---

[1] No. 45.

[2] Lord Shaftesbury, in his *Characteristicks* (III. v. 3), speaks of Jeremy Taylor's works as being the favourite good books of the most refined and politest devotees of either sex. 'They maintain', he writes, 'the principal place in the study of almost every elegant and high divine. They stand in folios and other volumes, adorned with variety of pictures, gildings, and other decorations, on the advanced shelves or glass-cupboards of the ladies' closets.'

What, then, is to be our attitude to 'these volumes of religion and mountains of piety', these immense unreadable books which Jeremy Taylor left behind him? There is much in the literature of old theology which is of permanent interest, even to the most secular-minded of modern readers. In the works of certain theologians we find ourselves in contact with original minds of great constructive power; while there are others who appeal to us either by their profound knowledge of the human heart or by the mystical illumination and fervour of their spirits. Jeremy Taylor cannot rank, however, with the great thinkers and original minds of the Church, nor with its profound psychologists or its saints and mystics. His most fervent admirers have to admit that his mental powers were somewhat limited and commonplace, and that he failed in handling the larger questions of religious thought. Even Coleridge, with all his veneration for Jeremy Taylor, confessed that what he expressed was little more than the theological commonplace of the time; that he 'had no ideas', that in contrast with his handling of other people's opinions his own thought is 'all weather eaten, dim, useless, a *Ghost* in *marble*'.[1]

Nor as a psychologist and analyst of the human heart is Jeremy Taylor worthy of our best attention. His treatment of human conduct, as his latest biographer says, 'is too often obvious, trite and starved', nor for all its pious fragrance is there much profound mystical fervour or illumination in his practical and somewhat utilitarian piety.

What, then, are we to say about the fame of Jeremy Taylor? His popularity among his own contemporaries we can understand; the controversies in which he was

[1] Coleridge, *Letters* (1895), p. 640.

Introduction.

engaged were to them of passionate interest, and the novelty of his devotional works made a strong appeal to the piety of that pious generation. But the revival of his reputation, his second crowning, the fact that his fame was so splendidly renewed, that his ghost was called up from the shades, and enthroned, by the King-makers of our literature, almost by the side of Shakespeare, and his name endowed with a posthumous glory that has once more grown dim—this is the extraordinary fate which demands an explanation, this the almost unprecedented fortune of an ancient divine, who, to borrow one of his own phrases, once wore a mitre and is now 'a little heap of dust'.

I quote these words—which fired Hazlitt's imagination —because the best way after all of approaching the problem of Jeremy Taylor's reputation is simply to copy out one of his own phrases. For the truth is that this devotional writer, though not endowed with the other qualities of genius, did possess one gift—the gift of handling words —which is perhaps the most essential gift of a great writer, and which was possessed by him so happily and to so supreme a degree, that it is of itself enough to explain and almost to justify the splendid praises which have been so liberally heaped upon him.

A distinction is often drawn between style and matter, between a writer's thought and his expression of that thought; and this distinction, although in the end it must prove to be a superficial one, will yet be of use to us in our consideration of a writer who is read, as far as he is read at all, for his style;—his subject-matter, or what he himself thought to be his subject-matter, what he deliberately attempted to inculcate and preach, being the well-known commonplaces of morals and religion, or controversial matters of little interest to us now.

In writing of Jeremy Taylor's style we must, however distinguish between his usual and his occasionally inspired way of writing. The great bulk of his work, and all his controversial volumes, are written in a harmonious, graceful Ciceronian style which stands midway between the elaborate but somewhat clumsy prose of the Elizabethan era, and the more correct and sober medium of the eighteenth century. This easy, harmonious prose is always adequate for its purpose; it tends, however, to be somewhat impersonal, and even dry and colourless at times; and for the most part it cannot be said to surpass in merit the prose of other divines of the Restoration period. But now and then as we read him an imagination, radiant and strange, seems to unfold its wings and soar aloft; now and then this painful clergyman, as he writes down his arguments and expositions, seems to dip his pen in enchanted ink; the words begin to dance and glitter, and a splendour falls upon the illuminated page. And when this happens the effect is so surprising that it seems the result of a spell, an incantation, a kind of magic.

Matthew Arnold has written of that magic of style, which is, he says, creative, and which being creative, possesses an extraordinary value. The phrase 'magic of style' is, like the word 'creative', somewhat vague in its meaning, but since Jeremy Taylor possessed this magic and this creative power of phrasing, since it is in fact his special quality, the thing that marks him out and makes him significant, any definition of his gift must involve an attempt to explain, or at least to describe, this strange evocative power of singing words and phrases.

That great master of prose-style, Flaubert, declared that
the criticism of literature fell behind that of science and
history because it rested on no firm foundation;—what
literary critics lacked, he said, was a knowledge of the
anatomy of style, of the nature and composition of the
phrase. And indeed, when the critic is met by phrases like
many of Jeremy Taylor's, with their haunting verbal
music, he finds himself led captive by a charm and spell
which he cannot analyse, an incalculable, incommuni-
cable art neither to be imitated nor explained. Yet
there are certain ingredients in this magic, certain ways
of producing these effects of beauty, which it is possible
to observe and isolate and define. Two main elements in
style may be thus distinguished, the sound and the image,
the verbal music which enchants the ear, and the picture
which fascinates the eye. There is a certain sensuous
charm, a texture of pleasurable sensation, to be derived
from the material qualities of the medium of any art; and
Jeremy Taylor was a master of that verbal music, that
felicity of sound and rhythm, which is the basis, the funda-
mental quality, of this audible art of language. 'No sigh
for the folly of an irrevocable word'—in the harmonious
variety of the vowel sounds of such a phrase we are
charmed by this music; and above all, in what Donne calls
the 'melodious fall of words', in the beautiful close of some
great sentence, we are conscious of his mastery of sound
and rhythm—as when, for instance, in describing the passage of an eagle through the air, he says, 'as long as her
flight lasted, the Air was shaken; but there remains no path
behind her'.

This wonder-working effect of sound and rhythm can
perhaps be best noted when Jeremy Taylor expresses the

same idea in a less, and then a more, perfect form. Thus in one of his earlier works he writes, 'Lucifer and many Angels walking upon the battlements of heaven grew top-heavy and fell into the state of devils';[1] but in the *Holy Dying* he says of these fallen angels, 'They grew vertiginous and fell from the battlements of heaven'. In the contrast of these phrases, they 'grew top-heavy and fell into the state of devils'—'they grew vertiginous and fell from the battlements of heaven', we can perceive the little changes of sound and rhythm which make so much difference—and how much it is! Another instance may be given. In one passage Jeremy Taylor compares the death of virtuous men to the 'descending of ripe and wholesome fruits from a pleasant and florid tree',[2] but in another to 'ripe and pleasant fruit falling from a fair tree and gathered into baskets for the planters use'.[3] Here again, with just a slight change of cadence, a new arrangement of epithets, the miracle happens, the crystallization takes place, and the phrase becomes a phrase of enchantment. Whether results like this are chance results, or the product of careful re-writing, it is impossible to say. But if we judge by what we know about the methods of other writers, we must think it likely that prose of this kind is seldom produced without pains and labour; and that Jeremy Taylor, like his contemporary Sir Thomas Browne, was an author who wrote commonly with a current pen, but who occasionally took a poet's pains to produce richer and more splendid passages and pages.

In addition to this music of phrase, we often note in Jeremy Taylor's fine passages a singular and happy audacity of diction. Although in the instructions he issued to

[1] *The Great Exemplar*, Part III, p. 103.   [2] No. 161.   [3] No. 22.

the clergymen of his diocese in Ireland, he warned them against 'fantastical' terms and instructed them to confine themselves in their sermons to 'primitive, known and accustomed words',[1] it cannot be said the Bishop always practised what he preached. His somewhat archaic use in his adjectives of the comparative degree, as when he writes of 'the air's looser garment', or the 'wilder fringes of the fire', is so frequent as to become a mannerism, though a happy one; and not infrequently, like Milton, he adorns his page with classicisms, or uses some word of classical derivation with its original and etymological meaning. But what above all gives its unique character to the diction of his finest pages is his audacity in using unexpected words, words which, being deprived by the context of their ordinary meaning, become luminous with the remoter associations usually latent in them, as the sun's penumbra is visible when the sun is itself eclipsed. Thus Jeremy Taylor writes of the fading rose falling at last on to the 'portion of weeds and *outworn* faces', and the falling tide deserting the '*unfaithful* dwelling of the sand'. This beauty of diction in which Jeremy Taylor embalmed his thoughts was noticed by Coleridge; his very words seeming, as Coleridge wrote, 'beauties and fragments of poetry from a Euripides or Simonides'.[2] The faults of great authors, the same critic has remarked, are generally their excellencies carried to an excess, and the fullness, overflow, superfluity, which Coleridge notes in Jeremy Taylor's prose, the over-abundant piling up of clauses, words, and epithets, provides nevertheless in his happier passages that richness of organ music which gives

[1] *Rules and Advices to the Clergy of the Diocesse of Down and Connor* (1661), p. 19.   [2] *Miscellanies*, 1911, p. 202.

a certain splendour to our older prose, and makes our modern way of writing sometimes seem short-breathed and jejune in comparison.

'We long for perishing meat, and fill our stomachs with corruption; we look after white and red, and the weaker beauties of the night; we are passionate after rings and seals, and enraged at the breaking of a Crystall... our hearts are hard, and inflexible to the softer whispers of mercy and compassion, having no loves for any thing but strange flesh, and heaps of money, and popular noises, for misery and folly; and therefore we are a huge way off from the Kingdome of God, whose excellencies, whose designs, whose ends, whose constitution is spiritual and holy, and separate, and sublime, and perfect.' [1]

This is one of Jeremy Taylor's more splendid pages; but he can write with an equal beauty in quieter passages, as, for instance, when he says of children, 'No man can tell but he that loves his children, how many delicious accents make a mans heart dance in the pretty conversation of those dear pledges; their childishnesse, their stammering, their little angers, their innocence, their imperfections, their necessities are so many little emanations of joy and comfort to him that delights in their persons and society'. [2]

English writing has no doubt gained much in precision and conciseness since these great periodic sentences have fallen out of fashion; but we have paid for our gain by the loss of that long-breathed eloquence, that great Atlantic roll of English prose with which no modern writers, save perhaps Landor and De Quincey and Ruskin, have attempted to enrich their pages. In addition to his mastery of verbal music, Jeremy Taylor possessed an extraordinarily rich and power-

[1] No. 166. [2] No. 56.

ful visual imagination, and his genius was, as Sir Edmund Gosse says, essentially sensorial, and 'when it ceased to be stirred by images and sensations, it ceased to be attractive'.[1] He renders the impressions of sight so vividly that we share in his visual impressions; he personifies abstractions and turns them into living creatures which we seem to see before us; a sin, for instance, that 'will look prettily, and talk flattering words, and entice thee with softnesses and easy fallacies',[2] or a grief that, if you stay but till to-morrow, 'will be weary, and will lie downe to rest'.[3]

But the main quality and magic of Jeremy Taylor's style is the rich and abundant use of his visual gift in the perpetual creation of similes and metaphors—the welling-forth, as from an inexhaustible fountain, of shining and flashing images. The command of simile and metaphor—and metaphors are only less explicit similes—was, Aristotle said, by far the most important element in style, for it was the gift of nature and could not be imparted by another, and was the mark of what he called the εὐφυής, the 'genius', as we translate the word, although our modern idea of genius is hardly a Greek conception.

Although there have been authors of eminence who have made but a sparing use of metaphors, yet the power of thinking in images, *le don des images*, has always been an important part of the endowment of the greatest writers. Indeed, the greater he is, the more richly, like Aeschylus, or Plato, or Shakespeare, he seems to be dowered with this splendid gift. As soon as a rich imagination begins to glow, it finds itself in need of metaphors and figurative expressions to convey its warmth of meaning; and these images, though sometimes derived from the other senses, are for

[1] Gosse, p. 218.   [2] *The Worthy Communicant*, II. iii. 3.   [3] No. 42.

the most part visual images, since thoughts and moods and feelings seem to find in visible objects both their most appropriate embodiment and their most potent means of impressing themselves upon the minds and sensibilities of others.

The use of metaphors and figured diction is, among prose-writers, most abundant in sermons and religious writings, for imagery, by its appeal to the imagination, is of especial value for the conveyance of religious ideas and transcendental experience.

'Reasons', Taylor's contemporary, Thomas Fuller, wrote, 'are the pillars of the fabrick of a Sermon; but similitudes are the windows which give the best light'; [1] and the sermons of all ages abound in windows of this kind. They are in Jeremy Taylor's sermons, however, so abundant and so vast, that the religious edifice often seems to be all windows, like some late-Gothic church. But what most distinguishes these windows is not only their great sun-illumined spaces but the richness elsewhere of their deeply-stained glass. Does not, for instance, his description of the soul in sickness possess the radiance of coloured detail which we find in some small medieval or Pre-Raphaelite church window?

'In sickness, the soul begins to dresse her self for immortality: and first she unties the strings of vanity . . . Then she drawes the curtains, and stops the lights from coming in, and takes the pictures down, those phantastic images of self-love, and gay remembrances of vain opinion, and popular noises. . . . Then she layes by all her vain reflexions, beating upon her Chrystall and pure mirrour from the fancies of strength and beauty, & little decayed prettinesses of the body.' [2]

[1] *The Holy State*, 1642, p. 84.   [2] No. 41.

Introduction.

The figures of other preachers, rich and abundant as
they often are, partake of the nature of rhetorical figures;
to produce their effect, to persuade the will, or satisfy the
understanding, they must be familiar to their audience,
and the sense of this appeal to an audience always accom-
panies them. But the images of Jeremy Taylor, although
he too was an orator, are a poet's images; they surprise us
by their novelty of expression, and his aim seems to be to
express his own emotions rather than to excite those of
others, to delight the imagination rather than to move the
will, to enrich and feed the mind with lyric tenderness and
beauty, rather than to furnish it with motives for action.

In his Oxford lectures on Poetry, Keble illustrates this
distinction between the rhetorical and the poetic use of
images by comparing Burke's description of Marie Antoi-
nette, 'decorating and cheering the elevated sphere she
just began to move in; glittering like the morning star',
with what Jeremy Taylor says, in his funeral sermon of
Lady Carbery, 'In all her Religion, in all her actions of
relation towards God, she had a strange evenness and untroubled passage, sliding towards her ocean of God and
infinity, with a certain and silent motion'.[1] Both illustrations, Keble says, are models of splendid style, 'but while
Burke speaks as an accomplished orator, Taylor touches the
heights of poetry'.[2]

Jeremy Taylor's poetic images flash out sometimes in
brief similes, as when he speaks of the wealth that 'flies
away like a bird from the hand of a child',[3] or compares the

[1] No. 10.
[2] *Keble's Lectures on Poetry*, 1832–41, translated by E. K. Francis
(1912), vol. i, p. 50. I owe this reference to Robert Willmott's biography
of Jeremy Taylor.
[3] *Holy Living*, p. 248.

charity and humility of the Virgin to 'the pure leaves of
the whitest Lilly',[1] or describes her grief at the Crucifixion
as being 'deep as the waters of the abysse, but smooth as
the face of a Pool'.[2] But more often he elaborates his
sermons and fills their windows with great pictures, great
epic similes, which, like those of Homer or of Milton, are
used for their poetic and decorative value, and are enriched
with details and ornaments which have little relevance to
the idea which they are supposed to illustrate. These
elaborate descriptions of the dawning sun or the fading
rose so delight the imagination and so fill it with images
of beauty, that we soon forget—as the preacher himself
seems to have almost forgotten—the moral and religious
meaning they are supposed to illustrate.

It is, then, this gift of splendid metaphor, of flashing
before our eyes pictures which are of the highest poetic
beauty, and are clothed in a soft radiance of words, which
is Jeremy Taylor's special gift and supreme endowment.
It is this, and almost this alone, which makes him a great
writer, and explains the otherwise almost fantastic comparison of his genius to that of Shakespeare. For lacking
as he lacked most of the other qualities of Shakespeare's
greatness, Jeremy Taylor nevertheless, as Coleridge
pointed out, almost rivals Shakespeare in that supremest
gift of the poet, the power of embodying his thought in
images of beauty and splendour.

Jeremy Taylor may therefore be described as a writer,
with one gift, and only one, of the highest quality; and for
this singularity his writings deserve a place among the
rarities and more precious curiosities of our literature.
But there is another and still more curious reason for

---

[1] *Great Exemplar*, Part I, p. 79.   [2] *Ibid.*, Part III, p. 165.

allotting him this place; for although endowed with
the poet's gifts of imagery and music, it was in prose
that he found his appropriate medium of expression; and
when he turned to verse, his light was eclipsed and his
power faded. We possess a number of poems of his composition; he tried to express many of his ideas, both in
verse and prose, and it is curious to compare his treatment
of the same themes in the different mediums. In his sermon on the Day of Judgement, for instance, he describes
the 'thunders of the dying and groaning heavens and the
crack of the dissolving world, when the whole fabrick of
nature shall shake into dissolution and eternall ashes':[1]

> When earth shall vanish from thy sight,
>   The heavens that never err'd,
>   But observ'd
> Thy laws, shal from thy presence take their flight,[2]

is the poor rendering he gives in verse of the same subject.

Or, to take another instance, let us compare Jeremy
Taylor's descriptions in verse and in prose of the rising sun.

>   What glorious light!
>   How bright a Sun after so sad a night
>   Does now begin to dawn! Bless'd were those eyes
>   That did behold
>   This Sun when he did first unfold
>   His glorious beams, and now begin to rise.[3]

In the *Holy Dying* he thus describes the sunrise:

'But as when the Sun approaches towards the gates of the
morning, he first opens a little eye of Heaven, and sends away
the spirits of darknesse, and gives light to a cock, and calls up the
lark to Mattins, and by and by gilds the fringes of a cloud and
peeps over the Eastern hills, thrusting out his golden horns, like

[1] No. 173.   [2] *The Golden Grove*, p. 156.   [3] *Ibid.*, p. 164.

those which decked the browes of *Moses* when he was forced to wear a vail, because himself had seen the face of God; and still while a man tells the story, the sun gets up higher, till he shows a fair face and a full light, and then he shines one whole day, under a cloud often, and sometimes weeping great and little showers, and sets quickly: so is a man's reason and his life.' [1]

We cannot compare these passages in prose and verse without being immediately aware that the verse is prose and the prose is poetry—poetry with no formal metre but with a rich music of its own, with a cadence, a harmony of sound which, as Sainte-Beuve said of Chateaubriand, almost justifies the masters of this large music in their disdain of verse, with its mechanical beats and ever-repeated rhythms.

Jeremy Taylor's contemporary, Thomas Traherne, has also expressed certain favourite ideas both in verse and prose, and with him, too, the renderings in prose are more beautiful and more poetical than those in verse.[2]

Let us take two other of Jeremy Taylor's famous prose lyrics, the similes of the Rose and of the Lark.

'But so have I seen a Rose newly springing from the clefts of its hood, and at first it was fair as the Morning, and full with the dew of Heaven, as a Lambs fleece; but when a ruder breath had forced open its virgin modesty, and dismantled its too youthful and unripe retirements, it began to put on darknesse, and to decline to softnesse, and the symptomes of a sickly age; it bowed the head, and broke its stalk, and at night having lost some of its leaves, and all its beauty, it fell into the portion of weeds and outworn faces.' [3]

[1] No. 19.
[2] We have, however, only to study the age-long attempts to versify the Psalms to see that in the prose-rhythms of their English versions there is a poetry which verse destroys.
[3] No. 156.

'For so have I seen a lark rising from his bed of grasse and soaring upwards singing as he rises, and hopes to get to heaven, and climbe above the clouds; but the poor bird was beaten back with the loud sighings of an eastern winde, and his motion made irregular and unconstant, descending more at every breath of the tempest, then it could recover by the libration and frequent weighing of his wings; till the little creature was forc'd to sit down and pant, and stay till the storm was over, and then it made a prosperous flight, and did rise and sing as if it had learned musick and motion from an Angell as he passed sometimes through the aire about his ministries here below.'[1]

What has English grammar to say about writing which so outrageously flouts its rules, and English criticism, with its neat distinctions between poetry and prose, and the respective domains of each—how is our criticism to deal with prose-lyrics like these, which are as musical and poetical as almost any verse?

[1] No. 110. It might be supposed that giant similes like those of Jeremy Taylor would be completely out of place in modern prose. One modern writer, however, has been able to handle them with admirable effect. When Henry James wishes, for instance, to describe the renunciation, on the part of a wronged lady, of all vindictive feelings, he says that these passions of fury and revenge, as she thought of them, 'figured nothing nearer to experience than a wild eastern caravan, looming into view with crude colours in the sun, fierce pipes in the air, high spears against the sky, all a thrill, a natural joy to mingle with, but turning off short before it reached her and plunging into other defiles'. *The Golden Bowl*, Book V, chap. ii.

Compare also in the same novel the earlier 'pagoda' simile: 'This situation has been occupying for months and months the very centre of the garden of her life, but it had reared itself there like some strange tall tower of ivory, or perhaps rather some wonderful beautiful but outlandish pagoda, a structure plated with hard bright porcelain, coloured and figured and adorned at the overhanging eaves with silver bells that tinkled ever so charmingly when stirred by chance airs. She had walked round and round it—that was what she felt; she had carried on her existence in the space left her for circulation, a space that sometimes seemed ample and sometimes narrow: looking up all the while at the fair structure that spread itself so amply and rose so high, but never quite making out as yet where she might have entered had she wished.' *Ibid.*, Book IV, chap. i.

It may say, and justly say, that, for any one who did not possess Jeremy Taylor's gifts of imagination, it would be a most fatal thing to try to imitate his imaginative prose; and it may note, as Matthew Arnold noted, passages—too many passages—in which, owing to a failure of sobriety and good taste, this prose becomes overadorned and florid and sometimes almost grotesque. And yet a judicious criticism, eager to welcome excellence in all its varied forms, cannot but pay a tribute of admiration to this high, unprecedented way of writing, so rich in images and colour, in beauty and pathos of expression.

Such, then, are the peculiarities of Jeremy Taylor's talent, the curious questions which his writings suggest. Equally curious is the fact that, although he must have been conscious of this special gift, he seems to have set no especial value upon it. His main purpose in writing was controversial and hortatory; his great work of moral casuistry was the work he believed would bring him lasting fame; of his splendid gifts of style and imagery, he made only an occasional and, as it were, a casual use; and there is not much evidence of them in the works of his earlier or his later period. It was really only during the few happy sequestered years which he spent in South Wales, amid the mountains and valleys and woodlands of that remote and romantic region, when, after the ruin, as he regarded it, of Church and State, and the shipwreck of his own private fortune, he so miraculously found refuge at Golden Grove, that he unfolded his golden talent from its napkin—that, as Sir Edmund Gosse puts it, his genius 'spread its branches and flowered like a magnolia under the shadow of a southern wall in a quiet courtyard'.[1]

---

[1] Gosse, p. 106.

I have spoken of the kindness shown to their chaplain by Lord Carbery and his young and saintly wife. The earl was his patron and protector, and in the countess he found a gentle friend and pious disciple; it was apparently for her that he filled his sermons at Golden Grove with radiant splendour and illuminated with gold-leaf the missals of devotion which he dedicated to her use; almost all his finest pages and passages were preached before her or written for her perusal; the most beautiful of all his books, the *Holy Dying*, was composed for her edification; and when she died in holiness before its printing, he produced, to use his own phrase, the sheets of that publication as a covering for her hearse;—as a purple pall, we may describe it, for this sainted lady, of sombre and splendid prose.

This holy friendship and spiritual devotion was thus the inspiration of Jeremy Taylor's genius, and it was in the sunshine of Lady Carbery's admiration that—if we may allow ourselves so profane an image—her chaplain spread before her the fan of his splendid talent, rich with colours dipped in heaven and many-tinted eyes. When this sunshine is darkened at her death, the display is over, the glittering round is folded up; the radiance begins to fade from Jeremy Taylor's pages, and their fine gold is dimmed.

The light of the sun he basked in for a few years of his overclouded life fills the sermons of those years with a bright illumination, and indeed it is from the sun itself that he borrows his fairest-shining similes and illustrations. His description of the sunrise I have already quoted—a passage which Coleridge knew by heart and which Hazlitt compared to a morning landscape of Claude Lorraine's.

We read elsewhere of the 'dispassionate and gentle sun of an autumn morning'; of the sun kissing the frozen earth in winter, or turning red in the mists it has drawn up from the fens, and darkened by them. But it is above all the full-blazing sun of noontide that he loves to celebrate; the sun that blinds the beholder's eye with looking upon 'too big a beauty'. Thus he says, for instance, in one of his large and shining similes, 'Repentance is like the Sun, which enlightens not onely the tops of the Eastern hils, or warms the wall-fruits of *Italy*; it makes the little Balsam tree to weep precious tears with staring upon its beauties; it produces rich spices in *Arabia*, and warms the cold Hermit in his grot'.[1] Friendship again, he says, is like the sun; some people have but a small share in his beams, only a dark day and a long night from him, snows and white cattle, a miserable life.

'But some have splendid fires, and aromatick spices, rich wines and well-digested fruits, great wit and great courage; because they dwell in his eye, and look in his face, and are the Courtiers of the Sun, and wait upon him in his Chambers of the East.'[2]

Such a courtier of the sun dwelt within the clerical garb of this Anglican divine, who celebrates the rites of sun-worship with an almost Persian fervour.

What often gives a freshness and vividness to these images is the loving notation of many minor and minute manifestations of the sun's glory; the sun's rays shining through little chinks and making little cones and pyramids of light in a darkened room, or reflected from a vessel full of water and flickering on the walls and roof of the room in which the vessel stands. Many other minute phenomena of illumination attracted his curious attention, the light of

[1] No. 112.   [2] No. 47.

a glow-worm, or the sparkling of a diamond; the dim illumination of the moon in eclipse, or the 'least spark of the Pleiades', the flickering or the steady light of candles, from which he draws many of his most curious elaborate similes.

Not only light itself, but the eye which receives it was the object of his interest and study; 'a mans, or a womans or a hauks eye' was, he said, 'more beauteous and excellent' than any jewel in the crown of a king; [1] there were eyes that looked healthily as a friendly planet, and innocent as flowers; [2] but others that were 'dim as a sullied mirror'. 'An eye', he says in one of the strangest of his similes, 'that dwells too long upon a starre must be refreshed with lesser beauties and strengthened with greens and looking-glasses, lest the sight become amazed with too great a splendor'; [3] and although this must be regarded as an observation remote from common experience, we can all recognize the accuracy of his description of those thousands of little fantastic fires which seem to burn when we press our eyeballs, [4] or the diffused light of the sun which penetrates into eyes closed with a thin eye-lid; a favourite and characteristic image of Jeremy Taylor's, which he uses to describe the hidden truths of Christ's parables shining through their veil, or even more beautifully the 'lustre of virtue' which men cannot help perceiving though they close their eyes against it.

Sir Edmund Gosse has finely noted this sensitiveness of Jeremy Taylor to the phenomena of light, and adds that he writes with equal happiness about water in almost all its forms. 'The sun reflecting upon a lympid fountain', [5] this phrase of Jeremy Taylor's gives us a picture in minia-

[1] No. 33.   [2] XXVIII Sermons, p. 51.   [3] No. 50.
[4] No. 79.   [5] The Great Exemplar, Part III, p. 125.

Introduction. xlv

ture of the luminous world in which his imagination delighted—a world gleaming with the ripple and the shine of water. In his observation of aqueous phenomena he employs the same minute, almost microscopic, observation, as when he writes, for instance, of a drop of water falling into dust.

'When a little water is spilt from a full vessel and falls into its enemy dust, it curles it self into a drop and so stands equally armed in every point of the circle dividing the forces of the enemy, that by that little union it may stand as long as it can; but if it be dissolved into flatnesse it is changed into the nature and possession of the dust.' [1]

Although Jeremy Taylor sometimes made use of metaphors and similes from the grander phenomena of nature, from clouds and storms and angry seas, from tempestuous winds roaring in the tree-tops of a forest, his world of images is for the most part composed of things luminous and minute and transitory and flickering; of glow-worms, shooting-stars, and the flames of tapers, of bees and dancing gnats, of the trembling needle, of birds' nests and the 'little rings of the vine when they begin to curl', of the morning mushroom, of the rose that fades, of 'the down of thistles, and the softest gossamer'.

We do not always remember how largely our modern love of nature is of theological origin, how much our delight in the creation is due to our belief, or the belief of our ancestors, in the beneficent design and loving purpose of its great Creator. Although sterner theologians like the Jansenists and the Calvinists regarded the world as under a curse and as an abyss of corruption, the gentler spirits

[1] *The Worthy Communicant*, 1660, p. 275.

of the Christian faith saw in the beauties of the natural
world reflections and emanations of the divine beauty ;—
these pious clergymen walking out (and surely the thought
of them is a holy one) to suck divinity from Nature's
flowers. God, Jeremy Taylor said, was the 'God of
beauties and perfections'; the beauteous frame of heaven
and earth was 'the glasse in which he beheld his wisedom'.
'God is glorified in the Sunne and Moon, in the rare fabrick
of the honeycombs, in the discipline of Bees, in the œconomy of Pismires, in the little houses of birds, in the
curiosity of an eye, God being pleased to delight in those
little images and reflexes of himself from those pretty
mirrours.'[1]

The similes of Jeremy Taylor's great contemporary,
Milton, are drawn for the most part from history, from
mythology, from travellers' tales or the writings of
astronomers ; they open vast and shadowy perspectives
and are full of remote resonances and echoes. Jeremy
Taylor makes use sometimes of these bookish and remote
images ; the Lybian lion, for instance, struck with a
Mauritanian spear,[2] the mice of Africa who hide golden
ore in their bowels,[3] the howling of 'a herd of Evening
wolves when they misse their draught of blood in their
midnight Revels',[4] or the Lapland witches, who 'dance
the round, but there is a horror and a harshnesse in the
Musick'.[5] For the most part, however, his images are drawn
from Nature as he observed its minute perfections with
careful and, it would seem, myopic eyes ; and, as his
latest biographer has said, 'with the solitary exception of
Shakespeare, there is no writer in all our early literature

[1] No. 148.   [2] No. 40.   [3] *Holy Living,* IV. viii. 3.
[4] No. 34.   [5] No. 92.

who has made so fresh and copious and effective a use of
metaphor taken directly from the observation of natural
objects'.[1]

Jeremy Taylor not only observed the things he saw
about him, and often, as Mr. Bridges has said of Keats,
drew his images from common things, which are for the
first time represented as beautiful, but he also possessed
another quality, a warmth or tenderness, which Mr.
Bridges noted as being of inestimable value in Keats's
poems. The gentle stream, 'that begs leave of every turfe to
let it passe',[2] the little breeze 'soft as the breath of heaven,
not willing to disturb the softest stalk of a violet',[3] the flies
that 'doe rise againe from their little graves in walls', and
dance awhile in the sun's winter beams,[4] the dashes of 'affectionate raine';[5] or 'the throbs and little beatings' of the
lover's watch[6]—these are a few instances of that warmth
of imagery which verges on the sentimental and yet so
exquisitely escapes it.

This delicate observation, this poetic use of concrete
detail, seem to lose, for the following generation, its interest
and be replaced by the hackneyed and generalized imagery
of poetic convention—it might almost seem indeed as if
the variegated world, with its richness of light and colour,
had faded away from the eyes of men. Wordsworth states
that with very few exceptions he could find, in the poetry
of the period between the publication of *Paradise Lost*
and Thomson's *Seasons*, no new images drawn from the
observation of external nature, or written with the poet's
eye steadily fixed upon its object. But with the 'return
to Nature' of the Romantic Movement, with the re-

[1] Gosse, p. 222. [2] No. 108. [3] *XXV Sermons*, p. 84.
[4] No. 42. [5] *XXVIII Sermons*, p. 176. [6] No. 22.

covered vision of external beauty, it was natural that
the fame of Jeremy Taylor, who, in his use of shining
imagery, may be regarded as the last of the Elizabethans,
should acquire a new lustre. His gift of imagination, his
perpetual evocation of pictorial images, is all the more
striking because this essentially poetic gift shines out, not
in poetry, but in didactic and controversial prose; we can
observe it there, as it were, in isolation; and we can observe
it there also in its excess. For it may be said of Jeremy
Taylor, as it was said of Chateaubriand, that his imagination, and his image-making power, are too potent; his metaphors and similes are too luminous for their moral purpose,
they outshine and over-adorn and almost obliterate the
moral thought they are meant to illustrate. We can indeed
hardly share with much confidence the hope of Jeremy
Taylor's pious editor that those who read his writings for
their beauties will appropriate to themselves the moral
lessons they convey.

The possession of a style full of magic is disadvantageous
in another way to the earnest preacher and writer of moral
prose. It is a dangerous thing for him to denounce evil in
lovely chimes of words; for the boundaries of invective and
panegyric approach each other more closely than they
ought to in a completely moral world, and thunders of
denunciation may be sometimes accompanied by brilliant
flashes that dazzle and delight our eyes. A sin which is
damned with too much eloquence may arouse more interest than holy execration; and when we read in Jeremy
Taylor of 'the falling stars and little glow-wormes of the
world',[1] we, too, are tempted to steal from the altar and
gaze on these 'little images of beauty and pleasure'; 'the

[1] No. 108.

harlots hands that build the fairy castle'[1] are hardly regarded by us with all the reprobation they deserve, and
a sinner who, with a heart seduced by wine and rage and
folly goes 'singing to his grave',[2] may seem to have made
what is after all a not inglorious end.

That the fineness of Jeremy Taylor's similes and the
quaintness of his sentences were regarded by some at least
of his contemporaries as inappropriate for the inculcation
of plain gospel truths, is evident from the well-known passage in one of Bishop South's sermons, in which he ridicules
such ear-tickling phrases as 'The fringes of the North Star',
the 'down of Angels' wings', or 'the beautiful locks of
Cherubims', or the use of 'starched similitudes, introduced
with a "Thus have I seen a cloud rolling in its airy mansion", and the like'.[3]   This was not, the severe bishop
remarks, the way the Apostles, poor mortals, preached
the Gospel; these sublimities were above the rise of the
apostolic spirit.

Jeremy Taylor tells us that in composing his *Holy Dying*
he had made a collection of passages from the Fathers,
preserving their meaning but changing their arrangement,
in order that, as he puts it, 'by placing some of their dispersed meditations into a chain, or sequell of discourse,
I may with their precious stones make an *Union*, and compose them into a jewel'.[4] To make some such 'union' or
composite jewel out of Jeremy Taylor's dispersed meditations is my primary object in this volume. Enough has
been said of his various and voluminous works, and of
their lack of interest for modern readers, and yet of

---

[1] *XXV Sermons*, p. 259.   [2] No. 87.
[3] Sermon preached at Christ Church, Oxon., 30 April 1668.
[4] *Holy Dying*, p. 72.

their occasional passages of great beauty, to show that if it is ever wise to submit any author to this sifting process, there is hardly any one who would more profit by it than the subject of this book. Bishop Heber, who edited Bishop Taylor's writings, said of his longest work, the *Ductor Dubitantium*, that it resembled in some degree those ancient inlaid cabinets, 'whose multifarious contents perplex our choice, and offer to the admiration or curiosity of a more accurate age a vast wilderness of trifles and varieties, with no arrangement at all, or an arrangement on obsolete principles; but whose ebony drawers and perfumed recesses contain specimens of every thing that is precious or uncommon, and many things for which a modern museum might be searched in vain'.[1]

This large Taylorian simile may be extended to contain all of Taylor's writings; all his works are old cabinets of this kind, full of trifles, but containing also much that is curious and of value; and if they are to be read at all, they must be read in selected passages and pages. For more than thirty years my eyes have been haunted by the glow of some of these jewels; in my ears have echoed, like the sound of far-off bells, the music of certain of his phrases, and I have long intended to make a selection from his writings. I am glad that I have now performed at last this pious task, although the piety may not be of a kind that the saintly bishop would have cared for very much.

But a mere collection of poetical passages and purple patches would but partially serve the purpose which the compiler of a book like this should make his aim. The man whose writings are thus sifted should be allowed to present himself involved as he was in the circumstances of his own

[1] *Works*, 1861, vol. i, p. ccxlii.

life and age and country; nor should all account be omitted of the views which he expounded, and the controversies in which he engaged, even if they have lost most of their interest for us now.

The writers of sermons and religious books were, moreover, the essayists of their time; and we find in their works much writing on familiar topics which is really secular in its tone, and concerns itself with human topics—with men's faults and virtues and their social relations—which are of perennial interest to us all.

Jeremy Taylor makes in his writings but few references to his personal history or the circumstances of his private life. Such as do occur are found, for the most part, in the dedications of his various works to his various patrons, and above all to Lord and Lady Carbery. These dedications are models of grace in their expression of personal esteem and affectionate gratitude, and in them are also to be found a few references to the evil times he lived in, and the persecuted state of the Church he loved and served.

As a disciple of Laud, Jeremy Taylor held the high views of episcopacy of his school, and was a convinced believer in institutional religion and what is called the Erastian point of view. The Church was, he said, the vine twined about the oak of the State; Religion being of itself soft and easy and defenceless, must lean upon the arm of Kings; [1] ritual and ceremonial, the pomp of religious services were great aids, he believed, to devotion; and during the eclipse of Church, and the persecution under the Commonwealth of what he called our 'poor afflicted Mother', he looked back with poignant regret to the beautiful old-established order, to Jerusalem and 'the pleasures of the Temple, the

[1] No. 74.

order of her services, the beauty of her buildings, the
sweetness of her songs'.[1] His eyes had almost grown old,
he wrote in 1655, with seeing the 'horrid mischiefs' due to
rebellion and disobedience; but when after the Restoration he dedicates his great work on casuistry to Charles II,
and when their duty stood, as he said, 'on the sunny side'
at last, he is able to rejoice in the restoration of the Throne
and Church. To his subsequent experiences, and to the
circumstances of his residence in Ireland, Jeremy Taylor
seldom refers in his writings: I have, however, reprinted
the pitying, uncomprehending account he gives of the
Irish Roman Catholics among whom he dwelt,[2] and also
some sentences from his funeral sermon on that great
divine, the aged John Bramhall, Anglican Archbishop of
Armagh.[3]

The passage from the same sermon, which follows this
extract, begins the next section of this book—the general
survey of man's life and our mortal condition, the vanity
of our desires, the folly and emptiness of our ambitions,
and the misery of our lives. We are made of dust, he tells
us; man is 'a lump of folly and unavoidable necessities',
and our hearts, so intricate and various and trifling,
so full of wantonness and foolish thoughts, come in
for many well-deserved if not altogether novel casti-
gations.

In his general survey of the nature of man and his mortal
condition he follows for the most part in the footsteps of
the old moralists and old theologians, and repeats, though
with a certain grace and freshness of diction, received
notions and well-established views. Sermons, he said, were
not like 'curious enquiries after new-nothings, but pur-

suance of old truths'; these truths he took for granted and asked no ultimate questions about them.

There are certain aspects, however, which, in addition to the beauty of his phrasing, lend an interest to his treatment of these ancient themes. His doctrine of disillusion, of the vanity of the world and the world's temptations, he seems to have derived more from classical than Christian sources; and learned in the classics as he was, the instances and exemplifications of human misery in his sermons, being copied from Greek and Latin literature, could hardly have caused much disquiet in the breasts of his hearers in South Wales. Whatever mundane temptations the rural solitudes of that locality might have afforded, it was hardly necessary, moreover, to warn them against corrupt longings for garments stained with the blood of the Tyrian fish, for oysters of Lucrinus, for the tender lard of Apulian swine, or condited bellies of the Scarus; for Galatian mules, or eunuchs for their slaves from Tunis.[1]

Jeremy Taylor's writings and sermons are like those of many divines of the period, loaded, and indeed overloaded, with classical quotations; but his immense knowledge of ancient literature, his 'oceanic reading', as Coleridge described it, was of service to him as more than a storehouse of recondite sins and appropriate quotations. His mind was filled with the noblest poetry of the ancients, his memory stored with all that was wise or beautiful or extraordinary in the ancient writers; and this constant reference to the classics, this borrowing of words and images and phrases from Greek and Latin writers, lends a great distinction, a kind of Miltonic richness to his style,

[1] No. 101.

and fills it with the murmur of far-off overtones and echoes. Perhaps of all modern divines Jeremy Taylor is the most steeped in the ancient classics; of all save Fénelon, that most Hellenic of ecclesiastics, who so miraculously contrived to fuse together in *Télémaque* a beautiful and almost impossible harmony of Christian piety and the soul of ancient Greece. But Jeremy Taylor was not a Hellenist like Fénelon; a spirit so Greek as Fénelon's has appeared only once in the Church of modern times; he was, however, deeply influenced by one element of Greek thought, of that Platonic philosophy which Christianity had early absorbed from Platonism, and which was so potent an influence in the Anglican theology of his time.[1] This religion of the spirit, this recognition of an unseen eternal world behind the flux of phenomena—a world of which the existing world is but an evanescent shadow, and which we apprehend, not with the senses but with the mind—this is the inspiration of that portion of Jeremy Taylor's writings which has for us the greatest spiritual value, since it is the expression of those permanent truths which underlie the shifting doctrines of the different ages of doctrinal history.

To pass from shadows to substances, from the pleasures of the senses to the contemplation of heavenly things and the joys of reason, from dwelling on this transitory earth to residence amid intellectual and eternal essences—this was for Jeremy Taylor the progress from earth to heaven, from death to eternal life. 'Children and fools', he wrote, 'choose to please their senses rather than their reason, because they still dwell within the regions of sense, and

[1] See Dean Inge, *The Platonic Tradition in English Religious Thought*, 1926.

have little residence amongst intellectuall essences'.[1] The growth in grace was for him the growth in this life of the spirit; for it was possible, he said, to taste of this perfection while in our mortal state on earth; a man's heart and eye may be in the state of perfection, that is, in Heaven, before he sets his feet upon 'that golden threshold'; and God, 'the eternal essence', would now grant his worshippers 'little antepasts of Heaven', opening for him little 'loopholes of eternity'; and sometimes 'draws aside the curtains of peace, and shews him his throne, and visits him with irradiations of glory, and sends him a little star to stand over his dwelling, and then again covers it with a cloud'.[2]

To feast as often as we can upon these 'glorious communications of eternity', to live as much as possible in heaven while we are still on earth, this was to Jeremy Taylor, in his higher moments of spiritual vision, the essence of religion; this our consolation in a world of sorrow, our redemption from its vanity and nothingness and dust. It was by means of prayer, which with all its wonder-working powers is, he says, nothing but an ascent to God, that the devout soul is enabled to participate in eternity; and it is when he writes of prayer that he writes with the sincerest unction, and floats heavenwards on the wings of his fairest images, like that symbol of prayer, the ascending lark, whose attempt he so beautifully describes 'to get to heaven, and climbe above the clouds'. Prayer, he says, 'is the peace of our spirit, the stilnesse of our thoughts, the evennesse of recollection, the seat of meditation, the rest of our cares, and the calme of our tempest; prayer is the issue of a quiet minde, of untroubled thoughts, it is the daughter of charity, and the sister of meeknesse';[3] and

---

[1] *The Great Exemplar*, Part III, p. 27. [2] *Ibid.*, Part III, p. 38. [3] No. 110.

some of Jeremy Taylor's loveliest writing is in the numerous prayers with which he fills his books of devotion, and a few of which will be found at the end of this volume. Each of these prayers, as Sir Edmund Gosse has said, is like a gush of music; they are the most exquisite of their kind in the English language, and display the 'delicate wholesomeness of his conscience and the inimitable distinction of his style'.[1]

Although we are told that he spent a large portion of each day in prayer, and in fact lived most of his life in heaven, Jeremy Taylor can hardly be counted a mystic of the quality of his contemporaries Traherne and Vaughan. He was too firmly planted in the familiar earth, too fond of its comforts and its commonplaces; and many of the secular ideas of the age he lived in found their expression in his pages. Among these currents of thought we may note the rising tide of that secular, common-sense, practical give-and-take religion which was destined to dominate English eighteenth-century theology, and replace the ancient and sublime platonic ladder to the serene heavens of eternal peace. 'Let no man be hasty', he writes, 'to eat the fruits of Paradise before his time'; [2] and in a curious sentence, in which we find the spirit of the prosaic eighteenth century, with its hatred and fear of enthusiasm, expressing itself in the poetic speech of the century which preceded it, 'It is more healthfull and nutritive', Jeremy Taylor writes, 'to dig the earth and to eat of her fruits then to stare upon the greatest glories of the heavens and live upon the beams of the Sun; so unsatisfying a thing is rapture and transportation to the soul; it often distracts the faculties, but seldom does advantage piety, and is full

[1] Gosse, p. 59.   [2] *The Great Exemplar*, Part I, p. 95.

of danger in the greatness of its lustre.'[1] Books of mystical theology had in them, he said, 'the most high, the most troublesome, and the most mysterious nothings in the world, and little better than the effluxes of a *religious madness*'.[2]

This more secular point of view, the light of this more modern common sense, modifies the gloom of Jeremy Taylor's vision; cheerfulness could not be completely banished; this scene of tears was after all not, it appeared, without its comforts and alleviations; time itself was chequered with black and white; and if our joys were ephemeral, our sorrows also did not last for ever. And in affliction, and the loss of all our worldly goods, how many sources of happiness remained! 'What now?' the impoverished parson asks with obvious reference to his own denuded state in Wales.

'Let me look about me. They have left me the Sun and the Moon, Fire and Water, a loving wife, and many friends to pity me, and some to relieve me, I can still discourse, . . . and still I sleep, and digest, I eat and drink, I reade and meditate, I can walk in my Neighbours pleasant fields, and see the varieties of natural beauties, and delight in all that in which God delights, that is, in virtue and wisdom, in the whole creation, and in God himself: and he that hath so many causes of joy, and so great, is very much in love with sorrow and peevishness, who loses all these pleasures, and chooses to sit down upon his little handful of thorns.'[3]

Healthy labour, the endearments of society, and the pleasantness of conversation, he mentions among the joys of life; and friendship, which he beautifully celebrates: marriage, that 'Queen of friendships', and the domestic

[1] *Ibid.*, p. 94.   [2] No. 122.   [3] No. 43.

joys, and above all the delight of children;—and no one has written more beautifully of the happiness which children bring.

This more secular point of view can be noted in Jeremy Taylor's attitude towards religious melancholy, and the scruples of a distressed conscience. He acknowledges the effect of physical states on our mental condition; the soul, he says, follows the tempers or distempers of the body, and he declares that much which passes for scrupulosity of conscience is nothing but the effect of fatigue and sleep-lessness and disease.

About ill-health and its consequences Jeremy Taylor is especially modern and observant, noting the enervation of the soul caused by the weakness of the body; and his accounts of illness, and of the psychological effects of bodily disorder, often read more like the notes of a modern doctor than those of an old-fashioned physician of souls. His attitude towards death is also modern; death being to him no longer the grisly horror of the old divines, but simply the end of a natural process of dissolution; as he says in a famous passage:

'Take away but the pomps of death, the disguises and solemn bug-bears, the tinsell, and the actings by candle-light, and proper and phantastic ceremonies, the minstrels and the noise-makers, the women and the weepers, the swoonings and the shrikings, the Nurses and the Physicians, the dark room and the Ministers, the Kinred and the Watchers, and then to die is easie, ready and quitted from its troublesome circumstances. It is the same harm-lesse thing, that a poor shepherd suffered yesterday, or a maid servant to-day.' [1]

These modern tendencies of his thought caused Jeremy

[1] No. 160.

Taylor, as we have seen, to be suspected of heresy; he was, his contemporaries thought, inadequately convinced of the total depravity of the human heart; and by questioning the doctrine of original sin, the imputation of Adam's transgression to posterity, he incurred the suspicion of Pelagianism, and became engaged in angry controversies with several divines of his own party. His denial of absolute Predestination and the damnation of unbaptized infants was regarded with horror by the Calvinists; his advocacy of religious toleration, his views on the inefficacy of death-bed repentance, shocked many devout Anglicans, and indeed, the Bishop of Calcutta tells us, he was led, on several of these points, to the expression of views which are irreconcilable with the Articles of the Church of England, and contrary to the plain sense of the scriptures.[1]

And yet Jeremy Taylor, although on some points a precursor of the rational and deistic divines of the eighteenth century, was not a real opponent of the orthodoxy of his day. A sacerdotalist, a believer in ceremonies and institutional religion, he maintained the high views of Episcopacy held by Laud and his supporters, and he accepted the orthodox doctrines of the Church to which he belonged. No one could see indeed, or state more clearly, the difficulties of accepting many of these doctrines; why an omnipotent God should permit evil to exist, or predestine souls to eternal torment, and damn the heathens and old Israelites to a Hell of which he never warned them—such doctrines were, he said, like the heads of the cherubim over the Mercy Seat; you could see their bright faces and golden wings, 'but there is no *body* to be handled'; the

[1] *Works,* vol. i, p. xlvi.

revelation is clear and the article plain, and yet the reason of it we cannot see at all.[1]

Jeremy Taylor did not hesitate, however, to inculcate these mysteries without a bottom; he accepted the existence of a personal Devil, although he admitted, 'we never heard his noises, nor have seen his affrighting shapes'[2]; and while daring to exclude unbaptized infants from its flaming precincts, he expatiated without reluctance on the horrors of Eternal Torment, and the unimaginable miseries of the countless millions 'roasting in the seats of the reprobate, and doomed to dwell with devils to eternal ages'.

The truth is that Jeremy Taylor was not a logical theologian; he accepted for the most part without questioning it the Anglican position of the seventeenth century, that *via media* between the corruptions of Roman Catholicism on the one hand, and the dangers of Puritan fanaticism on the other. In his ethical teaching also we find the same compromise between different ways of thinking; his ethics as well as his theology being an edifice composed, like the architecture of his time, of mingled classical, gothic, and more modern elements. The rules he gives for right conduct in practical affairs are, like most Christian ethics, a curious blend of Christian ideals, and the teachings of classical philosophers, of Aristotle and Plato, of the Epicureans and the Stoics: and he often quotes, along with the 'orthodox and ancient fathers', the sayings of the 'wise Heathens', 'the old brave philosophers and poets', who preached that 'contentedness which is the sum of all the old moral philosophy', and the wisdom of making our unavoidable fate our necessary religion.[3]

Good laws usually spring, Jeremy Taylor says, 'from ill

[1] No. 152.   [2] No. 151.   [3] *Holy Dying*, p. 19.

manners, and excellent Sermons are occasioned by men's
iniquities'; [1] but the excellence of his own sermons owe
but little to his realization of the sinfulness of man. Save
drunkenness and gluttony,[2] there are no sins which he
denounces at any length; he seems to have derived his
notions of iniquity, as I have said, from his classical reading,
and it is curious to note the contrast between his minute
observation of Nature and his own sensations, and his vague
and bookish notions of his fellow men, and their characters
and failings.

Jeremy Taylor's presentation of the Anglican doctrines
and the ethical thinking of his time has its historic interest;
it represents the views of a preacher and seventeenth-
century controversialist of great learning and of a liberal
mind. But this interest is after all only a secondary interest; we read Jeremy Taylor as we read Donne and other
preachers, and indeed the Hebrew prophets, less for their
subject-matter, than for their style. And yet this distinction between style and subject-matter, between manner
and meaning, is but a superficial distinction. The
form in any work of art cannot be divorced from its
content, for it is a part of that content; it expresses the
reaction of the artist's mind to the subject he is treating,
and cannot be separated from that totality of meaning
which his work conveys to our senses and imagination. In
Jeremy Taylor's best writing, when the poet emerged in
the preacher, what he really says, rather than what he
thinks he is saying—his unconscious rather than his conscious utterance—is the thing which is of real interest and

[1] *The Great Exemplar*, Part II, p. 24.
[2] Jeremy Taylor treats of over-eating in his *Holy Living*, and preached
two sermons on the subject at Golden Grove. Lord Carbery, Sir Edmund
Gosse suggests, may have been something of a gourmand. Gosse, p. 72.

importance to us. The preacher may be preaching with
the most solemn emphasis of the four great last things, of
Death and Judgement and Hell and Heaven, but if the
poet within his cassock is singing at the same time of the
dew on the leaves of the rose, it is to the song rather than
the sermon that we listen. So when we speak of Jeremy
Taylor's style we do not mean by style any mere technical
tricks or methods of adornment. Style, as one of its
modern masters has told us, is like the colouring of a
painter, a quality of the writer's vision, the rendering and
revelation of the world of his unique perception. The
special delight which each new artist gives us is due to the
enduring reality which is revealed to him, and which in
his turn he reveals to us.

It is Jeremy Taylor's possession of style in this sense,
the revelation in the music and magic of words of a unique
vision—it is this rarest of all gifts which we value in
him, although he seems to have set no value upon it
himself. We still read, or still should read, his tremulous
pages for the beauty of the world which hung upon his
pen, a world full of sun and the shimmer of water, a
world delicately tinted, fleeting, evanescent, and yet fixed
and made imperishable by the incantation of his words.

Imaginative prose, full of colour and music, is at present
out of fashion; in the view of our contemporary critics (at
least in England) prose should be lucid, logical, not difficult to write, and almost devoid of colour. Precision and
uniformity of texture are its merits, and it should never
dare to rise to special heights of imaginative vision. Such
is the accepted—and, to most authors, the acceptable and
labour-saving—theory; and since the fame of the im-
mortals is never really fixed, but must still follow the ebbs

and flows of sublunary fashions, our old writers of finely-wrought and imaginative prose have fallen out of favour. But when we read prose like the prose of the Prayer Book and the Bible, of Shakespeare and Milton, of Donne and Sir Thomas Browne and Jeremy Taylor, are we, as Hazlitt asks, to cut ourselves off from beauties like these with a theory? Is it not wiser to welcome excellence in all the expressive forms in which it presents itself to our appreciation? May we not admit the existence of great writers who, like Plato, were poets but not versifiers, and say of Jeremy Taylor, as was said of De Quincey—and might be also said of Sir Thomas Browne—that he has revealed new capacities of the language; has enlarged our conceptions concerning the possibilities of what Dryden described as 'the other harmony of prose'?

JEREMY TAYLOR
SELECTED PASSAGES

1. *To Archbishop Laud.*

My most Honourable good LORD.

May it please your GRACE,

T was obedience to my *Superiour* that ingaged me upon this last Anniversary commemoration of the great Goodnesse of God Almighty to our King and Country in the discouery of the most damnable *Powder-Treason.* It was a blessing which no tongue could expresse, much lesse mine, which had scarce learn'd to speake, at least, was most unfit to speake in the Schooles of the Prophets. *Delicata autem est illa obedientia quæ causas quærit.* It had beene no good argument of my obedience to have disputed the inconvenience of my person, and the unaptnesse of my parts for such an imployment. I knew God, out of the mouth of Infants, could acquire his praise, and if my heart were actually as *Votive* as my tongue should have beene, it might bee one of Gods *Magnalia* to perfect his owne praise out of the weaknesse and imperfection of the Organ. So as I was able, I endeavour'd to performe it, having my obedience ever ready for my excuse to men, and my willingnesse to performe my duty, for the assoylment of my selfe before God; part of which I hope was accepted, and I have no reason to thinke, that the other was not pardoned.

When I first thought of the Barbarisme of this Treason, I wondred not so much at the thing itselfe as by what meanes it was possible for the Divell to gaine so strong a party in mens resolutions, as to move them to undertake a businesse so abhorring from Christianity, so evidently full of extreame danger to their lives, and so certainly to incurre the highest wrath of God Almighty. My thoughts were thus rude at first; but after a strict inquisition I found it was apprehended as a businesse (perhaps full of danger to their bodies, but) advantagious to their soules, consonant to the obligation of all Christians, and meritorious of an exceeding weight of Glory, for now it was come to passe which our dear Master foretold, *men should kill us, and thinke they did God good service in it.* I could not thinke this to be a part of any mans religion, nor doe I yet believe it. For it is so apparently destructive of our deare Master his Royall lawes of *Charity* & *Obedience*, that I must not be so uncharitable as to thinke they speake their owne minde truly, when they professe their beliefe of the lawfullnesse and necessity in some cases of rebelling against their lawfull Prince, and using all meanes to throw him from his kingdome, though it be by taking of his life. But it is but iust that they who breake the bonds of duty to their Prince, should likewise forfeit the lawes of charity to themselves, and if they say not true, yet to bee more uncharitable to their owne persons, then I durst be, though I had their own warrant. Briefly (Most R. Father) I found amongst them of the Roman party such prevailing opinions, as could not consist with loyalty to their Prince, in case hee were not the Popes subiect, and these so generally believed, and somewhere obtruded under perill of their soules, that I could not but point at these dangerous rocks, at which I doubt not, but the loyalty of many hath suffered shipwrack, and of thousands more might, if a higher *Starre* had not guided them better, then their owne Pilots.

A Sermon upon the Anniversary of the Gunpowder-Treason, 1638, Dedication

2. *Jeremy Taylor in Wales. To Lord Hatton.*

My Lord,

IN this great Storm which hath dasht the Vessell of the Church all in pieces, I have been cast upon the Coast of *Wales,* and in a little Boat thought to have enjoyed that rest and quietnesse, which in *England* in a greater I could not hope for: Here I cast Anchor, and thinking to ride safely, the Storm followed me with so impetuous violence, that it broke a Cable, and I lost my Anchor: And here again I was exposed to the mercy of the Sea, and the gentlenesse of an Element that could neither distinguish things nor persons. And but that he who stilleth the raging of the Sea, and the noise of his Waves, and the madnesse of his people, had provided a Plank for me, I had been lost to all the opportunities of content or study. But I know not whether I have been more preserved by the courtesies of my friends, or the gentlenesse and mercies of a noble Enemy: Οἱ γὰρ βάρβαροι παρεῖχον οὐ τὴν τύχουσαν φιλανθρωπίαν ἡμῖν, ἀνάψαντες γὰρ πυρὰν προσελάβοντο πάντας ἡμᾶς διὰ τὸν ὑετὸν τὸν ἐφεστῶτα καὶ διὰ τὸ ψύχος. And now since I have come ashoar, I have been gathering a few sticks to warm me, a few books to entertain my thoughts, and divert them from the perpetuall Meditation of my private Troubles, and the publike Dyscrasy, but those which I could obtain were so few and so impertinent, and unusefull to any great purposes, that I began to be sad upon a new stock, and full of apprehension that I should live unprofitably, and die obscurely, and be forgotten, and my bones thrown into some common charnell house, without any name or note to distinguish me from those who only served their Generation by filling the number of Citizens, and who could pretend to no thanks or reward from the Publike, beyond a *ius trium liberorum*. While I was troubled with these thoughts, and busie to find out an opportunity of doing some good in my small proportion, still the cares of the publike did so intervene, that it was as impossible to separate my design from relating to the present, as to exempt my selfe from the participation of the common calamity; still halfe my thoughts was (in despite of all my diversions and arts of avocation) fixt upon and mingled with the present concernments: so that besides them I could not goe. . . .

Thus farre I discourst my selfe into imployment, and having come thus farre, I knew not how to get farther, for I had heard of a great experience, how difficult it was to make Brick without Straw, and here I had even seene my design blasted in the bud, and I despaired in the Calends of doing what I purposed in the Ides before: For I had no Books of my own here, nor any in the voisinage, and but that I remembered the result of some of those excellent Discourses, I had heard your Lordship make when I was so happy as in private to gather up what your temperance and modesty, forbids to be publick, I had come *in prælia inermis*, and like enough might have far'd accordingly. I had this only advantage besides; that I have chosen a Subject, in which, if my own reason does not abuse me, I needed no other books or aides, then what a man carries with him on horse-back, I meane the common principles of Christianity, and those ἀξιώματα which men use in the transactions of the ordinary occurrences of civill society; and upon the strength of them and some other collaterall assistances I have run through it *utcunque*, and the sum of the following Discourses, is nothing but the sense of these words of Scripture;

That since *we know in part, and prophesy in part, and that now we see through a glasse darkly*, wee should not *despise* or *contemn* persons not so knowing as our selves, but *him that is weak in the faith we should receive, but not to doubtfull disputations*; Therefore certainly to charity, and not to vexations, not to those which are the idle effects of impertinent wranglings.

The Liberty of Prophesying, 1647, pp. 1 and 5

3. *The Eclipse of the Church.*

WE have not onely felt the evils of an intestine Warre, but God hath smitten us in our spirit, and laid the scene of his judgements especially in Religion; he hath snuffed our lamp so near, that it is almost extinguished, and the sacred fire was put into a hole of the earth, even then when we were forced to light those tapers that stood upon our Altars, that by this sad truth better then by the old ceremony we might prove our succession to those holy men who were constrained to sing hymnes to Christ in dark places and retirements.

But I delight not to observe the correspondencies of such sad accidents, which as they may happen upon divers causes, or may be forc'd violently by the strength of fancy, or driven on by jealousy, and the too fond opinings of troubled hearts and afflicted spirits; so they doe but help to vex the offending part, and relieve the afflicted but with a phantastick and groundless comfort: I will therefore deny leave to my own affections to ease themselves by complaining of others: I shall onely crave leave that I may remember *Jerusalem* and call to minde the pleasures of the Temple, the order of her services, the beauty of her buildings, the sweetness of her songs, the decency of her Ministrations, the assiduity and Oeconomy of her Priests and Levites, the daily sacrifice, and that eternal fire of devotion that went not out by day nor by night; these were the pleasures of our peace, and there is a remanent felicity in the very memory of those spiritual delights which we then enjoyed as antepasts of heaven, and con-signations to an immortality of joyes. And it may be so again when it shall please God who hath the hearts of all Princes in his hand, and turneth them as the rivers of waters; and when men will consider the invaluable loss that is consequent, and the danger of sin that is appendant to the destroying such forms of discipline and devotion in which God was purely worshipped, and the Church was edified, and the people instructed to great degrees of piety, knowledge, and devotion.

A Collection of Offices, 1658, preface

4. *The Evils of the Age.*

THE Holy Scripture giving an account of the reasons of the divine providence taking Godly men from this world; and shutting them up in a hasty grave, sayes, that they are taken from the evils to come: and concerning our selves it is certain, if we had ten years agone taken seizure of our portion of dust, death had not taken us from good things, but from infinite evils, such which the sun hath seldom seen.

Holy Dying, 1651, p. 128

5. *To Lord Carbery.*

My Lord,

I HAVE now by the assistance of God, and the advantages of your many favours, finished a *Year of Sermons*; which if, like the first year of our Saviours preaching, it may be *annus acceptabilis*, an *acceptable year* to God, and his afflicted hand-maid the Church of *England*, a reliefe to some of her new necessities, and an institution or assistance to any soule; I shall esteem it among those honors and blessings, with which God uses to reward those good intentions which himselfe first puts into our hearts, and then recompenses upon our heads. My Lord, They were first presented to God in the ministeries of your family: For this is a blessing for which your Lordship is to blesse God, that your Family is like *Gideons* Fleece, irriguous with a dew from heaven, when much of the *voicinage* is dry; for we have cause to remember that *Isaac* complain'd of the *Philistims*, who fill'd up his wells with stones, and rubbish, and left no beauvrage for the Flocks; and therefore they could give no milke to them that waited upon the Flocks, and the flocks could not be gathered, nor fed, nor defended. It was a designe of ruine, and had in it the greatest hostility; and so it hath been lately;

—————————— *undiq; totis*
Vsque adeo turbatur agris. En! ipse capellas
Protenus æger ago; hanc etiam vix Tityre duco.

But, My Lord, this is not all: I would faine also complaine that men feele not their greatest evill, and are not sensible of their danger, nor covetous of what they want, nor strive for that which is forbidden them; but that this complaint would suppose an unnaturall evill to rule in the hearts of men; For who would have in him so little of a Man, as not to be greedy of the Word of God, and of holy Ordinances, even therefore because they are so hard to have? ...

I finde by the constitution of the Divine providence, and Ecclesiasticall affaires, that all the great necessities of the Church have been served by the zeale of preaching in publick, and other holy ministeries in publick or private, as they could be had. By this the Apostles planted the Church, and the primitive Bishops supported the faith of *Martyrs*, and the hardinesse of *Confessors*, and the austerity of the *Retired*. By this they confounded Hereticks, and evill livers, and taught them the wayes of the Spirit, and left them without pertinacy, or without excuse. It was Preaching that restored the splendour of the Church, when Barbarisme, and Warres, and Ignorance either sate in, or broke the Doctors Chaire in pieces: For then it was that divers Orders of *religious*, and especially of *Preachers* were erected; God inspiring into whole companies of men a zeal of Preaching: And by the same instrument God restored the beauty of the Church, when it was necessary shee should be reformed; it was the assiduous and learned preaching of those whom God chose for his Ministers in that work, that wrought the Advantages and persuaded those Truths, which are the *enamel* and beautie of our Churches. And because by the same meanes all things are preserved, by which they are produc'd, it cannot but be certaine, that the present state of the Church requires a greater care and prudence in this Ministerie

then ever; especially since by Preaching some endevour to
supplant Preaching, and by intercepting the fruits of the
flocks to dishearten the Shepheards from their attendances.

My Lord, your great noblenesse and religious charitie
hath taken from mee some portions of that glory which
I designed to my selfe in imitation of St. *Paul* towards the
Corinthian Church; who esteemed it his honour to preach
to them without a revenue; and though also like him I
have a trade, by which as I can be more usefull to others,
and lesse burthensome to you, yet to you also under God,
I owe the quiet and the opportunities and circumstances
of that, as if God had so interweaved the support of my
affaires with your charitie, that he would have no advantages passe upon mee, but by your interest; and that I
should expect no reward of the issues of my Calling, unlesse
your Lordship have a share in the blessing.

XXV Sermons, 1653, Epistle Dedicatory

6. *To Lady Carbery.*

Madam,

SINCE the Divine providence hath been pleased to bind
up the great breaches of my little fortune by your
charity and Noblenesse of a religious tendernesse, I account
it an excellent Circumstance and handsomnesse of condition that I have the fortune of S. *Athanasius* to have my
persecution relieved and comforted by an Honourable and
excellent Lady; and I have nothing to return for this
honour done to me, but to do as the poor paralyticks and
infirme people in the Gospell did when our B. Saviour
cured them, they went and told it to all the Country, and
made the voisinage full of the report, as themselves were
of health and joy. And although I know the modesty of

your person and religion, had rather do favours then own them, yet give me leave to draw aside the curtain and retirement of your charity; for I had rather your vertue should blush, then my unthankfulnesse make me ashamed. *Madam*, I intended by this addresse not onely to return you spirituals for your temporals, but to make your noble usages of me and mine, to become like your other charityes, productive of advantages to the standers by. For although the beams of the sun reflected from a marble, return not home to the body and fountain of light, yet they that walk below feel the benefit of a doubled heat: so whatever reflexions or returns of your favours I can make, although they fall short of what your worth does most reasonably challenge, and can proceed but towards you with forward desires and distant approaches, yet I am desirous to believe that those who walk between us may receive assistances from this entercourse, and the following papers may be Auxiliary to the enkindling of their piety, as to the confirming and establishing yours. For although the great prudence of your most noble Lord, and the modesties of your own temperate and sweeter dispositions become the great endearments of vertue to you, yet because it is necessary that you make Religion the businesse of your life, I thought it not an impertinent application, to expresse my thankfulnesse to your Honour by that which may best become my duty and my gratitude, because it may do you the greatest service. *Madam* I must beg your pardon, that I have opened the sanctuary of your retir'd vertues; but I was obliged to publish the endearments and favours of your Noble Lord and your self towards me and my relatives: For as your hands are so clasp'd that one ring is the ligature of them both, so I have found emanations from that conjuncture of hands with a consent so forward and apt, that nothing can satisfie for my obligations but by being in the greatest eminency of thankfulnesse and humility of person,

Madam,

Your Honours most

obliged, and most

humble Servant

TAYLOR

The Great Exemplar, 1649, Pt. III, Epistle Dedicatory

7. *To Lord Carbery.*

My Lord,

I NOW present to your Lordship a Copy of those Sermons the publication of which was first designed by the appetites of that *hunger and thirst of righteousnesse,* which made your Dear Lady (that rare soul) so dear to God, that he was pleased speedily to satisfie her, by carrying her from our shallow and impure cisterns to drink out of the fountains of our Saviour. My Lord, I shall but prick your tender eye, if I shall remind your Lordship, how diligent a hearer, how carefull a recorder, how prudent an observer, how sedulous a practiser of holy discourses she was, and that therefore it was, that what did slide thorow her ear, she was desirous to place before her eye, that by those windows they might enter in and dwell in her heart: But because by this truth I shall do advantage to the following discourses, give me leave (my Lord) to fancy, that this Book is derived upon your Lordship almost in the nature of a legacy from her, whose every thing was dearer to your Lordship, then your own eyes, and that what she was pleased to beleeve apt to minister to her devotions, and the religions of her pious and discerning soul, may also be allowed a place in your closet, and a portion of your retirement, and a lodging in your thoughts, that they may incourage and instruct your practise and promote that interest, which is and ought to be dearer to you then all those blessings and separations with which God hath remarked your family and person.

My Lord, I confess the publication of these Sermons can so little serve the ends of my reputation, that I am therefore pleased the rather to do it, because I cannot at all be tempted, in so doing, to minister to any thing of vanity. Sermons may please when they first strike the ear, and yet appear flat and ignorant when they are offered to the eye, and to an understanding that can consider at leisure. I remember that a young Gentleman of Athens being to answer for his life, hired an Orator to make his defence, and it pleased him well, at his first reading; but when the young man by often reading it that he might recite it publikely by heart, began to grow weary and displeased with it, the Orator bade him consider that the Judges and the people were to hear it but once, and then it was likely, they at that first instant might be as well pleased as he. This hath often represented to my mind the condition and fortune of Sermons, and that I now part with the advantage they had in their delivery, but I have sufficiently answered my self in that, and am at rest perfectly in my thoughts as to that particular, if I can in any degree serve the interest of souls, and (which is next to that) obey the piety, and record the memory of that dear Saint, whose name and whose soul is blessed: for in both these ministeries, I doubt not but your Lordship will be pleased, and account as if I had done also some service to

your self: your religion makes me sure of the first, and your
piety puts the latter past my fears.

XXVIII Sermons, 1651, Epistle Dedicatory

8. *To Lord Carbery.*

My Lord,

I AM treating your Lordship as a Roman Gentleman did
Saint *Augustine* and his Mother; I shall entertain you
in a Charnel house, and carry your meditations awhile into
the chambers of death, where you shall finde the rooms
dressed up with melancholy arts, and fit to converse with
your most retired thoughts, which begin with a sigh and
proceed in deep consideration, and end in a holy resolution. The sight that S. *Augustine* most noted in that house
of sorrow was the body of *Cæsar* clothed with all the dishonours of corruption, that you can suppose in a six
moneths burial. But I know that without pointing, your
first thoughts will remember the change of a greater beauty,
which is now dressing for the brightest immortality; and
from her bed of darknesse calls to you to dress your soul
for that change which shall mingle your bones with that
beloved dust, and carry your soul to the same Quire, where
you may both sit and sing for ever. My Lord it is your
dear Ladies *Anniversary,* and she deserved the *biggest
honour,* and the *longest memory,* and the *fairest monument,*
and the most *solemne mourning*; and in order to it give me
leave (My Lord) to cover her Hearse with these following
sheets; this book was intended first to minister to her
piety; and she desired all good people should partake of
the advantages which are here recorded: she knew how to
live rarely well, and she desired to know how to dye; and
God taught her by an experiment. But since her work is

done and God supplyed her with provisions of his own, before I could minister to her, and perfect what she desired, it is necessary to present to your Lordship those bundles of Cypresse which were intended to dresse her Closet, but come now to dresse her Hearse. (My Lord) both your Lordship and my self have lately seen and felt such sorrows of death, and such sad departure of Dearest friends, that it is more then high time we should think our selves neerly concerned in the accidents; Death hath come so neer to you as to fetch a portion from your very heart; and now you cannot choose but digge your own grave and place your coffin in your eye when the Angel hath dressed your scene of sorrow and meditation with so particular and so neer an object; and therefore as it is my duty, I am come to minister to your pious thoughts, and to direct your sorrows that they may turn into vertues and advantages. . . . My Lord, it is a great art to dye well. . . .

My work here is not to please the speculative part of men, but to minister to practise, to preach to the weary, to comfort the sick, to assist the penitent, to reprove the confident, to strengthen weak hands and feeble knees, having scarce any other possibilities left me of doing alms, or exercising that charity by which we shall be judged at Doomsday. It is enough for me to be an underbuilder in the House of God, and I glory in the imployment; I labour in the foundations, and therefore the work needs no Apology for being plain, so it be strong and well laid. But (My Lord) as mean as it is, I must give God thanks for the desires and the strength, and next to him, to you for that opportunity and little portion of leisure which I had to do it in; for I must acknowledge it publikely (and besides my prayers, it is all the recompence I can make you) my being quiet I owe to your Interest, much of my support to your bounty, and many other collaterall comforts I derive from your favour and noblenesse. (My Lord) because I much honour you, and because I would do honour to my self, I have written your Name in the entrance of my Book, I am sure you will entertain it because the designe related to your Dear Lady, and because it may minister to your spirit in the day of visitation when God shall call for you to receive your reward for your charity and your noble piety, by which you have not onely endeared very many persons, but in great degrees have obliged me to be

My Noblest Lord
Your Lordships most thankfull
and most humble servant
Taylor.

Holy Dying, 1651, Epistle Dedicatory

9. *Death of Lady Carbery.*

My lord,

I AM not asham'd to professe that I pay this part of service to your Lordship most unwillingly: for it is a sad office to be the chief Minister in a house of mourning, and to present an interested person with a branch of Cypresse and a bottle of tears. And indeed, my Lord, it were more proportionable to your needs to bring something that might alleviate or divert your sorrow, then to dresse the hearse of your Dear Lady, and to furnish it with such circumstances, that it may dwell with you, and lie in your closet, and make your prayers and your retirements more sad and full of weepings. But because the Divine providence hath taken from you a person so excellent, a woman fit to converse with Angels, and Apostles, with

Saints and Martyrs, give me leave to present you with her picture; drawn in little and in water-colours, sullyed indeed with tears and the abrupt accents of a reall and consonant sorrow; but drawn with a faithfull hand, and taken from the life: and indeed it were too great a losse, to be depriv'd of her example and of her rule, of the originall and of the copie too. The age is very evil and deserv'd her not; but because it is so evil, it hath the more need to have such lives preserv'd in memory to instruct our piety, or upbraid our wickednesse. For now that God hath cut this tree of paradise down from its seat of earth, yet so the dead trunk may support a part of the declining Temple, or at least serve to kindle the fire on the altar. My Lord, I pray God this heap of sorrow may swell your piety till it breaks into the greatest joyes of God and of religion: and remember, when you pay a tear upon the grave, or to the memory of your Lady (that Deare and most excellent Soule) that you pay two more: one of repentance for those things that may have caus'd this breach; and another of joy for the mercies of God to your Dear departed Saint, that he hath taken her into a place where she can weep no more. My Lord, *I think I shall,* so long as I live, that is so long as I am

Your Lordships

most humble Servant

TAYLOR.

Funeral Sermon for Lady Carbery, 1650, Dedication

10. *Character of Lady Carbery.*

NOW that we are come to weep over the grave of our Dear Sister, this rare personage, we cannot chuse but have many virtues to learn, many to imitate, and some to exercise.

I chose, not to declare her extraction and genealogy. It was indeed fair and Honourable; but having the blessing to be descended from worthy and Honoured Ancestors, and her self to be adopted and ingraffed into a more Noble family, yet she felt such outward appendages to be none of hers, because not of her choice, but the purchase of the virtues of others, which although they did ingage her to do noble things, yet they would upbraid all degenerate and lesse honourable lives then were those which began and increased the honour of the families. She did not love her fortune for making her noble; but thought it would be a dishonour to her if she did not continue a Noblenesse and excellency of virtue fit to be owned by persons relating to such Ancestors. It is fit for all us to honour the Noblenesse of a family: but it is also fit for them that are Noble to despise it, and to establish their honour upon the foundation of doing excellent things, and suffering in good causes, and despising dishonourable actions, and in communicating good things to others. For this is the rule in Nature: Those creatures are most Honourable which have the greatest power, and do the greatest good: And accordingly my self have been a witnesse of it, how this excellent Lady would by an act of humility, and Christian abstraction strip her self of all that fair appendage of exteriour honour which decked her person and her fortune; and desired to be owned by nothing but what was her own, that she might onely be esteemed Honourable according to that which is the honour of a Christian, and a wise person.

She had a strict and severe education, and it was one of Gods graces and favours to her. For being the Heiresse of a great fortune, and living amongst the throng of persons in the sight of vanities and empty temptations, that is, in that part of the Kingdome where greatnesse is too often expressed in great follies, and great vices, God had provided a severe and angry education to chastise the forwardnesses of a young spirit, and a fair fortune; that she might for ever be so far distant from a vice, that she might onely see it and loath it, but never tast of it, so much as to be put to her choice whether she would be virtuous or no. God intending to secure this soul to himself, would not suffer the follies of the world to seize upon her by way of too neer a triall, or busie temptation.

She was married young; and besides her businesses of religion seemed to be ordained in the providence of God to bring to this Honourable family a part of a fair fortune, and to leave behind her a fairer issue, worth ten thousand times her portion : and as if this had been all the publike businesse of her life ; when she had so far served Gods ends, God in mercy would also serve hers, and take her to an early blessednesse.

In passing through which line of providence, she had the art to secure her eternall interest, by turning her condition into duty, and expressing her duty in the greatest eminency of a virtuous, prudent and rare affection, that hath been known in any example. I will not give her so low a testimony, as to say onely, that she was chast ; She was a person of that severity, modesty, and close religion (as to that particular) that she was not capable of uncivill temptation ; and you might as well have suspected the sun to smell of the poppy that he looks on, as that she could have been a person apt to be sullyed by the breath of a foul question.

But that which I shall note in her, is that which I would

have exemplar to all Ladies, and to all women. She had
a love so great for her Lord, so intirely given up to a dear
affection, that she thought the same things, and loved the
same loves, and hated according to the same enmities, and
breathed in his soul, and lived in his presence, and lan-
guished in his absence: and all that she was or did, was
onely for and to her Dearest Lord,

Si gaudet, si flet, si tacet, hunc loquitur.
Cœnat, propinat, poscit, negat, innuit, unus
Nævius est:—and although this was a great enamell to
the beauty of her soul, yet it might in some degrees be
also a reward to the virtue of her Lord: For she would
often discourse it to them that conversed with her; that
he would improve that interest which he had in her affection to the advantages of God, and of religion: and she
would delight to say, that he called her to her devotions,
he incouraged her good inclinations, he directed her piety,
he invited her with good books: and then she loved religion, which she saw was not onely pleasing to God, and
an act or state of duty, but pleasing to her Lord, and an
act also of affection and conjugall obedience: and what at
first she loved the more forwardly for his sake; in the using
of religion left such relishes upon her spirit, that she found
in it amability enough, to make her love it for its own. So
God usually brings us to him by instruments of nature and
affections, and then incorporates us into his inheritance,
by the more immediate relishes of Heaven, and the secret
things of the Spirit. He onely was (under God) the light
of her eies, and the cordiall of her spirits, and the guide
of her actions, and the measure of her affections, till her
affections swelled up into a religion, and then it could go
no higher, but was confederate with those other duties

which made her dear to God. Which rare combination
of duty and religion, I choose to express in the words of
*Solomon: She forsook not the guide of her youth, nor brake the
Covenant of her God.*

As she was a rare wife: so she was an excellent Mother.
For in so tender a constitution of spirit as hers was, and
in so great a kindness towards her children, there hath
seldome been seen a stricter and more curious care of their
persons, their deportment, their nature, their disposition,
their learning, and their customes: And if ever kindness
and care did contest, and make parties in her, yet her care
and her severity was ever victorious; and she knew not
how to doe an ill turn to their severer part, by her more
tender and forward kindnesse. And as her custome was,
she turned this also into love to her Lord. For she was
not onely diligent to have them bred nobly and religiously,
but also was carefull and sollicitous, that they should be
taught to observe all the circumstances and inclinations,
the desires and wishes of their Father; as thinking, that
virtue to have no good circumstances which was not
dressed by his copy, and ruled by his lines, and his affections: And her prudence in the managing her children was
so singular and rare, that when ever you mean to blesse
this family, and pray a hearty and a profitable prayer for
it, beg of God, that the children may have those excellent
things which she designed to them, and provided for them
in her heart and wishes, that they may live by her purposes, and may grow thither, whither she would fain have
brought them. All these were great parts of an excellent
religion as they concerned her greatest temporall relations.

But if we examine how she demeaned her self towards
God, there also you will find her, not of a common, but

of an exemplar piety. She was a great reader of Scripture, confining her self to great portions every day; which she read, not to the purposes of vanity, and impertinent curiosities, not to seem knowing, or to become talking, not to expound and Rule; but to teach her all her duty, to instruct her in the knowledge and love of God and of her Neighbours; to make her more humble, and to teach her to despise the world, and all its gilded vanities; and that she might entertain passions wholly in design and order to heaven. I have seen a female religion that wholly dwelt upon the face and tongue; that like a wanton and an undressed tree spends all its juice in suckers and irregular branches, in leafs and gumme, and after all such goodly outsides you should never eat an apple, or be delighted with the beauties, or the perfumes of a hopefull blossome. But the religion of this excellent Lady was of another constitution; It took root downward in humility, and brought forth fruit upward in the substantiall graces of a Christian, in charity and justice, in chastity and modesty, in fair friendships and sweetnesse of society: She had not very much of the forms and outsides of godlinesse; but she was hugely carefull for the power of it, for the morall, essentiall, and usefull parts; such which would make her be, not seem to be religious.

She was a very constant person at her prayers, and spent all her time which Nature did permit to her choice, in her devotions, and reading and meditating and the necessary offices of houshold government, every one of which is an action of religion, some by nature, some by adoption. To these also God gave her *a very great love to hear the word of God preached*; in which because I had sometimes the honour to minister to her, I can give this certain testimony, that she was a diligent, watchfull and attentive hearer: and to this had so excellent a judgement, that if ever I saw a woman whose judgement was to be revered, it was hers alone: and I have sometimes thought that the eminency of her discerning faculties did reward a pious discourse, & placed it in the regions of honour and usefulnesse, and gathered it up from the ground, where commonly such homilies are spilt, or scattered in neglect and inconsideration. But her appetite was not soon satisfied with what was usefull to her soul: she was also *a constant Reader of Sermons*, and seldome missed to read one every day; and that she might be full of instruction and holy principles, she had lately designed to have a large Book in which she purposed to have a stock of Religion transcrib'd in such assistances as she would chuse, that she might be *readily furnished and instructed to every good work*. But God prevented that, and hath filled her desires not out of cisterns and little aquæducts, but hath carried her to the fountain, where *she drinks of the pleasures of the river*, and is full of God.

She alwaies liv'd a life of much Innocence, free from the violences of great sins: her person, her breeding, her modesty, her honour, her religion, her early marriage, the Guide of her soul & the Guide of her youth, were as so many fountains of restraining grace to her, to keep her from the dishonors of a crime. *Bonum est portare jugum ab adolescentiâ:* it is good to bear the yoke of the Lord from our youth; and though she did so, being guarded by a mighty providence, and a great favour & grace of God from staining her fair soul with the spots of hell, yet she had strange fears & early cares upon her; but these were not only for her self, but in order to others, to her neer'st

Relatives. For she was so great a lover of this Honorable
family of which now she was a Mother, that she desired to
become a chanel of great blessings to it unto future ages,
and was extremely jealous lest any thing should be done,
or lest any thing had been done, though an age or two
since, which should intail a curse upon the innocent posterity; and therefore (although I doe not know that ever
she was tempted with an offer of the crime) yet she did
infinitely remove all sacrilege *from her thoughts*, and delighted to see her estate of a clear and disintangled interest:
she would have no mingled rights with it; she would not
receive any thing from the Church, but religion and a
blessing: and she never thought a curse and a sin farre
enough off, but would desire it to be infinitely distant;
and that as to this family God had given much honour and
a wise head to Govern it, so he would also for ever give
many more blessings; And because she knew that the sins
of Parents descend upon Children, she endeavoured by
justice and religion, by charity and honour to secure that
her chanel should convey nothing but health, and a faire
example and a blessing.

And though her accounts to God was made up of
nothing but small parcels, little passions, and angry words,
and trifling discontents, which are the allayes of the piety
of the most holy persons, yet she was early at her repentance; and toward the latter end of her daies, grew so fast
in religion as if she had had a revelation of her approaching
end; and therefore that she must go a great way in a little
time: her discourses more full of religion, her prayers more
frequent, her charity increasing, her forgiveness more forward, her friendships more communicative, her passion
more under discipline, and so she trimm'd her lamp, not

thinking her night was so neer, but that it might shine also in the day time, in the Temple, and before the Altar of incense.

But in this course of hers there were some circumstances, and some appendages of substance, which were highly remarkable.

In all her Religion, and in all her actions of relation towards God, she had a strange evenness and untroubled passage, sliding toward her ocean of God and of infinity with a certain and silent motion. So have I seen a river deep and smooth passing with a still foot and a sober face, and paying to the *Fiscus*, the great Exchequer of the Sea, the Prince of all the watry bodies, a tribute large and full: and hard by it a little brook skipping and making a noise upon its unequall and neighbour bottom; and after all its talking and bragged motion, it payd to its common Audit no more then the revenues of a little cloud, or a contemptible vessel: So have I sometimes compar'd the issues of her religion to the solemnities and fam'd outsides of anothers piety. It dwelt upon her spirit, and was incorporated with the periodicall work of every day: she did not believe that religion was intended to minister to fame and reputation, but to pardon of sins, to the pleasure of God, and the salvation of souls. For religion is like the breath of Heaven; if it goes abroad into the open aire, it scatters and dissolves like camphyre: but if it enters into a secret hollownesse, into a close conveyance, it is strong and mighty, and comes forth with vigour and great effect at the other end, at the other side of this life, in the daies of death and judgment.

The other appendage of her religion, which also was a great ornament to all the parts of her life, was a rare modesty and humility of spirit, a confident despising and undervaluing of her self. For though she had the greatest judgment, and the greatest experience of things and persons that I ever yet knew in a person of her youth, and sex, and circumstances; yet as if she knew nothing of it she had the meanest opinion of her self; and like a fair taper when she shin'd to all the room, yet round about her own station she had cast a shadow and a cloud, and she shin'd to every body but her self. But the perfectnesse of her prudence and excellent parts could not be hid; and all her humility, and arts of concealment, made the vertues more amiable and illustrious. For as pride sullies the beauty of the fairest vertues, and makes our understanding but like the craft and learning of a Devil: so humility is the greatest eminency, and art of publication in the whole world; and she in all her arts of secrecy and hiding her worthy things, was but *like one that hideth the winde, and covers the oyntment of her right hand.*

I know not by what instrument it hapned; but when death drew neer, before it made any show upon her body, or reveal'd it self by a naturall signification, it was conveyed to her spirit: she had a strange secret perswasion that the bringing this Childe should be her last scene of life: and we have known, that the soul when she is about to disrobe her self of her upper garment, sometimes speaks rarely, *Magnifica verba mors propè admota excutit*; sometimes it is Propheticall; sometimes God by a superinduced perswasion wrought by instruments, or accidents of his own, serves the ends of his own providence and the salvation of the soul: But so it was, that the thought of death dwelt long with her, and grew from the first steps of fancy and feare, to a consent, from thence to a strange credulity, and expectation of it; and without the violence of sicknesse she died, as if she had done it voluntarily, and by design, and for feare her expectation should have been deceiv'd, or that she should seem to have had an unreasonable feare, or apprehension; or rather (as one said of *Cato*) *sic abiit è vitâ ut causam moriendi nactam se esse gauderet*, she died, as if she had been glad of the opportunity.

And in this I cannot but adore the providence and admire the wisdome and infinite mercies of God. For having a tender and soft, a delicate and fine constitution and breeding, she was tender to pain, and apprehensive of it, as a childs shoulder is of a load and burden: *Grave est teneræ cervici jugum*; and in her often discourses of death, which she would renew willingly and frequently, she would tell, that she fear'd not death, but she fear'd the sharp pains of death: *Emori nolo, me esse mortuam non curo:* The being dead, and being freed from the troubles and dangers of this world, she hop'd would be for her advantage; and therefore that was no part of her feare: But she believing the pangs of death were great, and the use and aids of reason little, had reason to fear lest they should doe violence to her spirit and the decency of her resolution. But God that knew her fears, and her jealousie concerning her self, fitted her with a death so easie, so harmlesse, so painlesse, that it did not put her patience to a severe triall. It was not (in all appearance) of so much trouble, as two fits of a common ague; so carefull was God to remonstrate to all that stood in that sad attendance, that this soule was dear to him: and that since she had done so much of her duty towards it, he that began, would also finish her redemption, by an act of a rare providence, and a singular mercy. *Blessed be that goodness of God, who does so carefull actions of mercy, for the ease and security of his servants.* But this one instance was a great demonstration that the apprehension of death is worse then the pains of death: and that God loves to reprove the unreasonablenesse of our feares, by the mightinesse, and by the arts of his mercy.

She had in her sickness (if I may so call it, or rather in the solemnities, and graver preparations towards death) some curious and well-becoming feares, concerning the finall state of her soul. But from thence she pass'd into a *deliquium*, or a kinde of trance, and as soon as she came forth of it, as if it had been a vision, or that she had convers'd with an Angel, and from his hand had receiv'd a labell or scroll of the *book of life*, and there seen her *name* enrolled, she cried out aloud, [*Glory be to God on high: Now I am sure I shall be saved.*] Concerning which manner of discoursing we are wholly ignorant what judgment can be made: but certainly there are strange things in the other world; and so there are in all the immediate preparations to it; and a little glimps of heaven, a minutes conversing with an Angel, any ray of God, any communication extraordinary from the Spirit of comfort which God gives to his servants in strange and unknown manners, are infinitely far from illusions; and they shall then be understood by us, when we feel them, and when our new and strange needs shall be refreshed by such unusuall visitations.

But I must be forced to use summaries and arts of abbreviature in the enumerating those things in which this rare Personage was dear to God & to all her Relatives.

If we consider her Person, she was in the flower of her age, *Jucundum cum ætas florida ver ageret*; of a temperate,

plain and naturall diet, without curiosity or an intemperate palate; she spent lesse time in dressing, then many
servants; her recreations were little & seldom, her prayers
often, her reading much: she was of a most noble and
charitable soul; a great lover of honourable actions, and as
great a despiser of base things; hugely loving to oblige
others, and very unwilling to be in arrear to any upon
the stock of courtesies and liberality; so free in all acts of
favour, that she would not stay to hear her self thank'd,
as being unwilling that what good went from her to a
needfull or an obliged person should ever return to her
again; she was an excellent friend, and hugely dear to very
many, especially to the best and most discerning persons,
to all that convers'd with her, and could understand her
great worth and sweetnesse: she was of an Honourable,
a nice and tender reputation; and of the pleasures of this
world which were laid before her in heaps she took a very
small and inconsiderable share, as not loving to glut her
self with vanity, or to take her portion of good things
here below.

If we look on her as a Wife, she was chast and loving,
fruitfull and discreet, humble and pleasant, witty and
complyant, rich and fair, and wanted nothing to the
making her a principall and a precedent to the best Wives
of the world, but a long life, and a full age.

If we remember her as a Mother, she was kinde and
severe, carefull and prudent, very tender, and not at all
fond, a greater lover of her Childrens soules, then of their
bodies, and one that would value them more by the strict
rules of honour and proper worth, then by their relation
to her self.

Her Servants found her prudent, and fit to Govern, and

yet open-handed and apt to reward; a just Exactor of their duty and a great Rewarder of their diligence.

She was in her house a comfort to her dearest Lord, a Guide to her Children, a Rule to her Servants, an example to all.

But as she related to God in the offices of Religion, she was even and constant, silent and devout, prudent and materiall: she lov'd what she now enjoyes, and she fear'd, what she never felt, and God did for her what she never did expect. Her fears went beyond all her evil; and yet the good which she hath receiv'd was, and is, and ever shall be beyond all her hopes.

She liv'd as we all should live, and she died as I fain would die——

Et cum supremos Lachesis perneverit annos,
Non aliter cineres mando jacere meos.

I pray God I may feel those mercies on my death-bed that she felt, and that I may feel the same effect of my repentance which she feels of the many degrees of her innocence. Such was her death that she did not die too soon; and her life was so usefull and so excellent that she could not have liv'd too long. *Nemo parum diu vixit qui virtutis perfectæ perfecto functus est munere:* and as now in the grave it shall not be inquired concerning her, how long she liv'd, but how well? so to us who live after her to suffer a longer calamity, it may be some ease to our sorrows, and some guide to our lives, and some security to our conditions, to consider that God hath brought the piety of a yong Lady to the early rewards of a never ceasing, and never dying eternity of glory. And we also, if we live as she did, shal partake of the same glories; not only having the honour of a good name and a dear and honour'd memory, but the glories of these glories, the end of all excellent labours, and all prudent counsels, and all holy religion, even the salvation of our souls in that day, when all the Saints, and amongst them this excellent Woman shall be shown to all the world to have done more, and more excellent things then we know of or can describe. *Mors illos consecrat, quorum exitum & qui timent, laudant:* Death consecrates and makes sacred that person whose excellency was such, that they that are not displeased at the death, cannot dispraise the life; but they that mourn sadly, think they can never commend sufficiently.

Funeral Sermon for Lady Carbery, 1650, p. 23

II. *The State of the Church.*

IN this sad declension of Religion, the *Seers* who are appointed to be the Watchmen of the Church, cannot but observe that the Supplanters and Underminers are gone out, and are digging down the Foundations: and having destroy'd all publick Forms of Ecclesiasticall Government, discountenanc'd an excellent Liturgie, taken off the hinges of Unity, disgrac'd the Articles of Religion, polluted publick Assemblies, taken away all cognisance of Schism, by mingling all Sects, and giving countenance to that, against which all Power ought to stand upon their guard. There is now nothing left, but that we take care that men be Christians: For concerning the Ornament and Advantages of Religion, we cannot make that provision we desire; *Incertis de salute, de gloriâ minimè certandum*; For since they who have seen *Jerusalem* in prosperity, and have forgotten the order of the Morning and Evening Sacrifice, and the beauty of the Temple, will be tempted to neglect so excellent a ministration, & their assembling themselves together for peace, and holy Offices, and be content with any thing that is brought to them, though it be but the husks and acorns of Prodigals and Swine, so they may enjoy their Lands and their Money with it; we must now take care that the young men who were born in the Captivity, may be taught how to worship the God of *Israel* after the manner of their fore-fathers, till it shall please God that Religion shall return into the Land, and dwell safely, and grow prosperously.

But never did the excellency of Episcopall Government appear so demonstratively and conspicuously as now: Under their conduct and order we had a Church so united, so orderly, so govern'd, a Religion so setled, Articles so true, sufficient, and confess'd, Canons so prudent and so obey'd, Devotions so regular and constant, Sacraments so adorn'd and ministred, Churches so beauteous and religious, Circumstances of Religion so grave and prudent, so useful and apt for edification, that the enemies of our Church, who serve the Pope in all things, and Jesus Christ in some, who dare transgress an Institution and Ordinance of Christ, but dare not break a Canon of the Pope, did despair of prevailing against Us *and Truth*, and knew no hopes but by setting their faces against us to destroy this Government, and then they knew they should triumph without any enemy: So *Balaam* the son of *Bosor* was sent for, to curse the people of the Lord, in hope that the son of *Zippor* might prevail against them that had long prospered under the conduct of *Moses* and *Aaron*.

But now in stead of this excellency of Condition and Constitution of Religion, the people are fallen under the harrows and saws of impertinent and ignorant Preachers, who think all Religion is a Sermon, and all Sermons ought

to be Libels against Truth and old Governours, and expound Chapters that the meaning may never be understood, and pray, that they may be thought able to talk,
but not to hold their peace, they casting not to obtain any
thing but Wealth and Victory, Power and Plunder; and
the people have reap'd the fruits apt to grow upon such
Crabstocks: they grow idle and false, hypocrites and careless, they deny themselves nothing that is pleasant, they
despise Religion, forget Government; and some never
think of Heaven; and they that do, think to go thither in
such paths which all the ages of the Church did give men
warning of, lest they should that way go to the Devil.

But when men have try'd all that they can, it is to be
suppos'd they will return to the excellency and advantages
of the Christian Religion, as it is taught by the Church of
England; for by destroying it, no end can be serv'd but
of Sin and Folly, Faction, and Death eternal. For besides
that, no Church that is enemy to this, does worship God
in that truth of Propositions, in that unblameable and
pious Liturgie, and in preaching the necessities of holy life,
so much as the Church of *England* does; besides this (I say)
it cannot be persecuted by any Governour that understands his own interest, unless he be first abus'd by false
Preachers, and then prefers his secret opinion before his
publick Advantage. For no Church in the World is so
great a friend to Loyalty and Obedience, as she, and her
Sisters of the same perswasion. They that hate Bishops
have destroy'd Monarchy, and they that would erect an
Ecclesiasticall Monarchy, must consequently subject the
Temporall to it. And both one and the other would be
Supreme in Consciences; and they that govern there, with
an opinion that in all things they ought to be attended to,

will let their Prince govern others, so long as he will be
rul'd by them: And certainly, for a Prince to persecute the
Protestant Religion, is as if a Physician should endevour
to destroy all Medicaments, and Fathers kill their Sons,
and the Master of Ceremonies destroy all Formalities and
Courtships; and as if the Pope should root out all the
Ecclesiastick State. Nothing so combines with Government, if it be of Gods appointment, as the Religion of the
Church of *England*, because nothing does more adhere to
the Word of God, and disregard the crafty advantages of
the world. If any man shall not decline to try his Title
by the Word of God, it is certain there is not in the world
a better guard for it, then the true Protestant Religion,
as it is taught in our Church. But let things be as it please
God; it is certain, that in that day when Truth gets her
Victory, in that day we shall prevail against all Gods
enemies and ours, not in the purchases and perquisites of
the world, but in the rewards and returns of Holiness and
Patience, and Faith and Charity; for by these we worship God, and against this interest we cannot serve any
thing else.

The Golden Grove, 1655, 'To the Reader'

12. *The Death of a Child.*

DEARE Sir, I am in some little disorder by reason of
the death of a little child of mine, a boy that lately
made us very glad: but now he rejoyces in his little orbe,
while we thinke, and sigh, and long to be as safe as he is.

Letter to John Evelyn, 19 July 1656

13. *The Restoration: to Charles II.*

Great Sir,

THE circles of the Divine Providence turn themselves upon the affairs of the world so, that every spondel of the wheels may mark out those Vertues which we are then to exercise; and every new event in the Oeconomy of God is God's finger to point out to us by what instances he will be served. We have been sorely smitten and for a long time; for (that I may use the words of the Prophet) *Alas, for that day was great, so that none was like it, it was even the time of Jacob's trouble;* and then, Faith and Patience, and all the passive Graces of Religion were in their own season. But since God hath left off to smite us with an iron rod, and hath once more said unto these Nations, *They shall serve the Lord their God, and David their King whom I have raised up unto them;* Now our duty stands on the Sunny side; it is our work to rejoice in *God* and in *God's Anointed*, and to be glad, and worthily to accept of our Prosperity is all our business: for so good a God we serve, that he hath made it our Duty to be happy, and we cannot please him unless we be infinitely pleased our selves. It was impossible to live without our King; but as Slaves live, that is, such who are civilly dead, and persons condemn'd to metalls: we lived to the lusts and insolency of others, but not at all to our selves, to our own Civil or Religious comforts. But now our joys are mere and unmixt; for that we may doe our duty and have our reward at once, God hath sent your Majesty amongst us, that we may feel the pleasures of Obedience, and reap the fruits of that Government which God loves and uses, which He hath constituted and adorned, which He hath restored to us by a conjugation of miracles, by the work of his hand and the light of his countenance, by changing the hearts of Men, and scattering the people that delight in War, by infatuating their Counsels and breaking their Cords asunder; that is, which He himself hath wrought amongst us by himself alone, and therefore will bless and will never interrupt: only we must be carefull never to provoke him any more by our Unthankfulness and infidel Apostasie.

Ductor Dubitantium, 1660, vol. i, Epistle Dedicatory, A 3 recto

14. *Rebellion and Disobedience.*

MY eyes are almost grown old with seeing the horrid mischiefs which came from Rebellion and Disobedience; and I would willingly now be blessed with observation of Peace and Righteousness, Plenty and Religion, which do already, and I hope shall for ever, attend upon Obedience to the best KING and the best CHURCH in the world.

Sermon preached at the Opening of Parliament, 1661,
Epistle Dedicatory

15. *The Irish.*

BUT we have observed amongst the generality of the *Irish*, such a declension of Christianity, so great credulity to believe every superstitious story, such confidence in vanity, such groundless pertinacy, such vitious lives, so little sense of true Religion and the fear of God, so much care to obey the Priests, and so little to obey God: such intolerable ignorance, such fond Oathes and manners of swearing, thinking themselves more obliged by swearing on the Mass-Book, than the Four Gospels, and S. *Patricks* Mass-Book more than any new one; swearing by their

Fathers Soul, by their Godsips hand, by other things which are the product of those many tales are told them; their not knowing upon what account they refuse to come to Church, but onely that now they are old and never did, or their Country-men do not, or their Fathers or Grand-fathers never did, or that their Ancestors were Priests, and they will not alter from their Religion; and after all, can give no account of their Religion, what it is: onely they believe as their Priest bids them, and go to Mass which they understand not, and reckon their beads to tell the number and the tale of their prayers, and abstain from eggs and flesh in Lent, and visit S. *Patricks* Well, and leave pins and ribbands, yarn or thred in their holy wells, and pray to God, S. *Mary* and S. *Patrick*, S. *Columbanus* and S. *Bridget*, and desire to be buried with S. *Francis*'s chord about them, and to fast on Saturdays in honour of our Lady. These and so many other things of like nature we see dayly, that we being conscious of the infinite distance which these things have from the spirit of Christianity, know that no Charity can be greater than to persuade the people to come to our Churches, were they shall be taught all the ways of godly wisdom, of peace and safety to their souls: whereas now there are many of them that know not how to say their prayers, but mutter like Pies and Parrots, words which they are taught, but they do not pretend to understand. But I shall give one particular instance of their miserable superstition and blindness.

I was lately within a few Moneths very much troubled with petitions and earnest requests, for the restoring a Bell which a Person of Quality had in his hands in the time of, and ever since the late Rebellion. I could not guess at the reasons of their so great and violent importunity, but told the petitioners, if they could prove that Bell to be theirs, the Gentleman was willing to pay the full value of it; though he had no obligation to do so (that I know of) but charity: but this was so far from satisfying them, that still the importunity encreased, which made me diligently to inquire into the secret of it. The first cause I found was, that a dying person in the parish desired to have it rung before him to Church, and pretended he could not die in peace if it were deny'd him; and that the keeping of that Bell did anciently belong to that family from father to son: but because this seem'd nothing but a fond and an unreasonable superstition, I enquired farther, and at last found that they believ'd this Bell came from heaven, that it used to be carryed from place to place, to end controversies by oath, wch the worst man durst not violate if they swore upon that Bell, and the best men amongst them durst not but believe him; that if this Bell was rung before the corpse to the grave, it would help him out of Purgatory, and that therefore when any one dyed, the friends of the deceased did, whilst the Bell was in their possession, hire it for the behoof of their dead, and that by this means that family was in part maintain'd. I was troubled to see under what spirit of delusion those poor souls do lie, how infinitely their credulity is abused, how certainly they believe in trifles, and perfectly rely on vanity, and how little they regard the truths of God, and how not at all they drink of the waters of Salvation. For the numerous companies of Priests and Friers amongst them, take care they shall know nothing of Religion but what they design for them, they use all means to keep them to the use of the *Irish* tongue, lest if they learn *English*, they might be supply'd with persons fitter to instruct them; the people are taught to make that also their excuse for not coming to our Churches, to hear our advises, or converse with us in religious intercourses, because they understand us not, and they will not understand us, neither will they learn, that they may understand and live. And this and many other evils are made greater and more irremediable by the affrightment which their Priests put upon them by the issues of Ecclesiastical Jurisdiction, by which (they now exercising it too publickly) they give them Laws, not onely for Religion, but even for Temporal things, and turn their Proselytes from the Mass, if they become farmers of the Tythes from the Minister or Proprietary without their leave. I speak that which I know to be true by their own confession and unconstrain'd and uninvited Narratives; so that as it is certain that the *Roman* Religion, as it stands in distinction and separation from us, is a body of strange Propositions, having but little relish of true primitive and pure Christianity (as will be made manifest if the importunity of our adversaries extort it) so it is here amongst us a faction and a State party and designe to recover their old Laws and barbarous manner of living, a device to enable them to dwell alone, and to be *populus unius labii*, a people of one language, and unmingled with others. And if this be Religion, it is such a one as ought to be reproved by all the severities of Reason and Religion, lest the people perish, and their souls be cheaply given away to them that make merchandize of souls, who were the purchase and price of Christs bloud.

A Dissuasive from Popery, 1664, Preface

16. *The Old Age of Archbishop Bramhall.*

HE thus having serv'd God and the King abroad, God was pleas'd to return to the King and to us all, as in the *dayes of old, and we sung the song of David.*

In convertendo captivitatem Sion: When King *David* and all his servants returned to *Jerusalem*, this great person having trode in the Wine-press was called to drink of the Wine, and as an honorary Reward of his great services and abilities was chosen Primate of this National Church: In which time we are to look upon him, as the King and the Kings great Vicegerent did, as a person concerning whose abilities the World had too great testimony ever to make a doubt. It is true, he was in the declension of his age and health; but his very Ruines were goodly; and they who saw the broken heaps of *Pompey's* Theatre, and the crushed Obelisks, and the old face of beauteous *Philænium*, could not but admire the disordered glories of such magnificent structures, which were venerable in their very dust.

Sermon at the Funeral of the Archbishop of Armagh (*John Bramhall*), 3rd ed., 1663, p. 57

17. *Our Mortal Condition.*

THE Condition of Man in this world is so limited and depressed, so relative and imperfect, that the best things he does he does weakly, and the best things he hath are imperfections in their very constitution. I need not tell how little it is that we know; the greatest indication of this is, That we can never tell how many things we know not: and we may soon span our own Knowledge, but our Ignorance we can never fathom. Our very Will, in which Mankind pretends to be most noble and imperial, is a direct state of imperfection; and our very liberty of Chusing good and evil is permitted to us, not to make us proud, but to make us humble; for it supposes weakness of Reason and weakness of Love. For if we understood all the degrees of Amability in the Service of God, or if we had such love to God as he deserves, and so perfect a conviction as were fit for his Services, we could no more Deliberate: For Liberty of Will is like the motion of a Magnetic Needle toward the North, full of trembling and uncertainty till it were fixed in the beloved Point; it wavers as long as it is free, and is at rest when it can chuse no more. And truly what is the hope of Man? It is indeed the resurrection of the Soul in this world from sorrow and her saddest pressures, and like the Twilight to the Day, and the Harbinger of joy; but still it is but a conjugation of Infirmities, and proclaims our present calamity, onely because it is uneasie here, it thrusts us forwards toward the light and glories of the Resurrection.

For as a Worm creeping with her belly on the ground, with her portion and share of *Adam's* curse, lifts up its head to partake a little of the blessings of the air, and opens the junctures of her imperfect body, and curles her little rings into knots and combinations, drawing up her tail to a neighbourhood of the heads pleasure and motion; but still it must return to abide the fate of its own nature, and dwell and sleep upon the dust: So are the hopes of a mortal Man; he opens his eyes and looks upon fine things at distance, and shuts them again with weakness, because they are too glorious to behold; and the Man rejoyces because he hopes fine things are staying for him; but his heart akes, because he knows there are a thousand wayes to fail and miss of those glories; & though he hopes, yet he enjoys not; he longs, but he possesses not, and must be content with his portion of dust; and being *a worm and no Man* must lie down in this portion, before he can receive the end of his hopes, the Salvation of his Soul in the resurrection of the dead.

Sermon at the Funeral of the Archbishop of Armagh (John Bramhall),
3rd ed., 1663, p. 1

18. *Birds of Paradise.*

MANKINDE now taking in his whole constitution, and designe is like the Birds of *Paradice* which travellers tell us of in the *Molucco Islands*; born without legs; but by a celestial power they have a recompence made to them for that defect; and they alwayes hover in the air, and feed on the dew of heaven: so are we birds of *Paradice*; but cast out from thence, and born without legs, without strength to walk in the laws of God, or to go to heaven; but by a power from above, we are adopted in our new birth to a celestial conversation, we feed on the dew of heaven.

Deus Justificatus, 1656, p. 79

19. *The Ages of Man.*

IN the accounts of a mans life we do not reckon that portion of dayes in which we are shut up in the prison of the womb: we tell our years from the day of our birth: and the same reason that makes our reckning to stay so long, sayes also that then it begins too soon. For then we are beholding to others to make the account for us: for we know not of a long time, whether we be alive or no, having but some little approaches and symptoms of a life. To feed, and sleep, and move a little, and imperfectly, is the state of an unborn childe; and when it is born, he does no more for a good while; and what is it that shall make him to be esteemed to live the life of a man? and when shall that account begin? For we should be loath to have the accounts of our age taken by the measures of a beast: and fools and distracted persons are reckoned as *civilly dead*; they are no parts of the Common-wealth, not subject to laws, but secured by them in Charity, and kept from violence as a man keeps his Ox; and a third part of our life is spent, before we enter into a higher order, into the state of a man.

Neither must we think, that the life of a Man begins when he can feed himself or walk alone, when he can fight, or beget his like; for so he is contemporary with a camel, or a cow; but he is first a man when he comes to a certain, steddy use of reason, according to his proportion, and when that is, all the world of men cannot tell precisely. Some are called *at age*, at fourteen, some at one and twenty, some never; but all men, late enough; for the life of a man comes upon him slowly and insensibly. But as when the Sun approaches towards the gates of the morning, he first opens a little eye of Heaven, and sends away the spirits of darknesse, and gives light to a cock, and calls up the lark to Mattins, and by and by gilds the fringes of a cloud and peeps over the Eastern hills, thrusting out his golden horns, like those which decked the browes of *Moses* when he was forced to wear a vail, because himself had seen the face of God; and still while a man tells the story, the sun gets up higher, till he showes a fair face and a full light, and then he shines one whole day, under a cloud often, and sometimes weeping great and little showers, and sets quickly: so is a mans reason and his life. He first begins to perceive himself to see or taste, making little reflections upon his actions of sense, and can discourse of flies and dogs, shells and play, horses and liberty; but when he is strong enough to enter into arts and little institutions, he is at first entertained with trifles and impertinent things, not because he needs them, but because his understanding is no bigger; and little images of things are laid before him, like a cock-boat to a whale onely to play withall: but before a man comes to be wise he is half dead with gouts and consumptions, with Catarrhes and aches, with sore eyes, and a worn out body: so that if we must not reckon the life of a man but by the accounts of his reason, he is long before his soul be dressed; and he is not to be called a man without a wise and an adorned soul, a soul at least furnished with what is necessary towards his well being; but by that time his soul is thus furnished, his body is decayed; and then you can hardly reckon him to be alive, when his body is possessed by so many degrees of death.

But there is yet another arrest. At first he wants strength of body, and then he wants the use of reason; and when that is come, it is ten to one, but he stops by the impediments of vice, and wants the strengths of the *spirit*; and we know that *Body* and *Soul* and *Spirit* are the constituent parts of every Christian man. And now let us consider, what that thing is, which we call *years of discretion*? The young man is passed his Tutors, and arrived at the bondage of a caytive spirit; he is run from discipline, and is let loose to passion; the man by this time hath wit enough to chuse his vice, to act his lust, to court his Mistresse, to talk confidently, and ignorantly, and perpetually, to despise his betters, to deny nothing to his appetite, to do things, that when he is indeed a man he must for ever be ashamed of; for this is all the discretion that most men show in the first stage of their Manhood; they can discern good from evil; and they prove their skill by leaving all that is good, and wallowing in the evils of folly, and an unbridled appetite. And by this time, the young man hath contracted vitious habits, and is a beast in manners, and therefore it will not be fitting to reckon the beginning of his life; he is a fool in his understanding, and that is a sad death; and he is dead in trespasses and sins, and that is a sadder: so that he hath no life but a natural, the life of a beast or a tree; in all other capacities he is dead; he neither hath the intellectual, nor the spiritual life, neither the life of a man, nor of a Christian; and this sad truth lasts too long. For old age seizes upon most men while they still retain the minds of boyes and vitious youth, doing actions from principles of great folly, and a mighty ignorance, admiring things uselesse and hurtfull, and filling up all the dimensions of their abode with businesses of empty affairs, being at leisure to attend no vertue: they cannot pray, because they are busie, and because they are passionate: they cannot communicate because they have quarrels and intrigues of perplexed causes, complicated hostilities, and things of the world; and therefore they cannot attend to the things of God, little considering, that they must find a time to die in; when death comes, they must be at leisure for that. Such men are like Sailers loosing from a port, and tost immediatly with a perpetual tempest lasting till their cordage crack, and either they sink, or return back again to the same place: they did not make a voyage, though they were long at sea.

Holy Dying, 1651, p. 21

20. *Man's Spirit.*

BUT so have I seen a fair structure begun with art and care, and raised to halfe its stature, and then it stood still by the misfortune or negligence of the owner, and the rain descended, and dwelt in its joynts, and supplanted the contexture of its pillars, and having stood a while like the antiquated Temple of a deceased Oracle, it fell into a hasty age, and sunk upon its owne knees, and so descended into ruine: So is the imperfect, unfinished spirit of a man; it layes the foundation of a holy resolution, and strengthens it with vows and arts of prosecution, it raises up the Sacraments, and Prayers, Reading, and holy Ordinances; and holy actions begin with a slow motion, and the building stays, and the spirit is weary, and the soul is naked, and exposed to temptation, and in the days of storm take in every thing that can doe it mischief; and it is faint and sick, listlesse and tired, and it stands till its owne weight wearies the foundation, and then declines to death and sad disorder, being so much the worse, because it hath not onely returned to its first follies, but hath superadded *unthankfulnesse* and *carelesnesse*, a positive neglect, and a despite of holy things, a setting a low price to the things of God, lazinesse and wretchlesnesse; all which are evills superadded to the first state of coldnesse, whither he is with all these loads and circumstances of death easily revolv'd.

XXV Sermons, 1653, p. 166

21. *The Day.*

FOR if we consider the disorders of every day, the multitude of impertinent words, the great portions of time spent in vanity, the daily omissions of duty, the coldnesse of our prayers, the indifference of our spirit in holy things, the uncertainty of our secret purposes, our infinite deceptions and hypocrisie, sometimes not known, very often not observed by our selves; our want of charity, our not knowing in how many degrees of action and purpose every vertue is to be exercised, the secret adherencies of pride, and too forward complacencie in our best actions, our failings in all our relations, the niceties of difference between some vertues and some vices, the secret undiscernable passages from lawfull to unlawfull in the first instances of change, the perpetuall mistakings of permissions for duty, and licentious practises for permissions, our daily abusing the liberty that God gives us, our unsuspected sins in the managing a course of life certainly lawfull, our little greedinesses in eating, our surprises in the proportions of our drinkings, our too great freedoms and fondnesses in lawfull loves, our aptnesse for things sensual, and our deadnesse and tediousnesse of spirit in spiritual employments, besides infinite variety of cases of conscience that do occur in the life of every man, and in all entercourses of every life, and that the productions of sin are numerous and increasing, like the families of the Northern people, or the genealogies of the first Patriarks of the world; from all this we shall find that the computations of a mans life are buisie as the Tables of Signes and Tangents, and intricate as the accounts of Eastern Merchants: and therefore it were but reason we should summe up our accounts at the foot of every page, I mean, that we call our selves to scrutiny every night when we compose our selves to the little images of Death.

Holy Dying, 1651, p. 55

22. *The Length of Life.*

*T*OSTATUS ABULENSIS was a very painful person and a great Cleark, and in the dayes of his manhood he wrote so many books, and they not ill ones, that the world computed a sheet for every day of his life; I suppose they meant, after he came to the use of reason, and the state of a man: and *John Scotus* died about the two and thirtieth year of his age; and yet besides his publike disputations, his dayly Lectures of Divinity in publike and private, the Books that he wrote being lately collected and printed at Lyons do equal the number of volumes of any two the most voluminous Fathers of the Latine Church. Every man is not inabled to such imployments, but every man is called and inabled to the works of a sober and a religious life; and there are many Saints of God that can reckon as many volumes of religion and mountains of piety, as those others did of good books. S. *Ambrose* (and I think from his example, S. *Augustine*) divided every day into three tertia's of imployment: eight hours he spent in the necessities of nature and recreation, eight hours in charity and doing assistance to others, dispatching their buisinesses, reconciling their enmities, reproving their vices, correcting their errors, instructing their ignorances, transacting the affairs of his Diocesse, and the other eight hours he spent in study and prayer. If we were thus minute and curious in the spending our time, it is impossible but our life would seem very long. For so have I seen an amorous person tell the minutes of his absence from his fancied joy, and while he told the sands of his hour-glasse, or the throbs and little beatings of his watch, by dividing an hour into so many members, he spun out its length by number, and so translated a day into the tediousnesse of a moneth. And if we tell our dayes by Canonical hours of prayer, our weeks by a constant revolution of fasting dayes, or dayes of special devotion, and over all these draw a black Cypresse a veil of penitential sorrow, and severe mortification, we shall soon answer the calumny and objection of a short life. He that governs the day and divides the hours hastens from the eyes and observation of a merry sinner; but loves to stand still, and behold, and tell the sighs, and number the groans, and sadly delicious accents of a grieved penitent. It is a vast work that any man may do if he never be idle; and it is a huge way that a man may go in vertue if he never goes out of his way by a vitious habit, or a great crime, and he that perpetually reads good books, if his parts be answerable, will have a huge stock of knowledge. It is so in all things else. Strive not to forget your time, and suffer none of it to passe undiscerned, and then measure your life, and tell me how you finde the measure of its abode. However, *the time we live, is worth the money we pay for it*: and therefore it is not to be thrown away.

When vitious men are dying, and scar'd with the affrighting truths of an evil conscience, they would give all the world for a year, for a moneth; nay we read of some that called out with amazement *inducias usq̃, ad mane, truce but till the morning*: and if that year, or some few moneths were given, those men think they could do miracles in it. And let us a while suppose what *Dives* would have done if he had been loosed from the pains of hell and permitted to live on earth one year. Would all the pleasures of the world have kept him one hour from the Temple? would he not perpetually have been under the hands of Priests, or at the feet of the Doctors, or by *Moses* chair, or attending as neer the Altar as he could get, or relieving poor *Lazars*, or praying to God, and crucifying all his sin? I have read of a Melancholy person who saw hell but in a dream or vision, and the amazement was such that he would have chosen ten times to die, rather then feel again so much of that horror: and such a person cannot be fancied but that he would spend a year in such holinesse, that the religion of a few moneths would equal the devotion of many years, even of a good man. Let us but compute the proportions. If we should spend all our years of reason so as such a person would spend that one, can it be thought that life would be short and trifling in which he had performed such a religion, served God with so much holinesse, mortified sin with so great a labour, purchased vertue at such a rate, and so rare an industry? It must needs be that such a man must dye when he ought to die, and be like ripe and pleasant fruit falling from a fair tree and gathered into baskets for the planters use: He that hath done all his businesse, and is begotten to a glorious hope by the seed of an immortal Spirit, can never die too soon, nor live too long.

Holy Dying, 1651, p. 28

23. *Growth in Wisdom.*

MEN at first think themselves wise, and are alwaies most confident when they have the least reason; and to morrow they begin to perceive yesterdayes folly, and yet they are not wise; But as the little Embryo in the naturall sheet and lap of its mother, first distinguishes into a little knot, and that in time will be the heart, and then into a bigger bundle, which after some dayes abode grows into two little spots, and they if cherished by nature will become eyes, and each part by order commences into weak principles, and is preserved with natures greatest curiosity; that it may assist first to distinction, then to order, next to usefulnesse, and from thence to strength, till it arrive at beauty, and a perfect creature: so are the necessities, and so are the discourses of men; we first learn the principles of reason, which breaks obscurely through a cloud, and brings a little light, and then we discern a folly, and by little and little leave it, till that enlightens the next corner of the soul; and then there is a new discovery; but the soul is still in infancy and childish follies; and every day does but the work of one day; but therefore art, and use, experience, and reason, although they do something, yet they cannot do enough; there must be something else: But this is to be wrought by a new principle, that is, by *the Spirit of grace*: Nature and reason alone cannot do it, and therefore the proper cure is to be wrought by those generall means of *inviting* and *cherishing*, of *getting* and *entertaining* Gods Spirit, which when we have observed, we may account our selves sufficiently instructed toward the repair of our breaches, and the reformation of our evill nature.

XXV Sermons 1653, p. 141

24. *Man's Heart.*

A MANS heart is infinitely deceitful, unknown to it self, not certain in his own acts, praying one way, and desiring another, wandring and imperfect, loose and various worshipping God and entertaining sin, following what it hates, and running from what it flatters, loving to be tempted and betrayed, petulant like a wanton girle, running from, that it might invite the fondnesse and enrage the appetite of the foolish young man or the evil temptation that followes it; cold and indifferent one while, and presently zealous and passionate, furious and indiscreet; not understood of it self or any one else, and deceitful beyond all the arts and numbers of observation.

Holy Dying, 1651, p. 302

25. *Man's Weakness.*

BECAUSE the heart of man is false, it suffers the fires of the Altar to go out, and the flames lessen by the multitude of fuel. But indeed it is because we put on strange fire, & put out the fire upon our hearths by letting in a glaring Sun beam, the fire of lust; or the heates of an angry spirit, to quench the fires of God, and suppresse the sweet cloud of incense. The heart of man hath not strength enough to think one good thought of it self, it cannot command its own attention to a prayer of ten lines long; but before its end it shall wander after some thing, that is to no purpose: and no wonder then that it grows weary of a holy religion, which consists of so many parts as make the businesse of a whole life. And there is no greater argument in the world of our spiritual weaknesse and falsnesse of our hearts in the matters of religion, then the backwardnesse which most men have alwayes, and all men have somtimes to say their prayers: so weary of their length, so glad when they are done, so wittie to excuse and frustrate an opportunity; and yet there is no manner of trouble in the duty, no wearinesse of bones, no violent

labours; nothing but begging a blessing, and receiving it;
nothing but doing our selves the greatest honour of speaking to the greatest person, and greatest king of the world;
and that we should be unwilling to do this, so unable to
continue in it, so backward to return to it; so without gust
and relish in the doing it, can have no visible reason in the
nature of the thing, but something within us, a strange
sicknesse in the heart, a spiritual nauseating or loathing of
Manna, something that hath no name; but we are sure it
comes from a weake, a faint, and false heart.

XXVIII Sermons, 1651, p. 83

26. *Man's Desires.*

FOR so have I seen a busie flame sitting upon a sullen
cole turn its point to all the angles and portions of its
neighbour-hood and reach at a heap of prepared straw,
which like a bold temptation called it to a restlesse motion
and activity, but either it was at too big a distance or a
gentle breath from heaven diverted the speare and the ray
of the fire to the other side, and so prevented the violence
of the burning, till the flame expired in a weak consumption, and dyed turning into smoak and the coolnesse of
death and the harmlesnesse of a Cinder: and when a mans
desires are winged with sailes and a lusty wind of passion
and passe on in a smooth chanel of opportunity, God often
times hinders the lust and the impatient desire from passing on to its port, and entring into action, by a suddain
thought, by a little remembrance of a word, by a fancy,
by a sudden disability, by unreasonable and unlikely fears,
by the suddain intervening of company, by the very wearinesse of the passion, by curiosity, by want of health, by
the too great violence of the desire, bursting it self with

its fulnesse into dissolution & a remisse easinesse, by a
sentence of scripture, by the reverence of a good man, or
else by the proper interventions of the spirit of grace
chastising the crime and representing its *appendant* mischiefs and its *constituent* disorder and irregularity; and
after all this, the very anguish and trouble of being defeated in the purpose hath rolled it self into so much
uneasinesse and unquiet reflections, that the man is grown
ashamed and vexed into more sober counsels.

XXVIII Sermons, 1651, p. 335

27. Man's Pleasures.

LOOK upon pleasures, not upon that side that is next the
Sunne, or where they look beauteously, that is, as they
come towards you to be enjoyed; for then they paint, and
smile, and dresse themselves up in tinsel & glasse, gems
and counterfeit imagery: but when thou hast rifled and
discomposed them with enjoying their false beauties, &
that they begin to go off, then behold them in their nakednesse and wearinesse. See what a sigh and sorrow, what
naked unhandsome proportions and a filthy carkasse they
discover; and the next time they counterfeit, remember
what you have already discovered, & be no more abused.
And I have known some wise persons have advised to cure
the passions and longings of their children by letting them
taste of every thing they passionately fancied: for they
should be sure to find lesse in it then they looked for, and
the impatience of their being denied would be loosened
and made slack; and when our wishings are no bigger then
the thing deserves, and our usages of them according to
our needs (which may be obtain'd by trying what they are,
and what good they can do us) we shall finde in all pleasures

so little entertainment, that the vanity of the possession will soon reprove the violence of the appetite. And if this permission be in innocent instances, it may be of good use: But *Solomon* tried it in all things, taking his fill of all pleasures: & soon grew weary of them all. The same thing we may do by reason which we do by experience, if either we will look upon pleasures as we are sure they will look when they go off, after their enjoyment, or if we will credit the experience of those men who have tasted them and loathed them.

Often consider, and contemplate the joyes of heaven, that when they have filled thy desires, which are the sails of the soul, thou mayest steer onely thither, and never more look back to *Sodom*. And when thy soul dwels above, and looks down upon the pleasures of the World, they seeme like things at distance, little and contemptible, and men running after the satisfaction of their sottish appetites seem foolish as fishes, thousands of them running after a rotten worme that covers a deadly hook; or at the best but like children with great noise pursuing a bubble rising from a wallnut shell, which ends sooner then the noise.

To this, the example of Christ and his Apostles, of *Moses* and all the Wise men of all ages of the world will much help: who understanding how to distinguish good from evil, did choose a sad and melancholy way to felicity, rather then the broad, pleasant and easie path to folly and misery.

Holy Living, 1650, p. 65

28. *Man's Joys.*

MENS joyes are troublesome, and besides that the fear of losing them takes away the present pleasure (and a man had need of another felicity to preserve this) they are also wavering and full of trepidation, not onely from their inconstant nature, but from their weak foundation: They arise from vanity, and they dwell upon ice, and they converse with the winde, and they have the wings of a bird, and are serious but as the resolutions of a childe, commenced by chance, and managed by folly and proceed by inadvertency, and end in vanity and forgetfulnesse. So that as *Livius Drusus* said of himself, *he never had any play-dayes, or dayes of quiet when he was a boy*, for he was troublesome and busie, *a restlesse and unquiet man*, the same may every man observe to be true of himself: he is alwayes restlesse and uneasy, he dwells upon the waters and leans upon thorns, and layes his head upon a sharp stone.

Holy Dying, 1651, p. 42

29. *The World.*

LEARN to despise the world; or, which is a better compendium in the duty, learn but truly to understand it; for it is a cousenage all the way; the head of it is a rainbow, and the face of it is flattery; its words are charmes, and all its stories are false; its body is a shadow, and its hands do knit spiders webs; it is an image and a noise, with a *Hyæna's* lip and a Serpents tail; it was given to serve the needs of our nature, and in stead of doing it, it creates strange appetites, and nourishes thirsts and feavers; it brings care and debauches our nature, and brings shame and death as the reward of all our cares. Our nature is a disease, and the world does nourish it; but if you leave to feed upon such unwholesome diet, your nature reverts to its first purities, and to the entertainments of the grace of God.

XXV Sermons, 1653, p. 148

30. *The Power of the World.*

WE see by the experience of the whole world, that the beliefe of an honest man in a matter of temporall advantage makes us do actions of such danger and difficulty, that half so much industry and sufferance would ascertain us into a possession of all the promises Evangelicall. Now let any man be asked, whether he had rather be *rich*, or be *saved*, he will tell you without all doubt, heaven is the better option, by infinite degrees: for it cannot be, that riches, or revenge or lust should be directly preferred, that is, be thought more eligible then the glories of immortality. That therefore men neglect so great salvation, and so greedily run after the satisfaction of their baser appetites, can be attributed to nothing, but want of faith, they do not *heartily believe*, that heaven is worth so much; there is upon them a stupidity of spirit, and their faith is dull, and its actions suspended most commonly, and often interrupted, and it never enters into the will: so that the propositions are considered nakedly and precisely in themselves, but not as referring to us or our interests, there is nothing of faith in it, but so much as is the first and direct act of understanding, there is no consideration, nor reflection upon the act or upon the person, or upon the subject: so that even as it is seated in the understanding, our faith is commonly lame, mutilous and imperfect, and therefore much more is it culpable, because it is destitute of all cooperation of the rationall appetite.

But let us consider the power and efficacy of worldly beliefe. If a man believes, that there is gold to be had in Peru for fetching, or pearles and rich Jewels in India for the exchange of trifles, he instantly, if he be in capacity leaves the wife of his bosom, and the pretty delights of children, and his own security, and ventures into the dangers of waters, and unknown seas, and freezings and calentures, thirst and hunger, pirates and shipwracks, and hath within him a principle strong enough to answer all objections, because he believes that riches are desirable, and by such meanes likely to be had. Our blessed Saviour comparing the Gospell to a Merchant man, that found a pearle of great price, and sold all to buy it, hath brought this instance home to the present discourse. For if we did as verily believe, that in heaven those great felicities, which transcend all our apprehensions are certainly to be obtained by leaving our vices, and lower desires, what can hinder us, but we should at least doe as much for obtaining those great felicities, as for the lesser, if the beliefe were equall; for if any man thinkes he may have them without holinesse and justice and charity, then he wants faith, for he believes not that saying of S. *Paul*; *follow peace with all men and holinesse, without which no man shall ever see* GOD. If a man believes learning to be the onely or chiefest Ornament and beauty of soules, that which will ennoble him to a faire imployment in his owne time, and an honourable memory to succeeding ages, this if he believes heartily, it hath power to make him endure *Catarrhes*, goutes, hypochondriacall passions, to read till his eyes almost fixe in their orbes, to despise the pleasures of idlenesse, or tedious sports, and to undervalue whatsoever does not cooperate to the end of his faith, the desire of learning. Why is the Italian so abstemious in his drinkings, or the Helvetian so valiant in his fight, or so true to the Prince that imployes him, but that they believe it to be noble *so* to be? If they believed the same, and had the same honourable thoughts of other vertues, they also would be as nationall as these. For faith will doe its proper worke: and when the understanding is peremptorily and fully determind upon the persvasion of a proposition, if the will should then dissent and choose the contrary, it were unnaturall and monstrous, and possibly no man ever does so; for that men doe things without reason and against their conscience, is because they have put out their light, and discourse their wills into the election of a sensible good, and want faith to believe truely all circumstances, which are necessary by way of predisposition for choice of the intellectuall.

But when mens faith is confident, their resolution and actions are in proportion; for thus the faith of Mahumetans makes them to abstaine from wine for ever: and therefore if we had the Christian faith, we should much rather abstaine from drunkennesse for ever; It being an expresse rule Apostolicall, *Be not drunke with wine, wherein is excesse*. The faith of the Circumcellians made them to run greedily to violent and horrid deaths as willingly, as to a crowne: for they thought it was the Kings high way to Martyrdome. And there was never any man zealous for his religion, and of an imperious bold faith, but he was also willing to dye for it; and therefore also by as much reason to live in it, and to be a strict observer of its prescriptions. And the stories of the strict sanctity, and prodigious sufferings and severe disciplines, and expensive religion, and complyant and laborious charity of the primitive Christians, is abundant argument to convince us, that the faith of Christians is infinitely more fruitfull, and productive of its vnivocall and proper issues, then the faith of hereticks, or the false religions of misbelievers, or the persuasions of secular persons, or the spirit of Antichrist; and therefore

when we see men serving their Prince with such difficult
and ambitious services, because they believe him able to
reward them, though of his will they are not so certain;
and yet so supinely negligent, and incurious of their services to GOD, of whose power and will to reward us
infinitely, there is certainty absolute and irrespective, is
certain probation, that we believe it not; for if we believe
there is such a thing as heaven, and that every single mans
portion of heaven is farre better then all the wealth of the
world, it is morally impossible we should preferre so little
before so great a profit.

The Great Exemplar, 1649, Pt. II, p. 16

31. *A Gentleman of Rome.*

I REMEMBER that *Arianus* tells of a Gentleman that
was banished from *Rome*, and in his sorrow visited the
Philosopher, and he heard him talk wisely, and believed
him, and promised him to leave all the thoughts of *Rome*
and splendours of the Court, and retire to the course of
a severe Philosophy: but before the good mans Lectures
were done, there came πινακίδες ἀπὸ τοῦ Καίσαρος, letters
from *Cæsar* to recall him home, to give him pardon, and
promise him great Imployment. He presently grew weary
of the good mans *Sermon*, and wished he would make an
end, thought his discourse was dull and flat; for his head
and heart were full of another storie and new principles;
and by these measures he could heare only and he could
understand.

Every man understands by his Affections more then by
his Reason: and when the *Wolfe* in the Fable went to
School to learn to spell, whatever letters were told him,
he could never make any thing of them but *Agnus*; he

thought of nothing but his belly: and if a man be very hungry, you must give him meate before you give him counsell. A mans mind must belike your proposition before it can be entertained: for whatever you put into a man it will smell of the Vessell: it is a mans mind that gives the *emphasis*, and makes your argument to prevail. . . .

Had not he lost his labour that would have discoursed wisely to *Apicius*, and told him of the books of Fate and the secrets of the other World, the abstractions of the Soul and its brisker Immortality, that Saints and Angels eate not, and that the Spirit of a man lives for ever upon wisdom and holinesse and contemplation? The fat *Glutton* would have stared a while upon the Preacher, and then have fallen asleep. But if you had discoursed well and knowingly of a Lamprey, a large Mullet, or a Boare, *animal propter Convivia natum*, and have sent him a Cook from *Asia* to make new *Sawces*, he would have attended carefully, and taken in your discourses *greedily*. And so it is in the Questions and secrets of Christianity: which made St. *Paul*, when he intended to convert *Felix*, discourse first with him about *Temperance, Righteousnesse* and *Judgement to come*. He began in the right point; he knew it was to no purpose to preach *Jesus Christ* crucified to an intemperate person, to an Usurper of other mens rights, to one whose soul dwelt in the World, and cared not for the sentence of the last day. The *Philosophers* began their Wisdom with the meditation of death, and St. *Paul* his with a discourse of the day of Judgment: to take the heart off from this world and the amabilities of it, which dishonour and baffle the understanding, and made *Solomon* himself become a child and fool'd into Idolatry, by the prettinesse of a talking woman. Men now-a-dayes love not a Religion that will cost them deare. If your Doctrine calls upon men to part with any considerable part of their estates, you must pardon them if they cannot believe you; they understand it not.

Via Intelligentiae, 1662, pp. 15 and 21

32. *The Coal of Fire.*

THE old Rabbins those Poets of religion report of Moses that when the courtiers of Pharaoh were sporting with the childe Moses in the chamber of Pharaohs daughter, they presented to his choice an ingot of gold in one hand, and a cole of fire in the other; and that the childe snatched at the coal, thrust it into his mouth, and so singed and parched his tongue, that he stammered ever after: and certainly it is infinitely more childish in us for the glittering of the small gloworms and the charcoal of worldly possessions, to swallow the flames of hell greedily, in our choice: such a bit will produce a worse stammering then Moses had: for so the accursed and lost souls have their ugly and horrid dialect, they *roare and blaspheme, blaspheme and roare for ever*. And suppose God should now at this instant send the great Archangel with his trumpet to summon all the world to judgement, would not all this seem a notorious visible truth, a truth, which you will then wonder that every man did not lay to his heart and preserve therein actual, pious and effective consideration?

XXVIII Sermons, 1651, p. 249

33. *Gaining the Whole World.*

FIRST, then suppose a man gets all the world, what is it that he gets? It is a bubble, and a Phantasme, and hath no reality beyond a present transient use; a thing that is impossible to be enjoyed, because its fruits and usages are transmitted to us, by parts and by succession; He that hath all the world, (if we can suppose such a man) cannot have a dish of fresh summer fruits in the midst of winter, not so much as a green fig: and very much of its possessions is so hid, so fugacious and of so uncertain purchase, that it is like the riches of the sea to the Lord of the shore, all the fish and wealth within all its hollownesses are his, but he is never the better, for what he cannot get. All the shell fishes that produce pearl, produce them not for him; and the bowels of the earth shall hide her treasures in undiscovered retirements; so that it will signifie as much to this great purchaser, to be intitled to an inheritance in the upper region of the aire; he is so far from possessing all its riches, that he does not so much as know of them, nor understand the Philosophy of her minerals.

I consider that he that is the greatest possessor in the world enjoyes its best and most noble parts and those which are of most excellent perfection but in common with the inferiour persons, and the most despicable of his kingdom. Can the greatest Prince inclose the Sun, and set one little star in his cabinet for his own use? or secure to himself the gentle and benigne influence of any one constellation? Are not his subjects fields bedewed with the same showers that water his gardens of pleasure?

Nay those things which he esteems his ornament and his singularity of his possessions, are they not of more use to others then to himself. For suppose his garments splendid and shining like the robe of a cherub or the clothing of the fields, all that he that wears them enjoyes, is that they keep him warm, and clean and modest; and all this is done by clean and lesse pompous vestments; & the beauty of them which distinguishes him from others, is made to please the eyes of the beholders; and he is like a fair bird, or the meretricious painting of a wanton woman made wholly to be looked on, that is to be enjoyed by every one but himself; and the fairest face and the sparkling eye cannot perceive or enjoy their own beauties but by reflection. It is I that am pleased with beholding his gayety, and the gay man in his greatest bravery is onely pleased because I am pleased with the sight: so borrowing his little and imaginary complacency, from the delight that I have, not from any inherency of his own possession.

The poorest Artizan of Rome walking in Cæsars gardens, had the same pleasures which they ministred to their Lord: and although it may be he was put to gather fruits to eat, from another place, yet his other senses were delighted equally with Cæsars: the birds made him as good musick, the flowers gave him as sweet smells, he there sucked as good aire, and delighted in the beauty and order of the place, for the same reason and upon the same perception, as the prince himselfe: save onely that Cæsar paid for all that pleasure vast summes of money, the blood and treasure of a province, which the poor man had for nothing.

Suppose a man Lord of all the world, (for still we are but in supposition) yet since every thing is received, not according to its own greatnesse and worth, but according to the capacity of the receiver, it signifies very little as to our content; or to the riches of our possession. If any man should give to a Lion a fair meadow full of hay, or a thousand quince trees, or should give to the goodly Bull, the master and the fairest of the whole heard, a thousand fair Stags; If a man should present to a childe a ship laden with Persian carpets, and the ingredients of the rich

scarlet, all these being either disproportionate to the appetite or to the understanding, could adde nothing of content, and might declare the freenesse of the presenter, but
they upbraid the incapacity of the receiver: and so it does
if God should give the whole world to any man; He knows
not what to do with it; he can use no more but according
to the capacities of a man. He can use nothing but meat
and drink and cloths; and infinite riches that can give him
changes of raiment every day, and a full table, do but give
him a clean trencher every bit he eats, it signifies no more
but wantonnesse, and variety to the same, not to any new
purposes; He to whom the world can be given to any purpose greater then a private estate can minister, must have
new capacities created in him; He needs the understanding
of an Angel to take the accounts of his estate; He had need
have a stomach like fire or the grave: for else he can eat
no more then one of his healthful subjects, and unlesse he
hath an eye like the Sun, and a motion like that of a
thought, and a bulk as big as one of the orbs of heaven;
the pleasures of his eye can be no greater then to behold
the beauty of a little prospect from a hill, or to look upon
the heap of gold packt up in a little room, or to dote upon
a cabinet of Jewels better then which there is no man that
sees at all but sees every day; For not to name the beauties
and sparkling diamonds of heaven, a mans or a womans or
a haukes eye is more beauteous and excellent, then al the
Jewels of his crown. And when we remember, that a beast
who hath quicker senses then a man, yet hath not so great
delight in the fruition of any object, because he wants
understanding and the power to make reflex acts upon his
perception, it will follow, that understanding and knowledge is the greatest instrument of pleasure, and he that

is most knowing hath a capacity to become happy, which a lesse knowing prince or a rich person hath not: and in this onely a mans capacity is capable of enlargement: but then although they onely have power to relish any pleasure rightly, who rightly understand the nature and degrees and essences, and ends of things, yet they do so understand also the vanity and the unsatisfyingnesse of the things of this world so that the relish which could not be great, but in a great understanding appears contemptible, because its vanity appears at the same time; the understanding sees all, and sees thorow it.

The greatest vanity of this world is remarkable in this, that all its joyes summed up together are not big enough to counterpoise the evil of one sharp disease, or to allay a sorrow. For imagine a man great in his dominion as Cyrus, rich as Solomon, victorious as David, beloved like Titus, learned as Trismegist, powerful as all the Roman greatnesse, all this, and the results of all this, give him no more pleasure in the midst of a feaver, or the tortures of the stone, then if he were only lord of a little dish, and a dishfull of fountain water. Indeed the excellency of a holy conscience is a comfort and a magazine of joy, so great, that it sweetens the most bitter potion of the world, and makes tortures and death not only tolerable, but amiable; and therefore to part with this whose excellency is so great, for the world that is of so inconsiderable a worth as not to have in it recompence enough, for the sorrows of a sharp disease, is a bargain fit to be made by none but fools and mad men. Antiochus, Epiphanes & Herod the great & his grand child Agrippa, were sad instances of this great truth; to every of which it happened that the grandeur of their fortune, the greatnesse of their possessions, and the encrease of their estate disappeared, and expired like Camphire at their arrest, by those several sharp diseases, which covered their head with Cypresse and hid their crowns in an inglorious grave.

For what can all the world minister to a sick person? If it represents all the spoils of nature and the choicest delicacies of land and sea. Alas his appetite is lost, and to see a pibble stone is more pleasing to him: For he can look upon that without loathing, but not so upon the most delicious fare that ever made famous the Roman luxury. Perfumes make his head ake; if you load him with jewels, you presse him with a burden as troublesome as his grave-stone: and what pleasure is in all those possessions, that cannot make his pillow easie, nor tame the rebellion of a tumultuous humour, nor restore the use of a withered hand, or straighten a crooked finger: vain is the hope of that man whose soul rests upon vanity, and such unprofitable possessions.

Suppose a man lord of all this world, an universal Monarch, as some princes have lately designed, all that cannot minister content to him; not that content which a poor contemplative man by the strength of Christian Philosophy, and the support of a very small fortune daily does enjoy. All his power and greatnesse cannot command the sea to overflow his shores or to stay from the retiring to the opposite strand. It cannot make his children dutiful or wise, & though the world admired at the greatness of Philip the second's fortune in the accession of Portugal and the East Indies to his principalities, yet this could not allay the infelicitie of his family, and the unhandsomenesse of his condition in having a proud and indiscreet and a vitious young prince likely to inherit all his greatnesse. And if

nothing appears in the face of such a fortune, to tell all
the world that it is spotted and imperfect; yet there is in
all conditions of the world, such wearinesse and tediousnesse of the spirits, that a man is ever more pleased with
hopes of going off for the present, then in dwelling upon
that condition which it may be others admire, and think
beauteous, but none knoweth the smart of it, but he that
drank off the little pleasure, and felt the ill relish of the
appendage. How many Kings have groaned under the
burden of their crowns, and have sunk down and died?
How many have quitted their pompous cares, and retired
into private lives, there to enjoy the pleasures of Philosophy and religion, which their thrones denied?

XXVIII Sermons, 1651, p. 226

34. *The Miseries of Life.*

HERE is no place to sit down in, but you must rise as
soon as you are set: for we have gnats in our chambers,
and worms in our gardens, and spiders and flies in the
palaces of the greatest Kings. How few men in the world
are prosperous? what an infinite number of slaves and
beggers, of persecuted and oppressed people fill all corners
of the earth with groans, and Heaven it self with weeping
prayers, and sad remembrances? how many Provinces and
Kingdoms are afflicted by a violent war, or made desolate
by popular diseases? some whole countreyes are remarked
with fatal evils, or periodical sicknesses. *Gran Cairo* in
Egypt feels the plague every three years, returning like a
Quartan ague, and destroying many thousands of persons.
All the inhabitants of Arabia the desert are in continuall
fear of being buried in huge heaps of sand, and therefore
dwell in tents and ambulatory houses or retire to unfruitful

mountains to prolong an uneasy and wilder life: and all
the Countreyes round about the Adriatic sea feel such
violent convulsions by Tempests and intolerable Earth-
quakes, that sometimes whole cities finde a Tombe, and
every man sinks with his own house made ready to become
his Monument, and his bed is crushed into the disorders
of a grave. Was not all the world drowned at one deluge,
and breach of the Divine anger? and shall not all the
world again be destroyed by fire? Are there not many
thousands that die every night, and that groan and weep
sadly every day? But what shall we think of that great
evil, which for the sins of men, God hath suffered to possess the greatest part of Mankinde? Most of the men that
are now alive, or that have been living for many ages, are
Jews, Heathens, or Turcs: and God was pleased to suffer
a base Epileptic person, a villain and a vitious to set up a
religion which hath filled almost all Asia, and Africa, and
some parts of Europe; so that the greatest number of men
and women born in so many kingdoms and provinces are
infallibly made Mahumetans, strangers and enemies to
Christ, by whom alone we can be saved. This consideration is extremely sad, when we remember how universal,
and how great an evil it is, that so many millions of sons
and daughters are born to enter into the possession of
Devils to eternal ages. These evils are the miseries of great
parts of mankinde, and we cannot easily consider more
particularly, the evils which happen to us, being the inseparable affections, or incidents to the whole nature of
man.

We finde that all the women in the world are either
born for barrennesse or the pains of Child-birth, and yet
this is one of our greatest blessings; but such indeed are

the blessings of this world: we cannot be well with, nor without many things. Perfumes make our heads ake, roses prick our fingers, and in our very blood where our life dwells is the Scene under which nature acts many sharp Feavers and heavy sicknesses. It were too sad if I should tell how many persons are afflicted with evil spirits, with spectres and illusions of the night; and that huge multitudes of men and women live upon mans flesh: Nay worse yet, upon the sins of men, upon the sins of their sons and of their daughters, and they pay their souls down for the bread they eat, buying this dayes meal with the price of the last nights sin.

Or if you please in charity to visit an Hospital, which is indeed a map of the whole world, there you shall see the effects of *Adams* sin and the ruines of humane nature, bodies laid up in heaps like the bones of a destroyed town, *homines precarii spiritus, & malè hærentis,* men whose souls seem to be borrowed, and are kept there by art and the force of Medicine; whose miseries are so great, that few people have charity or humanity enough to visit them, fewer have the heart to dresse them, and we pity them in civility or with a transient prayer, but we do not feel their sorrows by the mercies of a religious pity, and therefore as we leave their sorrows in many degrees unrelieved and uneased, so we contract by our unmercifulnesse a guilt by which our selves become liable to the same calamities. Those many that need pity, and those infinites of people that refuse to pity are miserable upon a several charge, but yet they almost make up all mankinde.

All wicked men are in love with that which intangles them in huge variety of troubles, they are slaves to the worst of Masters, to sin and to the Devil, to a passion, and

to an imperious woman. Good men are for ever persecuted, and God chastises every son whom he receives, and
whatsoever is easy is trifling and worth nothing, and whatsoever is excellent is not to be obtained without labour
and sorrow; and the conditions and states of men that are
free from great cares, are such as have in them nothing
rich and orderly, and those that have are stuck full of
thorns and trouble. Kings are full of care; and learned
men in all ages have been observed to be very poor, &
honestas miserias accusant; they complain of their honest
miseries.

But these evils are notorious and confessed; even they
also whose felicity men stare at and admire, besides their
splendour and the sharpnesse of their light, will with their
appendant sorrows wring a tear from the most resolved
eye. For not only the winter quarter is full of storms and
cold and darknesse, but the beauteous spring hath blasts
and sharp frosts, the fruitful teeming summer is melted
with heat, and burnt with the kisses of the sun her friend,
and choaked with dust, and the rich Autumn is full of
sicknesse, and we are weary of that which we enjoy, because sorrow is its biggest portion: and when we remember
that upon the fairest face is placed one of the worst sinks
of the body, *the nose*, we may use it, not only as a mortification to the pride of beauty, but as an allay to the fairest
outside of condition which any of the sons and daughters
of *Adam* do possesse. For look upon Kings and conquerours: I will not tell that many of them fall into the
condition of servants, and their subjects rule over them,
and stand upon the ruines of their families, and that to
such persons, the sorrow is bigger then usually happens in
smaller fortunes: but let us suppose them still conquerers,

and see what a goodly purchase they get by all their pains and amazing fears, and continual dangers. They carry their arms beyond Ister, and passe the Euphrates, and binde the Germans with the bounds of the river Rhyne: I speak in the stile of the Roman greatnesse: for now adayes, the biggest fortune swells not beyond the limits of a petty province or two, and a hill confines the progresse of their prosperity, or a river checks it: But whatsoever tempts the pride and vanity of ambitious persons is not so big as the smallest star which we see scattered in disorder, and unregarded upon the pavement and floor of Heaven. And if we would suppose the pismires had but our understandings, they also would have the method of a Mans greatnesse, and divide their little Mole-hils into Provinces and Exarchats: and if they also grew as vitious and as miserable, one of their princes would lead an army out, and kill his neighbour Ants that he might reign over the next handfull of a Turfe. But then if we consider at what price, and with what felicity all this is purchased, the sting of the painted snake will quickly appear, and the fairest of their fortunes will properly enter into this account of humane infelicities.

We may guesse at it by the constitution of *Augustus* fortune; who strugled for his power, first with the Roman Citizens, then with *Brutus* and *Cassius* and all the fortune of the Republike; then with his Collegue *Marc. Anthony*; then with his kinred and neerest Relatives; and after he was wearied with slaughter of the Romans, before he could sit down and rest in his imperial chair he was forced to carry armies into Macedonia, Galatia, beyond Euphrates, Rhyne, and Danubius: And when he dwelt at home in greatnesse and within the circles of a mighty power, he hardly escaped the sword of the *Egnatii*, of *Lepidus*, *Cæpio*, and *Muræna*: and after he had entirely reduced the felicity and *Grandeur* into his own family, his Daughter, his onely childe conspired with many of the young Nobility, and being joyned with adulterous complications as with an impious sacrament they affrighted and destroyed the fortune of the old man, and wrought him more sorrow then all the troubles that were hatched in the baths and beds of Egypt, between *Anthony* and *Cleopatra*. This was the greatest fortune that the world had then, or ever since, and therefore we cannot expect it to be better in a lesse prosperity.

The prosperity of this world is so infinitely sowred with the overflowing of evils, that he is counted the most happy who hath the fewest; all conditions being evil and miserable, they are onely distinguished by the Number of calamities. The Collector of the Roman and foreign examples, when he had reckoned two and twenty instances of great fortunes every one of which had been allayed with great variety of evils; in all his reading or experience he could tell but of two who had been famed for an intire prosperity; *Quintus Metellus*, and *Gyges* the King of *Lydia*; and yet concerning the one of them he tells that his felicity was so inconsiderable (and yet it was the bigger of the two) that the Oracle said that *Aglaus Sophidius* the poor *Arcadian* Shepherd was more happy then he, that is, he had fewer troubles; for so indeed we are to reckon the pleasures of this life; *the limit of our joy is the absence of some degrees of sorrow*, and he that hath the least of this, is the most prosperous person. But then we must look for prosperity, not in Palaces or Courts of Princes, not in the tents of Conquerers, or in the gaieties of fortunate and prevailing sinners; but something rather in the Cottages of honest innocent and contented persons, whose minde is no bigger then their fortune, nor their vertue lesse then their security. As for others whose fortune looks bigger, and allures fools to follow it like the wandring fires of the night, till they run into rivers or are broken upon rocks with staring and running after them, they are all in the condition of *Marius*, then whose condition *nothing was more constant, and nothing more mutable; if we reckon them amongst the happy, they are the most happy men, if we reckon them amongst the miserable, they are the most miserable*. For just as is a mans condition, great or little, so is the state of his misery; All have their share; but Kings and Princes, great Generals and Consuls, Rich men and Mighty, as they have the biggest businesse and the biggest charge, and are answerable to God for the greatest accounts, so they have the biggest trouble; that the uneasinesse of their appendage may divide the good and evil of the world, making the poor mans fortune as eligible as the Greatest; and also restraining the vanity of mans spirit which a great Fortune is apt to swell from a vapour to a bubble; but God in mercy hath mingled wormwood with their wine, and so restrained the drunkennesse and follies of prosperity. . . .

He that is no fool, but can consider wisely; if he be in love with this world; we need not despair but that a witty man might reconcile him with tortures, and make him think charitably of the Rack, and be brought to dwell with Vipers and Dragons, and entertain his Guests with the shrikes of Mandrakes, Cats and Scrich Owls, with the filing of iron, and the harshnesse of rending silk; or to admire the harmony that is made by a herd of Evening wolves when they misse their draught of blood in their midnight

Revels. The groans of a man in a fit of the stone are worse then all these; and the distractions of a troubled conscience are worse then those groans; and yet a carelesse merry sinner is worse then all that. But if we could from one of the battlements of Heaven espie how many men and women at this time lye fainting and dying for want of bread, how many young men are hewen down by the sword of war; how many poor Orphans are now weeping over the graves of their Father, by whose life they were enabled to eat. If we could but hear how many Mariners, and Passengers are at this present in a storm, and shrike out because their keel dashes against a Rock, or bulges under them; how many people there are that weep with want, and are mad with oppression, or are desperate by too quick a sense of a constant infelicity, in all reason we should be glad to be out of the noise and participation of so many evils. This is a place of sorrows and tears, of great evils and a constant calamity; let us remove from hence, at least in affections and preparation of minde.

Holy Dying, 1651, pp. 35 and 46

35. *Eternal Things.*

IT is the duty of Christian prudence to choose the end of a Christian, that which is perfective of a man, satisfactory to reason, the rest of a Christian, and the beatification of his spirit; and that is, to choose and desire, and propound to himself heaven, and the fruition of God, as the end of all his acts and arts, his designes and purposes. For in the nature of things that is most eligible, and most to be pursued, which is most perfective of our nature, and is the acquiescence, the satisfaction, and proper rest of our most reasonable appetites. Now the things of this world are difficult and uneasie, full of thornes, and empty of pleasures, they fill a diseased faculty, or an abused sense, but are an infinite dissatisfaction to reason, and the appetites of the soul: they are short, and transient, and they never abide, unlesse sorrow like a chain be bound about their leg, and then they never stir, till the grace of God and religion breaks it, or else that the rust of time eats the chain in pieces: they are dangerous and doubtfull, few and difficult, sordid and particular, not onely not communicable to a multitude, but not diffusive upon the whole man; there being no one pleasure or object in this world, that delights all the parts of man: and after all this, they are originally from earth, and from the creatures, onely that they oftentimes contract alliances with hell and the grave, with shame and sorrow; and all these put together make no great amability, or proportion to a wise mans choice: But on the other side, the things of God are the noblest satisfactions to those desires, which ought to be cherished and swelled up to infinite; their deliciousnesse is vast and full of relish, and their very appendant thorns are to be chosen, for they are gilded, they are safe and medicinall, they heal the wound they make, and bring forth fruit of a blessed and a holy life: The things of God and of religion are easie and sweet, they bear entertainments in their hand, and reward at their back, their good is certain and perpetual, and they make us cheerfull to day, and pleasant to morrow; and spiritual songs end not in a sigh and a groan; neither like unwholesome physick do they let loose a present humour, and introduce an habitual indisposition: But they bring us to the felicity of God, the same yesterday, and to day, and for ever; they do not give a private and particular delight, but their benefit is publike, like the incense of the altar, it sends up a sweet smell to heaven, and makes atonement for the religious man that kindled it, and delights all the standers by, and makes the very air wholesome; there is no blessed soul goes to heaven, but he makes a generall joy in all the mansions where the Saints do dwell, and in all the chappels where the Angels sing: and the joyes of religion are not univocal, but productive of rare and accidental, and præternatural pleasures; for the musick of holy hymnes delights the ear, and refreshes the spirit, and makes the very bones of the Saint to rejoyce: and charity, or the giving alms to the poor, does not onely ease the poverty of the receiver, but makes the giver rich, and heals his sicknesse, and *delivers from death*; and temperance though it be in the matter of meat, and drink, and pleasures, yet hath an effect upon the understanding, and makes the reason sober, and his will orderly, and his affections regular, and does things beside, and beyond their natural and proper efficacy; for all the parts of our duty are watered with the showers of blessing, and bring forth fruit according to the influence of heaven, and beyond the capacities of nature.

And now let the voluptuous person go and try whether putting his wanton hand to the bosome of his Mistris will get half such honour as Scævola put upon his head, when he put his hand into the fire. Let him see whether a drunken meeting will cure a fever, or make him wise? A hearty and a persevering prayer will. Let him tell me, if spending great summes of money upon his lusts will make him sleep soundly, or be rich? Charity will; Alms will increase his fortune, and a good conscience shall charme all his cares and sorrows into a most delicious slumber; well may a full goblet wet the drunkards tongue, and then the heat rising from the stomack will dry the spunge, and heat it into the scorchings and little images of hell: and the follies of a wanton bed will turn the itch into a smart, and empty the reins of all their lustfull powers; but can they do honour, or satisfaction in any thing that must last, and that ought to be provided for? No: All the things of this world are little, and trifling, and limited, and particular, and sometimes necessary because we are miserable, wanting and imperfect, but they never do any thing toward perfection, but their pleasure dies like the time in which it danced a while, and when the minute is gone, so is the pleasure too, and leaves no footstep but the impression of a sigh, and dwells no where, but in the same house where you shall finde *yesterday*, that is in forgetfulnesse, and annihilation, unlesse its onely childe, *sorrow*, shall marry, and breed more of its kinde, and so continue its memory and name to eternall ages. It is therefore the most necessary part of prudence to choose well in the main stake; and the dispute is not much; for if eternall things be better then temporall, the soul more noble then the body, vertue more honourable then the basest vices, a lasting joy to be chosen before an eternall sorrow, *much* to be preferred before *little*, *certainty* before *danger*, *publike good things*, before *private evils*, *eternity* before *moments*, then let us set down in religion, and make heaven to be our end, God to be our Father, Christ our elder Brother, the Holy Ghost the earnest of our inheritance, vertue to be our imployment, and then we shall never enter into the portion of fools and accursed ill-choosing spirits. Nazianzen said well, *Malim prudentiæ guttam quàm fœcundioris fortunæ pelagus*: One drop of prudence is more usefull, then an ocean of a smooth fortune; for prudence is a rare instrument towards heaven; and a great fortune is made often-times the high-way to hell and destruction. However, thus farre, prudence is our duty; every man can be so wise, and is bound to it, to choose heaven and a cohabitation with God, before the possessions and transient vanities of the world.

XXVIII Sermons, 1651, p. 254

36. *Tears.*

IF you do but see a Maiden carried to her grave a little before her intended marriage, or an Infant dye before the birth of Reason, Nature hath taught us to pay a tributary tear: Alas! your eyes will behold the ruine of many Families, which though they sadly have deserved, yet Mercy is not delighted with the spectacle; and therefore God places a watry cloud in the eye, that when the light of heaven shines upon it, it may produce a rain-bow to be a Sacrament and a memorial that God and the sons of God do not love to see a man perish.

Sermon preached at the Opening of Parliament, 1661, p. 43

37. *Adversity.*

NO man is more miserable then he that hath no adversity; that man is not tryed whether he be good or bad; and God never crowns those vertues which are onely *faculties,* and *dispositions:* but *every act* of vertue is an ingredient into reward. And we see many children fairly planted, whose parts of nature were never dressed by art, nor called from the furrowes of their first possibilities by discipline, and institution, and they dwell for ever in ignorance, and converse with beasts: and yet if they had been dressed and exercised, might have stood at the chairs

of Princes, or spoken parables amongst the rulers of cities?
Our vertues are but in the seed, when the grace of God
comes upon us first: but this grace must be thrown into
broken furrowes, and must *twice feel the cold, and twice feel
the heat*, and be softned with storms and showers, and then
it will arise into fruitfulnesse and harvests: And what is
there in the world to distinguish vertues from dishonours,
or the valour of *Cæsar* from the softnesse of the Egyptian
Eunuchs, or that can make any thing rewardable, but the
labour and the danger, the pain and the difficulty? Vertue
could not be any thing but sensuality, if it were the entertainment of our senses and fond desires; and *Apicius* had
been the noblest of all the Romans, if feeding a great
appetite and despising the severities of temperance had
been the work and proper imployment of a wise man. But
otherwise do fathers, and otherwise do mothers handle
their children: These soften them with kisses and imperfect noises, with the pap and breast milk of soft endearments, they rescue them from Tutors, and snatch them
from discipline, they desire to keep them fat and warm,
and their feet dry and their bellies full; and then the
children govern, and cry, and prove fools, and troublesome, so long as the feminine republike does endure. But
fathers, because they designe to have their children wise
and valiant, apt for counsel, or for arms, send them to
severe governments, and tye them to study, to hard labour,
and afflictive contingencies. They rejoyce when the bold
boy strikes a lyon with his hunting spear, and shrinks not
when the beast comes to affright his early courage. Softnesse is for slaves and beasts, for minstrels and uselesse
persons, for such who cannot ascend higher then the state
of a fair ox, or a servant entertained for vainer offices: But

the man that designes his son for noble imployments, to honours, and to triumphs, to consular dignities and presidences of counsels, loves to see him pale with study or panting with labour, hardned with sufferance or eminent by dangers: and so God dresses us for heaven. He loves to see us strugling with a disease, and resisting the Devil, and contesting against the weaknesses of nature, and against hope to believe in hope, resigning our selves to Gods will, praying him to choose for us, and dying in all things but *faith* and *its blessed consequents, ut ad officium cum periculo simus prompti*; and the *danger* and the *resistance* shall endeare the office. For so have I known the boysterous north-winde passe thorough the yielding aire which opened its bosome, and appeased its violence by entertaining it with easie compliance in all the regions of its reception. But when the same breath of Heaven hath been checked with the stiffnesse of a tower, or the united strength of a wood; it grew mighty, and dwelt there, and made the highest branches stoop, and make a smooth path for it on the top of all its glories: So is sicknesse, and so is the grace of God. When sicknesse hath made the difficulty, then Gods grace hath made a triumph, and by doubling its power hath created new proportions of a reward; and then shews its biggest glory, when it hath the greatest difficulty to Master, the greatest weaknesse to support, the most busie temptations to contest with: For so God loves that *his strength should be seen in our weaknesse*, and our danger. Happy is that state of life in which our services to God are the dearest, and the most expensive.

Holy Dying, 1651, p. 113

38. *Job*.

IT was the fire that did honour to *Mutius Scevola*, poverty made *Fabritius* famous, *Rutilius* was made excellent by banishment, *Regulus* by torments, *Socrates* by prison, *Cato* by his death: and God hath crowned the memory of *Job* with a wreath of glory because he sate upon his dunghil wisely and temperatly: and his potsheard and his groans mingled with praises and justifications of God, pleased him like an Anthem sung by Angels in the morning of the resurrection.

Holy Dying, 1651, p. 113

39. *Sickness*.

WE carry about us the body of death, and we bring evils upon our selves by our follies, and then know not how to bear them; and the flesh forsakes the spirit. And indeed in sicknesse the infirmity is so very great, that God in a manner at that time hath reduced all Religion into one vertue, *Patience* with its appendages is the summe totall of almost all our duty that is proper to the days of sorrow: and we shall find it enough to entertain all our powers, and to imploy all our aids; the counsels of wise men, and the comforts of our friends, the advices of Scripture, and the results of experience, the graces of God, and the strength of our own resolutions are all then full of imployments, and find it work enough to secure that one grace. For then it is that a cloud is wrapped about our heads, and our reason stoops under sorrow, the soul is sad, and its instrument is out of tune, the auxiliaries are disorder'd, and every thought sits heavily; then a comfort cannot make the body feel it, and the soule is not so abstracted to rejoyce much without its partner; so that

G

the proper joyes of the soul, such as are hope, and wise discourses, and satisfactions of reason, and the offices of Religion, are felt, just as we now perceive the joyes of heaven, with so little relish, that it comes as news of a victory to a man upon the Rack, or the birth of an heir to one condemned to dye; he hears a story which was made to delight him, but it came when he was dead to joy and all its capacities; and therefore sicknesse, though it be a good *Monitor*, yet it is an ill stage to act some vertues in; and a good man cannot *then* doe much, and therefore he that is in the state of flesh and blood, can doe nothing at all.

XXV Sermons, 1653, p. 131

40. *The Lybian Lion.*

AT the first addresse and presence of sicknesse, *stand still and arrest thy spirit,* that it may without amazement, or affright consider that this was that thou lookedst for, and wert alwayes certain should happen, and that now thou art to enter into the actions of a new religion, the agony of a strange constitution; but at no hand suffer thy spirits to be dispersed with fear, or wildnesse of thought, but stay their loosenesse and dispersion by a serious consideration of the present and future imployment. For so doth the Lybian Lion spying the fierce huntsman, first beats himself with the stroaks of his tail, and curles up his spirits, making them strong with union and recollection, till being strook with a Mauritanian spear, he rushes forth into his defence and noblest contention; and either scapes into the secrets of his own dwelling, or else dies, the bravest of the forrest: Every man when shot with an arrow from Gods quiver, must then draw in all the auxiliaries of reason, and know, that then is the time to try his strength,

and to reduce the words of his religion into action, and
consider that if he behaves himself weakly and timerously,
he suffers never the lesse of sicknesse; but if he turns to
health he carries along with him the mark of a coward and
a fool; and if he descends into his grave, he enters into the
state of the *faithlesse* and *unbeleevers*. Let him set his heart
firm upon this resolution, *I must bear it inevitably; and
I will by Gods grace do it nobly.*

Holy Dying, 1651, p. 157

41. *The Advantages of Sickness.*

SICKNESSE is the more tolerable because it cures very
many evils, and takes away the sense of all the crosse
fortunes which amaze the spirits of some men, and trans
port them certainly beyond all the limits of patience. Here
all losses and disgraces, domestick cares and publick evils,
the apprehensions of pity, and a sociable calamity, the fears
of want and the troubles of ambition, lie down and rest
upon the sick mans pillow. One fit of the stone takes away
from the fancies of men, all relations to the world and
secular interests; at least they are made dull and flat, without sharpnesse and an edge.

And he that shall observe the infinite variety of troubles
which afflicts some busie persons, & almost all men in very
busie times, will think it not much amisse that those huge
numbers were reduced to certainty, to method, and an
order; and there is no better compendium for this, then
that they be reduced to one. And a sick man seems so
unconcerned in the things of the world, that although this
separation be done with violence; yet it is no otherwise
then all noble contentions are, and all honours are purchased, and all vertues are acquired, and all vices mortified,

and all appetites chastised, and all rewards obtained: there
is infallibly to all these a difficulty and a sharpnesse annexed, without which there could be no proportion between a work and a reward. To this adde, that sicknesse
does not take off the sense of secular troubles, and worldly
cares from us, by imploying all the perceptions, and apprehensions of men, by filling all faculties with sorrow, and
leaving no room for the lesser instances of troubles; as little
rivers are swallowed up in the Sea: But sicknesse is a messenger of God, sent with purposes of abstraction and
separation, with a secret power and a proper efficacie to
draw us off from unprofitable and uselesse sorrows: and
this is effected *partly* by reason that it represents the use-
lessenesse of the things of this world, and that there is a
portion of this life in which honours and things of the
world cannot serve us to many purposes, partly by preparing us to death, and telling us that a man shall descend
thither whence this world cannot redeem us, & where the
goods of this world cannot serve us.

And yet after all this, sicknesse leaves in us appetites
so strong, and apprehensions so sensible, and delights so
many, and good things in so great a degree, that a healthlesse body, and a sad disease do seldome make men weary
of this world; but still they would fain find an excuse to
live. The gout, the stone, and the toothach, the *sciatica*,
sore eyes, and an aking head, are evils indeed; But such,
which rather then die, most men are willing to suffer, and
Mecenas added also a wish, rather to be crucified then to
die; and though his wish was low, timerous, and base, yet
we find the same desires in most men, dressed up with
better circumstances. It was a cruell mercy in *Tamerlan*
who commanded all the leprous persons to be put to

death, as we knock some beasts quickly on their head, to put them out of pain, and lest they should live miserably. The poor men would rather have endured another leprosie, and have more willingly taken two diseases then one death; therefore *Cæsar* wondred that the old crazed souldier begged leave he might kill himself, and asked him, *Doest thou think then to be more alive then now thou art?* We do not die suddenly, but we descend to death by steps, and slow passages; and therefore men (so long as they are sick) are unwilling to proceed and go forward in the finishing that sad imployment. Between a disease and death, there are many degrees, and all those are like the reserves of evil things, the declining of every one of which is justly reckoned amongst those good things, which alleviate the sicknesse and make it tolerable. Never account that sick-nesse intolerable, in which thou hadst rather remaine, then die: And yet if thou hadst rather die then suffer it, the worst of it that can be said is this, that this sicknesse is worse then death; that is, it is worse then that which is the best of all evils, and the end of all troubles; and then you have said no great harme against it. . . .

We finde in story that many Gentiles who walked by no light but that of reason, opinion, and humane examples, did bear their sicknesse nobly, and with great contempt of pain, and with huge interests of vertue. When *Pompey* came from Syria and called at Rhodes, to see *Posidonius* the Philosopher, he found him hugely afflicted with the gout, and expressed his sorrow, that he could not hear his Lectures from which by this pain he must needs be hindred. *Posidonius* told him, *but you may hear me for all this*; and he discours'd excellently in the midst of his tortures, even then, *when the torches were put to his feet,* that *nothing was good but what was honest*; and therefore *nothing could be an evil, if it were not criminal*, and summed up his Lectures with this saying; *O pain, in vain doest thou attempt me; for I will never confesse thee to be an evil as long as I can honestly bear thee.* And when *Pompey* himself was desperately sick at Naples, the *Neopolitans* wore crowns and triumphed; and the men of *Puteoli* came to congratulate his sicknesse, not because they loved him not, but because it was the custome of their countrey to have better opinions of sicknesse then we have. The boyes of *Sparta* would at their Altars endure whipping till their very entrails saw the light thorow their torn flesh; and some of them to death, without crying or complaint. *Cæsar* would drink his potions of Rhubarb rudely mixt, and unfitly allayed with little sippings, and tasted the horror of the medicine spreading the loathsomnesse of his physick so, that all the parts of his tongue and palate might have an intire share: and when *C. Marius* suffered the veins of his leg to be cut out for the curing his gout, and yet shrunk not, he declared not onely the rudenesse of their physick, but the strength of a mans spirit, if it be contracted and united by the aids of reason or Religion, by resolution or any accidentall harshnesse, against a violent disease.

All impatience howsoever expressed, is perfectly uselesse to all purposes of ease, but hugely effective to the multiplying the trouble; and the impatience and vexation is another, but the sharper disease of the two; it does mischief *by it self*, and mischief *by the disease*. For *men grieve themselves as much as they please*, and when by impatience they put themselves into the retinue of sorrows, they become solemne mourners. For so have I seen the rayes of the Sun or Moon dash upon a brazen vessel whose lips kissed the face of those waters that lodged within its bosome, but being turned back and sent off with its smooth pretences, or rougher waftings, it wandred about the room and beat upon the roof, and still doubled its heat and motion: So is a sicknesse and a sorrow entertained by an unquiet and a discontented man, turned back either with anger, or with excuses; but then the pain passes from the stomack to the liver, and from the liver to the heart, and from the heart to the head, and from feeling to considera-tion, from thence to sorrow, and at last ends in impatience, and uselesse murmur, and all the way the man was im-potent, and weak; but the sicknesse was doubled and grew imperious and tyrannicall over the soul and body. *Mas-surius Sabinus* tels, that the image of the goddesse *Angerona* was with a mufler upon her mouth placed upon the Altar of *Volupia*, to represent, that those persons who bear their sicknesses and sorrows without murmur, shall certainly passe from sorrow to pleasure, and the ease and honours of felicity; but they that with spite and indignation bite the burning coal, or shake the yoak upon their necks, gall their spirits, and fret the skin, and hurt nothing but themselves.

Remember that this sicknesse is but for a short time; If it be sharp it will not last long; If it be long, it will be easie and very tolerable. And although S. *Eadsine* Arch-bishop of *Canterbury* had twelve years of sicknesse, yet all that while he ruled his Church prudently, gave example of many vertues, and after his death was enrolled in the Calender of Saints, who had finished their course pros-perously. Nothing is more unreasonable then to intangle our spirits in wildnesse, and amazement, like a Partrich fluttering in a net, which she breaks not, though she breaks her wings. . . .

In sicknesse, the soul begins to dresse her self for immortality: and first she unties the strings of vanity that
made her upper garment cleave to the world and sit
uneasily. First she puts off the light and phantastic summer robe of lust, and wanton appetite, and as soon as that
Cestus that lascivious girdle is thrown away, then the *reins
chasten us and give us warning in the night*: then that which
called us formerly to serve *the manlinesse of the body*, and
the childishnesse of the soul, keeps us waking, to divide the
hours with the intervals of prayer, and to number the
minutes with our penitential groans: Then the flesh sits
uneasily and dwells in sorrow, and then the spirit feels it
self at ease, freed from the petulant sollicitations of those
passions which in health were as buisie and as restlesse as
atomes in the sun, alwayes dancing and alwayes busie and
never sitting down till a sad night of grief and uneasinesse
draws the vail, and lets them dye alone in secret dishonour.

Next to this; *the soul by the help of sicknesse knocks off
the fetters of pride and vainer complacencies*. Then she
drawes the curtains, and stops the lights from coming in,
and takes the pictures down, those phantastic images of
self-love, and gay remembrances of vain opinion, and
popular noises. Then the Spirit stoops into the sobrieties
of humble thoughts and feels corruption chiding the for-
wardnesse of fancy, and allaying the vapours of conceit and
factious opinions. For humility is the souls grave into
which he enters, not to die, but to meditate and interre
some of its troublesome appendages. There she sees the
dust, and feels the dishonours of the body, and reads the
Register of all its sad adherencies; and then she layes by
all her vain reflexions, beating upon her Chrystall and pure
mirrour from the fancies of strength and beauty, & little

decayed prettinesses of the body. And when in sicknesse we forget all our knotty discourses of Philosophy, and a Syllogisme makes our head ake, and we feel our many and loud talkings served no lasting end of the soul, no purpose that now we must abide by; and that the body is like to descend to the land, where all things are forgotten, then she layes aside all her remembrances of applauses, all her ignorant confidences, and cares onely to *know Christ Jesus and him crucified*, to know him plainly, and with much heartinesse, and simplicity. . . .

Next to these; *As the soul is still undressing, she takes off the roughnesse of her great and little angers, and animosities,* and receives the oil of mercies, and smooth forgivenesse, fair interpretations, and gentle answers, designes of recon- cilement, and Christian atonement in their places. For so did the wrastlers in *Olympus*, they stripped themselves of all their garments, and then anointed their naked bodies with oil, smooth and vigorous, with contracted nerves and enlarged voice, they contended vehemently, till they ob- tained their victory, or their ease, and a crown of Olive, or a huge pity was the reward of their fierce contentions.

Holy Dying, 1651, pp. 91, 95, 105, 108

42. *Comforts.*

OUR Conversation must be παράκλητος, apt to com- fort the disconsolate; and *then this*, men in present can feel no greater charity. For since halfe the duty of a Christian in this life consists in the exercise of passive graces, and the infinite variety of providence, and the per- petuall adversity of chances, and the dissatisfaction and emptynesse that is in things themselves, and the weary- nesse and anguish of our spirit does call us to the trial and exercise of patience even in the dayes of sunshine, and much more in the violent storms that shake our dwellings, and make our hearts tremble; God hath sent some Angels into the world, whose office it is to refresh the sorrowes of the poore, and to lighten the eyes of the disconsolate; he hath made some creatures whose powers are chiefly ordain'd to comfort; *wine*, and *oyle*, and *society*, *cordials* and *variety*; and *time* it selfe is checker'd with black and white; stay but till to morrow, and your present sorrow will be weary, and will lie downe to rest. But this is not all. The third person of the holy Trinity is known to us by the name and dignity of the *Holy Ghost the Comforter*, and God glories in the appellative, that he is *the Father of mercies*, and *the God of all comfort*, and therefore to minister in the office is to become like God, and to imitate the charities of heaven; and God hath fitted mankinde for it; he most needs it, and he feels his brothers wants by his owne experience, and God hath given us speech, and the endearments of society, and pleasantness of conversation, and powers of seasonable discourse, arguments to allay the sorrow, by abating our apprehensions and taking out the sting, or telling the periods of comfort, or exciting hope, or urging a precept, and reconciling our affections, and reciting promises, or telling stories of the Divine mercy, or changing it into duty, or making the burden lesse by comparing it with greater, or by proving it to be lesse then we deserve, and that it is so intended, and may become the instrument of vertue. And certain it is, that as nothing can better doe it, so there is nothing greater, for which God made our tongues, next to reciting his prayses, then to minister comfort to a weary soul. And what greater measure can we have, then that we should bring joy to our brother, who with his dreary eyes looks to heaven and round about, and cannot finde so much rest as to lay his eye-lids close together, then that thy tongue should be tun'd with heavenly accents, and make the weary soul *to listen* for light and ease, and when he perceives that there is such a thing in the world, and in the order of things, as comfort and joy, *to begin* to break out from the prison of his sorrows at the dore of sighs and tears, and by little and little melt into showres and refreshment? This is glory to thy voyce, and imployment fit for the brightest Angel. But so have I seen the sun kisse the frozen earth which was bound up with the images of death, and the colder breath of the North, and then the waters break from their inclosures, and melt with joy, and run in usefull channels, and the flies doe rise againe from their little graves in walls, and dance a while in the aire, to tell that there is joy within, and that the great mother of creatures will open the stock of her new refreshment, become usefull to man-kinde, and sing prayses to her Redeemer: So is the heart of a sorrowfull man under the discourses of a wise Com-forter, he breaks from the despairs of the grave, and the fetters and chains of sorrow, he blesses God, and he blesses thee, and he feels his life returning; for to be miserable is death, but nothing is life but to be comforted; and God is pleased with no musick from below so much as in the thanksgiving songs of relieved Widows, of supported Or-phans, of rejoycing, and comforted, and thankfull persons.

XXV Sermons, 1653, p. 327

43. *Contentedness.*

FOR since all the evil in the World consists in the dis-
agreeing between the object and the appetite, as when
a man hath what he desires not, or desires what he hath
not, or desires amisse; he that composes his spirit to the
present accident, hath variety of instances for his vertue,
but none to trouble him, because his desires enlarge not
beyond his present fortune: and a wise man is placed in
the variety of chances like the Nave or Centre of a wheel,
in the midst of all the circumvolutions and changes of
posture, without violence or change, save that it turns
gently in complyance with its changed parts, and is indifferent which part is up and which is down; for there is
some vertue or other to be exercised what ever happens,
either patience or thanksgiving, love or fear, moderation
or humility, charity or contentednesse, and they are every
one of them equally in order to his great end, an immortal
felicity: and beauty is not made by white or red, by black
eyes & a round face, by a strait body and a smooth skin;
but by a proportion to the fancy: No rules can make
amability, our mindes & apprehensions make that; and so
is our felicity; and we may be reconcil'd to poverty and
a low fortune, if we suffer contentednesse and the grace of
God to make the proportions. . . .

Contentednesse in all accidents brings great peace of
spirit, and is the great and onely instrument of temporal
felicity. It removes the sting from the accident, and makes
a man not to depend upon chance, and the uncertain dispositions of men for his well being, but onely on G O D
and his own Spirit. Wee our selves make our fortunes good
or bad, and when God lets loose a Tyrant upon us, or a

sicknesse, or scorne, or a lessened fortune, if we fear to dye, or know not to be patient, or are proud, or covetous, then the calamity sits heavy on us. But if we know how to manage a noble principle, and fear not Death so much as a dishonest action, and think impatience a worse evil then a Feaver, and Pride to be the biggest disgrace, and poverty to be infinitely desirable before the torments of covetousnesse; then we who now think vice to be so easie, and make it so familiar, and think the cure so impossible, shall quickly be of another minde, and reckon these accidents amongst things eligible. . . .

Now suppose thy self in as great a sadnesse, as ever did load thy spirit, wouldest thou not beare it cheerfully and nobly, if thou wert sure that within a certain space some strange excellent fortune would relieve thee, and enrich thee, and recompence thee so as to overflow all thy hopes and thy desires, and capacities? Now then, when a sadnesse lies heavy upon thee, remember that thou art a Christian designed to the inheritance of Jesus: and what dost thou think concerning thy great fortune, thy lot and portion of eternity? Doest thou think thou shalt be saved or damned? Indeed if thou thinkest thou shalt perish, I cannot blame thee to be sad, sad till thy heart-strings crack: but then why art thou troubled at the losse of thy money? what should a damned man do with money, which in so great a sadnes it is impossible for him to enjoy? Did ever any man upon the rack, afflict himself because he had received a crosse answer from his Mistresse? or call for the particulars of a purchase upon the gallows? If thou doest really believe thou shalt be damned, I do not say it will *cure* the sadnesse of thy poverty, but it will *swallow* it up. But if thou believest thou shalt be saved, consider how great is that joy, how infinite is that change, how unspeak-able is the glory, how excellent is the recompence for all the sufferings in the world, if they were all laden upon thy spirit? So that let thy condition be what it will, if thou considerest thy own present condition, and compare it to thy future possibility, thou canst not feel the present smart of a crosse fortune to any great degree, either because thou hast a far bigger sorrow, or a far bigger joy. Here thou art but a stranger travelling to thy Countrey where the glories of a kingdom are prepared for thee, it is therefore a huge folly to be much afflicted because thou hast a lesse con-venient Inne to lodge in by the way.

But these arts of *looking forwards and backwards* are more then enough to support the spirit of a Christian: there is no man but hath blessings enough in present possession to outweigh the evils of a great affliction. Tell the joynts of thy body, and do not accuse the universal providence for a lame leg, or the want of a finger, when all the rest is perfect: and you have a noble soul, a particle of Divinity, the image of G O D himself: and by the want of a finger you may the better know how to estimate the remaining parts, and to account for every degree of the surviving blessings. *Aristippus* in a great suit at law lost a Farm, and to a Gentleman who in civility pitied and deplored his losse, He answered, I have two Farms left still, and that is more then I have lost, and more then you have by one. If you misse an Office for which you stood Candidate, then besides that you are quit of the cares and the envy of it, you still have all those excellencies which rendred you capable to receive it, and they are better then the best Office in the Common-wealth. If your estate be lessened, you need the lesse to care who governs the Province, whether he be rude or gentle. I am cross'd in my journey, and yet I scaped robbers; and I consider, that if I had been set upon by Villanes I would have redeem'd that evil by this which I now suffer, and have counted it a deliverance: or if I did fall into the hands of theeves, yet they did not steal my land: or I am fallen into the hands of Publicans and Sequestrators, and they have taken all from me, what now? let me look about me. They have left me the Sun and the Moon, Fire and Water, a loving wife, and many friends to pity me, and some to relieve me, and I can still discourse, and unlesse I list they have not taken away my merry countenance, and my cheerful spirit, and a good conscience: they still have left me the providence of God, and all the promises of the Gospel, and my Religion, and my hopes of Heaven, and my charity to them too: and still I sleep, and digest, I eat and drink, I reade and meditate, I can walk in my Neighbours pleasant fields, and see the varieties of natural beauties, and delight in all that in which God delights, that is, in vertue and wisdom, in the whole creation, and in God himself: and he that hath so many causes of joy, and so great, is very much in love with sorrow and peevishness, who loses all these pleasures, and chooses to sit down upon his little handful of thorns: such a person were fit to bear *Nero* company in his funeral sorrow for the losse of one of *Poppeas* hairs, or help to mourn for *Lesbia*'s sparrow: and because he loves it, he deserves to starve in the midst of plenty, and to want comfort while he is encircled with blessings. . . .

If you will secure a contented spirit, you must measure your desires by your fortune and condition, not your fortunes by your desires. That is, be governed by your needs not by your fancy; by Nature, not by evil customes and

ambitious principles. He that would shoot an arrow out
of a Plow, or hunt a Hare with an Elephant, is not unfortunate for missing the mark or prey; but he is foolish for
choosing such unapt instruments: and so is he that runs
after his content with appetites not springing from natural
needs, but from artificial, phantastical and violent necessities: These are not to be satisfied; or if they were, a
man hath chosen an evill instrument towards his content:
Nature did not intend rest to a Man by filling of such
desires. Is that Beast better that hath two or three Mountains to graze on, then a little Bee that feeds on Dew or
Manna, and lives upon what falls every morning from the
Store-houses of Heaven *Clouds and Providence*: Can a Man
quench his thirst better out of a River then a full Urn, or
drink better from the Fountain when it is finely paved
with Marble, then when it swels over the green Turfe?
Pride and artificial gluttonies do but adulterate Nature,
making our diet healthlesse, our appetites impatient and
unsatisfiable, and the taste mixt, phantastical, and meretricious. But that which we miscal poverty, is indeed
Nature: and its proportions are the just measures of a
Man, and the best instruments of content: But when we
create needs that God or Nature never made, we have
erected to our selves an infinite stock of trouble that can
have no period.

Sempronius complained of want of clothes, and was much
troubled for a new suit, being ashamed to appear in the
Theatre with his Gown a little thread-bare: but when he
got it and gave his old clothes to *Codrus*, the poor man
was ravisht with joy, and went and gave God thanks for
his new purchase: and *Codrus* was made richly fine and
cheerfully warm by that which *Sempronius* was asham'd to

wear; and yet their natural needs were both alike, the difference onely was, that *Sempronius* had some artificial and phantastical necessities superinduced, which *Codrus* had not; and was harder to be reliev'd, and could not have joy at so cheap a rate; because the one liv'd according to Nature, the other by Pride and ill customes, and measures taken by other mens eyes and tongues, and artificial needs. He that propounds to his fancy things greater then himself, or his needs, and is discontent and troubled when he fails of such purchases, ought not to accuse Providence, or blame his fortune but his folly. God and Nature made no more needs then they mean to satisfie: and he that will make more must look for satisfaction where he can.

Holy Living, 1650, pp. 128, 130, 138, 144

44. *Labour*.

GOD hath sent no greater evil into the world, then that *in the sweat of our brows we shall eat our bread*, and in the difficulty and agony, in the sorrows and contention of our souls we shall *work out our salvation*. But see how in the first of these God hath out done his own anger and defeated the purposes of his *wrath* by the inundation of his *mercy*; for this labour and sweat of our brows is so far from being a curse that without it our very bread would not be so great a blessing. Is it not labour that makes the Garlick and the pulse, the Sycamore and the Cresses, the cheese of the Goats and the butter of the sheep to be savoury and pleasant, as the flesh of the Roebuck or the milk of the Kine, the marrow of Oxen or the thighs of birds? If it were not for labour, men neither could eat so much, nor relish so pleasantly, nor sleep so

soundly nor be so healthful, nor so useful, so strong nor
so patient, so noble, or so untempted.

XXVIII Sermons, 1651, p. 322

45. *Cheerfulness.*

A CHEERFULL spirit is the best convoy for Religion;
and though sadnesse does in some cases *become a Christian*, as being an *Index* of a pious minde, of compassion,
and a wise proper resentment of things, yet it serves but
one end, being useful in the onely instance of repentance;
and hath done its greatest works, not when it weeps and
sighs, but when it hates and grows carefull against sin.
But *cheerfulnesse* and a *festivall spirit* fills the soule full of
harmony, it composes musick for Churches and hearts, it
makes and publishes glorifications of God, it produces
thankfulnesse and serves the ends of charity, and when the
oyle of gladnesse runs over, it makes bright and tall emissions of light and holy fires, reaching up to a cloud, and
making joy round about: And therefore since it is so innocent, and may be so pious and full of holy advantage,
whatsoever can innocently minister to this holy joy does
set forward the work of Religion and Charity. And indeed
charity it selfe, which is the verticall top of all Religion,
*is nothing else but an union of joyes, concentred in the heart,
and reflected from all the angles of our life· and entercourse.*
It is a rejoycing in God, a gladnesse in our neighbors good,
a pleasure in doing good, a rejoycing with him; and without love we cannot have any joy at all. It is this that
makes children to be a pleasure, and friendship to be so
noble and divine a thing; and upon this account it is certaine that all that which can innocently make a man cheerfull, does also make him charitable; for *grief*, and *age*, and

sicknesse, and *wearinesse,* these are peevish and troublesome; but *mirth* and cheerfulnesse is *content,* and *civil,* and
compliant, and *communicative,* and loves to doe good, and
swels up to felicity onely upon the wings of charity. In
this account here is pleasure enough for a Christian in
present, and if a facete discourse and an amicable friendly
mirth can refresh the spirit, and take it off from the vile
temptations of peevish, despairing, uncomplying melancholy, it must needs be innocent and commendable. And
we may as well be refreshed by a clean and a brisk discourse, as by the aire of *Campanian* wines; and our faces
and our heads may as well be anointed and look pleasant
with wit and friendy entercourse, as with the fat of the
Balsam tree; and such a conversation no wise man ever
did, or ought to reprove. But when the jest hath teeth
and nails, biting or scratching our Brother, when it is loose
and wanton, when it is unseasonable, and much, or many,
when it serves ill purposes, or spends better time, then it
is *the drunkennesse of the soul,* and makes the spirit fly away,
seeking for a Temple where the mirth and the musick is
solemne and religious.

XXV Sermons, 1653, p. 304

46. *Friendship.*

XΡΗΣΤΟΣ ἀνὴρ *the good man* is a profitable, useful person, and that's the band of an effective friendship.
For I do not think that friendships are Metaphysical
nothings, created for contemplation, or that men or
women should stare upon each others faces, and make dialogues of news and prettinesses, and look babies in one
anothers eyes. Friendship is the allay of our sorrows, the
ease of our passions, the discharge of our oppressions, the

sanctuary to our calamities, the counsellor of our doubts, the clarity of our minds, the emission of our thoughts, the exercise and improvement of what we meditate: And although I love my friend because he is worthy, yet he is not worthy if he can do no good. I do not speak of accidental hinderances and misfortunes by which the bravest man may become unable to help his Childe; but of the natural and artificial capacities of the man. He only is fit to be chosen for a friend, who can do those offices for which friendship is excellent. For (mistake not) no man can be loved for himselfe; our perfections in this world cannot reach so high; it is well if we would love God at that rate, and I very much fear, that if God did us no good, we might admire his Beauties, but we should have but a small proportion of love towards him; and therefore it is, that God to endear *the obedience*, that is, *the love* of his servants signifies what benefits he gives us, what great good things he does for us.

Discourse of Friendship, 1657, p. 23

47. *Friendship.*

SO that to your question, how far a Dear and perfect friendship is authoris'd by the principles of Christianity? The answer is ready and easy. It is warranted to extend to all mankind; and the more we love, the better we are, and the greater our friendships are, the dearer we are to God; let them be as Dear, and let them be as perfect, and let them be as many as you can; there is no danger in it; only where the restraint begins, there begins our imperfection; it is not ill that you entertain brave friendships and worthy societies: it were well if you could

love, and if you could *benefit* all mankinde; for I conceive
that is the sum of all friendships.

I confess this is not to be expected of us in this world;
but as all our graces here are but imperfect, that is, at the
best they are but tendencies to glory, so our friendships
are imperfect too, and but beginnings of a celestial friendship, by which we shall love every one as much as they can
be loved. But then so we must here *in our proportion*; and
indeed that is it that can make the difference; we must be
friends to all: That is, apt to do good, loving them really,
and doing to them all the benefits which we can, and
which they are capable of. The friendship is equal to all
the world, and of it selfe hath no difference; but is dif-
ferenc'd only by accidents and by the capacity or incapacity of them that receive it: *Nature* and the *Religion* are
the *bands* of friendships; *excellency* and *usefulness* are its
great *indearments*: *society* and *neighbourhood*, that is, the
possibilities and the circumstances of converse are the
determinations and *actualities* of it. Now when men either
are unnatural, or irreligious, they *will not* be friends; when
they are neither excellent nor useful, *they are not worthy*
to be friends; where they are strangers or unknown, they
cannot be friends actually and practically; but yet, as any
man hath any thing of the good, contrary to those evils,
so he can have and must have his share of friendship. For
thus the Sun is the eye of all the World; and he is indifferent to the Negro, or the cold Russian, to them that
dwell under the line, and them that stand neer the
Tropics, the scalded Indian or the poor boy that shakes
at the foot of the Riphean hills; but the fluxures of the
heaven and the earth, the conveniency of aboad, and
the approaches to the North or South respectively change the

emanations of his beams; not that they do not pass alwayes
from him, but that they are not equally received below,
but by periods and changes, by little inlets and reflections,
they receive what they can; and some have only a dark
day and a long night from him, snowes and white cattel,
a miserable life, and a perpetual harvest of Catarrhes and
consumptions, apoplexies and dead-palsies; but some have
splendid fires, and aromatick spices, rich wines, and well
digested fruits, great wit and great courage; because they
dwell in his eye, and look in his face, and are the Courtiers
of the Sun, and wait upon him in his Chambers of the
East; just so is it in friendships: some are worthy, and
some are necessary; some dwell hard by and are fitted for
converse; Nature joyns some to us, and Religion combines
us with others; society and accidents, parity of fortune,
and equal dispositions do actuate our friendships: which
of themselves and in their prime disposition are prepared
for all mankind according as any one can receive them.
We see this best exemplified by two instances and expressions of friendships and charity: *viz. Almes* and *Prayers*;
Every one that needs relief is equally the object of our
charity; but though to all mankind in equal needs we
ought to be alike in charity; yet we signifie this severally
and by limits, and distinct measures: the poor man that
is near me, he whom I meet, he whom I love, he whom
I fancy, he who did me benefit, he who relates to my
family, he rather then another, because my expressions
being finite and narrow, and cannot extend to all in equal
significations, must be appropriate to those whose circumstances best fit me: and yet even to all I give my almes:
to all the world that needs them; I pray for all mankind,
I am grieved at every sad story I hear; I am troubled when

I hear of a pretty bride murdered in her bride-chamber
by an ambitious and enrag'd Rival; I shed a tear when
I am told that a brave King was misunderstood, then
slandered, then imprisoned, and then put to death by evil
men: and I can never read the story of the Parisian Massacre, or the Sicilian vespers, but my blood curdles and
I am disorder'd by two or three affections. A good man
is a friend to all the world; and he is not truly charitable
that does not wish well, and do good to all mankind in
what he can; but though we must pray for all men, yet
we say speciall Letanies for brave Kings and holy Prelates,
and the wise Guides of souls; for our Brethren and Relations, our Wives and Children.

Discourse of Friendship, 1657, p. 8

48. *Friendship and Fancy.*

BUT if you yet enquire further, whether fancy may be
an ingredient in your choice? I answer, that fancy
may minister to this as to all other actions in which there
is a liberty and variety; and we shall finde that there may
be peculiarities and little partialities, a *friendship, impro-
perly so called*, entring upon accounts of an innocent passion and a pleas'd fancy; even our Blessed Saviour himself
loved S. *John* and *Lazarus* by a special love, which was
signified by special treatments; and of the young man that
spake well and wisely to Christ, it is affirmed, *Jesus loved
him*: that is, he fancied the man; and his soul had a certain
cognation and similitude of temper and inclination. For
in all things where there is a latitude, every faculty will
endeavour to be pleased, and sometimes the meanest persons in a house have a festival; even sympathies and natural
inclinations to some persons, and a conformity of humors,

and proportionable loves, and the beauty of the face, and a witty answer may first strike the flint and kindle a spark, which if it falls upon tender and compliant natures may grow into a flame; but this will never be maintained at the rate of friendship, unless it be fed by pure materials, by *worthinesses* which *are the food of friendship.* Where these are not, men and women may be pleased with one anothers company, and lie under the same roof, and make themselves companions of equal prosperities, and humour their friend; but if you call this friendship, you give a sacred name to humour or fancy; for there is a Platonic friendship as well as a Platonic love; but they being but the Images of more noble bodies are but like tinsell dressings, which will shew bravely by candle-light, and do excellently in a mask, but are not fit for conversation, and the material entercourses of our life. These are the prettinesses of prosperity and good-natur'd wit; but when we speak of friendship, which is the best thing in the world (for it is love and beneficence; it is charity that is fitted for society) we cannot suppose a brave pile should be built up with nothing; and they that build Castles in the aire, and look upon friendship, as upon a fine Romance, a thing that pleases the fancy, but is good for nothing else, will do well when they are asleep, or when they are come to Elysium; and for ought I know in the mean time may be as much in love with *Mandana* in the *Grand Cyrus,* as with the *Countess of Exeter;* and by dreaming of perfect and abstracted friendships, make them so immaterial that they perish in the handling and become good for nothing.

But I know not whither I was going; I did only mean to say that because friendship is that by which the world is most blessed and receives most good, it ought to be chosen amongst the worthiest persons, that is, amongst those that can do greatest benefit to each other; and though in equal worthiness I may choose by my eye, or ear, that is, into the consideration of the essential I may take in also the accidental and extrinsick worthinesses; yet I ought to give every one their just value; when the internal beauties are equal, these shall help to weigh down the scale, and I will love a worthy friend that can delight me as well as profit me, rather then him who cannot delight me at all, and profit me *no more*; but yet I will not weigh the gayest flowers, or the wings of butterflies against wheat; but when I am to choose wheat, I may take that which looks the brightest: I had rather see Time and Roses, Marjoram and Julyflowers that are fair and sweet and medicinal, then the prettiest Tulips that are good for nothing: And my Sheep and Kine are better servants then race-Horses and Grayhounds: And I shall rather furnish my study with *Plutarch* and *Cicero*, with *Livy* and *Polybius*, then with *Cassandra* and *Ibrahim Bassa*; and if I do give an hour to these for divertisement or pleasure, yet I will dwell with them that can instruct me and make me wise, and eloquent, severe and useful to my selfe, and others. I end this with the saying of *Lælius* in *Cicero*: *Amicitia non debet consequi utilitatem, sed amicitiam utilitas.* When I choose my friend, I will not stay till I have received a kindness; but I will choose such a one that can doe me many if I need them: But I mean such kindnesses which make me wiser, and which make me better; that is, I will when I choose my friend, choose him that is the bravest, the worthiest and the most excellent person: and then your first Question is soon answered; to love such a person and to contract such friendships is just so author-

ized by the principles of Christianity, as it is warranted to
love wisdome and vertue, goodness and beneficence, and
all the impresses of God upon the spirits of brave men.

Discourse of Friendship, 1657, p. 35

49. *Brothers.*

A BROTHER if he be worthy is the readiest and the
nearest to be a friend, but till he be so, he is but
the twi-light of the day, and but the blossom to the fairest
fruit of Paradise.

Discourse of Friendship, 1657, p. 68

50. *Old Friends.*

WHEN all things else are equal preferre an old friend
before a new. If thou meanest to spend thy friend,
and make a gain of him till he be weary, thou wilt esteem
him as a beast of burden, the worse for his age: But if thou
esteemest him by noble measures, he will be better to thee
by thy being used to him, by tryall and experience, by
reciprocation of indearments, and an habitual worthiness.
An old friend is like old wine, which when a man hath
drunk, he doth not desire new, because he saith the old is
better. But every old friend was new once; and if he be
worthy keep the new one till he become old.

After all this, treat thy friend nobly, love to be with
him, do to him all the worthinesses of love and fair endearment, according to thy capacity and his; Bear with his
infirmities till they approach towards being criminal; but
never dissemble with him, never despise him, never leave
him. Give him gifts and upbraid him not, and refuse
not his kindnesses, and be sure never to despise the small-
ness or the impropriety of them. *Confirmatur amor bene-*

ficio accepto: A gift (saith *Solomon*) fastneth friendships; for as an eye that dwells long upon a starre must be refreshed with lesser beauties and strengthened with greens and looking-glasses, lest the sight become amazed with too great a splendor; so must the love of friends sometimes be refreshed with material and low Caresses; lest by striving to be *too divine* it becomes *less humane*: It must be allowed its share of *both*: It is *humane* in giving pardon and fair construction, and opennesse and ingenuity, and keeping secrets; it hath *something* that is *Divine*, because it is *beneficent*; but *much* because it is *Eternall*.

Discourse of Friendship, 1657, p. 98

51. *The Death of a Friend*.

IT is certainly a sad thing in nature to see a friend trembling with a palsie, or scorched with feavers, or *dried up like a potsheard* with immoderate heats, and rowling upon his uneasie bed without sleep which cannot be invited with musick, or pleasant murmurs, or a decent stillnesse; nothing but the servants of cold death, *poppy and wearinesse* can tempt the eyes to let their curtains down; and then they sleep onely to tast of death, and make an essay of the shades below; and yet we weep not here: the period and opportunity for tears we choose when our friend is fallen asleep, when he hath laid his neck upon the lap of his mother, and let his head down to be raised up to heaven.

Holy Dying, 1651, p. 325

52. *Marriage*.

MARRIAGE was ordained by God, instituted in Paradise, was the relief of a naturall necessity, and the first blessing from the Lord; he gave to Man not a friend,

but a wife, that is, a friend and a wife too: (for a good
woman is in her soul the same that a man is, and she is
a woman only in her body; that she may have the excellency of the one, and the usefulnesse of the other, and
become amiable in both:) it is the seminary of the Church,
and daily brings forth sons and daughters unto God; it
was ministred to by Angels, and *Raphael* waited upon a
young man that he might have a blessed marriage, and
that that marriage might repair two sad families, and blesse
all their relatives. Our blessed Lord, though he was born
of a maiden, yet she was vail'd under the cover of marriage,
and she was marryed to a widower; for *Joseph* the supposed Father of our Lord had children by a former wife.
The first Miracle that ever *Jesus* did, was to doe honour
to a wedding; marriage was in the world before sin, and
is in all ages of the world the greatest and most effective
antidote against sin, in which all the world had perished
if God had not made a remedy; and although sin hath
sour'd marriage, and stuck the mans head with cares, and
the womans bed with sorrowes in the production of
children, yet these are but throes of life and glory; and
*she shall be saved in child-bearing, if she be found in faith
and righteousnesse.* Marriage is a Schoole and exercise of
vertue; and though *Marriage* hath *cares*, yet *the single
life* hath *desires* which are more troublesome and more
dangerous, and often end in sin, while the cares are but
instances of duty and exercises of piety; and therefore if
single life hath more privacy of devotion, yet marriage
hath more necessities and more variety of it, and is an
exercise of more graces. In two vertues *celibate* or single
life may have the advantage of degrees ordinarily and commonly, that is, in *chastity* and *devotion*: but as in some per-

sons this may fail, and it does in very many, and a marryed man may spend as much time in devotion as any virgins or widowes do, yet as in marriage even those vertues of chastity and devotion are exercised: so in other instances, this state hath proper exercises and trials for those graces, for which single life can never be crown'd; Here is the proper scene of piety and patience, of the duty of Parents and the charity of relatives; here kindnesse is spread abroad, and love is united and made firm as a centre: Marriage is the nursery of heaven; the virgin sends prayers to God, but she carries but one soul to him; but the state of marriage fils up the numbers of the elect, and hath in it the labour of love, and the delicacies of friendship, the blessing of society, and the union of hands and hearts; it hath in it lesse of beauty, but more of safety then the single life; it hath more care, but lesse danger; it is more merry, and more sad; is fuller of sorrowes, and fuller of joyes; it lies under more burdens, but it is supported by all the strengths of love and charity, and those burdens are delightfull. Marriage is the mother of the world, and preserves Kingdomes, and fils Cities, and Churches, and Heaven it self: Celibate, like the flie in the heart of an apple, dwels in a perpetuall sweetnesse, but sits alone, and is confin'd and dies in singularity; but marriage, like the usefull Bee, builds a house and gathers sweetnesse from every flower, and labours and unites into societies and republicks, and sends out colonies, and feeds the world with delicacies, and obeys their king, and keeps order, and exercises many vertues, and promotes the interest of man-kinde, and is that state of good things to which God hath designed the present constitution of the world.

XXV Sermons, 1653, p. 222

53. *Man and Wife.*

MAN and wife are equally concerned to avoid all offences of each other in the beginning of their conversation: every little thing can blast an infant blossome; and the breath of the south can shake the little rings of the Vine, when first they begin to curle like the locks of a new weaned boy; but when by age and consolidation they stiffen into the hardnesse of a stem, and have by the warm embraces of the sun and the kisses of heaven brought forth their clusters, they can endure the storms of the North, and the loud noises of a tempest, and yet never be broken: so are the early unions of an unfixed marriage; watchfull and observant, jealous and busie, inquisitive and carefull, and apt to take alarum at every unkind word. For infirmities do not manifest themselves in the first scenes, but in the succession of a long society; and it is not chance or weaknesse when it appears at first, but it is want of love or prudence, or it will be so expounded; and that which appears ill at first usually affrights the unexperienced man or woman, who makes unequall conjectures, and fancies mighty sorrowes by the proportions of the new and early unkindnesse. It is a very great passion, or a huge folly, or a certain want of love, that cannot preserve the colours and beauties of kindnesse, so long as publick honesty requires man to wear their sorrows for the death of a friend. *Plutarch* compares a new marriage to a vessell before the hoops are on. . . .

The dominion of a man over his wife is no other then as the soul rules the body; for which it takes a mighty care, and uses it with a delicate tendernesse, and cares for it in all contingencies, and watches to keep it from all evils, and studies to make for it fair provisions, and very often is led by its inclinations and desires, and does never contradict its appetites, but when they are evill, and then also not without some trouble and sorrow; and its government comes only to this, it furnishes the body with light and understanding, and the body furnishes the soul with hands and feet; the soul governs, because the body cannot else be happy, but the *government* is no other then *provision*; as a nurse governs a childe when she causes him to eat and to be warm, and dry and quiet; and yet even the very government it self is divided; for man and wife in the family are as the Sun and Moon in the firmament of heaven; He rules by day, and she by night, that is, in the lesser and more proper circles of her affairs; in the conduct of domestick provisions and necessary offices, and shines only by his light and rules by his authority: and as the Moon in opposition to the Sun shines brightest, that is, then, when she is in her own circles and separate regions; so is the authority of the wife then most conspicuous when she is separate and in her proper sphere, in *Gynæceo* in the nursery and offices of domestick employment; but when she is in conjunction with the Sun her Brother, that is, in that place and employment in which his care and proper offices are imployed, her light is not seen, her authority hath no proper businesse.

XXV Sermons, 1653, pp. 227, 233

54. *The Bunch of Myrrh.*

REMEMBER the dayes of darknesse, for they are many; The joyes of the bridal chambers are quickly past, and the remaining portion of the state is a dull progresse without variety of joyes, but not without the change of sorrowes; but that portion that shall enter into the grave must be eternall. It is fit that I should infuse a bunch of myrrhe into the festivall goblet, and after the Egyptian manner serve up a dead mans bones at a feast; I will only shew it and take it away again; it will make the wine bitter, but wholesome; But those marryed pairs that live, as remembring that they must part again, and give an account how they treat themselves and each other, shall at the day of their death be admitted to glorious espousals, and when they shall live again, be marryed to their Lord, and partake of his glories, with *Abraham* and *Joseph*, S. *Peter* and St. *Paul*, and all the marryed Saints.

XXV Sermons, 1653, p. 243

55. *Virginity.*

CHASTITY is either *abstinence* or *continence*. *Abstinence* is that of Virgins or Widows: *Continence* of married persons. *Chaste marriages* are honourable and pleasing to God: *Widowhood* is pitiable in its solitariness and losse, but amiable and comely when it is adorned with gravity and purity, and not sullied with remembrances of the passed license, nor with present desires of returning to a second bed. But *Virginity* is a life of Angels, the enamel of the soul, the huge advantage of religion, the great opportunity for the retirements of devotion: and being empty of cares, it is full of prayers: being unmingled with the World, it is apt to converse with God: and by not feeling the warmth of a too forward and indulgent nature, flames out with holy fires, till it be burning like the Cherubim and the most ecstasied order of holy and unpolluted Spirits.

Holy Living, 1650, p. 181

56. *Children.*

NO man can tell but he that loves his children, how many delicious accents make a mans heart dance in the pretty conversation of those dear pledges; their child-ishnesse, their stammering, their little angers, their inno-cence, their imperfections, their necessities are so many little emanations of joy and comfort to him that delights in their persons and society; but he that loves not his wife and children, feeds a Lionesse at home, and broods a nest of sorrowes.

XXV Sermons, 1653, p. 236

57. *Children.*

WHEN we see a childe strike a servant rudely, or jeere a silly person, or wittily cheat his play-fellow, or talk words light as the skirt of a summer garment, we laugh and are delighted with the wit and confidence of the boy; and incourage such hopeful beginnings; and in the mean time we consider not that from these beginnings he shall grow up till he become a Tyrant, an oppressor, a Goat and a Traytor. *Nemo simul malus fit & malus esse cernitur; sicut nec scorpijs tum innascuntur stimuli cum pungunt* No man is discerned to be vitious so soon as he is so, and vices have their infancy and their childe-hood and it cannot be expected that in a childs age should be the vice of a man; that were monstrous as if he wore a beard in his cradle; and we do not believe that a serpents sting does just then grow when he stricks us in a vital part: The venome and the little spear was there, when it first began to creep from his little shell: And little boldnesses and looser words and wranglings for nuts, and lying for trifles, are of the same proportion to the malice of a childe, as impudence and duels and injurious law-suits, and false witnesse in judgement & perjuries are in men.

XXVIII Sermons, 1651, p. 203

58. *Body, Soul, and Spirit.*

IT is very requisite that we should understand the state of our own infirmity, the weakness of the flesh, the temptations and diversions of the spirit, that by understanding our present state we may prevent the evils of carelesness and security. Our evils are the imperfections and sorrows inherent in, or appendant to our bodies, our souls, our spirits.

In our bodies we finde weakness, and imperfection, sometimes crookedness, sometimes monstrosity; filthiness, and weariness, infinite numbers of diseases, and an uncertain cure, great pain, and restless night, hunger and thirst, daily necessities, ridiculous gestures, madness from passions, distempers and disorders, great labour to provide meat and drink, and oftentimes a loathing when we have them; if we use them they breed sicknesses, if we use them not, we die; and there is such a certain healthlesness in many things to all, and in all things to some men and at some times, that to supply a need, is to bring a danger: and if we eat like beasts onely of one thing, our souls are quickly weary; if we eat variety, we are sick, and intemperate; and our bodies are inlets to sin, and a stage of temptation. If we cherish them, they undoe us; if we doe not cherish them, they die: we suffer illusion in our dreams, and absurd fancies when we are waking; our life is soon done, and yet very tedious; it is too long, and too short; darkness and light are both troublesome; and those things which are pleasant, are often unwholesome. Sweet smels make the head ake, and those smels which are medicinal in some diseases, are intolerable to the sense. The pleasures of our body are bigger in expectation, then in the possession; and yet while they are expected, they torment us with the delay, and when they are enjoyed, they are as if they were not, they abuse us with their vanity, and vex us with their volatile and fugitive nature. Our pains are very frequent alone, and very often mingled with pleasures to spoil them; and he that feels one sharp pain, feels not all the pleasures of the world, if they were in his power to have them. We live a precarious life, begging help of every thing, and needing the repairs of every day, and being beholding to beasts and birds, to plants and trees, to dirt and stones, to the very excrements of beasts, and that which dogs and horses throw forth. Our motion is slow and dull, heavy and uneasy; we cannot move but we are quickly tired, and for every days labour, we need a whole night to recruit our lost strengths; we live like a lamp, unless new materials be perpetually poured in, we live no longer than a fly; and our motion is not otherwise then a clock; we must be pull'd up once or twice in twenty four hours; and unless we be in the shadow of death for six or eight hours every night, we shall be scarce in the shadows of life the other sixteen. Heat and cold are both our enemies; and yet the one always dwels within, and the other dwels round about us. The chances and contingencies that trouble us, are no more to be numbred then the minutes of eternity. The Devil often hurts us, and men hurt each other oftner, and we are perpetually doing mischief to our selves. The stars doe in their courses fight against some men, and all the elements against every man; the heavens send evil influences, the very beasts are dangerous, and the air we suck in does corrupt our lungs: many are deformed, and blinde, and ill coloured; and yet upon the most beauteous face is plac'd one of the worst sinks of the body; and we are forc'd to pass that through our mouthes oftentimes, which our eye and our stomack hates. *Pliny* did wittily and elegantly represent this state of evil things. *Itaque fœlicitèr homo natus jacet manibus pedibúsque devinctis, flens, animal cæteris imperaturum, & à suppliciis vitam auspicatur, unam tantum ob culpam quia natum est.* A man is born happily, but at first he lies bound hand and foot by impotency and cannot stir; the creature weeps that is born to rule over all other creatures, and begins his life with punishments, for no fault, but that he was born. In short. The body is a region of diseases, of sorrow and nastiness, and weakness and temptation. Here is cause enough of being humbled.

Neither is it better in the soul of man, where ignorance dwells and passion rules. μετὰ γὰρ τὸν θάνατον καὶ πολὺς παθῶν εἰσῆλθεν ἐσμός. After death came in, there entred also a swarm of passions. And the will obeys every thing but God. Our judgement is often abused in matters of sense, and one faculty guesses at truth by confuting another; and the error of the eye is corrected by something of reason or a former experience. Our fancy is often abus'd, and yet creates things of it self, by tying disparate things together, that can cohere no more then Musick and a Cable, then Meat and Syllogisms: and yet this alone does many times make credibilities in the understandings. Our Memories are so frail, that they need instruments of recollection, and laborious artifices to help them; and in the use of these artifices sometimes we forget the meaning of those

instruments: and of those millions of sins which we have
committed, we scarce remember so many as to make us
sorrowful, or asham'd. Our judgements are baffled with
every Sophism, and we change our opinion with a wind,
and are confident against truth, but in love with error.
We use to reprove one error by another, and lose truth
while we contend too earnestly for it. Infinite opinions
there are in matters of Religion, and most men are confident, and most are deceived in many things, and all in
some; and those few that are not confident, have onely
reason enough to suspect their own reason. We do not
know our own bodies, nor what is within us, nor what ails
us when we are sick, nor whereof we are made; nay we
oftentimes cannot tell what we think, or believe, or love.
We desire and hate the same thing, speak against and run
after it. We resolve, and then consider; we binde our
selves, and then finde causes why we ought not to be
bound, and want not some pretences to make our selves
believe we were not bound. Prejudice and Interest are our
two great motives of believing; we weigh deeper what is
extrinsical to a question, then what is in its nature; and
oftner regard who speaks, then what is said. The diseases
of our soul are infinite; τὴν ἀνθρωπείαν φύσιν ἀρχῆθεν ἀπὸ
τῶν θείων ἀγαθῶν ἀνοήτως ἐξολισθήσασαν ἡ πολυπαθεστάτη
ζωὴ διαδέχεται, καὶ τοῦ φθοροποιοῦ θανάτου πέρας, said
Dionysius of *Athens*. Mankinde of old fell from those good
things which God gave him, and now is fallen into a life of
passion, and a state of death. In sum, it follows the temper
or distemper of the body, and sailing by such a Compass, and
being carried in so rotten a vessell, especially being empty,
or fill'd with lightness, and ignorance, and mistakes, it must
needs be exposed to the danger and miseries of every

storm; which I choose to represent in the words of *Cicero*. *Ex humanæ vitæ erroribus & ærumnis fit, ut verum sit illum quod est apud Aristotelem, sic nostros animos cum corporibus copulatos, ut vivos cum mortuis esse conjunctos.* The soul joyned with the body, is like the conjunction of the living and the dead; the dead are not quickened by it, but the living are afflicted and die.

But then if we consider what our spirit is, we have reason to lie down flat upon our faces, and confess Gods glory and our own shame. When it is at the best, it is but willing, but can do nothing without the miracle of Grace. Our spirit is hindred by the body, and cannot rise up whither it properly tends, with those great weights upon it. It is foolish and improvident; large in desires, and narrow in abilities; naturally curious in trifles, and inquisitive after vanities; but neither understands deeply, nor affectionately relishes the things of God; pleas'd with forms, cousen'd with pretences, satisfi'd with shadows, incurious of substances and realities. It is quick enough to finde doubts, and when the doubts are satisfied, it raises scruples, that is, it is restless after it is put to sleep, and will be troubled in despight of all arguments of peace. It is incredibly negligent of matters of Religion, and most solicitous and troubled in the things of the world. We love our selves, and despise others; judging most unjust sentences, and by peevish and cross measures; Covetousness and Ambition, Gain and Empire are the proportions by which we take account of things. We hate to be govern'd by others, even when we cannot dress our selves; and to be forbidden to do or have a thing, is the best art in the world to make us greedy of it. The flesh and the spirit perpetually are at strife; the spirit pretending that his ought to be the dominion, and the flesh alleaging that this is her state, and her day. We hate our present condition, and know not how to better our selves, our changes being but like the tumblings and tossings in a Feaver, from trouble to trouble, that's all the variety. We are extremely inconstant, and alwayes hate our own choice: we despair sometimes of Gods mercies, and are confident in our own follies; as we order things, we cannot avoid little sins, and doe not avoid great ones. We love the present world, though it be good for nothing, and undervalue infinite treasures, if they be not to be had till the day of recompences. We are peevish, if a servant does but break a glass, and patient when we have thrown an ill cast for eternity; throwing away the hopes of a glorious Crown for wine, and dirty silver. We know that our prayers, if well done, are great advantages to our state, and yet we are hardly brought to them, and love not to stay at them, and wander while we are saying them, and say them without minding, and are glad when they are done, or when we have a reasonable excuse to omit them. A passion does quite overturn all our purposes, and all our principles, and there are certain times of weakness in which any temptation may prevail, if it comes in that unlucky minute.

This is a little representment of the state of man; whereof a great part is a natural impotency, and the other is brought in by our own folly. Concerning the first when we discourse, it is as if one describes the condition of a Mole, or a Bat, an Oyster, or a Mushrome, concerning whose imperfections, no other cause is to be inquired of, but the will of God, who gives his gifts as he please, and is unjust to no man, by giving or not giving any certain proportion of good things: And supposing this loss was brought first upon *Adam*, and so descended upon us, yet we have no cause to complain, for we lost nothing that was ours.

Unum Necessarium, 1655, p. 427

59. *Reason.*

REASON is such a boxe of Quicksilver that it abides no where; it dwells in no setled mansion; it is like a doves neck, or a changeable Taffata; it looks to me otherwise then to you who doe not stand in the same light that I doe: and if we inquire after the law of Nature by the rules of our reason, we shall be uncertain as the discourses of the people, or the dreams of disturbed fancies. For some having (as *Lucian* calls it) weighed reasons in a pair of scales thought them so even, that they concluded no truth to be in the reasonings of men; or if there be, they knew not on which side it stood, and then it is, as if it were not at all; these were the *Scepticks*: and when *Varro* reckoned two hundred eighty eight opinions concerning the cheefest good or end of mankinde, that were entertained by the wisest and most learned part of mankinde, it is not likely that these wise men should any more agree about the intricate ways and turnings that lead thither, when they so little could agree about the journeys end, which all agreed could have in it no variety, but must be one, and ought to stand fair in the eyes of all men, and to invite the industry of all mankinde to the pursuit of it.

Ductor Dubitantium, 1600, vol. i, p. 231

60. *The Reynolds's.*

BESIDES these things, there is a strange spring, and secret principle in every man's Understanding, that it is oftentimes turned about by such impulses, of which no man can give an account. But we all remember a most wonderful Instance of it, in the Disputation between the two *Reynolds's, John* and *William*; the former of which being a Papist, and the later a Protestant, met, and disputed, with a purpose to confute, and to convert each other; and so they did: for those Arguments which were us'd, prevail'd fully against their adversary, and yet did not prevail with themselves. The Papist turned Protestant, and the Protestant became a Papist, and so remain'd to their dying day.

A Dissuasive from Popery, 1664, Pt. II, p. 207

61. *Proverbs.*

BE curious to avoid all proverbs and propositions, or odde sayings, by which evil life is incouraged, and the hands of the spirit weakned. It is strange to consider what a prejudice to a mans understanding of things is a contrary proverb. *Can any good thing come out of Galilee? And when Christ cometh, no man knoweth whence he is.* Two or three proverbs, did in despight of all the miracles, and holy doctrines, and rare example of Christ hinder many of the Jews from beleeving in him. The words of S. *Paul* misunderstood, and worse applied, have been so often abused to evil purposes, that they have almost passed into a proverbial excuse, *The evil that I would not that I doe.* Such sayings as these, are to be tried by the severest measures, and all such senses of them which are enemies to holiness of life are to be rejected, because they are against the whole Oeconomy and design of the Gospel, of the life and death of Christ. But a proverb being used by every man, is supposed to contain the opinion and belief, or experience of mankinde: and then that evil sense that we are pleased to put to them, will be thought to be of the same authority. I have heard of divers persons who have been strangely intic'd on to finish their revellings, and drunken conventicles by a catch, or a piece of a song, by a humor, and a word, by a bold saying, or a common proverb: and whoever take any measures of good evil, but the severest discourses of reason and religion, will be like a ship turned every way by a little piece of wood; by chance, and by half a sentence, because they dwell upon the water, and a wave of the Sea is their foundation.

Unum Necessarium, 1655, p. 523

62. *Dreams.*

WE suffer the Arguments of Religion to have so little impression upon our spirits, that they operate but like the discourses of childhood, or the Problems of uncertain Philosophy: A man talks of Religion but as of a dream, and from thence he awakens into the Businesses of the world, and acts them deliberately, with perfect Action and full Resolution, and contrives, and considers, and lives in them: But when he falls asleep again, or is taken from the Scene of his own employment and choice; then he dreams again, and Religion makes such Impressions as is the conversation of a Dreamer, and he acts accordingly. *Theocritus* tells of a Fisherman that dreamed he had taken οὐ σάρκινον ἰχθύν, ἀλλὰ χρύσεον, a Fish of gold, upon which being over-joyed he made a vow, that he would never fish more: But when he waked, he soon declared his vow to be

null, because he found his golden Fish was scaped away
through the holes of his eyes, when he first opened them.
Just so we do in the purposes of Religion; sometimes in
a good mood we seem to see Heaven opened, and all the
streets of Heavenly Jerusalem paved with gold and precious
stones, and we are ravished with spirituall apprehensions,
and resolve never to return to the low affections of the
world, and the impure adherencies of sin, but when this
flash of lightning is gone, and we converse again with the
Inclinations, and habituall desires of our false hearts, those
other desires and fine considerations disband, and the
Resolutions taken in that pious fit melt into Indifferency,
and old Customes. He was prettily and fantastically
troubled, who having used to put his trust in Dreams, one
night dreamed, that all dreams were vain; For he considered, If so, then This was vain, and then dreams might
be true for all this: But if they might be true, then this
dream might be so upon equall reason; And then dreams
were vain, because This dream, which told him so, was
true, and so round again. In the same Circle runs the
Heart of man; All his cogitations are vain, and yet he
makes especiall use of this, that, that Thought which thinks
so, That is vain; and if That be vain, then his other
Thoughts, which are vainly declared so, may be Reall, and
Relied upon; And so we do. Those religious thoughts,
which are sent into us, to condemne and disrepute the
thoughts of sin and vanity, are esteemed the onely dreams;
And so all those Instruments, which the grace of God hath
invented for the destruction of Impiety, are rendred in-
effectuall, either by our direct opposing them, or (which
happens most commonly) by our want of considering them.

XXVIII Sermons, 1651, p. 96

63. *Forgetfulness.*

HE that had an ill memory did wisely comfort himselfe by reckoning the advantages he had by his forgetful- nesse. For by this means he was hugely secured against malice, and ambition; for his anger went off with the short notice and observation of the injury; and he saw himself unfit for the businesses of other men, or to make records in his head, & undertake to conduct the intrigues of affairs of a multitude, who was apt to forget the little accounts of his own seldom reading. He also remembred this, that his pleasures in reading books were more frequent, while he remembred but little of yesterdays study, and to mor- row the book is newes, and with its novelties gives him fresh entertainment, while the retaining brain layes the book aside, and is full already. Every book is new to an ill memory, and one long book is a Library, and its parts return fresh as the morning, which becomes a new day, though by the revolution of the same sun. Besides these, it brought him to tell truth for fear of shame, and in meer necessity made his speech little and his discourses short; because the web drawn from his brain was soon spun out, and his fountain grew quickly dry, and left running through forgetfulnesse.

XXV Sermons, 1653, p. 286

64. *The Imagination.*

LAY fetters and restraints upon the imaginative and phantastick part: because our fancie being an imper- fect and higher facultie is usually pleased with the enter- tainment of shadowes and gauds; and because the things of the world fill it with such beauties and phantastick imagery, the fancy presents such objects as amiable to the affections, and elective powers. Persons of fancy, such as are women and children have alwayes the most violent loves; but therefore if we be careful with what represent-ments we fill our fancy, we may the sooner rectifie our loves. To this purpose, it is good that we transplant the instruments of fancy into religion: and for this reason musick was brought into Churches, and ornaments, and perfumes, and comely garments, and solemnities, and decent ceremonies, that the busie and lesse discerning fancy being bribed with its proper objects may be instru-mental to a more cœlestial and spiritual love.

Holy Living, 1650, p. 253

65. Day-dreams.

ENTERTAIN no fancies of vanity and private whispers of this Devil of pride: such as was that of *Nebuchodo-nosor*; *Is not this great Babylon which I have built for the honour of my name, and the might of my majesty, and the power of my kingdom?* Some phantastick spirits will walk alone, and dream waking, of greatnesses, of palaces, of excellent orations, full theatres, loud applauses, sudden advancement, great fortunes: and so will spend an hour with imaginative pleasure, all their imployment being nothing but fumes of pride, and secret, indefinite desires, and significations of what their heart wishes: In this, al-though there is nothing of its own nature directly vitious, yet it is either an ill mother, or an ill daughter, an ill signe or an ill effect; and therefore at no hand consisting with the safety and interests of humility.

Holy Living, 1650, p. 106

66. *Astrology*.

ALTHOUGH it is lawful to beleeve a truth which the devil tels us, yet it is not lawful to goe to School to the devil, or to make inquiries of him, because he that does so, makes him his Master, and gives something of Gods portion to Gods enemy. As for Judicial Astrology and Genethliacal predictions, for my part I therefore reprove them, not because their reason is against Religion, for certainly it cannot be; but because I think they have not reason enough in what they say; they goe upon weak principles which they cannot prove; they reduce them to practice by impossible mediums: they draw conclusions with artless and unskilful heads, they argue about things with which they have little conversation, they cannot make scientifical progress in their profession, but out of greediness to doe something; they usually, at least are justly suspected to take in auxiliaries from the spirits of Darkness; they have always spoken uncertainly, and most part falsly; and have always lived scandalously in their profession: they have by all Religions been cried down, trusted by none but fools, and superstitious people; and therefore although the art may be very lawful, if the starres were upon the earth, or the men were in heaven, if they had skill in what they profess, and reason in all their pretences, and after all that their principles were certain, and that the starres did really signify future events, and that those events were not overruled by every thing in heaven and in earth, by God, and by our own will and wisdome, yet because here is so little reason, and less certainty, and nothing but confidence and illusion, therefore it is that Religion permits them not; and it is not the reason in this art, that is against Religion, but the folly or the knavery of it, and the dangerous and horrid consequents, which they feel that run a whoring after such Idols of imagination.

Ductor Dubitantium, 1660, vol. i, p. 61

67. *The Pagans.*

THE unlearned and ruder Nations had fewer vertues, but they had also fewer vices then the wise Empires, that ruled the World with violence and wit together. The softer Asians had lust and intemperance in a full Chalice; but their understandings were ruder then the finer Latines, for these mens understandings distill'd wickednesse, as through a Limbeck, and the Romans drank spirits and the sublim'd quintessences of villany, whereas the other made themselves drunk with the lees and cheaper instances of sinne: so that the understanding is not an idle and uselesse faculty but naturally derives to practice, and brings guests into the inward Cabinet of the will, and there they are entertained and feasted. And those understandings which did not serve the baser end of vices, yet were unprofitable for the most part, and furnished their inward rooms with glasses and beads and trifles fit for an American Mart.

The Great Exemplar, 1649, Pt. I, p. 84

68. *Heathen Religions.*

BUT for the Heathen religions it is evidently to be seen, that they are nothing but an abuse of the natural inclination which all men have to worship a God, whom because they know not, they guess at in the dark; for that they know there is and ought to be something that hath the care and providence of their affairs. But the body of their Religion is nothing but little arts of Governments,

and stratagems of Princes, and devices to secure the
Government of new Usurpers, or to make obedience to
the Laws sure, by being sacred, and to make the yoke that
was not natural, pleasant by something that is. But yet
for the whole body of it who sees not that their worshippings could not be sacred, because they were done by
something that is impure, they appeased their gods with
adulteries and impure mixtures, by such things which *Cato*
was ashamed to see, by gluttonous eatings of flesh, and
impious drinkings, and they did *litare in humano sanguine,*
they sacrificed men and women and children to their
Dæmons, as is notorious in the rites of *Bacchus Omesta*
amongst the Greeks, and of *Jupiter,* to whom a Greek and
a Greekess, a Galatian and a Galatess were yearly offered;
in the answers of the Oracles to *Calchas* as appears in
Homer and *Virgil*; who sees not that crimes were warranted by the example of their immortal gods, and that
what did dishonour themselves, they sang to the honour of
their gods, whom they affirmed to be passionate and proud,
jealous and revengefull, amorous and lustfull, fearfull and
impatient, drunken and sleepy, weary and wounded, that
the Religions were made lasting by policy and force, by
ignorance, and the force of custome, by the preferring an
inveterate error, and loving of a quiet and prosperous evil,
by the arguments of pleasure, and the correspondencies of
sensuality, by the fraud of Oracles, and the patronage of
vices, and because they feared every change as an Earth-
quake, as supposing overturnings of their old error to be
the eversion of their well established Governments: and it
had been ordinarily impossible that ever Christianity
should have entred, if the nature and excellency of it had
not been such as to enter like rain into a fleece of wooll,

or the Sun into a window without noise or violence, without emotion and disordering the political constitution, without causing trouble to any man but what his own ignorance or peevishness was pleased to spin out of his own bowels, but did establish Governments, secure obedience, made the Laws firm, and the persons of Princes to be sacred; it did not oppose force by force, nor *strike Princes for Justice*; it defended it self against enemies by patience, and overcame them by kindness, it was the great instrument of God to demonstrate his power in our weaknesses, and to doe good to Mankinde by the imitation of his excellent goodness.

Lastly, he that considers concerning the Religion and person of Mahomet, that he was a vicious person, lustful and tyrannical, that he propounded incredible and ridiculous propositions to his Disciples, that it entred by the sword, by blood and violence, by murder and robbery, that it propounds sensual rewards and allures to compliance by bribing our basest lusts, that it conserves it self by the same means it entred; that it is unlearned and foolish, against reason, and the discourses of all wise men, that it did no miracles and made false Prophecies: in short, that in the person that founded it, in the article it perswades in the manner of prevailing, in the reward it offers it is unholy and foolish and rude; it must needs appear to be void of all pretence, and that no man of reason can ever be fairly perswaded by arguments, that it is the daughter of God and came down from heaven.

Ductor Dubitantium, 1660, vol. i, p. 139

69. *The Triumph of Christianity.*

PRESENTLY it came to pass that the Religion of the despised Jesus did infinitely prevail: a Religion that taught Men to be meek and humble, apt to receive injuries, but unapt to do any; a Religion that gave countenance to the poor and pitiful, in a time when riches were ador'd, and ambition and pleasure had possessed the heart of all Mankind; a Religion that would change the face of things, and the hearts of Men, and break vile habits into gentleness and counsel; that such a Religion, in such a time, by the Sermons and Conduct of Fishermen, Men of mean breeding and illiberal Arts, should so speedily triumph over the Philosophy of the World, and the arguments of the subtil, and the Sermons of the Eloquent; the Power of Princes and the Interests of States, the inclinations of Nature and the blindness of zeal, the force of custom and the solicitation of passions, the pleasures of sin and the busie Arts of the Devil; that is, against Wit and Power, Superstition and Wilfulness, Fame and Money, Nature and Empire, which are all the causes in this World that can make a thing impossible; this, this is to be ascrib'd to the power of God, and is the great demonstration of the Resurrection of Jesus. Every thing was an Argument for it, and improv'd it; no Objection could hinder it, no Enemies destroy it; whatsoever was for them, it made the Religion to increase; whatsoever was against them, made it to increase; Sunshine and Storms, Fair Weather or Foul, it was all one as to the event of things: for they were instruments in the hands of God, who could make what himself should chuse to be the product of any cause; So that if the Christians had peace, they went abroad and brought in Converts; if they had no peace but persecution; the Converts came in to them. In prosperity they allur'd and intic'd the World by the beauty of holiness: in affliction and trouble they amaz'd all men with the splendour of their Innocence, and the glories of their patience; and quickly it was that the World became Disciple to the glorious *Nazarene*, and men could no longer doubt of the Resurrection of Jesus, when it became so demonstrated by the certainty of them that saw it, and the courage of them that died for it, and the multitude of them that believ'd it; who by their Sermons, and their Actions, by their publick Offices and Discourses, by Festivals and Eucharists, by Arguments of Experience and Sense, by Reason and Religion, by perswading rational Men, and establishing believing Christians, by their living in the obedience of Jesus, and dying for the testimony of Jesus, have greatly advanc'd his Kingdom, and his Power, and his Glory, into which he entered after his Resurrection from the dead. For he is the first fruits; and if we hope to rise through him, we must confess that himself is first risen from the dead. That's the first particular.

There is an order for us also. We also shall rise again.

> *Combustusque senex tumulo procedit adultus,*
> *Consumens dat membra rogus;——*

The ashes of old *Camillus* shall stand up spritely from his Urne; and the Funeral fires shall produce a new warmth to the dead bones of all those who died under the arms of all the Enemies of the Roman greatness.

Sermon at the Funeral of the Archbishop of Armagh (John Bramhall),
3rd ed., 1663, p. 11

70. *The Change.*

BUT when Christian religion was *planted and had taken root, and had filled all lands*, then all the nature of things, *the whole creation* became servant to the kingdom of grace, and *the Head of the religion* is also the Head of the creatures, and ministers all the things of the world in order to the Spirit of grace: and now *Angels are ministring spirits*, sent forth to minister for the good of them that fear the Lord, and all the violences of men, and things of nature, and choice, are forced into subjection and lowest ministeries, and to cooperate as with an united designe to verifie all the promises of the Gospel, and to secure and advantage all the children of the kingdom, and now he that is made poor by chance, or persecution, is made rich by religion, and he that hath nothing, yet possesses all things, and sorrow it self is the greatest comfort, not only because it ministers to vertue, but because *it self is one*, as in the case of repentance; and *death* ministers to *life*, and *bondage* is *freedom*, and *losse is gain*, and our *enemies* are our *friends*, and every thing turns into religion, and religion turns into felicity, and all manner of advantages. But that I may not need to enumerate any more particulars in this observation: certain it is that Angels of light and darknesse, all the influences of heaven, and the fruits and productions of the earth, the stars, and the elements, the secret things that lie in the bowels of the Sea, and the entrails of the earth, the single effects of all efficients, and the conjunction of all causes, all events foreseen, and all rare contingencies, every thing of chance, and every thing of choice, is so much a servant to him whose greatest desire, and great interest, is by all means to save our souls, that we are thereby made sure, that all the whole creation shall be made to bend in all the flexures of its nature and accidents, that it may minister to religion, to the good of the Catholike Church, and every person within its bosom, who are the body of him that rules over all the world, and commands them as he chooses.

XXVIII Sermons, 1651, p. 341

71. *The Martyrs.*

IF we had seen S. *Policarp* burning to death, or S. *Laurence* rosted upon his gridiron, or S. *Ignatius* exposed to lions, or S. *Sebastian* pierced with arrowes, or S. *Attalus* carried about the theatre with scorn unto his death for the cause of Jesus, for religion, for God and a holy conscience, we should have been in love with flames, and have thought the gridiron fairer then the *spondæ, the ribs of a maritall bed*: and we should have chosen to converse with those beasts rather then those men that brought those beasts forth; and estimated the arrows to be the rayes of light brighter then the moon; and that disgrace and mistaken pageantry were a solemnity richer and more magnificent then *Mordecai's* procession upon the Kings horse, and in the robes of majesty; for so did these holy men account them: they kissed their stakes, and hugged their deaths, and ran violently to torments, and counted whippings and secular disgraces to be the enamel of their persons, and the ointment of their heads, and the embalming their names, and securing them for immortality.

Holy Dying, 1651, p. 144

72. *The Fathers.*

THE Ancients were nearer to the fountains Apostolical, their stream was less pudled, their thred was not fine but plain and strong, they were troubled with fewer heresies; they were not so wittily mistaken as we have been since; they had better and more firm tradition, they had pass'd through fewer changes, and had been blended with fewer interests; they were united under one Prince, and consequently were not forc'd to bend their doctrines to the hostile and opposite designs of fighting, and crafty Kings; their questions were concerning the biggest articles of Religion, and therefore such in which they could have more certainty and less deception; their piety was great, their devotion high and pregnant, their discipline regular and sincere, their lives honest, their hearts simple, their zeal was for souls, and the blood of the Martyrs made the Church irriguous, and the Church was then a garden of the fairest flowers, it did daily germinate with blessings from heaven, and Saints sprung up, and one Saint could know more of the secrets of Christs Kingdom, the mysteriousnesses of godly wisdome then a hundred disputing Sophisters; *and above all*, the Church of *Rome* was then *holy* and *Orthodox*, *humble* and *charitable*, her authority dwelt in the house of its birth, that is, in the advantages of *an excellent faith* and an *holy life*; to which the advantages of an accidental authority being added by the Imperial seat, she was made able to doe all the good she desired, and she desired all that she ought; and the greatness of this advantage we can best judge by feeling those sad effects which have made Christendome to groan, since the Pope became a temporal Prince, and hath possess'd

the rights of some Kings, and hath invaded more, and
pretends to all, and is become the great Fable, and the
great Comet of Christendome, useless and supreme, high
and good for nothing in respect of what he was at first,
and still might have been, if he had severely judged the
interest of Jesus Christ to have been his own.

Ductor Dubitantium, 1660, vol. i, p. 163

73. *The Roman Catholic Church.*

SUCH as are the beauty and splendor of their Church;
their pompous Service; the statelinesse and solemnity
of the Hierarchy; their name of Catholick, which they
suppose their own due, and to concern no other Sect of
Christians; the Antiquity of many of their Doctrines; the
continuall Succession of their Bishops; their immediate
derivation from the Apostles; their Title to succeed
S. *Peter*; the supposall and pretence of his personall Pre-
rogatives; the advantages which the conjunction of the
Imperiall Seat with their Episcopall hath brought to that
Sea; the flattering expressions of minor Bishops, which by
being old Records, have obtain'd credibility; the multitude and variety of people which are of their perswasion;
apparent consent with Antiquity in many Ceremonialls
which other Churches have rejected; and a pretended, and
sometimes an apparent consent with some elder Ages in
many matters doctrinall; the advantage which is derived
to them by entertaining some personall opinions of the
Fathers, which they with infinite clamours see to bee cryed
up to be a Doctrine of the Church of that time; The great
consent of one part with another in that which most of
them affirm to be *de fide*; the great differences which
are commenc'd amongst their Adversaries, abusing the

Liberty of Prophecying unto a very great licentiousnesse; their happinesse of being instruments in converting divers Nations; the advantages of Monarchicall Government, the benefit of which as well as the inconveniences (which though they feele they consider not) they daily doe enjoy; the piety and the austerity of their Religious Orders of men and women; the single life of their Priests and Bishops; the riches of their Church; the severity of their Fasts and their exteriour observances; the great reputation of their first Bishops for Faith and sanctity; the known holinesse of some of those persons whose Institutes the Religious Persons pretend to imitate; their Miracles false or true, substantiall or imaginary; the casualties and accidents that have hapned to their Adversaries, which being chances of humanity are attributed to severall causes according as the fancies of men and their Interests are pleased or satisfied; the temporall felicity of their Professors; the oblique arts & indirect proceedings of some of those who departed from them; and amongst many other things, the names of Heretick and Schismatick, which they with infinite pertinacy fasten upon all that disagree from them; These things and divers others may very easily perswade persons of much reason and more piety, to retain that which they know to have been the Religion of their fore-Fathers, which had actuall possession and seizure of mens understandings before the opposite professions had a name; And so much the rather because Religion hath more advantages upon the fancy and affections, then it hath upon Philosophy and severe discourses, and therefore is the more easily perswaded upon such grounds as these, which are more apt to amuse then to satisfie the understanding.

The Liberty of Prophesying, 1647, p. 250

74. *Church and State.*

ABOVE all things those sects of Christians whose pro-
fessed doctrine brings destruction and diminution to
government, give the most intolerable scandal, and dishonour to the institution; and it had been impossible that
Christianity should have prevailed over the wisdom and
power of the Greeks and Romans, if it had not been
humble to superiours, patient of injuries, charitable to the
needy, a great exactour of obedience to Kings, even *to
heathens,* that they might be won, and convinced; and
to persecutours that they might be sweetned in their anger,
or upbraided for their cruel injustice: for so doth the
humble vine creep at the foot of an oak, and leans upon
its lowest base, and begs shade and protection, and leave
to grow under its branches, and to give and take mutuall
refreshment, and pay a friendly influence for a mighty
patronage, and they grow and dwell together, and are the
most remarkable of friends and married pairs of all the
leavie nation. Religion of it self is soft, easie and defenselesse, and God hath made it grow up with empire, and to
leane upon the arms of Kings, and it cannot well grow
alone; and if it shall like the *Ivy* suck the heart of the
oak upon whose body it grew and was supported, it will
be pulled down from its usurped eminency, and fire and
shame shall be its portion. We cannot complain if Princes
arm against those Christians, who if they are suffered to
preach will disarm the Princes; and it will be hard to perswade that Kings are bound to protect and nourish those
that will prove ministers of their own exauctoration: And
no Prince can have juster reason to forbid, nor any man
have greater reason to deny communion to a family, then

if they go about to destroy the power of the one, or corrupt
the duty of the other.

XXVIII Sermons, 1651, p. 266

75. *The Beauty of Services.*

I CONSIDER, that those riches and beauties in Churches
and religious solemnities, which adde nothing to GOD,
adde much devotion to us, and much honour and efficacy
to devotion. For since impression is made upon the soul
by the intervening of corporall things, our religion and
devotion of the soul receives the addition of many degrees
by such instruments. Insomuch that we see persons of the
greatest fancy, and such who are most pleased with outward fairnesses are most religious. Great understandings
make religion lasting and reasonable, but great fancies
make it more scrupulous, strict, operative, and effectuall,
And therefore it is strange, that we shall bestow such great
expences to make our owne houses convenient and delect-
able, that we may entertaine our selves with complacency
and appetite, and yet think that religion is not worth the
ornament, nor our fancies fit to be carried into the choyce,
and prosecution of religious actions with sweetnesse, entertainments, and fair propositions. If we say that GOD is
not the better for a rich house, or a costly service; we may
also remember, that neither are we the better for rich
clothes; and the sheep will keep us as modest, as warme,
and as cleane, as the silk-worm; and a gold chaine, or a
carkenet of pearle does no more contribute to our happinesse, then it does to the service of Religion. For if we
reply, that they help to the esteem, and reputation of our
persons, and the distinction of them from the vulgar, from
the servants of the lot of *Issachar,* and adde reverence and

veneration to us; how great a shame is it, if we study by
great expences to get reputation, and accidentall advantages to our selves, and not by the same meanes to purchase
reverence and esteem to religion? since we see that Religion amongst persons of ordinary understandings receives
as much externall and accidentall advantages by the accession of exteriour ornaments and accommodation, as we our
selves can, by rich clothes, and garments of wealth, ceremony and distinction. And as in Princes Courts the
reverence to Princes is quickned, and increased by an outward state and glory: So also it is in the service of GOD;
although the understandings of men are no more satisfied
by a pompous magnificence, then by a cheap plainnesse,
yet the eye is, and the fancy, and the affections, and the
sences, that is, many of our faculties are more pleased
with Religion, when Religion by such instruments and
conveyances pleases them. And it was noted by *Sozomen*
concerning *Valens* the Arrian Emperour, that when he
came to *Cæsarea* in *Cappadocia* he praised S. *Basil* their
Bishop, and upon more easie termes revoked his banishment: because he was a grave person, and did his holy
offices with reverent, and decent addresses, and kept his
Church-assemblies with much ornament and solemnity.

But when I consider that saying of S. *Gregory*, That the
Church is Heaven within the Tabernacle, Heaven dwelling
among the sonnes of men, and remember that GOD hath
studded all the Firmament, and paved it with starres,
because he loves to have his house beauteous, and highly
representative of his Glory, I see no reason we should not
do as *Apollinaris* sayes GOD does, *In earth do the works of
heaven.* For he is the GOD of beauties, and perfections,
and every excellency in the Creature is a portion of in-

fluence from the Divinity, and therefore is the best instrument of conveying honour to him, who made them for no other end, but for his own honour, as the last resort of all other ends for which they were created.

The Great Exemplar, 1649, Pt. II, p. 35

76. *The Accumulations of Theology.*

SO long as Christian Religion was a simple profession of the articles of beliefe, and a hearty prosecution of the rules of good life, the fewnesse of the articles and the clearnesse of the rule, was cause of the seldome prevarication. But when divinity is swell'd up to so great a body, when the severall questions which the peevishnesse and wantonnesse of sixteene ages have commenc'd, are concentred into one, and from all these questions something is drawne into the body of *Theologie* till it hath ascended up to the greatnesse of a mountaine, and the summe of Divinity collected by *Aquinas*, makes a volume as great as was that of *Livy* mock'd at in the *Epigramme*,

> *Quem mea vix totum bibliotheca capit.*

It is impossible for any industry to consider so many particulars in the infinite numbers of questions as are necessary to be consider'd before we can with certainty determine any. And after all the considerations which we can have in a whole age, we are not sure *not to be deceived*. The obscurity of some questions, the nicety of some articles, the intricacy of some revelations, the variety of humane understandings, the windings of *Logicke*, the tricks of adversaries, the subtilty of Sophisters, the ingagement of educations, personall affections, the portentous number of writers, the infinity of authorities, the vastnesse of some arguments, as consisting in enumeration of many

particulars, the uncertainty of others, the severall degrees
of probability, the difficulties of Scripture, the invalidity
of probation of tradition, the opposition of all exteriour
arguments to each other, and their open contestation, the
publicke violence done to authors and records, the private
arts and supplantings, the falsifyings, the indefatigable
industry of some men to abuse all understandings, and all
perswasions into their owne opinions, these and thousands
more, even all the difficulty of things, and all the weaknesses of man & all the arts of the Devill, have made it
impossible for any man in so great variety of matter not to
be deceived. No man pretends to it but the Pope, and no
man is more deceived then he is in that very particular.

The Liberty of Prophesying, 1647, p. 191

77. *Men's Notions.*

IF the Spirit of God be your Teacher, he will teach you
such truths as will make you know and love God, and
become like to him, and enjoy him for ever, by passing
from similitude to union and eternal fruition. But what
are you the better if any man should pretend to teach you
whether every Angel makes a *species*? and what is the
individuation of the Soul in the state of separation? what
are you the wiser if you should study and find out what
place *Adam* should for ever have lived in if he had not
fallen? and what is any man the more learned if he heares
the disputes, whether *Adam* should have multiplied Children in the state of Innocence, and what would have been
the event of things if one Child had been born before his
Fathers sin?

Too many Scholars lived upon Air and empty notions
for many ages past, and troubled themselves with tying

and untying Knots, like *Hypochondriacs* in a fit of Melancholy, thinking of *nothing*, and troubling themselves with *nothing*, and falling out about *nothings*, and being very wise and very learned in things that are not and work not, and were never planted in *Paradise* by the finger of God. Mens notions are too often like the Mules, begotten by æquivocall and unnaturall Generations; but they make no *species*: they are begotten, but they can beget nothing: they are the effects of long study, but they can do no good when they are produced: they are not that which *Solomon* calls *viam intelligentiæ, the way of understanding.*

Via Intelligentiae, 1662, p. 47

78. *Books of Controversy.*

I REMEMBER that *Agricola* in his Book *de animalibus subterraneis* tells of a certain kind of spirits that use to converse in Mines and trouble the poor Labourers: They dig metals, they cleanse, they cast, they melt, they separate, they joyn the Ore; but when they are gone the men find just nothing done, not one step of their work set forward: So it is in the Books and Expositions of many men; They study, they argue, they expound, they confute, they reprove, they open secrets, and make new discoveries; and when you turn the bottom upwards, up starts nothing; no man is the wiser, no man is instructed, no truth discover'd, no proposition clear'd, nothing is alter'd, but that much labour and much time is lost; and this is manifest in nothing more than in Books of Controversie, and in mystical Expositions of Scripture: *Quærunt quod nusquam est, inveniunt tamen*; Like *Isidore*, who in contemplation of a Pen observ'd that the nib of it was divided into two, but yet the whole body remain'd one: *Credo propter myste-*

rium; he found a knack in it, and thought it was a mystery. Concerning which I shall need to say no more, but that they are safe when they are necessary; and they are useful when they teach better; and they are good when they do good: but this is so seldom and so by chance, that oftentimes if a man be taught truth, he is taught it by a lying Master; it is like being cur'd by a good witch, an evil spirit hath a hand in it; and if there be not error and illusion in such interpretations, there is very seldom any certainty.

A Supplement to the 'Eνιαυτός, 1678, p. 181

79. *Reason and Faith.*

FAITH gives a new light to the soul, but it does not put our eyes out; and what God hath given us in our nature could never be intended as a snare to Religion, or engage us to believe a lie. . . .

Whatsoever is against right reason, that no faith can oblige us to believe. For although reason is not the positive and affirmative measures of our faith, and God can do more then we can understand, and our faith ought to be larger then our reason, and take something into her heart that reason can never take into her eye; yet in all our Creed, there can be nothing against reason. . . .

If therefore any society of men calls upon us to believe in our Religion what is false in our experience, to affirm that to be done which we know is impossible it ever can be done, to wink hard that we may see the better, to be unreasonable men that we offer to God a reasonable sacrifice, they make religion so to be seated in the will, that our understanding will be uselesse and can never minister to it. But as he that shuts the eye hard and with violence curles the eye-lid, forces a phantastick fire from the Crystalline humor, and espies a light that never shines, and sees thousands of little fires that never burn: So is he that blinds the eye of his reason and pretends to see by an eye of faith; he makes little images of notion, and some atomes dance before him, but he is not guided by the light, nor instructed by the proposition; but sees like a man in his sleep, and growes as much the wiser as the man that dreamt of a *Lycanthropy*, and was for ever after wisely wary not to come neer a river. He that speaks against his own reason speaks against his own conscience; and therefore it is certain, no man serves God with a good conscience, that serves him against his reason.

The Worthy Communicant, 1660, pp. 243, 244, 245

80. *Probable Arguments.*

PROBABLE arguments are like little starres, every one of which will be useless as to our conduct and enlightening, but when they are tyed together by order and vicinity, by the finger of God and the hand of an Angel, they make a Constellation, and are not onely powerful in their influence, but like a bright Angel to guide and to enlighten our way. And although the light is not great as the light of the Sun or Moon, yet Mariners sail by their conduct; and though with trepidation and some danger, yet very regularly they enter into the haven. This heap of probable inducements, is not of power as a Mathematical and Physical demonstration, which is in discourse as the Sun is in heaven, but it makes a Milky and a white path, visible enough to walk securely.

And next to these tapers of effective reason, drawn from the nature and from the events, and the accidents and the expectations and experiences of things, stands the grandeur of a long and united authority: The understanding thus reasoning, That it is not credible that this thing should have escaped the wiser heads of all the great personages in the world, who stood at the chairs of Princes, or sate in the Rulers chair, and should onely appear to two or three bold, illiterate, or vicious persons, ruled by lusts, and overruled by evil habits; but in this we have the same security and the same confidence that timorous persons have in the dark; they are pleased and can see what is and what is not, if there be a candle, but in the dark they are less fearful if they be in company.

Ductor Dubitantium, 1660, vol. i, p. 122

81. *Conscience.*

NOTHING is more usual, then to pretend *Conscience* to all the actions of men which are publick, and whose nature cannot be concealed. If arms be taken up in a violent warre; inquire of both sides, why they ingage on that part respectively? they answer, because of their Conscience. Ask a Schismatick why he refuses to joyn in the Communion of the Church? he tels you, it is against his Conscience: And the disobedient refuse to submit to Laws; and they also in many cases pretend Conscience. Nay, some men suspect their brother of a crime, and are perswaded (as they say) in Conscience that he did it: and their Conscience tels them that *Titius* did steal their goods, or that *Caia* is an adulteress. And so Suspicion; and Jealousie, and Disobedience, and Rebellion are become *Conscience*; in which there is neither knowledge, nor revelation, nor truth, nor charity, nor reason, nor religion.

Quod volumus sanctum est, was the Proverb of *Tichonius* and the *Donatists.*

> *Nemo suæ mentis motus non æstimat æquos,*
> *Quódque volunt homines se bene velle putant.*

Every mans way seems right in his own eyes; and what they think is not against Conscience, they think or pretend to think, it is an effect of Conscience, and so their fond per-swasions and fancies are made sacred, and Conscience is pretended, and themselves and every man else is abused. But in these cases and the like, men have found a sweetness in it to serve their ends upon Religion, and because Con-science is *the Religious Understanding,* or *the Minde of a man as it stands dress'd in and for Religion,* they think that some sacredness or authority passes upon their passion or design, if they call it *Conscience.*

Ductor Dubitantium, 1660, vol. i, p. 26

82. *An Extraordinary Spirit.*

BESIDES all this, an extraordinary spirit is extremely unnecessary, and God does not give immissions and miracles from heaven to no purpose, and to no necessities of his Church; for the supplying of which he hath given *Apostles* and *Evangelists, Prophets* and *Pastors, Bishops* and *Priests,* the *spirit of Ordination,* and *the spirit of instruction, Catechists,* and *Teachers, Arts* and *Sciences, Scriptures* and *a constant succession of Expositors,* the testimony of Churches, and a constant line of *tradition,* or delivery of Apostolical Doctrine in all things necessary to salvation. And after all this, to have a *fungus* arise from the belly of mud and darknesse, and nourish a gloworm, that shall challenge to out-shine the lantern of Gods word, and all the candles which God set upon a hill, and all that the

Spirit hath set upon the candlesticks; and all *the starres in Christs right hand*, is to annull all the excellent, established, orderly, and certain effects of the Spirit of God, and to worship the false fires of the night. He therefore that will follow a Guide that leads him by an extraordinary spirit, shall go an extraordinary way, and have a strange fortune, and a singular religion, and a portion by himself, a great way off from the common inheritance of the Saints, who are all led by the Spirit of God, and have one heart, and one minde, one faith, and one hope, the same baptisme, and the helps of the Ministery, leading them to the common countrey, which is the portion of all that are the sons of adoption, consigned by the Spirit of God, *the earnest of their inheritance*.

XXVIII Sermons, 1651, p. 281

83. *Virtues and Vices.*

VERTUES and Vices have not in all their instances a great land-mark set between them, like warlike nations separate by prodigious walls, vast seas and portentous hills; but they are oftentimes like the bounds of a Parish; men are fain to cut a cross upon the turfe, and make little marks and annual perambulations for memorials: so it is in lawful and unlawful: by a little mistake a man may be greatly ruin'd.

Righteousness Evangelical, 1663, p. 50

84. *Small Sins.*

FOR who is there amongst us almost, who cals himself to an account for trifling words, loose laughter, the smallest beginnings of intemperance, careless spending too great portions of our time in trifling visits and courtships, balls, revellings, phantastick dressings, sleepiness, idleness, and useless conversation, neglecting our times of prayer frequently, or causlesly, slighting religion and religious persons, siding with factions indifferently, forgetting our former obligations upon trifling regards, vain thoughts, wandrings and weariness at our devotion, love of praise, laying little plots and snares to be commended; high opinion of our selves, resolutions to excuse all, and never to confess an error; going to Church for vain purposes, itching ears, love of flattery, and thousands more? The very kinds of them put together are a heap; and therefore the so frequent and almost infinite repetition of the acts of all those are, as *Davids* expression is, without hyperbole, more then the hairs upon our head; they are like the number of the sands upon the Sea shore for multitude.

Unum Necessarium, 1655, p. 154

85. *The Love of Temptation.*

THERE are some men more in love with the temptation then with the sin; and because this rushes against the Conscience rudely, and they see death stand at the end of the progression, therefore they onely love to stand upon *Mount Ebal* and view it. They resolve they will not commit the sin, they will not be overcome, but they would fain be tempted. If these men will but observe the contingencies of their own own state, they shall finde that when they have set the house on fire, they cannot prescribe its measures of burning. *But there is a secret iniquity in it.* For he that loves to stand and stare upon the fire that burnt him formerly, is pleas'd with the warmth and splendour, and *the temptation it self hath some little correspondencies to the appetite.* The man dares not fornicate, but

loves to look upon the beauties of a woman, or sit with her
at the wine, till his heart is ready to drop asleep. He will
not enter into the house, because it is infected with the
plague, but he loves to stand at the door, and fain would
enter if he durst; *It is impossible that any man should love
to abide by a temptation for a good end. There is some little
sensuality in being tempted:* And the very consideration
concerning it, sometimes strikes the fancy too unluckily,
and pleases some faculty or other, as much as the man
dares admit. I doe not say, that to be tempted is always
criminal, or in the neighbourhood of it; but it is the best
indication of our love to God, for his sake to deny its
importunity, and to overcome it: but that is onely, when
it is unavoidable and from without, against our wils, or at
least besides our purposes.

Unum Necessarium, 1655, p. 308

86. *The Memory of Sin.*

THERE is sometimes a fantastick pleasure in the remembrances of sin, in the approaches of it, in our
addresses to it: and there are some men who dare not act
the foul crime, who yet love to look upon its fair face;
and they drive out sin as *Abraham* did *Ismael,* with an
unwilling willingness (God knows) and therefore give it
bread and water abroad though no entertainment at home,
and they look after it, and are pleased with the stories of
it, and love to see the place of its acting,

> *Hic locus, hæc eadem sub qua requiescimus arbor
> Scit quibus ingemui curis, quibus ignibus arsi.*

And they roll it in their minds: now they that goe but
thus farre and love to tempt themselves by walking upon
the brink of the river, and delight themselves in viewing

the instrument of their sin, though they use it no further, they have given demonstration of their love of sin when they make so much of its Proxy.

Ductor Dubitantium, 1660, vol. i, p. 415

87. *Drunkenness.*

I PRAY consider, what a strange madness and prodigious folly possesses many men, that they love to swallow death, and diseases, and dishonour, with an appetite which no reason can restrain. We expect our servants should not dare to touch what we have forbidden to them; we are watchfull that our children should not swallow poysons, and filthinesse, and unwholesome nourishment; we take care that they should be well manner'd and civil and of fair demeanour; and we our selves desire to be, or at least to be accounted wise; and would infinitely scorne to be call'd fooles; and we are so great lovers of health, that we will buy it at any rate of money or observance; and then for honour, it is that which the children of men pursue with passion, it is one of the noblest rewards of vertue, and the proper ornament of the wise and valiant, and yet all these things are not valued or considered, when a merry meeting, or a looser feast calls upon the man to act a scene of *folly* and *madnesse,* and *healthlesnesse* and *dishonour.* We doe to God what we severely punish in our servants; we correct our children for their medling with dangers, which themselves preferre before immortality; and though no man think himselfe fit to be despised, yet he is willing to make himselfe a beast, a sot, and a ridiculous monkey, with the follies and vapors of wine; and when he is high in drinke or fancy, proud as a *Grecian* Orator in the midst of his popular noyses, at the same time he shall talk such dirty language, such mean low things, as may well become a changeling and a foole, for whom the stocks are prepared by the laws, and the just scorne of men. . . .

Much safer it is to go to the severities of a watchfull and a sober life; for all that time of life is lost, when wine, and rage, and pleasure, and folly steale away the heart of a man, and make him goe singing to his grave.

XXV Sermons, 1653, pp. 215, 218

88. *Drunkenness.*

IF we consider how many drunken meetings the Sunne sees every day, how many Markets and Faires and Clubs, that is, so many solemnities of drunkennesse, are at this instant under the eye of heaven; that many *Nations* are marked for intemperance, and that it is lesse noted because it is so popular, and universall, and that even in the midst of the glories of Christianity there are so many persons drunk, or too full with meat, or greedy of lust, even now that the Spirit of God is given to us to make us sober, and temperate, and chaste, we may well imagine, since all men have flesh, and all men have not the spirit, the flesh is the parent of sin, and death, and it can be nothing else.

XXV Sermons, 1653, p. 130

89. *Gluttony.*

STRANGE therefore it is that for the stomach which is scarce a span long, there should be provided so many furnaces and ovens, huge fires and an army of cooks, cellars swimming with wine, and granaries sweating with corn; and that into one belly should enter the vintage of many Nations, the spoils of distant Provinces, and the shell-fishes of severall seas. When the Heathens feasted their Gods, they gave nothing but a fat oxe, a ram, or a kid, they powred a little wine upon the Altar, and burned a handfull of gum; but when they feasted themselves, they had many vessels fill'd with Campanian wine, turtles of *Liguria*, *Sicilian beeves*, and *wheat* from *Egypt*, wilde boars from *Illyrium*, and *Grecian* sheep, variety, and load, and cost, and curiosity: and so do we. It is so little we spend in Religion, and so very much upon our selves, so little to the poor, and so without measure to make our selves sick, that we seem to be in love with our own mischief, and so passionate for necessity and want, that we strive all the wayes we can to make our selves need more then nature intended. I end this consideration with the saying of the *Cynic*; It is to be wondred at, that men eat so much for pleasures sake; and yet for the same pleasure should not give over eating, and betake themselves to the delights of temperance, since to be *healthfull* and *holy* is so great a pleasure. However, certain it is that no man ever repented that he arose from the table sober, healthfull, and with his wits about him; but very many have repented that they sate so long, till their bellies swelled, and their *health*, and their *vertue*, and their *God* is departed from them.

XXV Sermons, 1653, p. 202

90. *Reason at a Feast.*

THE senses languish, the spark of Divinity that dwels within is quenched, and the mind snorts, dead with sleep and fulnesse in the fouler regions of the belly.

So have I seen the eye of the world looking upon a fenny bottome, and drinking up too free draughts of moysture gather'd them into a cloud, and that cloud crept about his face, and made him first look red, and then cover'd him with darknesse and an artificiall night: so is our reason at a feast.

XXV Sermons, 1653, p. 208

91. *The Sons of Eli.*

FOR the manner of dressing, the sons of *Eli* were noted of indiscreet curiosity: they would not have the flesh boiled, but raw that they might *rost it with fire*. Not that it was a sin to eat it, or desire meat rosted; but that when it was appointed to be boil'd, they refused it; which declared an intemperate and a nice palate. It is lawful in all senses to comply with a weak and a nice stomach: but not with a nice and curious palate. When our health requires it, that ought to be provided for; but not so, our sensuality and intemperate longings. *Whatsoever is set before you, eat*; if it be provided for you, you may eat it be it never so delicate; and be it plain and common, so it be wholsom and fit for you, it must not be refus'd upon curiosity; for every degree of that is a degree of intemperance. Happy and innocent were the ages of our forefathers, who ate herbs and parched corne, and drank the pure stream, and broke their fast with nuts and roots; and when they were permitted flesh, eat it onely dressed with hunger and fire; and the first sauce they had was bitter herbs, and sometimes bread dipt in vinegar.

Holy Living, 1650, p. 69

92. *Lapland Witches.*

FOR the pleasures of intemperance, they are nothing but the reliques and images of pleasure, after that nature hath been feasted; For so long as she needs, that is, so long as temperance waits, so long pleasure also stands there. But as temperance begins to go away, having done the ministeries of Nature, every morsell, and every new goblet is still lesse delicious, and cannot be endured but as men force nature by violence to stay longer then she would: How have some men rejoyced when they have escaped a cup! and when they cannot escape, they pour it in, and receive it with as much pleasure as the old women have in the Lapland dances; they dance the round, but there is a horror and a harshnesse in the Musick; and they call it pleasure, because men bid them do so: but there is a *Devill* in the company, and such as is his pleasure, such is theirs: he rejoyces in the thriving sin, and the swelling fortune of his darling drunkennesse, but his joyes are the joyes of him that knowes and alwayes remembers that he shall infallibly have the biggest damnation; and then let it be considered how forc'd a joy that is, that is at the end of an intemperate feast.

> *Non benè mendaci risus componitur ore,*
> *Nec benè sollicitis ebria verba sonant.*

Certain it is, intemperance takes but natures leavings; when the belly is full and nature cals to take away, the pleasure that comes in afterwards is next to loathing: it is like the relish and taste of meats at the end of the third course, or the sweetnesse of honey to him that hath eaten til he can endure to take no more; and in this, there is no other difference of these men from them that die upon another cause, then was observed among the *Phalangia* of old, τὰ μὲν ποιεῖ γελῶντας ἀποθνήσκειν, τὰ δὲ κλαίοντας, some of these serpents make men die laughing, and some to die weeping: so does the intemperate, and so does his brother that languishes of a consumption; this man dies weeping, and the other dies laughing: but they both die infallibly, and all his pleasure is nothing but the sting of a serpent, *immixto liventia mella veneno*, it wounds the heart, and he dies with a *Tarantula* dancing and singing till he bowes his neck, and kisses his bosome with the fatall noddings and declensions of death.

XXV Sermons, 1653, p. 249

93. *The Thorn in the Flesh.*

GOD often punishes ambition and pride with lust; and he sent a thorne in the flesh as a corrective to the elevations and *grandezza* of S. *Paul*, growing up from the multitude of his revelations; and it is not likely the punishment should have lesse trouble then the crime, whose pleasures and obliquity this was designed to punish. And indeed every experience can verifie, that an adulterer hath in him the impatience of desires, the burnings of lust, the fear of shame, the apprehensions of a jealous, abused, and an enraged Husband. He endures affronts, mistimings, tedious waytings, the dulnesse of delay, the regret of interruption, the confusion and amazements of discovery, the scorn of a reproached vice, the debasings of contempt upon it, unlesse the man growes impudent, and then he is more miserable upon another stock. But David was so put to it to attempt, to obtain, to enjoy Bathsheba, and to prevent the shame of it, that the difficulty was greater then all his wit and power, and it drove him into base and unworthy arts, which discovered him the more and multiplied his crime. But while he enjoyed the innocent pleasures of his lawfull bed, he, had no more trouble in it, then there was in inclining his head upon his pillow. *The wayes of sin are crooked, desert, rocky and vneven*, they are broad indeed and there is variety of ruins, and allurements to entice fools, and a large theatre to act the bloody tragedies of souls upon: but they are nothing smooth, or safe, or delicate. The wayes of vertue are *streight* but *not crooked*; *narrow*, but *not unpleasant*.

The Great Exemplar, 1649, Pt. III, p. 11

94. *The Widow of Ephesus.*

THE *Ephesian Woman* that the souldier told of in *Petronius*, was the talk of all the town, and the rarest example of a dear affection to her husband; she descended with the corps into the vault, and there being attended with her maiden resolved to weep to death, or dye with famine, or a distempered sorrow: from which resolution nor his, nor her friends, nor the reverence of the principal citizens, who used the intreaties of their charity and their power, could perswade her. But a souldier that watched seven dead bodies hanging upon trees just over against this monument, crept in, and a while stared upon the silent and comely disorders of the sorrow: and having let the wonder a while breath out at each others eyes, at last he fetched his supper and a bottle of wine with purpose to eat and drink, and still to feed himself with that sad prettinesse; His pity and first draught of wine made him bold and curious to try if the maid would drink, who having many hours since felt her resolution faint as her wearied body, took his kindnesse, and the light returned into her eyes and danced like boyes in a festival; and fearing lest the pertinaciousnesse of her Mistresse sorrows should cause her evil to revert, or her shame to approach, assayed whether she would endure to hear an argument to perswade her to drink and live. The violent passion had layed all her spirits in wildness and dissolution and the maid found them willing to be gathered into order, at the arrest of any new object; being weary of the first, of which like leeches they had sucked their fill, till they fell down and burst. The weeping woman took her cordial and was not angry with her maid, and heard the souldier talk, and he was so pleased with the change, that he who first lov'd the silence of the sorrow was more in love with the musick of her returning voice, especially which himself had strung and put in tune; and the man began to talk amorously, and the womans weak heart and head was soon possessed with a little wine, and grew gay, and talked, and fell in love, and that very night in the morning of her passion, in the grave of her husband, in the pompes of mourning, and in her funeral garments, married her new and stranger Guest. For so the wilde forragers of *Lybia* being spent with heat, and dissolved by the too fond kisses of the sun, do melt with their common fires, and die with faintnesse, and descend with motions slow and unable to the little brooks that descend from heaven in the wildernesse; and when they drink they return into the vigor of a new life, & contract strange marriages; & the Lioness is courted by a Panther, and she listens to his love, and conceives a monster that all men call unnatural, and the daughter of an equivocal passion and of a sudden refreshment: and so also it was in the Cave at *Ephesus*: for by this time the souldier began to think it was fit he should return to his watch, and observe the dead bodies he had in charge; but when he ascended from his mourning bridal chamber, he found that one of the bodies was stolne by the friends of the dead, and that he was fallen into an evil condition, because by the laws of *Ephesus* his body was to be fixed in the place of it. The poor man returns to his woman, cryes out bitterly, and in her presence resolves to dye to prevent his death, and *in secret to prevent his shame*; but now the womans *love was raging* like her former sadnesse, and grew witty, and she comforted her souldier, and perswaded him to live, lest by losing him who had brought her from death and a more grievous sorrow, she should return to her old solemnities of dying and lose her honour for a dream, or the reputation of her constancy without the change and satisfaction of an enjoyed love. The man would fain have lived if it had been possible, and she found out this way for him, that he should take the body of her first husband whose funeral she had so strangely mourned, and put it upon the gallows in the place of the stolne thief; he did so and escaped the present danger to possesse a love which might change as violently as her grief had done: But so have I seen a croud of disordered people rush violently and in heaps till their utmost border was restrained by a wall, or had spent the fury of the first fluctuation and watry progress, and by & by it returned to the contrary with the same earnestness, only because it was violent & ungoverned; a raging passion is this croud, which when it is not under discipline and the conduct of reason, and the proportions of temperate humanity, runs passionatly the way it happens, and by and by as greedily to another side, being swayed by its own weight, and driven any whither by chance, in all its pursuits having no rule, but to do all it can, and spend it self in haste and expire with some shame and much undecency.

Holy Dying, 1651, p. 326

95. *The Lust of the Tongue.*

WHEN S. John reckoned the principles of evil actions, he told but of three, *The lust of the flesh, the lust of the eyes, and the pride of life.* But there was then also in the world (and now it is grown into age, and strength, and faction) another lust, *the lust of the ear,* and a fift also, *the lust of the tongue.* Some people have an insatiable appetite in hearing, and hear onely that they may hear, and talk and make a party: They enter into their neighbours house to kindle their candle, and espying there, a glaring fire, sit down upon the hearth and warm themselves all day, and forget their errand, and in the mean time, their own fires are not lighted, nor their families instructed, or provided for, nor any need served, but a lazie pleasure, which is uselesse and impudent.

XXVIII Sermons, 1651, Epistle Dedicatory

96. *Stultiloquy.*

DOE not many men talke themselves into anger, skrewing up themselves with dialogues and fancy, till they forget the company and themselves? and some men hate to be contradicted, or interrupted, or to be discovered in their folly; and some men being a little conscious, and not striving to amend it by silence, they make it worse by discourse; a long story of themselves, a tedious praise of another collaterally to do themselves advantage, a declamation against a sin to undoe the person, or oppresse the reputation of their neighbour, unseasonable repetition of that which neither profits nor delights, trifling contentions about a goats beard, or the blood of an oyster, anger and animosity, spite and rage, scorn and reproach begun

upon Questions, which concern neither of the litigants,
fierce disputations, strivings for what is past, and for what
shall never be, these are the events of the loose and unwary
tongue; which are like flies and gnats upon the margent
of a poole, they doe not sting like an Aspic, or bite deep
as a Bear, yet they can vex a man into a feaver and impatience, and make him uncapable of rest and counsel.

XXV Sermons, 1653, p. 301

97. *Revealing Secrets.*

THE third instance of the *vain trifling conversation,* and
immoderate talking is, *revealing secrets;* which is a dis-
mantling and rending off the robe from the privacies of
humane entercourse; and it is worse then denying to
restore that which was intrusted to our charge; for this
not onely injures his neighbors right, but throws it away,
and exposes it to his enemy; it is a denying to give a man
his own arms, and delivering them to another, by whom
he shall suffer mischief. He that intrusts a secret to his
friend, goes thither as to sanctuary, and to violate the rites
of that is *sacriledge,* and *profanation of friendship,* which is
the sister of Religion, and *the mother of secular blessing;* a
thing so sacred, that it changes a Kingdome into a Church,
and makes Interest to be Piety, and Justice to become
Religion. But this mischief growes according to the subject matter and its effect; and the tongue of a babbler
may crush a mans bones, or break his fortune upon her
owne wheel; and whatever the effect be, yet of it self it
is the betraying of a trust, and by *reproach,* oftentimes
passes on to intolerable calamities, like a criminal to his
scaffold through the execrable gates of Cities; And though
it is infinitely worse when the secret is laid open out of

spite or treachery, yet it is more foolish when it is discovered for no other end but to serve the itch of talking,
or to seem to know, or to be accounted worthy of a trust;
for so some men open their cabinets to shew onely that
a treasure is laid up, and that themselves were valued by
their friend, when they were thought capable of a secret;
but they shall be so no more; for he that by that means goes
in pursuit of reputation, loses the substance by snatching
at the shadow, and by desiring to be thought worthy of
a secret, proves himselfe unworthy of friendship or society.
D' Avila tels of a *French* Marquesse, young and fond, to
whom the Duke of *Guise* had conveyed notice of the
intended massacre, which when he had whispered into the
Kings ear, where there was no danger of publication, but
onely would seem a person worthy of such a trust, he was
instantly murder'd, lest a vanity like that might unlock so
horrid a mysterie.

XXV Sermons, 1653, p. 305

98. *Curiosity.*

EVERY man hath in his own life sins enough, in his
own minde trouble enough, in his own fortune evils
enough, and in performance of his offices failings more
then enough to entertain his own enquiry: so that curi-
ositie after the affairs of others, cannot be without envy and
an evil minde. What is it to me if my Neighbours Grand-
father were a Syrian, or his Grandmother illegitimate, or
that another is indebted five thousand pounds, or whether
his wife be expensive? But commonly curious persons, (or
as the Apostles phrase is) *busie-bodies* are not sollicitous,
or inquisitive into the beauty and order of a well governed
family, or after the vertues of an excellent person; but if

there be any thing for which men keep locks and bars and porters, things that blush to see the light, and either are shameful in manners, or private in nature, these things are their care and their businesse. But if great things will satisfie our enquiry, the course of the Sun and Moon, the spots in their faces, the Firmament of Heaven, and the supposed Orbs, the ebbing and flowing of the Sea, are work enough for us: or if this be not, let him tell me, whether the number of the stars be even or odde, and when they began to be so? since some ages have discovered new stars which the former knew not, but might have seen, if they had bin where now they are fix'd. If these be too troublesome, search lower, and tell me, why this turfe this year brings forth a Daisie, and the next year a Plantane: why the apple bears his seed in his heart, and wheat bears it in his head: let him tell, why a graft taking nourishment from a crab-stock shall have a fruit more noble then its nurse and parent: let him say, why the best of oyl is at the top, the best of wine in the middle, and the best of hony at the bottom, otherwise then it is in some liquors that are thinner, and in some that are thicker? But these things are not such as please busie bodies. They must feed upon Tragedies, and stories of misfortunes & crimes; & yet tell them ancient stories of the ravishment of chast maidens, or the debauchment of nations, or the extream poverty of learned persons, or the persecutions of the old Saints, or the changes of government, and sad accidents hapning in Royal families amongst the *Arsacidæ*, the *Cæsars*, the *Ptolomies*, these were enough to scratch the itch of knowing sad stories. But unlesse you tell them something *sad and new*, something that is done within the bounds of their own knowledge or relation, it seems tedious and unsatisfying; which showes plainly it is an evil spirit: envie and idlenesse married together, and begot curiosity. Therfore *Plutarch* rarely well compares, curious and inquisitive ears to the execrable gates of cities, out of which onely Malefactors, and hangmen and tragedies passe, nothing that is chast or holy. If a Physitian should go from house to house unsent for and enquire what woman hath a Cancer in her bowels, or what man hath a fistula in his colick gut, though he could pretend to cure it, he would be almost as unwelcome as the disease it self: and therefore it is inhumane to enquire after crimes and disasters without pretence of amending them, but onely to discover them. We are not angry with Searchers and Publicans when they look onely on publick merchandise; but when they break open trunks, and pierce vessels, and unrip packs, and open sealed letters.

Curiosity is the direct incontinency of the spirit: and adultery it self in its principle is many times nothing but a curious inquisition after, and envying another mans inclosed pleasures: and there have been many who refused fairer objects that they might ravish an inclosed woman, from her retirement and single possessour. But these inquisitions are seldom without danger, never without basenesse; they are neither just nor honest, nor delightful, and very often uselesse to the curious inquirer. For men stand upon their guards against them, as they secure their meat against Harpyes and Cats, laying all their counsels and secrets out of their way; or as men clap their garments close about them when the searching and saucy winds would discover their nakednesse: as knowing that what men willingly hear, they do willingly speak of. Knock therefore at the door before you enter upon your neigh-

bours privacy; and remember that there is no difference
between entring into his house, and looking into it.

Holy Living, 1650, p. 120

99. *Hypocrisy.*

WE do not live in an age in which there is so much
need to bid men be wary, as to take care that they
be innocent: Indeed in religion we are usually too loose,
and ungirt, exposing our selves to temptation, and others
to offence, and our name to dishonour, and the cause it
self to reproach, and we are open and ready to every evil
but persecution: from that we are close enough, and that
alone we call prudence; but in the matter of interest we
are wary as serpents, subtil as foxes, vigilant as the birds
of the night, rapacious as Kites, tenacious as grapling hooks
and the weightiest anchors, and above all, false and hypo-
critical as a thin crust of ice, spread upon the face of a
deep, smooth, and dissembling pit; if you set your foot,
your foot slips, or the ice breaks, and you sink into death,
and are wound in a sheet of water, descending into mischief or your grave; suffering a great fall, or a sudden death
by your confidence and unsuspecting foot. There is an
universal crust of hypocrisie, that covers the face of the
greatest part of mankinde. Their religion consists in forms
and outsides, and serves reputation or a designe, but does
not serve God: Their promises are but fair language, and
the civilities of the Piazzas or Exchanges, and disband and
unty like the air that beat upon their teeth, when they
spake the delicious and hopefull words. Their oaths are
snares to catch men, and make them confident: Their contracts are arts and stratagems to deceive, measured by
profit and possibility; and every thing is lawfull that is

gainfull; and their friendships are trades of getting; and
their kindnesse of watching a dying friend, is but the office
of a vulture, the gaping for a legacy, the spoil of the
carcasse; and their sicknesses are many times policies of
state, sometimes a designe to shew the riches of our bed-
chamber; and their funeral tears are but the paranymphs
and pious solicitors of a second Bride; and every thing that
is ugly must be hid, and every thing that is handsome must
be seen, and that will make a fair cover for a huge de-
formity; and therefore it is (as they think) necessary that
men should alwayes have some pretences and forms, some
faces of religion, or sweetnesse of language, confident
affirmatives, or bold oaths, protracted treaties, or multitude of words, affected silence, or grave deportment, a
good name, or a good cause, a fair relation, or a worthy
calling, great power, or a pleasant wit; any thing that can
be fair, or that can be usefull, any thing that can do good,
or be thought good, we use it to abuse our brother, or
promote our interests.

XXVIII Sermons, 1651, p. 290

100. *Worldliness.*

ARE not most men of the world made miserable at a
lesse price then a thousand pound a year? Do not all
the usurers and merchants, all tradesmen and labourers
under the Sun toil and care, labour and contrive, venture
and plot for a little money, and no man gets, and scarce
any man desires so much of it as he can lay upon three
acres of ground; not so much as will fill a great house; and
is this sum, that is such a trifle, such a poor limited heap
of dirt, the reward of all the labour, and the end of all the
care, and the design of all the malice, and the recompence

of all the wars of the world; and can it be imaginable, that
life it self, and a long life, an eternall and a happy life,
a kingdome, a perfect kingdome, and glorious, that shall
never have ending, nor ever shall be abated with rebellion,
or fears, or sorrow, or care, that such a kingdome should
not be worth the praying for, and quitting of an idle company, and a foolish humour, or a little drink, or a vicious
silly woman for it? surely men beleeve no such thing.
They do not relye upon those fine stories that are read in
books, and published by Preachers, and allow'd by the
lawes of all the world. If they did, why do they choose
intemperance and a feaver, lust and shame, rebellion and
danger, pride and a fall, sacriledge and a curse, gain and
passion, before humility and safety, religion and a constant
joy, devotion and peace of conscience, justice and a quiet
dwelling, charity and a blessing, and at the end of all this,
a Kingdome more glorious then all the beauties the Sun
did ever see.

XXV Sermons, 1653, p. 142

101. *Covetousness.*

RICHES are troublesome: but the satisfaction of those
appetites which God and nature hath made are cheap
and easy: for who ever paid use-money for bread and
onions and water to keep him alive: but when we covet
after houses of the frame and designe of *Italy*, or long for
jewels, or for my next neighbours field, or horses from
Barbary, or the richest perfumes of *Arabia*, or *Galatian*
mules, or fat Eunuchs for our slaves from *Tunis*, or rich
coaches from *Naples*, then we can never be satisfied till we
have the best thing that is fancied, and all that can be had,
and all that can be desired, and that we can lust no more:

but before we come to the one half of our first wilde
desires, we are the bondmen of Usurers, and of our worse
tyrant appetites, and the tortures of envy and impatience.

Holy Living, 1650, p. 326

102. *Luxuries.*

AND therefore it was not without mystery observ'd
among the Ancients, that they who made gods of gold
and silver, of hope and fear, peace and fortune, Garlic and
Onions, Beasts and Serpents, and a quartan Ague, yet
never deified money: meaning, that however wealth was
admired by common or abused understandings; yet from
riches, that is, from that proportion of good things which
is beyond the necessities of Nature, no moment could be
added to a mans real content or happinesse. Corn from
Sardinia, herds of *Calabrian* cattel, meadows through
which pleasant *Liris* glides, silkes from *Tyrus*, and golden
Chalices to drown my health in, are nothing but instruments of vanity or sinne, and suppose a disease in the soul
of him that longs for them, or admires them.

Holy Living, 1650, p. 298

103. *Revenge.*

IF thy Brother sins against thee in words and offers thee
satisfaction seven times in a day, receive him. *Simon* his
Disciple saith unto him, seven times in a day? The Lord
answers, yea, I say unto you, seventy times seven times.
For even amongst the Prophets also, after they were
anointed with the holy Ghost, there was found the word
of sin; that is, they also offended in their tongues.'

Against this there is no objection, but what is made by
the foolish discourses of young men, fighters and malicious,

who by the evil manners of the world are taught to call revenge, gallantry, and the pardoning of injuries to be pusillanimity and cowardice: for this Devil that dwells in tombs and cannot be bound with chaines, prevailes infinitly upon this account amongst the more glorious part of mankinde; but (as all other things are, which oppose the wisdome of God) is infinitely unreasonable; there being nothing in the world a greater testimony of impotency and effeminacy of spirit then a desire of revenge. Who are so cruel as Cowards, and who so revengeful as the weakest and the most passionate women? Wise *Chrysippus*, and gentle *Thales*, and the good old man who being to drink his poyson refused to give any of it to his persecutor; these men did not think revenge a pleasure, or a worthy satisfaction. For what man is so barbarous as to recover his leprosy by sucking the life-blood from dying infants? a good man would rather endure ten leprosies then one such remedie. Such a thing is revenge; it pretends to cure a wound but does it with an intolerable remedy. It was the song of *Cyclops* to his sheep: *feed you upon the tender herbs, I mean to feed upon the flesh and drink the blood of the Greeks*; this is a violence not onely to the laws and manners, but even to the very nature of men. Lyons indeed and Tygres do with a strange curiosity eye and observe him that struck them, and they fight with him above all the hunters; to strike again is the return of beasts; but to pardon him that smote me, is the bravest amends and the noblest way of doing right unto our selves; whilest in the wayes of a man and by the methods of God, we have conquered our enemy into a friend. But revenge is the disease of honour, and is as contrary to the wisdom and bravery of men as dwelling in rivers and wallowing in

fires is to their natural manner of living, and he who out
of pretence of valour pursues revenge is like to him, who
because fire is a glorious thing, is willing to have a St.
Anthonies fire in his face.

The Worthy Communicant, 1660, p. 301

104. *Domitian's Feast.*

DOMITIAN was a cruel man, false and bloudie; and
to be nere him was a perpetual danger: enough to
try the constancy of the bravest Roman. But once that
he might be wanton in his crueltie; he invited the chiefest
of the *Patricii* to supper; who coming in obedience and
fear enough, entred into a court all hanged with blacks,
and from thence were conducted into dining rooms by the
Pollinctors, who used to dresse the bodies unto funeralls:
the lights of heaven (we may suppose) were quite shut out
by the approaching night and arts of obscuritie; when they
were in those charnel houses (for so they seemed) every
one was placed in order, a black pillar or coffin set by him,
and in it a dim taper besmeared with brimstone that it
might burn faint and blue and solemn; where when they
had stood a while like designed sacrifices, or as if the Prince
were sending them on solemn Embassie to his brother the
Prince of darknesse; on a sudden entred so many naked
black-moors or children besmear'd with the horrid juice
of the *sepia*, who having danced a little in phantastick and
Divils postures, retired a while, and then returned serving
up a banquet as at solemn funerals, and wine brought to
them in Urnes instead of Goblets; with deepest silence,
now and then interrupted with fearful groans and shriek-
ings. Here the Senators, who possibly could have strugled
with the abstracted thoughts of death, seeing it dressed in

all the fearful imagerie and ceremonies of the grave, had
no powers of Philosophie or Roman courage; but falling
into a *lipothymie* or deep swooning, made up this pageantry
of death with a representing of it unto the life. This scene
of sorrows was over-acted, and it was a witty cruelty to
kill a wise man by making him too imaginative and phantastical. It is not good to break a staffe by too much trying
the strength of it, or to undo a mans soul by a uselesse and
so phantastick a temptation. For he that tries himself
further then he hath need of, is like *Palæmons* shepherd,
who fearing the foot-bridge was not strong enough, to trie
it, loaded it so long, till by his unequal trial he broke that
which would have born a bigger burden then he had to
carry over it. *Some things will better suffer a long usage, then
an unequal trial.*

The Worthy Communicant, 1660, p. 154

105. *The Prosperity of Sinners.*

THERE is no age, no history, no state, no great change
in the world, but hath ministred an example of *an
afflicted truth*, and *a prevailing sin*: For I will never more
call that sinner prosperous, who after he hath been permitted to finish his businesse, shall die, and perish miserably: for at the same rate, we may envie the happinesse of
a poor fisherman, who while his nets were drying, slept
upon the rock and dreamt that he was made a King; on
a sudden starts up, and leaping for joy, fals down from the
rock, and in the place of his imaginary felicities, loses his
little portion of pleasure, and innocent solaces, he had from
the sound sleep and little cares of his humble cottage. . . .

But if we should look under the skirt of the prosperous
and prevailing Tyrant, we should finde even in the dayes

of his joyes, such allayes and abatements of his pleasure, as may serve to represent him *presently miserable*, besides his final infelicities. For I have seen a young and healthful person warm and ruddy under a poor and a thin garment, when at the same time, an old rich person hath been cold, and paralytick, under a load of sables and the skins of foxes; it is the body that makes the clothes warm, not the clothes the body: and the spirit of a man makes felicity and content, not any spoils of a rich fortune wrapt about a sickly and an uneasie soul. Apollodorus was a Traitor, and a Tyrant, and the world wondered to see a bad man have so good a fortune; But knew not that he nourished Scorpions in his brest, and that his liver and his heart were eaten up with Spectres and images of death; his thoughts were full of interruptions, his dreams of illusions, his fancie was abused with real troubles, and phantastick images, imagining that he saw the Scythians flaying him alive, his daughters like pillars of fire dancing round about a cauldron in which himself was boyling, and that his heart accused it self to be the cause of all these evils: And although all tyrants have not imaginative and phantastick consciences, yet all tyrants shall die and *come to judgement*; and such a man is not to be feared, nor at all to be envied: and in the mean time can he be said to escape, who hath an unquiet conscience, who is already designed for hell, he whom God hates and the people curse, and who hath an evil name, and against whom all good men pray, and many desire to fight, and all wish him destroyed, and some contrive to do it? is this man a blessed man? Is that man prosperous who hath stolen a rich robe, & is in fear to have his throat cut for it, and is fain to defend it with the greatest difficulty and the greatest danger? Does not he drink more sweetly, that takes his beaverage in an earthen vessel, then he that looks and searches into his golden chalices for fear of poison, and looks pale, at every sudden noise, and sleeps in armour, and trusts no body, and does not trust God for his safety, but does greater wickednesse onely to escape a while unpunished for his former crimes? *Auro bibitur venenum,* No man goes about to poison a poor mans pitcher, nor layes plots to forrage his little garden made for the hospital of two bee hives, and the feasting of a few Pythagorean herbe eaters.

XXVIII Sermons, 1651, pp. 127, 129

106. *The Faithful Compass.*

BUT as the needle of a compasse, when it is directed to its beloved star, at the first addresses waves on either side, and seems indifferent in his courtship of the rising or declining sun, and when it seems first determined to the North, stands a while trembling, as if it suffered inconvenience in the first fruition of its desires and stands not still in a full enjoyment till after, first, a great variety of motion, and then an undisturbed posture: so is the piety, and so is the conversion of a man; wrought by degrees and several steps of imperfection; and at first our choices are wavering, convinced by the grace of God and yet not perswaded, and then perswaded but not resolved, and then resolved but deferring to begin, and then beginning, but (as all beginnings are) in weaknesse and uncertainty, and we flie out often into huge indiscretions and look back to Sodom and long to return to Egypt; and when the storm is quite over we finde little bublings and unevennesses upon the face of the waters, we often weaken our own purposes by the returns of sin, and we do not call our

selves *conquerours* till by the long possession of vertues it
is a strange and unusual, and therefore an uneasy and
unpleasant thing to act a crime.

XXVIII Sermons, 1651, p. 211

107. *The Rising Tide.*

AND indeed if we consider upon how trifling and inconsiderable grounds most men hope for pardon (if at
least that may be call'd hope, which is nothing but a carelesse boldnesse, and an unreasonable wilfull confidence) we
shall see much cause to pity very many who are going
merrily to a sad and intolerable death. Pardon of sins is
a mercy which Christ purchased with his dearest blood,
which he ministers to us upon conditions of an infinite
kindnesse, but yet of great holinesse and obedience, and
an active living faith; it is a grace, that the most holy
persons beg of God with mighty passion, and labour for
with a great diligence, and expect with trembling fears,
and concerning it many times suffer sadnesses with uncertain soules, and receive it by degrees, and it enters upon
them by little portions, and it is broken as their sighs and
sleeps. But so have I seen the returning sea enter upon
the strand, and the waters rolling towards the shore, throw
up little portions of the tide, and retire as if nature meant
to play, and not to change the abode of waters; but still
the floud crept by little steppings, and invaded more by
his progressions then he lost by his retreat, and having told
the number of its steps, it possesses its new portion till the
Angell calls it back, that it may leave its unfaithfull dwelling of the sand: so is the pardon of our sins, it comes by
slow motions, and first quits a present death, and turnes,
it may be, into a sharp sicknesse; and if that sicknesse prove

not health to the soul, it washes off, and it may be will
dash against the rock again, and proceed to take off the
severall instances of anger, and the periods of wrath; but
all this while it is uncertain concerning our finall interest,
whether it be *ebbe* or *floud*; and every hearty prayer, and
every bountifull almes still enlarges the pardon, or addes
a degree of probability and hope; and then a drunken
meeting, or a covetous desire, or an act of lust, or looser
swearing, idle talk, or neglect of Religion, makes the pardon retire; and while it is disputed between Christ and
Christs enemy who shall be Lord, the pardon fluctuates
like the wave, striving to climbe the rock, and is wash'd
off like its own retinue, and it gets possession by time
and uncertainty, by difficulty, and the degrees of a hard
progression.

XXV Sermons, 1653, p. 96

108. *Imperfect Prayers.*

OUR prayers and devotions must be fervent and
zealous, not cold, patient, easie, and soon rejected;
but supported by a patient spirit, set forwards by importunity, continued by perseverance, waited on by attention,
and a present mind, carryed along with holy but strong
desires, and ballasted with resignation, and conformity to
the divine will; and then it is, as God likes it, and does
the work to Gods glory and our interest effectively. He
that asks with a doubting mind, and a lazy desire, begs for
nothing but to be denyed; we must in our prayers be
earnest, and fervent, or else we shall have but a cold
answer; for God gives his grace according as we can receive
it; and whatsoever evill returnes we meet in our prayers,
when we ask for good things, is wholly by reason of our

wandring spirits, and cold desires; we have reason to complain that our minds wander in our prayers, and our diversions are more prevailing then all our arts of application, and detention; and we wander sometimes even when we pray against wandring: and it is in some degrees naturall, and unevitable: but although the evill is not wholly to be cured, yet the symptomes are to be eased; and if our desires were strong, and fervent, our minds would in the same proportion be present; we see it by a certain and regular experience; what we love passionately, we perpetually think on, and it returnes upon us whether we will or no; and in a great fear the apprehension cannot be shaken off; and therefore if our desires of holy things were strong and earnest, we should most certainly attend our prayers: it is a more violent affection to other things that carries us off from this; and therefore if we lov'd passionately what we aske for daily, we should aske with hearty desires, and an earnest appetite, and a present spirit; and however it be very easie to have our thoughts wander, yet it is our indifferency and lukewarmnesse that makes it so naturall: and you may observe it, that so long as the light shines bright, and the fires of devotion, and desires flame out, so long the mind of a man stands close to the altar, and waits upon the sacrifice; but as the fires die and desires decay, so the mind steals away and walks abroad to see the little images of beauty and pleasure, which it beholds in the falling stars and little glow-wormes of the world. The river that runs slow and creeps by the banks, and begs leave of every turfe to let it passe, is drawn into little hollownesses, and spends it selfe in smaller portions, and dies with diversion; but when it runs with vigorousnesse and a ful stream, and breaks down every obstacle, making it even as

its own brow, it stays not to be tempted by little avoca-
tions, and to creep into holes, but runs into the sea through
full and usefull channels: So is a mans prayer, if it moves
upon the feet of an abated appetite, it wanders into the
society of every trifling accident, and stays at the corners
of the fancy, and talks with every object it meets, and
cannot arrive at heaven; but when it is carryed upon the
wings of passion and strong desires, a swift motion and
a hungry appetite, it passes on through all the intermediall
regions of clouds, and stays not till it dwells at the foot of
the Throne, where mercy sits, and thence sends holy
showers of refreshment.

XXV Sermons, 1653, p. 170

109. *Aversion from Prayer.*

FOR it is a sad consideration, and of secret reason, that
since *prayer* of all duties is certainly the sweetest and
the easiest, it having in it no difficulty or vexatious labour;
no wearinesse of bones, no dimnesse of eyes, or hollow
cheeks is directly consequent to it, no naturall desires of
contradictory quality, nothing of disease, but much of
comfort & more of hope in it; yet we are infinitely averse
from it, weary of its length, glad of an occasion to pre-
termit our offices, and yet there is no visible cause of such
indisposition; nothing in the nature of the thing, nor in
the circumstances necessarily appendant to the duty.
Something is amisse in us and it wanted a name till the
spirit of GOD by enjoyning us the duty of mortification,
hath taught us to know that immortification of spirit is
the cause of all our secret and spiritual indispositions: we
are so incorporated to the desires of *sensuall* objects, that
we feel no relish or gust of the *spirituall*. It is as if a Lyon

should eat hay, or an Ox venison, there is no proportion between the object and the appetite, till by mortification of our first desires, our wills are made spirituall, and our apprehensions supernatural and clarified. For as a Cook told *Dionysius* the Tyrant, the black broth of *Lacedæmon* would not do well at *Syracusa*, unlesse it be tasted by a Spartans palate; so neither can the excellencies of heaven be discerned, but by a spirit disrelishing the sottish appetites of the world, and accustomed to diviner banquets: and this was mystically signified by the two altars in *Solomons* temple, in the outer court whereof beasts were sacrificed, in the inner court an altar of incense: the first representing Mortification or slaying of our beastly appetites; the second the offering up our prayers, which are not likely to become a pleasant offertory, unlesse our impurities be removed by the atonement made by the first Sacrifices; without our spirit be mortified, we neither can love to pray, nor GOD love to hear us.

The Great Exemplar, 1649, Pt. I, p. 121

110. *Angry Prayer.*

THE first thing that hinders the prayers of a good man from obtaining its effect is a violent anger, a violent storm in the spirit of him that prayes. For anger sets the house on fire, and all the spirits are busie upon trouble, and intend propulsion, defence, displeasure or revenge; it is a short madnesse, and an eternall enemy to discourse, and sober counsels, and fair conversation; it intends its own object with all the earnestnesse of perception, or activity of designe, and a quicker motion of a too warm and distempered bloud; it is a feaver in the heart, and a calenture in the head, and a fire in the face, and a sword in the hand, and a fury all over; and therefore can never suffer a man to be in a disposition to pray. For prayer is an action and a state of entercourse, and desire, exactly contrary to this character of anger. Prayer is an action of likenesse to the holy Ghost, the Spirit of gentlenesse and dove-like simplicity; an imitation of the holy Jesus, whose Spirit is meek up to the greatnesse of the biggest example, and a conformity to God whose anger is alwaies just, and marches slowly, and is without transportation, and often hindred, and never hasty, and is full of mercy; prayer is the peace of our spirit, the stilnesse of our thoughts, the evennesse of recollection, the seat of meditation, the rest of our cares, and the calme of our tempest; prayer is the issue of a quiet minde, of untroubled thoughts, it is the daughter of charity, and the sister of meeknesse; and he that prayes to God with an angry, that is, with a troubled and discomposed spirit, is like him that retires into a battle to meditate, and sets up his closet in the out quarters of an army, and chooses a frontier garrison to be wise in. Anger is a perfect alienation of the minde from prayer, and therefore is contrary to that attention which presents our prayers in a right line to God. For so have I seen a lark rising from his bed of grasse and soaring upwards singing as he rises, and hopes to get to heaven, and climbe above the clouds; but the poor bird was beaten back with the loud sighings of an eastern winde, and his motion made irregular and unconstant, descending more at every breath of the tempest, then it could recover by the libration and frequent weighing of his wings; till the little creature was forc'd to sit down and pant, and stay till the storm was over, and then it made a prosperous flight, and did rise and sing as if it had learned musick and motion from an

Angell as he passed sometimes through the aire about his ministeries here below: so is the prayers of a good man; when his affairs have required businesse, and his businesse was matter of discipline, and his discipline was to passe upon a sinning person, or had a design of charity, his duty met with the infirmities of a man, and anger was its instrument, and the instrument became stronger then the prime agent, and raised a tempest, and overrul'd the man; and then his prayer was broken, and his thoughts were troubled, and his words went up towards a cloud, and his thoughts pull'd them back again, and made them without intention; and the good man sighs for his infirmity, but must be content to lose that prayer, and he must recover it when his anger is removed and his spirit is becalmed, made even as the brow of *Jesus*, and smooth like the heart of God; and then it ascends to heaven upon the wings of the holy dove, and dwels with God till it returnes like the usefull Bee, loaden with a blessing and the dew of heaven.

XXV Sermons, 1653, p. 59

iii. *Unholy Prayer.*

FOR so an impure vapor begotten of the slime of the earth, by the feavers and adulterous heats of an intemperate Summer sun, striving by the ladder of a mountaine to climbe up to heaven, and rolling into various figures by an uneasy, unfixed revolution, and stop'd at the middle region of the aire, being thrown from his pride and attempt of passing towards the seat of the stars, turnes into an unwholsome flame, and like the breath of hell is confin'd into a prison of darknesse, and a cloud, till it breaks into diseases, plagues and mildews, stink and blastings: so is the prayer of an unchast person, it strives to climbe the battlements of heaven, but because it is a flame of sulphur, salt and *bitumen*, and was kindled in the dishonorable regions below, deriv'd from hell, and contrary to God, it cannot passe forth to the element of love, but ends in barrennesse and murmur, fantastick expectations, and trifling imaginative confidences, and they at last end in sorrows and despaire.

XXV Sermons, 1653, p. 54

112. *Repentance.*

REPENTANCE is like the Sun, which enlightens not onely the tops of the Eastern hils, or warms the wall-fruits of *Italy*; it makes the little Balsam tree to weep precious tears with staring upon its beauties; it produces rich spices in *Arabia*, and warms the cold Hermit in his grot, and calls the religious man from his dorter in all the parts of the world where holy religion dwels; at the same time it digests the American gold, and melts the snows from the Riphæan mountains, because he darts his rays in every portion of the air, and the smallest atome that dances in the air, is tied to a little thread of light, which by equal emanations fils all the capacities of every region: so is repentance; it scatters its beams and holy influences; it kils the lust of the eyes, and mortifies the pride of life; it crucifies the desires of the flesh, and brings the understanding to the obedience of Jesus: the *fear* of it, bids war against the sin, and the *sorrow* breaks the heart of it: the *hope* that is mingled with *contrition*, enkindles our desires to return; and the *love* that is in it procures our pardon, and the *confidence* of that pardon does increase our *love,* and that *love* is *obedience,* and that *obedience* is *sanctification,* and that *sanctification* supposes the man to be *justified* before; and *he that is justified must be justified still*; and thus repentance is a holy life. But the little drops of a beginning sorrow, and the pert resolution to live better, never passing into act and habit; the quick and rash vows of the newly returning man, and the confusion of face espied in the convicted sinner, if they proceed no further, are but like the sudden fires of the night, which glare for a while within a little continent of air bigge enough to make a fire-ball, or the revolution of a minutes walk. These when they are alone, and do not actually, and with effect minister to the wise counsels and firm progressions of a holy life, are as far from procuring pardon, as they are from a life of piety and holiness.

Unum Necessarium, 1655, p. 668

113. *The Good Repentance.*

THATS a good repentance that bears fruit, and not that which produces leaves onely. When the heathen gods were to choose what trees they would have sacred to them and used in their festivals; *Jupiter* chose the Oake, *Venus* the Myrtle, *Apollo* loved the Laurel, but wise *Minerva* took the Olive. The other trees gave no fruit; an uselesse apple from the Oak, or little berries from the Laurel and the Myrtle; but besides the show, they were good but for very little: but the Olive gives an excellent fruit, fit for food and Physick, which when *Jupiter* observed, he kissed his daughter, and called her wise: for all pompousnesse is vain, and the solemn religion stands for nothing, unlesse that which we do, be profitable and good for material uses.

The Worthy Communicant, 1660, p. 394

114. *Miracles of Grace.*

WHEN *Horatius Cocles* had won that glorious victory over the three *Sabine* Brothers, & entring gloriously into *Rome* espied his sister wetting his Laurel with her unseasonable tears for the death of one of them whom she loved with the honour of a wife and the passion of a lover; and being mad with rage and pride, because her sorrow allayd his joyes and glory, kild her with that sword by which her servant died: Sometimes passion makes a prodigious excursion and passes on to the greatest violence, and the most prodigious follies; and though it be usually so restrained by reason and religion that such transvolations are not frequent; yet one such act is an eternal testimony how weak we are, and how mischievous a passion can be. It is a miracle of providence that in the midst of all the rudenesses and accidents of the world, a man preserves his eyes, which every thing can extinguish and put out: and it is no lesse a miracle of grace, that in the midst so many dishonourable loves there are no more horrid tragœdies: and that so many brutish angers do not produce more cruel sudden murders; and that so much envy does not oftener break out into open hostilities; it is indeed a mighty grace that pares the nails of these wild beasts and makes them more innocent in their effects, then they are in their nature; but still the principle remaines: there is in us the same evil nature, and the same unruly passion; and therefore as there ought to be continual guards upon them, so there must be continual inquiries made concerning them; and every thing is to be examined, lest all be lost upon a sudden.

The Worthy Communicant, 1660, p. 182

115. *Saving Souls.*

THERE is no greater charity in the world then to save a soul, nothing that pleases God better, nothing that can be in our hands greater or more noble, nothing that can be a more lasting and delightfull honour, then that a perishing soul, snatched from the flames of an intolerable Hell, and born to Heaven upon the wings of piety and mercy, by the Ministery of Angels, and the graces of the holy Spirit, shall to eternall ages blesse God and blesse thee, *Him*, for the *Author and finisher* of salvation, and thee for the Minister and charitable instrument; that bright starre must needs look pleasantly upon thy face for ever, which was by thy hand plac'd there, and had it not been by thy Ministery might have been a sooty coal, in the regions of sorrow.

XXV Sermons, 1653, p. 184

116. *The Soul.*

FIRST if we consider what the soul is in its own capacity to happinesse, we shall finde it to be an excellency greater then the sun; of an angelicall substance, sister to a cherubin, an image of the divinity, and the great argument of that mercy, whereby God did distinguish us from the lower form of beasts and trees and minerals.

For so it was the scripture affirmes, that *God made man after his own image*, that is, *secundum illam imaginem & ideam quam concepit ipse*, not according to the likenesse of any of those creatures which were prexistent to mans production; not according to any of those images or ideas whereby God created the heavens, and the earth; but by a new form; to distinguish him, from all other substances;

he made him by a new idea of his own, by an uncreated exemplar; and besides that this was a donation of intelligent faculties, such as we understand to be perfect, and essential, or rather the essence of God, it was also a designation of him to a glorious immortality and a communication of the rayes and reflections of his own essential felicities.

But the soul is al that whereby we may be, and without which we cannot be happy. It is not the eye that sees the beauties of the heaven, nor the ear that hears the sweetnesses of musick, or the glad-tidings of a prosperous accident, but the soul that perceives all the relishes of sensual and intellectual perfections and the more noble and excellent the soul is the greater and more savory are its perceptions; and if a childe beholds the rich Ermine, or the Diamonds of a starry night, or the order of the world, or hears the discourses of an Apostle, because he makes no reflex acts upon himself, and sees not that he sees; he can have but the pleasure of a fool or the deliciousnesse of a mule. But although the reflection of its own acts be a rare instrument of pleasure or pain respectively, yet the souls excellency is upon the same reason not perceived by us, by which the sapidnesse of pleasant things of nature, are not understood by a childe; even because the soul cannot reflect far enough. For as the Sun which is the fountain of light and heat, makes violent and direct emission of his rayes from himself but reflects them no further then to the bottom of a cloud, or the lowest imaginary circle of the middle region, and therefore receives [not] a duplicate of his own heat; so is the soul of man, it reflects upon its own inferiour actions of particular sense or general understanding; but because it knows little of its own nature, the manners of volition the immediate instruments of understanding, the way how it comes to meditate, and cannot discern how a sudden thought arrives, or the solution of a doubt, not depending upon preceding premises, therefore above halfe its pleasures are abated, and its own worth lesse understood; and possibly it is the better, it is so. If the Elephant knew his strength, or the horse the vigorousnesse of his own spirit, they would be as rebellious against their rulers, as unreasonable men against government: nay the Angels themselves, because their light reflected home to their orbs, and they understood all the secrets of their own perfection, they grew vertiginous and fell from the battlements of heaven. But the excellency of a humane soul shall then be truly understood, when the reflection will make no distraction of our faculties, nor enkindle any irregular fires; when we may understand our selves without danger.

XXVIII Sermons, 1651, p. 238

117. *The Weakness of the Soul.*

AND indeed (Madam) this is in a manner the sum total of the evill of our abused and corrupted nature; Our soul is in the body as in a Prison; it is there *tanquam in alienâ domo*, it is a sojourner, and lives by the bodies measures, and loves and hates by the bodies Interests and Inclinations; that which is pleasing and nourishing to the body, the soul chooses and delights in: that which is vexatious and troublesome, it abhorres, and hath motions accordingly; for Passions are nothing else but acts of the Will, carried to or from materiall Objects, and effects and impresses upon the man, made by such acts; consequent motions and productions from the Will.

Deus Justificatus, 1656, p. 20

118. *The Canes of Egypt.*

FOR so the Canes of Egypt when they newly arise from their bed of mud and slime of Nilus, start up into an equal and continual length, and are interrupted but with few knots, and are strong and beauteous with great distances, and intervals: but when they are grown to their full length they lessen into the point of a pyramis, and multiply their knots and joynts, interrupting the finenesse and smoothnesse of its body: so are the steps & declensions of him that does not grow in grace: at first when he springs up from his impurity, by the waters of baptisme and repentance, he grows straight and strong, and suffers but few interruptions of piety, and his constant courses of religion are but rarely intermitted; till they ascend up to a full age or towards the ends of their life, then they are weak and their devotions often intermitted, and their breaches are frequent, and they seek excuses, and labour for dispensations, and love God and religion lesse and lesse, till their old age instead of a crown of their vertue and perseverance ends in levity and unprofitable courses; light and uselesse as the tufted feathers upon the cane, every winde can play with it and abuse it, but no man can make it useful.

XXVIII Sermons, 1651, p. 180

119. *The Little Boat.*

IF the righteous scarcely be saved, where shall the wicked and the sinner appear.

These words are taken out of the proverbs according to the translation of the 70. *If the righteous scarcely is safe:* where the word μόλις implyes that he is safe; but by intermedial difficulties: and σώζεται he is safe in the midst of his persecutions, they may disturb his rest, and discompose his fancy, but they are like the firy chariot to Elias; he is encircled with fire and rare circumstances, and strange usages, but is carried up to Heaven in a robe of flames: and so was Noah safe when the flood came; and was the great type and instance too of the verification of this proposition, he was ὁ δίκαιος & δικαιοσύνης κήρυξ, he was put into a strange condition, perpetually wandring, shut up in a prison of wood, living upon faith, having never had the experience of being safe in flouds. And so have I often seen young and unskilful persons sitting in a little boat, when every little wave sporting about the sides of the vessel, and every motion and dancing of the barge seemed a danger, and made them cling fast upon their fellows, and yet all the while they were as safe as if they sat under a tree, while a gentle winde shaked the leaves into a refreshment, and a cooling shade: And the unskilful unexperienced Christian strikes out when ever his vessel shakes, thinking it alwayes a danger, that the watry pavement is not stable and resident like a rock; and yet all his danger is in himself, none at all from without: for he is indeed moving upon the waters, but fastned to a rock; faith is his foundation, and hope is his anchor and death is his harbour, and Christ is his pilot, and heaven is his countrey, and all the evils of poverty, or affronts of tribunals: and evil judges, of fears and sadder apprehensions are but like the loud wind blowing from the right point, they make a noise and drive faster to the harbour: and if we do not leave the ship and leap into the sea, quit the interests of religion and run to the securities of the world, cut our cables, and dissolve our hopes, grow impatient and hug a wave and die in its embraces, we are as safe at sea, safer in the storm which

God sends us, then in a calm, when we are befriended with the world.

XXVIII Sermons, 1651, p. 139

120. *Free Will.*

ALL this state of things thus represented must needs signify a state much more perfect then that of beasts, but very imperfect in respect of that of Angels, and of that which we our selves expect hereafter; and therefore that liberty which is made in just proportion to fit this imperfection must also of it self needs be imperfect, and need not be envied to mankind as if it were a jewel of the celestial crown. Alas it is an imperfection, fit to humble us, not to make us proud; it is not too much to be given us, it is a portion of our imperfect condition; it onely sets us higher then a Tulip, and enlarges our border beyond the folds of sheep or the Oxens stall, but it keeps us in our just station, servants to God, inferior to Angels, and in possibility of becoming Saints. For in moral or spiritual things *liberty* and *indetermination* is *weaknesse*, and supposes a great infirmity of our reason and a great want of love. For if we understood all the degrees of amability in the service of God, and if we could love God as he deserves, we could not deliberate concerning his service, and we could not possibly *chuse* or be in love with disobedience, we should have no liberty left, nothing concerning which we could deliberate; for there is no deliberation but when something is to be refus'd, and something is to be preferr'd, which could not be but that we understand good but little, and love it lesse. For the Saints and Angels in heaven and God himself love good and cannot chuse evil, because to doe so were imperfection and infelicity; and

the Devils and accursed souls hate all good, without liberty
and indifferency: but between these is the state of Man
in the days of his pilgrimage, untill he comes to a confirmation in one of the opposite termes. Liberty of will
is like the motion of a Magnetic needle toward the North,
full of trembling and uncertainty till it be fixt in the
beloved point: It wavers as long as it is free, and is at rest
when it can chuse no more. It is humility and truth to
allow to man this liberty; and therefore for this we may
lay our faces in the dust, and confesse that our dignity
and excellence supposes misery and is imperfection, but
the instrument and capacity of all duty and all vertue.

Ductor Dubitantium, 1660, vol. ii, p. 440

121. *Scruple.*

SCRUPLE is a little stone in the foot, if you set it upon
the ground it hurts you, if you hold it up you cannot
goe forward; it is a trouble where the trouble is over, a
doubt when doubts are resolved; it is a little party behinde
a hedge when the main army is broken and the field
cleared, and when the conscience is instructed in its way,
and girt for action, a light trifling reason, or an absurd
fear hinders it from beginning the journey, or proceeding
in the way, or resting at the journeys end.

Very often it hath no reason at all for its inducement,
but proceeds from indisposition of body, pusillanimity,
melancholly, a troubled head, sleepless nights, the society
of the timorous from solitariness, ignorance, or unseasoned
imprudent notices of things, indigested learning, strong
fancy and weak judgement; from any thing that may abuse
the reason into irresolution and restlesness. It is indeed
a direct walking in the dark, where we see nothing to

affright us, but we fancy many things, and the phantasms
produced in the lower regions of fancy, and nursed by
folly, and born upon the arms of fear doe trouble us.

But if reason be its parent, then it is born in the twi-
light, and the mother is so little that the daughter is a' fly
with a short head and a long sting, enough to trouble a
wise man, but not enough to satisfy the appetite of a little
bird. The reason of a scruple is ever as obscure as the light
of a Gloworm, not fit to govern any action, and yet is
suffered to stand in the midst of all its enemies, and like
the flies of *Egypt* vex and trouble the whole Army.

This disease is most frequent in women, and monastick
persons, in the sickly and timorous, and is often procured
by excess in religious exercises, in austerities and disciplines, indiscreet fastings and pernoctations in prayer,
multitude of humane Laws, variety of opinions, the impertinent talk and writings of men that are busily idle:
the enemy of mankinde by the weaknesses of the body and
understanding enervating the strengths of the spirit, and
making Religion strike it self upon the face by the palsies,
and weak tremblings of its own fingers.

Ductor Dubitantium, 1660, vol. i, p. 209

122. *Mystical Books.*

THE scrupulous man must avoid *those companies*, and
those *imployments*, and those *books* from whence the
clouds arise, especially the books of ineffective and phantastick notion, such as are *Legends* of Saints, *ridiculously*
and *weakly invented*, furnished out for *Idea's*, not for
actions of common life, with dreams and false propositions; for the scrupulous and fearful will easily be troubled,
if they finde themselves fall short of those fine images of

virtue which some men describe, that they might make
a fine picture, but *like no body*. Such also are the Books of
mystical Theology, which have in them the most high, the
most troublesome, and the most mysterious nothings in
the world, and little better then the effluxes of a *religious
madness*.

Ductor Dubitantium, 1660, vol. i, p. 218

123. *Joy and Fear*.

DO not seek for deliciousnesse and sensible consolations
in the actions of religion, but onely regard the duty
and the conscience of it. For although in the beginning of
religion most frequently, and at some other times irregu-
larly, God complyes with our infirmity, and encourages
our duty with little overflowings of spiritual joy, and
sensible pleasure, and delicacies in prayer, so as we seem
to feel some little beam of Heaven and great refreshments
from the spirit of consolation; yet this is not alwayes safe
for us to have, neither safe for us to expect and look for:
and when we do it, it is apt to make us cool in our enquiries
and waitings upon Christ when we want them: It is a
running after him, not for the miracles, but for the loaves;
not for the wonderful things of God, and the desires of
pleasing him, but for the pleasures of pleasing our selves.
And as we must not judge our devotion to be barren or
unfruitful when we want the overflowings of joy running
over: so neither must we cease for want of them; If our
spirits can serve God choosingly and greedily out of pure
conscience of our duty, it is better in it self, and more
safe to us.

Let him use to soften his spirit with frequent meditation
upon sad and dolorous objects, as of death, the terrours of

the day of judgement; fearful judgements upon sinners, strange horrid accidents, fear of Gods wrath, the pains of Hell, the unspeakable amazements of the damned, the intolerable load of a sad Eternity. For whatsoever creates fear, or makes the spirit to dwell in a religious sadnesse, is apt to entender the spirit, and make it devout and plyant to any part of duty. For a great fear, when it is ill managed, is the parent of superstition; but a discreet and well guided fear produces religion.

Holy Living, 1650, p. 298

124. *Godly Fear.*

FEAR is the duty we owe to God as being the God of power and Justice, the great Judge of heaven and earth, the avenger of the cause of Widows, the Patron of the poor, and the Advocate of the oppressed, a mighty God and terrible, and so essentiall an enemy to sin, that he spared not his own Son, but gave him over to death, and to become a sacrifice, when he took upon him our Nature, and became a person obliged for our guilt. *Fear* is the great bridle of intemperance, the modesty of the spirit, and the restraint of gaieties and dissolutions; it is the *girdle* to the soul, and the handmaid to repentance, the arrest of sin, and the cure or antidote to the spirit of reprobation; it preserves our apprehensions of the divine Majesty, and hinders our single actions from combining to sinfull habits; it is the mother of consideration, and the nurse of sober counsels, and it puts the soul to fermentation and activity, making it to passe from trembling to caution, from caution to carefulnesse, from carefulnesse to watchfulnesse, from thence to prudence, and by the gates and progresses of repentance, it leads the soul on to love, and to felicity, and to joyes in God that shall never cease again. Fear is the guard of a man in the dayes of prosperity, and it stands upon the watch-towers and spies the approaching danger, and gives warning to them that laugh loud, and feast in the chambers of rejoycing, where a man cannot consider by reason of the noises of wine, and jest, and musick: and if prudence takes it by the hand, and leads it on to duty, it is a state of grace, and an universall instrument to infant Religion, and the only security of the lesse perfect persons; and in all senses is that homage we owe to God who sends often to demand it, even then when he speaks in thunder, or smites by a plague, or awakens us by threatning, or discomposes our easinesse by sad thoughts, and tender eyes, and fearfull hearts, and trembling considerations.

But this so excellent grace is soon abused in the best and most tender spirits; in those who are softned by Nature and by Religion, by infelicities or cares, by sudden accidents or a sad soul; and the Devill observing, that fear like spare diet starves the feavers of lust, and quenches the flames of hell, endevours to highten this abstinence so much as to starve the man, and break the spirit into timorousnesse and scruple, sadnesse and unreasonable tremblings, credulity and trifling observation, suspicion and false accusations of God; and then vice being turned out at the gate, returns in at the postern, and does the work of hell and death by running too inconsiderately in the paths which seem to lead to heaven. But so have I seen a harmlesse dove made dark with an artificiall night, and her eyes ceel'd and lock'd up with a little quill, soaring upward and flying with amazement, fear and an undiscerning wing, she made toward heaven, but knew not that she was made a train and an instrument, to teach her enemy to prevail upon her and all her defencelesse kindred: so is a superstitious man, zealous and blinde, forward and mistaken, he runs towards heaven as he thinks, but he chooses foolish paths; and out of fear takes any thing that he is told or fancies; and guesses concerning God by measures taken from his own diseases and imperfections.

XXV Sermons, 1653, p. 116

125. *Superstitions.*

THERE is no man more miserable in the world, then the man who fears God as his enemy, and Religion as a snare, and duty as intolerable, and the Commandements as impossible, and his Judge as implacable, and his anger as certain, unsufferable, and unavoidable: whither shall this man goe? where shall he lay his burden? where shall he take sanctuary? for he fears the Altars as the places where his soul bleeds and dies; and God who is his Saviour he looks upon as his enemy; and because he is Lord of all, the miserable man cannot change his service unlesse it be apparently for a worse. And therefore of all the evils of the minde, *fear* is certainly the worst and the most intolerable; *levity* and *rashnesse* have in it some spritefulnesse, and greatnesse of action; *anger* is valiant; *desire* is busie and apt to hope; *credulity* is oftentimes entertain'd and pleased with images and appearances: But *fear* is dull, and sluggish, and treacherous, and flattering, and dissembling, and miserable, and foolish. Every false opinion concerning God is pernicious and dangerous; but if it be joyned with trouble of spirit, as fear, scruple or superstition are, it is like a wound with an inflamation, or a strain of a sinew with a contusion, or contrition of the part, painfull and unsafe; it puts on to actions when it self is driven; it urges reason, and circumscribes it, and makes it pityable, and ridiculous in its consequent follies; which if we consider it, will sufficiently reprove the folly, and declare the danger.

Almost all ages of the world have observed many instances of fond perswasions and foolish practises proceeding from violent fears and scruples in matter of Religion. *Diomedon* and many other Captains were condemned to dye, because after a great *Naval victory* they pursued the flying enemies, and did not first bury their dead. But *Chabrias* in the same case first buryed the dead, and by that time the enemy rallyed, and returned and beat his Navy, and made his masters pay the price of their importune superstition; they fear'd where they should not, and where they did not, they should. From hence proceeds observation of signs, and unlucky dayes; and the people did so when the *Gregorian* account began, continuing to call those unlucky dayes which were so signed in their tradition or *Erra pater*, although the day upon this account fell 10 dayes sooner; and men were transported with many other trifling contingencies and little accidents; which when they are once entertain'd by weaknesse, prevail upon their own strength, and in sad natures and weak spirits have produced effects of great danger and sorrow. *Aristodemus* King of the *Messenians* in his warre against the *Spartans*, prevented the sword of the enemies by a violence done upon himself, only because his dogs howl'd like wolves, and the Soothsayers were afraid because the *Briony* grew up by the wals of his Fathers house: and *Nicias* Generall of the *Athenian* forces sate with his armes in his bosome, and suffered himself and 40000 men tamely to fall by the insolent enemy, only because he was afraid of the labouring and eclipsed Moon. When the Marble statues in *Rome* did sweat (as naturally they did against all rainy weather) the *Augures* gave an alarum to the City; but if lightning struck the spire of the Capitoll, they thought *the summe of affairs*, and the Commonwealth it self was indanger'd. And this *Heathen folly* hath stuck so close to the *Christian*, that all the Sermons of the Church for 1600 years have not cured them all: But the practises of weaker people and the artifice of ruling Priests have superinduced many new ones. When Pope *Eugenius* sang Masse at *Rhemes*, and some few drops from the Chalice were spilt upon the pavement, it was thought to foretell mischief, warres, and bloud, to all Christendome, though it was nothing but carelesnesse and mischance of the Priest: and because *Thomas Becket* Archbishop of *Canterbury* sang the Masse of *Requiem* upon the day he was reconcil'd to his Prince, it was thought to foretell his own death by that religious office: and if men can listen to such whispers, and have not reason and observation enough to confute such trifles, they shall still be afrighted with the noise of birds, and every night-raven shall foretell evill as *Micaiah* to the King of Israel, and every old woman shall be a Prophetesse, and the events of humane affairs which should be managed by the conduct of counsell, of reason, and religion, shall succeed by chance, by the flight of birds, and the meeting with an evill eye, by the falling of the salt, or the decay of reason, of wisdome, and the just religion of a man.

XXV Sermons, 1653, p. 119

126. *Constant Zeal.*

TO that fervour and zeal that is necessary and a duty, *it is required that we be constant and persevering. Esto fidelis ad mortem*, said the Spirit of God to the Angel of the Church of *Smyrna*, *Be faithfull unto death, and I will give thee a crown of life*: For he that is warm to day, and cold to morrow, zealous in his resolution and weary in his practises, fierce in the beginning, and slack and easie in his progresse, hath not yet well chosen what side he will be of; he sees not reason enough for Religion, and he hath not confidence enough for its contrary; and therefore he is *duplicis animi*, as St. *James* calls him, *of a doubtfull mind*. For Religion is worth as much to day as it was yesterday, and that cannot change though we doe; and if we doe, we have left God, and whither he can goe that goes from God, his owne sorrowes will soon enough instruct him. This fire must never goe out, but it must be like the fire of heaven, it must shine like the starres, though sometimes cover'd with a cloud, or obscur'd by a greater light; yet they dwell for ever in their orbs, and walk in their circles, and observe their circumstances, but goe not out by day nor night, and set not when Kings die, nor are extinguish'd when Nations change their Government: So must the zeal of a Christian be, a constant incentive of his duty, and though sometimes his hand is drawne back by violence or need, and his prayers shortned by the importunity of businesse, and some parts omitted by necessities, and just complyances, yet still the fire is kept alive, it burns within when the light breaks not forth, and is eternall as the orb of fire, or the embers of the Altar of Incense.

XXV Sermons 1653, p. 176

127. *The Silkworm.*

FOR as the silk-worm eateth it self out of a seed to become a little worm, and there feeding on the leaves of mulberies, it grows till its coat be off, and then works it self into a house of silk, then casting its pearly seeds for the young to breed, it leaveth its silk for man, and dieth all white and winged in the shape of a flying creature: So is the progresse of souls: when they are regenerated by Baptisme, and have cast off their first stains and the skin of worldly vanities, by feeding on the leaves of Scriptures, and the fruits of the vine, and the joyes of the Sacrament, they incircle themselves in the rich garments of holy and vertuous habits; then by leaving their blood, which is the Churches seed, to raise up a new generation to God, they leave a blessed memory, and fair example, and are themselves turned into Angels, whose felicity is to do the will of God, as their imployments was in this world to suffer it.

XXVIII Sermons, 1651, p. 136

128. *Faith.*

FROM these premises we may see but too evidently, that though a great part of mankind pretend to be sav'd by Faith, yet they know not what it is, or else wilfully mistake it, and place their hopes upon sand or the more Unstable water. Believing is the least thing in a justifying Faith. For Faith is a conjunction of many Ingredients; and Faith is a Covenant, and faith is a law, and Faith is Obedience, and Faith is a work, and indeed is a sincere cleaving to and a closing with the termes of the Gospel in every instance, in every particular. Alas! the niceties of a spruce understanding, and the curious nothings of useless speculation, and all the opinions of Men that make the divisions of heart, and do nothing else, cannot bring us one drop of comfort in the day of tribulation; and therefore are no parts of the strength of faith. Nay, when a man begins truly to fear God, and is in the Agonies of mortification, all these new nothings and curiosities will lye neglected by as baubles do by children when they are deadly sick. But that only is Faith that makes us to love God, to do his will, to suffer his impositions, to trust his promises, to see thorough a cloud, to overcome the World, to resist the Devil, to stand in the day of trial, and to be comforted in all our sorrows.

Righteousness Evangelical, 1663, p. 205

129. *True Faith.*

IF you are willing even in death to confesse not onely the articles, but in affliction and death to trust the promises; If in the lowest nakednesse of poverty you can cherish your selves with expectation of Gods promises and dispensation, being as confident of food and rayment, and deliverance or support, when all is in Gods hand; as you are, when it is in *your own*; If you can be cheerfull in a storme, smile when the world frownes; be content in the midst of spirituall desertions, and anguish of spirit, expecting all should worke together for the best according to the promise; If you can strengthen your selves in GOD, when you are weakest, believe when ye see no hope, and entertain no jealousies or suspicions of GOD, though you see nothing to make you confident; then, and then onely, you have faith, which in coniunction with its other parts is able to save your soules.

The Great Exemplar, 1649, Pt. II, p. 19

130. *St. Paul's Vision.*

ALTHOUGH God was pleased in all times to communicate to mankind notices of the other World, sufficient to encourage Virtues, and to contest against the

rencounters of the World, yet he was ever sparing in telling
the secrets of it; and when St. *Paul* had his rapture into
Heaven, he saw fine things, and heard strange words, but
they were ἄρρητα ῥήματα, words that he could not speak,
and secrets that he could not understand, and secrets that
he could not communicate. For as a Man staring upon
the broad eye of the Sun, at his noon of Solstice, feels his
heat, and dwels in light, and loses the sight of his Eyes,
and perceives nothing distinctly, but the Organ is confounded, and the faculty amazed with too big a beauty:
So was St. *Paul* in his extasie; he saw that he could see
nothing to be told below, and he perceived the glories
were too big for flesh and blood, and that the beauties of
separate Souls were not to be understood by the Soul in
Conjunction; and therefore after all the fine things that
he saw, we only know what we knew before, *viz*. That
the Soul can live when the Body is dead; that it can subsist
without the Body; that there are very great glories re-
served for them that serve God; that they who die in
Christ shall live with him; that the body is a prison and
the Soul is in fetters while we are alive; and that when
the body dies the Soul springs and leaps from her Prison,
and enters into the first liberty of the Sons of God. Now
much of this did relie upon the same argument, upon
which the wise Gentiles of old concluded the immortality
of the Soul; even because we are here very miserable and
very poor: we are sick and we are afflicted; we do well
and we are disgraced; we speak well and we are derided;
we tell truths and few believe us; but the proud are
exalted, and the wicked are delivered, and evil men reign
over us, and the covetous snatch our little bundles of
Money from us, and the *Fiscus* gathers our Rents, and

every where the wisest and the best men are oppressed;
but therefore because it is thus, and thus it is not well, we
hope for some great good thing hereafter. For if in this
life only we had hope, then we Christians, all we to whom
persecution is allotted for our portion, we who must be
patient under the Cross, and receive Injuries, and say
nothing but prayers, we certainly were of all men the most
miserable.

The Worthy Communicant, 3rd ed., 1683, p. 394

131. *Grace.*

DO not we see this by a daily experience? Even those
things which a good man and an evil man know, they
do not know them both alike. A wicked man does know
that good is lovely, and sin is of an evill and destructive
nature; and when he is reproved, he is convinced; and
when he is observed, he is ashamed; and when he hath
done, he is unsatisfied; and when he pursues his sin, he
does it in the dark. Tell him he shall dye, and he sighs
deeply, but he knows it as well as you: proceed, and say
that after death comes Judgement, and the poor man
believes and trembles. He knows that God is angry with
him; and if you tell him that for ought he knows he may
be in Hell to morrow, he knows that it is an intolerable
truth, but it is also undeniable. And yet after all this he
runs to commit his sin with as certain an event and resolution, as if he knew no argument against it. These
notices of things terrible and true passe through his understanding as an Eagle through the Air: as long as her flight
lasted, the Air was shaken; but there remains no path
behind her.

Now since at the same time we see other persons, not

so learned it may be, not so much versed in Scriptures, yet they say a thing is good and lay hold of it, they believe glorious things of Heaven, and they live accordingly, as men that believe themselves; halfe a word is enough to make them understand; a nod is a sufficient reproof; the Crowing of a Cock, the singing of a Lark, the dawning of the day, and the washing their hands are to them competent memorialls of Religion and warnings of their duty: What is the reason of this difference? They both read the Scriptures, they read and heare the same *Sermons*, they have capable understandings, they both believe what they heare and what they read, and yet the event is vastly different. The reason is that which I am now speaking of: the one understands by one Principle, the other by another; the one understands by Nature, and the other by Grace; the one by humane Learning, and the other by Divine; the one reads the Scriptures without, and the other within; the one understands as a son of man, the other as a son of *God*; the one perceives by the proportions of the World, and the other by the measures of the Spirit; the one understands by Reason, and the other by Love; and therefore he does not only understand the *Sermons* of the Spirit, and perceives their meaning, but he pierces deeper, and knows the meaning of that meaning, that is, the secret of the Spirit, that which is spiritually discerned, that which gives life to the Proposition, and activity to the Soul.

And the reason is, because he hath a Divine principle within him, and a new understanding: that is plainly, he hath Love, and that 's more then Knowledge; as was rarely well observed by St. Paul, *Knowledge puffeth up, but Charity edifieth*; that is, Charity makes the best Scholars. No

Sermons can edify you, no Scriptures can build you up a holy building to God, unlesse the love of God, be in your hearts; and *purifie your souls from all filthinesse of the Flesh and spirit.*

But so it is in the régions of *Starrs*, where a vast body of fire is so divided by excentric motions, that it looks as if Nature had parted them into Orbes and round shells of plain and purest materialls: but where the cause is simple and the matter without variety, the motions must be uniforme; and in Heaven we should either espy no motion, or no variety. But God, who designed the Heavens to be the causes of all changes and motions here below, hath placed his Angels in their houses of light, and given to every one of his appointed officers a portion of the fiery matter to circumagitate and roll; and now the wonder ceases: for if it be enquired why this part of the fire runs Eastward and the other to the South, they being both indifferent to either, it is because an Angel of God sits in the Centre, and makes the same matter turne, not by the bent of its own mobility and inclination, but in order to the needs of Man and the great purposes of God; and so it is in the understandings of men: When they all receive the same notions, and are taught by the same Master, and give full consent to all the propositions, and can of themselves have nothing to distinguish them in the events, it is because God hath sent his Divine spirit, and kindles a new fire, and creates a braver capacity, and applies the actives to the passives, and blesses their operation. For there is in the heart of man such a dead sea, and an indisposition to holy flames, like as in the cold Rivers in the North, so as the fires will not burn them, and the Sun it self will never warme them, till Gods holy Spirit does from the

Temple of the new *Ierusalem* bring a holy flame, and make
it shine and burn.

Via Intelligentiae, 1662, p. 31

132. *Prayer.*

SINCE prayer can obtain every thing, it can open the
windows of heaven and shut the gates of hell; it can
put a holy constraint upon God, and detain an Angel till
he leave a blessing; it can open the treasures of rain, and
soften the iron ribs of rocks, till they melt into tears and
a flowing river; prayer can unclasp the girdles of the
North, saying to a mountain of ice; be thou removed
hence, and cast into the bottom of the Sea; it can arrest
the Sun in the midst of his course, and send the swift
winged winds upon our errand; and all those strange
things and secret decrees and unrevealed transactions
which are above the clouds and far beyond the regions of
the starrs shall combine in ministery and advantages for
the praying man: it cannot be but we should feel lesse
evil, and much more good then we do, if our prayers were
right.

The Worthy Communicant, 1660, p. 160

133. *The Essence of Prayer.*

THE prayers of men have saved cities and kingdoms
from ruine; prayer hath raised dead men to life, hath
stopped the violence of fire, shut the mouths of wilde
beasts, hath altered the course of nature, caused rain in
Egypt, and drowth in the sea, it made the Sun to go from
West to East, and the Moon to stand still, and rocks and
mountains to walk, and it cures diseases without physick,
and makes physick to do the work of nature, and nature

to do the work of grace, and grace to do the work of God; and it does miracles of accident and event: and yet prayer that does all this, is of it self nothing but an ascent of the minde to God, a desiring things fit to be desired, and an expression of this desire to God as we can, and as becomes us: And our unwillingnesse to pray, is nothing else but a not desiring what we ought passionately to long for; or if we do desire it, it is a choosing rather to misse our satisfaction and felicity, then to ask for it.

Holy Living, 1650, p. 282

134. *The Prayer of a Good Man.*

FOR a man of an ordinary piety is like *Gideons* fleece, wet in its own locks; but it could not water a poor mans Garden. But so does a thirsty land drink all the dew of heaven that wets its face, and a great shower makes no torrent, nor digs so much as a little furrow that the drils of the water might passe into rivers, or refresh their neighbours wearinesse; but when the earth is full, and hath no strange consumptive needs, then at the next time when God blesses it with a gracious shower, it divides into portions, and sends it abroad in free and equall communications, that all that stand round about may feel the shower. So is a good mans prayer; his own cup is full, it is crowned with health, and overflowes with blessings, and all that drink of his cup, and eat at his table are refreshed with his joys, and divide with him in his holy portions. And indeed he hath need of a great stock of piety, who is first to provide for his own necessities, and then to give portions to a numerous relation.

XXV Sermons, 1653, p. 72

135. *True Theology.*

MY *Text* is simple as Truth it self, but greatly Comprehensive, and contains a truth that alone will enable you to understand all *Mysteries*, and to expound all *Prophecies*, and to interpret all *Scriptures*, and to search into all Secrets, all (I mean) which concern our happinesse and our duty: and it being an affirmative hypotheticall, is plainly to be resolved into this Proposition, *The way to judge of Religion is by doing of our duty, and Theology is rather a Divine life then a Divine knowledge.* In Heaven indeed we shall first see, and then love; but here on Earth we must first love, and love will open our eyes as well as our hearts, and we shall then see and perceive and understand.

Via Intelligentiae, 1662, p. 13

136. *Water in the Desert.*

BUT happy is that soul which comes to these springs of salvation, as the Hart to the water brooks, panting and thirsty, longing and passionate, weary of sin and hating vanity, and reaching out the heart and hands to Christ; and this we are taught by the same mystery represented under other Sacraments; the waters of the spiritual rock of which our Fathers drank in the wildernesse; the rock was Christ; and those waters were his blood in Sacrament: and with the same appetite they drank those Sacramental waters withal, we are to receive these divine mysteries Evangelical.

Now let us by the aides of memory and fancy consider the children of Israel in the wildernesse in a barren and dry land where no water was, marching in dust and fire, not wet with the dew of heaven, wholly without moisture save onely what dropt from their own brows; the aire was fire, and the vermin was fire; the flying serpents were of the same cognation with the firmament, their sting was a flame, their venome was a feaver, and the feaver a calenture, and their whole state of abode and travel was a little image of the day of judgement, when the elements shall melt with fervent heat: These men like Salamanders walking in fire, dry with heat, and scorched with thirst, and made yet more thirsty by calling upon God for water; suppose I say these thirsty souls hearing *Moses* to promise that he will smite the rock, and that a river should break forth from thence: observe how presently they ran to the foot of the springing stone, thrusting forth their heads and tongues to meet the water, impatient of delay; crying out that the water did not move like light, all at once, and then suppose the pleasure of their drink, the unsatiablenesse of their desire; the immensity of their appetite; they took in as much as they could, & they desired much more. This was their Sacrament of the same mystery; and this was their manner of receiving it; and this teaches us to come to the same Christ with the same desires; for if that water was a type of our Sacrament, or a Sacrament of the same secret blessing, then that thirst is a signification of our duty; that we come to receive Christ in all the wayes of reception with longing appetites; preferring him before all the interests of the world, as birds do corn above jewels, or hungry men meat before long orations.

The Worthy Communicant, 1660, p. 132

137. *The Holy Supper.*

THE holy Communion, or Supper of the Lord is the most sacred, mysterious and useful conjugation of secret and holy things and duties in the Religion. It is not easie to be understood, it is not lightly to be received: it is not much opened in the writings of the New Testament, but still left in its mysterious nature; it is too much untwisted and nicely handled by the writings of the Doctors; and by them made more mysterious: and like a Doctrine of Philosophy made intricate by explications, and difficult by the aperture and dissolution of distinctions. So we sometimes espie a bright cloud form'd into an irregular figure; when it is observed by unskilful and phantastick travellers, looks like a centaure to some, & as a Castle to others: some tell that they saw an Army with Banners and it signifies war; but another wiser then his fellow sayes it looks for all the world like a flock of sheep, and foretells plenty, and all the while it is nothing but a shining cloud by its own mobility and the activity of a wind cast into a contingent and inartificial shape: So it is in this great mystery of our Religion; in which some espie strange things which God intended not, and others see not what God hath plainly told: some call that part of it a mystery, which is none, and others think all of it nothing but a mere ceremony and a signe: some say it signifies, and some say it effects; some say it is a sacrifice, and others call it a Sacrament; some Schooles of learning make it the instrument of Grace in the hand of God; others say that it is God himself in that instrument of Grace; some call it venerable, and others say as the vain men in the Prophet, that *the Table of the Lord is contemptible*: some come to it,

with their sins on their head, and others with their sins
in their mouth: Some come to be cured, some to be
quicknd; some to be nourished, and others to be
made alive; some out of fear and reverence take it but
seldom, others out of devotion take it frequently; some
receive it as a means to procure great graces and blessings,
others as an Eucharist, and an office of thanksgiving for
what they have received: some call it an act of obedience
merely, others account it an excellent devotion and the
exercising of the virtue of Religion; some take it to
strengthen their faith, others to beget it, and yet many
affirm that it does neither, but supposes faith beforehand
as a disposition; faith in all its degrees according to the
degree of grace whither the communicant is arrived: Some
affirme the Elements are to be blessed by prayers of the
Bishop or other Minister; others say, it is onely by the
mystical words, the words of institution; and when it is
blessed, some believe it to be the natural body of Christ;
others, to be nothing of that; but the blessings of Christ,
his word and his spirit, his passion in representment, and
his grace in real exhibition: and all these men have something of reason for what they pretend; and yet the words
of Scripture from whence they pretend, are not so many,
as are the several pretensions.

My purpose is not to dispute, but to persuade; not to
confute any one, but to instruct those that need; not
to make a noise, but to excite devotion; not to enter into
curious, but material inquiries; and to gather together
into an union all those several portions of truth, & differing
apprehensions of mysteriousnesse and various methods and
rules of preparation, & seemingly opposed Doctrines by
which even good men stand at distance and are afraid of

each other: for since all societies of Christians pretend to the greatest esteem of this above all the rites or external parts and ministeries of Religion, it cannot be otherwise but that they will all speak honourable things of it, & suppose holy things to be in it, and great blessings one way or other to come by it; & it is contemptible only among the prophane & the Atheistical; all the innumerable differences which are in the discourses and consequent practises relating to it, proceed from some common truthes and universal notions and mysterious or inexplicable words, and tend all to reverential thoughts and pious treatment of these rites, and holy offices; & therefore it will not be impossible to finde honey or wholesome dewes upon all this variety of plants; and the differing opinions and several understandings of this mystery, which (it may be) no humane understanding can comprehend, will serve to excellent purposes of the spirit; if, like men of differing interest, they can be reconciled in one Communion, at least the ends and designes of them all can be conjoyned in the designe & ligatures of the same reverence and piety and devotion.

The Worthy Communicant, 1660, p. 8

138. *Mysteries*.

BUT if any man will search into the harder things, or any more secret Sacrament of Religion, by that means to raise up his mind to the contemplation of heavenly things, and to a contempt of things below, he may do it if he please, so that he do not impose the belief of his own speculations upon others, or compel them to confess what they know not, and what they cannot find in Scriptures, or did not receive from the Apostles. We find by experience, that a long act of Parliament, or an Indenture and

Covenant that is of great length, ends none, but causes many contentions; and when many things are defin'd, and definitions spun out into declarations, men believe less, and know nothing more. And what is Man, that he who knows so little of his own body, of the things done privately in his own house, of the nature of the meat he eates; nay, that knows so little of his own Heart, and is so great a stranger to the secret courses of Nature? I say, what is man, that in the things of God he should be asham'd to say, This is a secret; This God onely knows; This he hath not reveal'd; This I admire, but I understand not; I believe, but I understand it to be a mystery? And cannot a man enjoy the gift which God gives, and do what he commands, but he must dispute the Philosophy of the gift, or the Metaphysicks of a Command? Cannot a man eat Oysters, unless he wrangle about the number of the senses which that poor animal hath? and will not condited Mushromes be swallowed down, unless you first tell whether they differ specifically from a spunge? Is it not enough for me to believe the words of Christ, saying, *This is my body*? and cannot I take it thankfully, and believe it heartily, and confess it joyfully; but I must pry into the secret, and examine it by the rules of *Aristotle* and *Porphyry*, and find out the nature and the undiscernable philosophy of the manner of its change, and torment my own brains, and distract my heart, and torment my Brethren, and lose my charity, and hazard the loss of all the benefits intended to me, by the Holy Body; because I break those few words into more questions, than the holy bread is into particles to be eaten? Is it not enough, that I believe, that, whether we live or die, we are the Lord's, in case we serve him faithfully? but we must descend into hell, and inquire after the

secrets of the dead, and dream of the circumstances of the
state of separation, and damn our Brethren if they will not
allow us and themselves to be half damn'd in Purgatory?

A Dissuasive from Popery, 1664, Pt. II, p. 167

139. *The Name of Christ.*

THIS miraculous name is above all the powers of
Magicall inchantments, the nightly rites of sorcerers,
the secrets of *Memphis*, the drugs of *Thessaly*, the silent
and mysterious murmures of the wise *Caldees*, and the
spels of *Zoroastres*, This is the name at which the Devills
did tremble, and pay their inforced and involuntary adora-
tions, by confessing the Divinity, and quitting their possessions and usurped habitations. If our prayers be made
in this name G O D opens the windows of heaven and rains
down benediction: at the mention of this name the blessed
Apostles, and *Hermione* the daughter of S. *Philip*, and
Philotheus the son of *Theophila*, and S. *Hilarion* and S. *Paul*
the Hermite, and innumerable other lights who followed
hard after the sun of righteousnesse, wrought great and
prodigious miracles: *Signes and wonders and healings were
done by the name of the holy Childe JESUS.* This is the
name which we should engrave in our hearts, and write
upon our foreheads, and pronounce with our most harmonious accents, and rest our faith upon, and place our
hopes in, and love with the overflowings of charity, and
joy, and adoration. And as the revelation of this name
satisfied the hopes of all the world, so it must determine
our worshippings, and the addresses of our exteriour and
interiour religion: it being that name whereby G O D and
G O D S mercies are made presentiall to us and propor-
tionate objects of our religion and affections.

The Great Exemplar, 1649, Pt. I, p. 61

140. *God's Love.*

NOW (Madam) be pleased to say, whether I had not reason and necessity for what I have taught: You are a happy Mother of an Honorable Posterity, your Children and Nephews are Deare to you as your right eye, and yet you cannot love them so well as God loves them, and it is possible that a Mother should forget her Children, yet God even then will not, cannot; but if our Father and Mother forsake us, God taketh us up: Now Madam consider, could you have found in your heart when the Nurses and Midwives had bound up the heads of any of your Children, when you had born them with pain and joy upon your knees, could you have been tempted to give command that murderers should be brought to slay them alive, to put them to exquisite tortures, and then in the middest of their saddest groans, throw any one of them into the flames of a fierce fire, for no other reason, but because he was born at Latimers, or upon a Friday, or when the Moon was in her prime, or for what other reason you had made, and they could never avoid? could you have been delighted in their horrid shrieks and out-cries, and taking pleasure in their unavoidable and their intollerable calamity? could you have smiled, if the hangman had snatched your Eldest Son from his Nurses breasts, and dashed his brains out against the pavement; and would you not have wondred that any Father or Mother could espie the innocence and pretty smiles of your sweet babes, and yet tear their limbs in pieces, or devise devilish artifices to make them roar with intollerable convulsions? could you desire to be thought good, and yet have delighted in such cruelty? I know I may answer for you; you would first have dyed your self. And yet say again, God loves mankind better then we can love one another, and he is essentially just, and he is infinitely mercifull, and he is all goodness, and therefore though we might possibly do evil things, yet he cannot, and yet this doctrine of the Presbyterian reprobation, saies he both can and does things, the very apprehension of which hath caused many in despair to drown or hang themselves.

Deus Justificatus, 1656, p. 35

141. *The Love of God.*

Means of exciting contrition, or repentance of sins, proceeding from the love of God.

TO which purpose the sick man may consider, and is to be reminded (if he does not) that there are in God, all the motives and causes of amability in the world; that God is so infinitely good, that there are some of the greatest and most excellent spirits of heaven, whose work, and whose felicity, and whose perfections, and whose nature it is, to flame and burn in the brightest and most excellent love; that to love God is the greatest glory of Heaven, that in him there are such excellencies, that the smallest rayes of them communicated to our weaker understandings are yet sufficient to cause ravishments and transportations, and satisfactions, and *joyes unspeakeable, and full of glory* ; that all the wise Christians of the world know and feel such causes to love God that they all professe themselves ready to die for the love of God, and the Apostles and millions of the Martyrs did die for him ; And although it be harder to live in his love then to die for it, yet all the good people that ever gave their names to Christ did for his love endure the crucifying their lusts, the mortification of their appetites, the contradictions and death of their most passionate, naturall desires; that Kings and Queens have quitted their Diadems, and many married Saints have turned their mutuall vowes into the love of Jesus, and married him onely, keeping a virgin chastity in a married life, that they may more tenderly expresse their love to God; that all the good we have, derives from Gods love to us, and all the good we can hope for is the effect of his love, and can descend onely upon them that love him; that by his love it is that we receive the holy Jesus, and by his love we receive the Holy Spirit, and by his love we feel peace and joy within our spirits, and by his love we receive the mysterious Sacrament: And what can be greater, then that from the goodnesse and love of God, we receive Jesus Christ, and the Holy Ghost, and Adoption, and the inheritance of sons, and to be coheirs with Jesus, and to have pardon of our sins, and a divine nature, and restraining grace, and the grace of sanctification, and a rest and peace within us, and a certain expectation of glory, who can choose but love him, who when we had provoked him exceedingly, sent his Son to die for us, that we might live with him; who does so desire to pardon us and save us, that he hath appointed his Holy Son continually to intercede for us? That his love is so great that he offers us great kindnesse, and intreats us to be happy, and makes many decrees in heaven concerning the interest of our soul, and the very provision and support of our persons; That he sends an Angel to attend upon every of his servants, and to be their guard, and their guide, in all their dangers and hostilities; That for our sakes he restrains the Devil, and puts his mightinesse in fetters and restraints, and chastises his malice with decrees of grace and safety; That he it is who makes all the creatures serve us, and takes care of our sleeps, and preserves all plants and elements, all mineralls and vegetables, all beasts and birds, all fishes and *insects* for food to us, and for ornament, for physick and instruction, for variety and wonder, for delight and for religion; That as God is all good in himself, and all good to us, so sin is directly contrary to God, to reason, to religion, to safety and pleasure, and felicity; That it is a great dishonour to a mans spirit to have been made a fool, by a weak temptation, and an empty lust; and to have rejected God, who is so rich, so wise, so good, and so excellent, so delicious, and so profitable to us; That all the repentance in the world of excellent men does end in contrition, or a sorrow for sins proceeding from the love of God; because they that are in the state of grace do not fear hell violently, and so long as they remain in Gods favour, although they suffer the infirmities of men, yet they are Gods portion, and therefore all the repentance of just and holy men which is certainly the best, is a repentance not for lower ends, but because they are the friends of God, and they are full of indignation that they have done an act against the honour of their Patron, and their dearest Lord and Father; That it is a huge imperfection and a state of weaknesse, to need to be moved with fear or temporall respects, and they that are so, as yet are either immerged in the affections of the world, or of themselves; and those men that bear such a character, are not yet esteemed laudable persons, or men of good natures, or the sons of vertue. That no repentance can be lasting, that relies upon any thing but the love of God; for temporal motives may cease, and contrary contingencies may arise, and fear of hell, may be expelled by natural or acquired hardnesses, and is alwayes the least when we have most need of it, and most cause of it; for the more habitual our sins are, the more cauterized our conscience is, the lesse is the fear of hell, and yet our danger is much the greater, that although fear of hell or other temporal motives may be the first inlet to a repentance, yet repentance in that constitution and under those circumstances cannot obtain pardon; because there is in that no union with God, no adhesion to Christ, no endeerment of passion, or of spirit, no similitude, or conformity to the great instrument of our peace, our glorious Mediatour: for as yet a man is turned from his sin, but not converted to God; the first and last of our returns to God being love, and nothing but love: for obedience is the first part of love, and fruition is the last, and because he that does not love God cannot obey him, therefore he that does not love him cannot enjoy him.

Holy Dying, 1651, p. 200

142. *God's Mercy.*

AND as the Sun passing to its Southern Tropic looks with an open eye upon his sun-burnt Æthiopians, but at the same time sends light from its posterns and collateral influences from the backside of his beams, and sees the corners of the East, when his face tends towards the West, because he is a round body of fire, and hath some little images and resemblances of the infinite; so is Gods mercy; when it looked upon *Moses* it relieved S. *Paul*, and it pardoned *David*, and gave hope to *Manasses*, and might have restored *Judas*, if he would have had hope and used himself accordingly.

Holy Dying, 1651, p. 297

143. *God's Mercies.*

MAN having destroyed that which God delighted in, that is, the beauty of his soul, fell into an evil portion, and being seized upon by the divine justice, grew miserable, and condemned to an incurable sorrow. Poor Adam being banished and undone, went and lived a sad life in the mountains of *India*, and turned his face and his prayers towards Paradise; thither he sent his sighes, to that place he directed his devotions; there was his heart now, and his felicity sometimes had been; but he knew not how to return thither, for God was his enemy, and by many of his attributes opposed himself against him. *Gods power* was armed against him; and *poor man*, whom a fly, or a fish could kill, was assaulted and beaten with a sword of fire in the hand of a Cherubim. *Gods eye* watched him, *his omniscience* was mans accuser, *his severity* was the Judge, *his justice* the executioner. It was a mighty calamity that man was to undergo, when he that made him, armed himself against his creature, which would have died or turned to nothing, if he had but withdrawn the miracles and the Almightinesse of his power. If God had taken his arm from under him, man had perished; but it was therefore a greater evil when God laid his arm upon him and against him, and seemed to support him that he might be longer killing him. In the midst of these sadnesses God remembered his own creature, and pitied it, and by his *mercy* rescued him from *the hand of his power*, and *the sword of his justice*, and *the guilt of his punishment*, and *the disorder of his sin*, and placed him in that order of good things where he ought to have stood: It was *mercy* that preserved the noblest of Gods creatures here below; he who stood

condemned and undone under all the other attributes of
God, was onely saved and rescued by his *mercy*: that it
may be evident that *Gods mercy is above all his works*, and
above *all ours*, greater then the creation, and greater then
our sins; *as is his Majesty, so is his mercy*, that is, without
measures, and without rules, sitting in heaven and filling
all the world, calling for a duty that he may give a blessing,
making man that he may save him, punishing him that
he may preserve him: and Gods *justice* bowed down to
his *mercy*, and all his *power* passed into *mercy*, and his
omniscience converted into *care and watchfulnesse*, into *providence*, and *observation* for mans avail, and Heaven gave
its influence for man, and rained showers for our food and
drink, and the Attributes and Acts of God *sat at the foot
of mercy*, and *all that mercy descended upon the head of man*:
For so the light of the world in the morning of the creation
was spread abroad like a curtain, and dwelt no where, but
filled the *expansum* with a dissemination great as the un-
foldings of the airs looser garment, or the wilder fringes
of the fire, without knots, or order or combination; but
God gathered the beams in his hand, and united them into
a globe of fire, and all the light of the world became the
body of the Sun, and he lent some to his weaker sister that
walks in the night, and guides a traveller and teaches him
to distinguish a house from a river, or a rock from a plain
field; so is the mercy of God; a vast *expansum* and a huge
Ocean, from eternall ages it dwelt round about the throne
of God, and it filled all that infinite distance and space,
that hath no measure but the will of God; untill God
desiring to communicate that excellency and make it
relative, *created Angels*, that he might have persons capable
of huge gifts, *and man*, who he knew would need forgive-

nesse; for so the Angels our elder Brothers dwelt for ever in the house of their Father, and never brake his commandements; but we the younger like prodigals, forsook our fathers house, and went into a strange countrey, and followed stranger courses, and spent the portion of our nature, and forfeited all our title to the family, and came to need another portion: for ever since the fall of Adam, who like an unfortunate man spent all that a wretched man could need, or a happy man could have, *our life is repentance*, and *forgivenesse is all our portion*: and though Angels were objects of Gods *bounty*, yet man onely is (in proper speaking) the object of his *mercy*. And the mercy which dwelt in an infinite circle, became confin'd to a little ring, and dwelt here below, and here shall dwell below, till it hath carried all Gods portion up to heaven, where it shall reigne and glory upon our crowned heads for ever and ever.

But for him that considers Gods mercies, and dwels a while in that depth, it is hard not to talk wildly and without art, and order of discoursings: Saint Peter talked he knew not what, when he entered into a cloud with Jesus upon mount Tabor, though it passed over him like the little curtains that ride upon the North-winde, and passe between the Sun and us: And when we converse with a light greater then the Sun, and tast a sweetnesse more delicious then the dew of heaven, and in our thoughts entertain the ravishments and harmony of that atonement which reconciles God to man, and man to felicity, it will be more easily pardoned, if we should be like persons that admire much, and say but little: and indeed we can best confesse the glories of the Lord by dazeled eyes and a stammering tongue, and a heart overcharged with the miracles of this infinity; For so those little drops that *run over*, though they be not much in themselves, yet they tell that the vessell was full, and could expresse the greatnesse of the shower no otherwise, but by spilling, and inartificiall expressions and runnings over. . . .

It is a sad calamity to see a kingdom spoiled, and a church afflicted, the Priests slain with the sword, and the blood of Nobles mingled with cheaper sand, religion made a cause of trouble, and the best men most cruelly persecuted, Government confounded, and laws ashamed, Judges decreeing causes in fear and covetousnesse, and the ministers of holy things setting themselves against all that is sacred, and setting fire upon the fields, and turning in little foxes on purpose to destroy the vineyards; and what shall make recompence for this heap of sorrows, when ever God shall send such swords of fire? even *the mercies of God*, which then will be made publick, when we shall hear such afflicted people sing *In convertendo captivitatem Sion* with the voice of joy and festival eucharist, *among such as keep holy day*; and when peace shall become sweeter and dwell the longer; and in the mean time it serves religion, and the affliction shall try the children of God, and God shall crown them, and men shall grow wiser, and more holy, and leave their petty interests, and take sanctuary in holy living and be taught temperance by their want, and patience by their suffering, and charity by their persecution, and shall better understand the duty of their relations, and at last the secret worm that lay at the root of the plant, shall be drawn forth and quite extinguished. For so have I known a luxuriant Vine swell into irregular twigs, and bold excrescencies, and spend it self in leaves and little rings, and affoord but trifling clusters to the wine-presse, and a faint return to his heart which longed to be refreshed with a full vintage: But when the Lord of the vine had caused the dressers to cut the wilder plant and made it bleed, it grew temperate in its vain expense of uselesse leaves, and knotted into fair and juicy bunches, and made accounts of that losse of blood by the return of fruit: So is an afflicted Province, cured of its surfets, and punished for its sins, and bleeds for its long riot, and is left ungoverned for its disobedience, and chastised for its wantonnesse, and when the sword hath let forth the corrupted blood, and the fire hath purged the rest, then it enters into the double joyes of restitution, and gives God thanks for his rod, and confesses the mercies of the Lord in making the smoke be changed into fire, and the cloud into a perfume, the sword into a staffe, and his anger into mercy. . . .

Is not all the earth our orchard, and our granary, our vineyard, and our garden of pleasure? and the face of the Sea is our traffique, and the bowels of the Sea is our *vivarium*, a place for fish to feed us, and to serve some other collaterall appendant needs; and all the face of heaven is a repository for influences and breath, fruitfull showers and fair refreshments; and when God made provisions for his other creatures, he gave it of one kinde, and with variety no greater, then the changes of day and night, one devouring the other, or sitting down with his draught of blood, or walking upon his portion of grasse: But man hath all the food of beasts, and all the beasts themselves that are fit for food; and *the food of Angels, and the dew of heaven, and the fatnesse of the earth*; and every part of his body hath a provision made for it, and the smoothnesse of the olive, and the juice of the vine refresh the heart and make the face cheerfull, and serve the ends of joy, and the festivity of man, and are not onely to cure hunger or to allay thirst, but to appease a passion, and allay a sorrow. It is an infinite variety of meat with which God furnishes out the table of mankinde; and in the covering our sin, and clothing our nakednesse, God passed from fig-leaves to the skins of beasts, from aprons to long-robes, from leather to wool, and from thence to the warmth of furres, and the coolnesse of silks, he hath dressed not onely our needs, but hath fitted the severall portions of the yeer, and made us to go dressed like our mother; leaving off the winter sables when the florid spring appears, and as soon as the Tulip fades we put on the robe of Summer, and then shear our sheep for Winter; and God uses us as Joseph did his brother *Benjamin*, we have many changes of raiment, and our messe is five times bigger then the provision made for our brothers of the Creation. . . .

Does not God plant remedies there where the diseases are most popular, and every Countrey is best provided against its own evils? Is not the Rhubarb found where the Sun most corrupts the liver, and the Scabious by the shore of the Sea, that God might cure as soon as he wounds, and the inhabitants may see their remedy against the leprosie, and the scurvy, before they feel their sicknesse? And then to this we may adde, Natures commons and open fields, the shores of rivers, and the strand of the Sea, the unconfined air, the wildernesse that hath no hedge, and that in these every man may hunt, and fowl and fish respectively; and that God sends some miracles and extraordinary blessings so for the publike good, that he will not endure they should be inclosed and made severall: Thus he is pleased to dispense with *Manna of*

Calabria, the medicinall waters of Germany, the Musles at *Sluce* at this day, and the Egyptian beans in the marishes of Albania, and the salt at Troas of old; which God to defeat the covetousnesse of man, and to spread his mercy over the face of the indigent, as the Sun scatters his beams over the bosome of the whole earth, did so order that as long as every man was permitted to partake, the bosome of heaven was open; but when man gathered them into single handfulls, and made them impropriate, God gathered his hand into his bosome, and bound the heavens with ribs of brasse, and the earth with decrees of iron, and the blessing reverted to him that gave it, since they might not receive it, to whom it was sent. And in general, this is the excellency of this mercy, that all our needs are certainly supplied, and secured by a promise which God cannot break, but he that cannot breake the lawes of his own promises, can break the lawes of nature, that he may perform his promise, and he will do a miracle rather then forsake thee in thy needs: So that our security and the relative mercy, is bound upon us by all the power and the truth of God.

But because such is the bounty of God, that he hath provided a better life for the inheritance of man, if God is so mercifull in making fair provisions for our lesse noble part, in order to the transition toward our Countrey, we may expect that the mercies of God hath rare arts to secure to us his designed bounty, in order to our inheritance, to that which ought to be our portion for ever. And here I consider, that it is an infinite mercy of the Almighty Father of mercies that he hath appointed to us such a religion that leads us to a huge felicity, through pleasant wayes. For the felicity that is designed to us is so above our present capacities and conceptions, that while we are so ignorant as not to understand it, we are also so foolish as not to desire it with passions great enough to perform the little conditions of its purchase; God therefore knowing how great an interest it is, and how apt we would be to neglect it, hath found out such conditions of acquiring it which are eases and satisfaction to our present appetites. God hath bound our salvation upon us by the endearment of temporall prosperities; and because we love this world so well, God hath so ordered it, that even this world may secure the other. And of this, God in old time made open profession, for when he had secretly designed to bring his people to a glorious immortality in another world, he told them nothing of that, it being a thing bigger then the capacity of their thoughts, or of their Theology, but told them that which would tempt them most, and endear obedience: *If you will obey, ye shall eat the good things of the land*: Ye shall possesse a rich countrey, ye shall triumph over your enemies, ye shall have numerous families, blessed children, rich granaries, over-running wine-presses; for God knew the cognation of most of them was so dear, between their affections and the good things of this world, that if they did not obey in hope of that they did need, and fancy, and love, and see, and feel, it was not to be expected they should quit their affections for a secret in another world, whither before they come they must die, and lose all desire and all capacities of enjoyment. But this designe of God which was bare-faced in the dayes of the law, is now in the Gospel interwoven secretly (but yet plain enough to be discovered by an eye of faith and reason) into every vertue, and temporal advantage is a great ingredient in the constitution of every

Christian grace for so the richest tissue dazles the beholders eye when the Sun reflects upon the mettal, the silver and the gold weaved into phantastic imagery, or a wealthy plainnesse, but the rich wire and shining filaments are wrought upon the cheaper silk, the spoil of worms and flies: so is the imbroidery of our vertue; the glories of the spirit dwell upon the face and vestment, upon the fringes and the borders; and there we see the Beril and the Onyx, the Jasper and the sardyx, order and perfection, love and peace and joy, mortification of the passions and ravishment of the will, adherencies to God and imitation of Christ, reception and entertainment of the Holy Ghost and longings after heaven, humility, and chastity, temperance, and sobriety; these make the frame of the garment, the cloaths of the soul that it may not be found naked in the day of the Lords visitation; but through these rich materials a thrid of silk is drawn, some compliance with worms and weaker creatures, something that shall please our bowels, and make the lower man to rejoyce: they are wrought upon secular content, and material satisfactions, and now we cannot be happy unlesse we be pious, and the religion of a Christian is the greatest security and the most certain instrument of making a man *rich*, and *pleased*, and *healthful* and *wise* and *beloved* in the whole world.

XXVIII Sermons, 1651, pp. 313, 324, 328, 329

144. *God's Favour.*

WHAT a prodigy of favour is it to us, that he hath passed by, so many formes of his creatures, and hath not set us down in the rank of any of them, till we came to be *paulo minores angelis*, a little lower then the angels: and yet from the meanest of them God can perfect his own praise; The deeps and the snows, the hail and the rain, the birds of the air, and the fishes of the sea, they can and do glorifie God, and give him praise in their capacity; and yet he gave them no speech, no reason, no immortall spirit, or capacity of eternall blessednesse; but he hath distinguished us from them by the absolute issues of his predestination, and hath given us a lasting and eternall spirit, excellent organs of perception, and wonderfull instruments of expression, that we may joyn in consort with the morning star, and bear a part in the *Chorus* with the Angels of light, to sing *Alleluiah* to the great Father of men and Angels. . . .

He causeth us to be born of Christian parents, under whom we were taught the mysteriousnesse of its goodnesse and designes, for the redemption of man: And by the designe of which religion *repentance* was taught to mankind, and an excellent law given for distinction of good and evil; and this is a blessing which though possibly we do not often put into our eucharisticall Letanies to give God thanks for, yet if we sadly consider, what had become of us, if we had been born under the dominion of a *Turkish* Lord, or in *America* where no Christians do inhabite, where they worship the Devil, where witches are their priests, their prophets, their phisitians, and their Oracles, can we choose but apprehend a visible notorious necessity of perishing in those sins which we then should not have understood by the glasse of a divine law, to have declined, nor by a revelation have been taught to repent of?

XXVIII Sermons, 1651, pp. 148, 149

145. *Mercy*.

*L*ET *us take heed:* for Mercy is like a rainbowe, which God set in the clouds to remember mankinde; it shines here as long as it is not hindered; but we must never look for it after it is night, and it shines not in the other world; if we refuse mercy here, we shall have justice to eternity.

XXVIII Sermons, 1651, p. 354

146. *God's Omnipresence*.

*G*OD is every where present *by his power*. He roules the Orbs of Heaven with his hand, he fixes the Earth with his Foot, he guides all the Creatures with his Eye, and refreshes them with his influence: He makes the powers of Hell to shake with his terrours, and binds the Devils with his Word, and throws them out with his command; and sends the Angels on Embassies with his decrees: He hardens the joynts of Infants, and confirms the bones when they are fashioned beneath secretly in the earth: He it is that assists at the numerous productions of fishes, and there is not one hollownesse in the bottom of the sea, but he shows himself to be Lord of it, by sustaining there the Creatures that come to dwell in it: And in the wildernesse, the Bittern and the Stork, the Dragon and the Satyr, the Unicorn and the Elk live upon his provisions, and revere his power, and feel the force of his Almightinesse. . . .

God is *by grace and benediction* specially present *in holy places*, and in the solemn assemblies of his servants. If holy people meet in grots and dens of the earth, when persecution or a publick necessity disturbs the publick order, circumstance, and convenience, God fails not to come thither to them: but God is also by the same or a greater reason present there where they meet *ordinarily*, *by order*, *and publick authority*: There God is present ordinarily, that is, at every such meeting. God will go out of his way to meet his Saints, when themselves are forced out of their way of order by a sad necessity: but else, Gods *usual way* is to be present in those places where his servants are appointed *ordinarily* to meet. But his presence there signifies nothing but his *readinesse* to hear their prayers, to blesse their persons, to accept their offices, and to like even the circumstance of orderly and publick meeting. For thither, the prayers of consecration, the publick authority separating it, and Gods love of order, and the reasonable customes of Religion, have in ordinary, and in a certain degree fixed this manner of his presence; and he loves to have it so.

God is *especially present* in the hearts of his people *by his Holy Spirit*: and indeed the hearts of holy men are Temples in the truth of things, and in type and shadow they are of Heaven it self. For God *reigns* in the hearts of his servants. *There is his Kingdom.* The power of grace hath *subdued* all his enemies. There is, *his power.* They *serve* him night and day and give him thanks and praise: that is, *his glory*: This is the religion and worship of God in the Temple. The temple it self is the heart of man; Christ is the High Priest, who from thence sends up the incense of prayers and joyns them to his own intercession, and presents all together to his Father; and the Holy Ghost by his dwelling there, hath also consecrated it into a Temple; and God dwells in our hearts by faith, and Christ by his Spirit, and the Spirit by his purities; so that we are also Cabinets of the Mysterious Trinity; and what is this short of Heaven it self, but as infancy is short of manhood, and letters of words? The same state of life it is, but not the same age. It is *Heaven in a Looking-glasse*, (dark, but yet true) representing the beauties of the soul, and the graces of God, and the images of his eternal glory by the reality of a special presence.

Holy Living, 1650, p. 29

147. *Joan of Arc.*

HIS providence is extraregular and produces strange things beyond common rules: and he that led Israel through a Sea, and made a Rock powre forth waters, and the Heavens to give them bread and flesh, and whole Armies to be destroyed with phantastick noises, and the fortune of all *France* to be recovered and intirely revolv'd by the arms and conduct of a Girle against the torrent of the *English* fortune and Chivalry; can do what he please, and still retains the same affections to his people, and the same providence over mankinde as ever.

Holy Living, 1650, p. 242

148. *God's Glory.*

GOD is the eternall fountain of honour, and the spring of glory; in him it dwells essentially, from him it derives originally; and when an action is glorious, or a man is honourable, it is because the action is pleasing to God, in the relation of obedience or imitation, and because the man is honoured by God, or by Gods Vicegerent; and therefore God cannot be dishonoured, because all honour comes from himself; he cannot but be glorified, because to be himself is to be infinitely glorious. And yet he is pleased to say, that our sins dishonour him, and our obedience does glorifie him. But as the Sun, the great eye of the world, prying into the recesses of rocks, and the hollow-nesse of valleys, receives species, or visible forms from these objects, but he beholds them onely by that light which proceeds from himself: So does God who is the light of that eye; he receives reflexes and returns from us, and these he calls *glorifications* of himself, but they are such which are made so by his own gracious acceptation. For God cannot be glorified by any thing but by himself, and by his own instruments, which he makes as mirrours to reflect his own excellency, that by seeing the glory of such emanations, he may rejoyce in his own works, because they are images of his infinity. Thus when he made the beauteous frame of heaven and earth, he rejoyced in it, and glorified himself, because it was the glasse in which he beheld his wisedom, and Almighty power: And when God destroyed the old world, in that also he glorified himself; for in those waters he saw the image of his justice; they were the looking glasse for that Attribute; and God is said *to laugh at*, and *rejoyce in the destruction of a sinner*, because he is pleased with the Oeconomy of his own lawes, and the excellent proportions he hath made of his judgements, consequent to our sins. But above all, God rejoyced in his Holy Son, for he was the image of the Divinity, *the character and expresse image of his person*, in him he beheld his own Essence, his wisedom, his power, his justice, and his person, and he was that excellent instrument, designed from eternall ages to represent as in a double mirrour, not onely the glories of God to himself, but also to all the world; and he glorified God by the instrument of obe-dience, in which God beheld his own dominion, and the sanctity of his lawes clearly represented; and he saw his justice glorified, when it was fully satisfied by the passion of his Son; and so he hath transmitted to us a great manner of the Divine glorification, being become to us the Authour, and the Example of giving glory to God after the manner of men, that is, by well-doing, and patient suffering, by obeying his lawes, and submitting to his power, by imitating his holinesse, and confessing his goodnesse, by remaining innocent, *or becoming penitent*; for this also is called in the Text

GIVING GLORY TO THE LORD OUR GOD.

For he that hath dishonoured God by sins, that is, hath denied, by a morall instrument of duty, and subordination, to confesse the glories of his power, and the goodnesse of his lawes, and hath dishonoured, and despised his mercy, which God intended as an instrument of our piety, hath no better way to glorifie God, then by returning to his duty, to advance the honour of the Divine Attributes in which he is pleased to communicate himself, and to have entercourse with man. He that repents, confesses his own errour, and the righteousnesse of Gods lawes, and by judging himself confesses that he deserves punishment, and therefore that God is righteous if he punishes him: and by returning, confesses God to be the fountain of felicity, and the foundation of true, solid, and permanent joyes, saying in the sense and passion of the Disciples, *Whither shall we go? for thou hast the words of eternall life:* and by humbling himself, exalts God by making the proportions of distance more immense, and vast: and as repentance does contain in it all the parts of holy life which can be performed by a returning sinner (all the acts, and habits of vertue, being but parts, or instances, or effects of repentance): so all the actions of a holy life do constitute the masse and body of all those instruments whereby God is pleased to glorifie himself. For if God is glorified in the Sunne and Moon, in the rare fabrick of the honeycombs, in the discipline of Bees, in the œconomy of Pismires, in the little houses of birds, in the curiosity of an eye, God being pleased to delight in those little images and reflexes of himself from those pretty mirrours, which like a crevice in a wall thorow a narrow perspective transmit the species of a vast excellency: much rather shall God be pleased to behold himself in the glasses of our obedience, in the emissions of our will and understanding; these being rationall and apt instruments to expresse him, farre better then the naturall, as being neerer communications of himself.

XXVIII Sermons, 1651, p. 52

149. *God's Disposal.*

THAT great wise disposer of all things in Heaven and Earth, who makes twins in the little continent of their Mothers Wombe to lie at ease and peace, and the Eccentric motions of the Orbes, and the regular and irregular progressions of the starres, not to crosse or hinder one another, and in all the variety of humane actions, cases and contingencies, hath so wisely dispos'd his laws that no contradiction of chance can infer a contradiction of duty, and it can never be necessary to sin, but on one hand or other it may for ever be avoided; cannot be supposed to have appointed two powers in the hands of his servants to fight against or to resist each other: but as good is never contrary to good, nor truth to truth, so neither can those powers which are ordain'd for good.

Ductor Dubitantium, 1660, vol. ii, p. 199

150. *Reverence.*

LET us alwayes bear about us such impressions of reverence and fear of God as to tremble at his voice, to expresse our apprehensions of his greatnesse in all great accidents, in popular judgements, loud thunders, tempests, earth quakes, not onely for fear of being smitten our selves, or that we are concerned in the accident, but also that we may humble our selves before his Almightinesse, and expresse that infinite distance between his infinitenesse and our weaknesses, at such times especially when he gives such visible arguments of it. He that is merry and ayry at shore when he sees a sad and a loud tempest on the sea, or dances briskly when God thunders from heaven, regards not when God speaks to all the world, but is possessed with a firm immodesty.

Holy Living, 1650, p. 123

151. *The Devil.*

GOD hath given *his laws* to rule us, *his word* to instruct us, *his spirit* to guide us, *his Angels* to protect us, *his ministers* to exhort us; he *revealed* all our duty and he hath *concealed* whatsoever can hinder us, he hath *affrighted* our follies with feare of death and engaged our watchfulnesse by its secret coming; he hath exercised our faith by keeping private the state of souls departed, and yet hath confirmed our faith by a promise of a resurrection and entertained our hope by some general significations of the state of interval: His mercies make contemptible means instrumental to great purposes, and a small herb the remedy of the greatest diseases; he impedes the Devils rage and infatuates his counsels, he diverts his malice, and defeats his purposes, he bindes him in the chaine of darknesse and gives him no power over the children of light; he suffers him to walk in solitary places and yet fetters him that he cannot disturb the sleep of a childe; he hath given him mighty power & yet a young maiden that resists him shall make him flee away; he hath given him a vast knowledge and yet an ignorant man can confute him with the twelve articles of his creed, he gave him power over the winds and made him Prince of the air and yet the breath of a holy prayer can drive him as far as the utmost sea; and he hath so restrained him, that (except it be by faith) we know not whether there be any Devils yea, or no: for we never heard his noises, nor have seen his affrighting shapes.

XXVIII Sermons, 1651, p. 343

152. *The Limitations of Reason.*

WHO can tell why the Devil, who is a wise and intelligent creature, should so spitefully, and for no end but for mischief, tempt so many souls to ruine, when he knows it can doe him no good, no pleasure, but phantastick? or who can tell why he should be delighted in a pleasure that can be nothing but phantastick, when he knows things by *intuition*, not by *phantasm*, and hath no low conceit of things as we have? or why he should doe so many things against God, whom he knows he cannot hurt, and against souls, whose ruine cannot adde one moment of pleasure to him? and if it makes any change, it is infinitely to the worse: That these things are so, our Religion tels us; but our reason cannot reach it why it is so, or how: Whose reason can give an account why, or understand it to be reasonable, that God should permit evil for good ends, when he hates that evil, and can produce that good without that evil? and yet that he does so we are taught by our Religion: Whose reason can make it intelligible, that God who delights not in the death of a sinner, but he and his Christ, and all their Angels rejoyce infinitely in the salvation of a sinner, yet that he should not cause that every sinner should be saved, working in him a mighty and a prevailing grace, without which grace he shall not in the event of things be saved, and yet this grace is wholly his own production. . . . Why does not he work in us all to will and to doe, not onely that we can will, but that we shall will? for if the actual willing be any thing, it is his creation; we can create nothing, we cannot will unless he effect it in us, and why he does not doe that which so well pleases him, and for the want of the doing of which he is so displeased, and yet he alone is to doe it some way or other; humane reason cannot give a wise or a probable account. . . . Where is the wise Discourser, that can tell how it can be, that God foreknows certainly what I shall doe ten years hence, and yet it is free to me at that time, to will or not to will, to doe or not to doe that thing? Where is the discerning Searcher of secrets, that can give the reason why God should determine for so many ages before, that *Judas* should betray Christ, and yet that God should kill him eternally for effecting the Divine purpose, and fore-determined counsel? Well may we wonder that God should wash a soul with water, and with bread and wine nourish us up to immortality, and make real impresses upon our spirits by the bloud of the vine, and the kidneys of wheat; but who can tell why he should choose such mean instruments to effect such glorious promises? since even the greatest things of this world had not been disproportionable instruments to such effects, nor yet too great for our understanding; and that we are fain to stoop to make these mean elements be even with our faith, and with our understanding. Who can divine, and give us the cause, or understand the reason, why God should give us so great rewards for such nothings, and yet damne men for such insignificant mischiefs, for thoughts, for words, for secret wishes, that effect no evil abroad, but onely might have done, or it may be were resolved to be unactive? For if the goodness of God be so overflowing in some cases, we in our reason should not expect, that in such a great goodness, there should be so great an aptness to destroy men greatly for little things: and if all mankinde should joyn in search, it could never be told, why God should adjudge the Heathen or the Israelites to an eternal hell, of which he never gave them warning, nor created fears great enough, to produce caution equal to their danger; and who can give a reason why for temporal and transient actions of sin, the world is to expect never ceasing torments in hell to eternal ages? That these things are thus, we are taught in Scripture, but here our reason is not instructed to tell why or how; and therefore our reason is not the positive measure of mysteries, and we must beleeve what we cannot understand.

Thus are they to be blamed, who make intricacies and circles in mysterious articles, because they cannot wade thorough them; it is not to be understood why God should send his holy Son from his bosome to redeem us, to pay our price; nor to be told why God should exact a price of himself for his own creature; nor to be made intelligible to us, why he who loved us so well, as to send his Son to save us, should at the same time so hate us, as to resolve to damne us, unless his Son should come and save us. But the *Socinians* who conclude that this was not thus, because they know not how it can be thus, are highly to be reproved for their excess in the inquiries of reason, not where she is not a competent Judge, but where she is not competently instructed; and that is the second reason.

The reason of man is a right Judge always when she is truly informed; but in many things she knows nothing but the face of the article: the mysteries of faith are oftentimes like Cherubims heads placed over the Propitiatory, where you may see a clear and a bright face and golden wings, but there is no *body* to be handled; there is light and splendor upon the brow, but you may not grasp it; and though you see the revelation clear, and the article plain, yet the reason of it we cannot see at all; that is, the whole knowledge which we can have here is dark and obscure; *We see as in a glass darkly*, saith S. *Paul*, that is, we can see *what*, but not *why*, and what we doe see is the least part of that which does not appear; but in these cases our understanding is to submit, and wholly to be obedient, but not to inquire further.

Ductor Dubitantium, 1660, vol. i, p. 48

153. *The Atheist.*

WHO in the world is a verier fool, a more ignorant wretched person then he that is an Atheist? A man may better beleeve there is no such man as himself, and that he is not in being, then that there is no God: for himself can cease to be, and once was not, and shall be changed from what he is, and in very many periods of his life knowes not that he is; and so it is every night with him when he sleeps: but none of these can happen to God;

and if he knowes it not, he is a fool. Can any thing in this world be more foolish then to think that all this rare fabrick of heaven and earth can come by chance, when all the skill of art is not able to make an Oyster? To see rare effects and no cause; an excellent government and no Prince; a motion without an immovable; a circle without a centre; a time without eternity; a second without a first; a thing that begins not from it self, and therefore not to perceive there is something from whence it does begin, which must be without beginning; these things are so against Philosophy, and naturall reason, that he must needs be a beast in his understanding that does not assent to them. This is the Atheist: *the fool hath said in his heart, there is no God.* That's his character: the thing framed saies that nothing framed it; the tongue never made it self to speak, and yet talks against him that did; saying, that which is made, *is,* and that which made it, *is not.* But this folly is as infinite as hell, as much without light or bound, as the *Chaos* or the *primitive nothing.* But in this, the Devill never prevailed very farre; his Schooles were alwaies thin at these Lectures: some few people have been witty against God, that taught them to speak before they knew to spell a syllable; but either they are monsters in their manners, or mad in their understandings, or ever finde themselves confuted by a thunder or a plague, by danger or death.

But the Devill hath infinitely prevail'd in a thing that is almost as senselesse and ignorant as Atheisme, and that is *idolatry;* not only making *God after mans image,* but in the likenesse of a calf, of a cat, of a serpent; making men such fools as to worship a quartan ague, fire and water, onions and sheep. This is the skill man learned, and the Philosophy that he is taught by beleeving the Devill. What wisedome can there be in any man, that cals good evill, and evill good; to say *fire is cold*, and the *Sun black*, that fornication can make a man happy, or drunkennesse can make him wise? And this is the state of a sinner, of every one that delights in iniquity; he cannot be pleased with it if he thinks it evill; he cannot endure it, without beleeving this proposition, that *there is in drunkennesse, or lust, pleasure enough, good enough to make him amends for the intolerable pains of damnation.*

XXV Sermons, 1653, p. 262

154. *Secret Sins.*

LET the sick man in the scrutiny of his conscience and confession of his sins, be carefully reminded to consider those sins which are onely condemned *in the court of conscience*, and no where else. For there are certain secrecies and retirements, places of darknesse, and artificiall veils, with which the Devil uses to hide our sins from us, and to incorporate them into our affections by a constant uninterrupted practise, before they be prejudiced or discovered. 1. There are many sins which have reputation and are accounted honour, as *fighting a duel, answering a blow with a blow, carrying armies into a neighbour countrey, robbing with a navy, violently seizing upon a kingdom.* 2. Others are permitted by law; as *Usury* in all countreys; and because every excesse of it is a certain sin, the permission of so suspected a matter makes it ready for us, and instructs the temptation. 3. Some things are not forbidden by lawes, as *lying* in ordinary discourse, *jeering, scoffing, intemperate eating, ingratitude, selling too dear, circumventing another in contracts, importunate intreaties,* and *tempta-*

tion of persons to many instances of sin, pride, and ambition.
4. Some others do not reckon the sin against God, if the
lawes have seized upon the person; and many that are
imprisoned for debt, think themselves disobliged from pay-
ment; and when they pay the penalty, think they owe
nothing for the scandal and disobedience. 5. Some sins are
thought not considerable, but go under the title of sins of
infirmity, or inseparable accidents of mortality; such as
*idle thoughts, foolish talking, looser revellings, impatience,
anger,* and all the events of evil company. 6. Lastly, many
things are thought to be no sins; such as mispending of
their time, whole dayes or moneths of uselesse and impertinent imployment, long gaming, winning mens money in
greater portions, censuring mens actions, curiosity, æqui-
vocating in the prices and secrets of buying and selling,
rudenesse, speaking truths enviously, doing good to evil
purposes, and the like: Under the dark shadow of these
unhappy, and fruitlesse Yew-trees, the enemy of mankind
makes very many to lie hid from themselves, sewing before
their nakednesse the fig-leaves of popular and *idle reputation,* and *impunity, publike permission, a temporall penalty,
infirmity, prejudice,* and *direct errour in judgement,* and
ignorance.

Holy Dying, 1651, p. 262

155. *Life Shortened by Sin.*

SIN brought Death in first, and yet Man lived almost
a thousand yeers. But he sinned more, and then Death
came neerer to him; for when all the World was first
drownd in wickednesse, and then in water, GOD cut him
shorter by one half, and five hundred yeers was his ordinary
period. And Man sinned still, and had strange imagina-

tions, and built towers in the air, and then about *Pelegs* time GOD cut him shorter by one half yet, two hundred and odde yeers was his determination. And yet the generations of the World returned not unanimously to GOD, and GOD cut him off another half yet, and reduced him to one hundred twenty yeers. And by *Moses* time, one half of the final remanent portion was par'd away, reducing him to threescore yeers and ten. So that unlesse it be by special dispensation, Men live not beyond that term, or thereabout, but if GOD had gone on still in the same method, and shortned our dayes as we multiplyed our sins, we should have been but as an Ephemeron, Man should have lived the life of a Fly, or a Gourd, the morning should have seen his birth, his life have been the term of a day, and the evening must have provided him of a shroud.

The Great Exemplar, 1649, Pt. III, p. 21

156. *Dust and Ashes.*

IT will be very material to our best and noblest purposes, if we represent this scene of change and sorrow a little more dressed up in Circumstances, for so we shall be more apt to practice those Rules, the doctrine of which is consequent to this consideration. It is a mighty change that is made by the death of every person, and it is visible to us who are alive. Reckon but from the spritefulnesse of youth, and the fair cheeks and full eyes of childhood, from the vigorousnesse, and strong flexure of the joynts of five and twenty, to the hollownesse and dead palenesse, to the loathsomnesse and horrour of a three dayes burial, and we shall perceive the distance to be very great, and very strange. But so have I seen a Rose newly springing from the clefts of its hood, and at first it was fair as the Morning, and full with the dew of Heaven, as a Lambs fleece; but when a ruder breath had forced open its virgin modesty, and dismantled its too youthful and unripe retirements, it began to put on darknesse, and to decline to softnesse, and the symptomes of a sickly age; it bowed the head, and broke its stalk, and at night having lost some of its leaves, and all its beauty, it fell into the portion of weeds and outworn faces: The same is the portion of every man, and every woman; the heritage of worms and serpents, rottennesse and cold dishonour, and our beauty so changed that our acquaintance quickly knew us not, and that change mingled with so much horrour, or else meets so with our fears and weak discoursings, that they who six hours ago tended upon us, either with charitable or ambitious services cannot without some regret stay in the room alone where the body lies stripped of its life and Honour. I have read of a fair young German Gentleman, who living, often refused to be pictured, but put off the importunity of his friends desire, by giving way that after a few dayes burial they might send a painter to his vault, and if they saw cause for it, draw the image of *his death unto the life*. They did so, and found his face half eaten, and his midriffe and back bone full of serpents, and so he stands pictured among his armed Ancestours. So does the fairest beauty change, and it will be as bad with you and me; and then, what servants shall we have to wait upon us in the grave, what friends to visit us, what officious people to cleanse away the moist and unwholsom cloud reflected upon our faces from the sides of the weeping vaults, which are the longest weepers for our funeral.

This discourse will be useful, if we consider and practise by the following Rules and Considerations respectively.

All the Rich, and all the Covetous men in the world will perceive, and all the world will perceive for them, that it is but an ill recompence for all their cares, that by this time all that shall be left will be this, that the Neighbours shall say he died a rich man: and yet his wealth will not profit him in the grave, but hugely swell the sad accounts of Doomsday; And he that kills the Lords people with unjust or ambitious wars for an unrewarding interest, shall have this character, that he threw away all the dayes of his life, that one year might be reckoned with his Name, and computed by his reign, or consulship; and many men by great labors and affronts, many indignities and crimes labour onely for a pompous Epitaph, and a loud title upon their Marble; whilest those into whose possessions their heirs, or kinred are entred, are forgotten, and lye unregarded as their ashes, and without concernment or relation, as the turf upon the face of their grave. A man may read a sermon, the best and most passionate that ever men preached, if he shall but enter into the sepulchres of Kings. In the same Escurial where the Spanish Princes live in greatnesse and power, and decree war or peace, they have wisely placed a cœmeterie where their ashes and their glories shall sleep till time shall be no more: and where our Kings have been crowned, their Ancestours lay interred, and they must walk over their Grandsires head to take his crown. There is an acre sown with royal seed, the copy of the greatest change, from rich to naked, from cieled roofs to arched coffins, from *living like Gods* to *dye like Men*. There is enough to cool the flames of lust, to abate the heights of pride, to appease the itch of covetous desires, to sully and dash out the dissembling colours of a lustful, artificial, and imaginary beauty. There the warlike and

the peaceful, the fortunate and the miserable, the beloved
and the despised Princes mingle their dust, and pay down
their symbol of Mortality, and tell all the world, that when
we die, our ashes shall be equal to Kings, and our accounts
easier, and our pains or our crowns shall be lesse. To my
apprehension it is a sad record which is left by *Athenæus*
concerning *Ninus* the great Assyrian Monarch, whose life
and death is summed up in these words: '*Ninus* the Assyrian had an Ocean of gold, and other riches more then
the sand in the Caspian sea: he never saw the stars, and
perhaps he never desired it; he never stirred up the holy
fire among the *Magi*, nor touched his God with the sacred
rod according to the Laws; he never offered sacrifice nor
worshipped the Deity, nor administred justice, nor spake
to his people, nor numbred them; but he was most valiant
to eat and drink, and having mingled his wines he threw
the rest upon the stones: This man is dead; Behold his
Sepulchre, and now hear where *Ninus* is. Some times I
was *Ninus*, and drew the breath of a living man, but now
am nothing but clay. I have nothing, but what I did eat,
and what I served to my self in lust [that was and is all
my portion;] the wealth with which I was [esteemed]
blessed, my enemies meeting together shall bear away, as
the mad *Thyades* carry a raw Goat. I am gone to Hell,
and when I went thither, I neither carried Gold, nor
Horse, nor silver Chariot. I that wore a Miter, am now
a little heap of dust.' I know not any thing that can
better represent the evil condition of a wicked man, or
a changing greatnesse. From the greatest secular dignity
to dust, and ashes, his nature bears him; and from thence
to Hell his sins carry him, and there he shall be for ever
under the dominion of chains and devils, wrath, and an

intollerable calamity. This is the reward of an unsancti-
fied condition, and a greatnesse ill gotten, or ill administred.

Let no man extend *his thoughts*, or let *his hopes* wander
towards future and far distant events and accidental contingencies. This day is mine and yours, but *ye know not
what shall be on the morrow*: and every morning creeps out
of a dark cloud, leaving behinde it an ignorance and silence
deep as midnight and undiscerned as are the phantasms
that make a Chrysome childe to smile: so that we cannot
discern what comes hereafter, unlesse we had a light from
Heaven, brighter then the vision of an Angel, even the
Spirit of Prophesie. Without revelation we cannot tell
whether we shal eat to morrow, or whether a Squinzy shall
choak us: and it is written in the unrevealed folds of Divine
Predestination, that many who are this day alive, shall to
morrow be laid upon the cold earth, and the women shall
weep over their shrowd, and dresse them for their funeral.

Holy Dying, 1651, p. 10

157. *Mortality.*

WE are as water spilt on the ground, which cannot be
gathered up again. Stay. We are as water, weak and
of no consistence, alwaies descending, abiding in no certain
place, unlesse where we are detained with violence: and
every little breath of winde makes us rough and tempestuous, and troubles our faces: every trifling accident
discomposes us; and as the face of the waters wafting in
a storm so wrinkles it self that it makes upon its forehead
furrows deep, and hollow like a grave: so doe our great
and little cares and trifles, first make the wrinkles of old
age, and then they dig a grave for us: And there is in
nature nothing so contemptible, but it may meet with us

in such circumstances, that it may be too hard for us in our weaknesses: and the sting of a Bee is a weapon sharp enough to pierce the finger of a childe, or the lip of a man: and those creatures which nature hath left without weapons, yet they are arm'd sufficiently to vex those parts of men which are left defenselesse and obnoxious to a sun beame, to the roughness of a sowre grape, to the unevenness of a gravel-stone, to the dust of a wheel, or the unwholsome breath of a starre looking awry upon a sinner.

But besides the weaknesses and naturall decayings of our bodies, if chances and contingencies be innumerable, then no man can reckon our dangers, and the præternaturall causes of our deaths. So that he is a vain person whose hopes of life are too confidently increased by reason of his health: and he is too unreasonably timorous, who thinks his hopes at an end when he dwels in sicknesse. For men die without rule; and with, and without occasions; and no man suspecting or foreseeing any of deaths addresses, and no man in his whole condition is weaker then another. A man in a long Consumption is fallen under one of the solemnities and preparations to death: but at the same instant the most healthfull person is as neer death, upon a more fatall, and a more sudden, but a lesse discerned cause. There are but few persons upon whose foreheads every man can read the sentence of death written in the lines of a lingring sicknesse, but they (sometimes) hear the passing bell ring for stronger men, even long before their own knell cals at the house of their mother to open her womb and make a bed for them. No man is surer of to morrow then the weakest of his brethren: and when *Lepidus* and *Aufidius* stumbled at the threshold of the Senate and fell down and dyed, the blow came from heaven in a cloud but it struck more suddenly then upon the poor slave that made sport upon the Theatre with a præmeditated and foredescribed death: *Quod quisque vitet, nunquam homini satis cautum est in horas.* There are sicknesses that walk in darknesse, and there are exterminating Angels that fly wrapt up in the curtains of immateriality and an uncommunicating nature; whom we cannot see, but we feel their force and sink under their sword, and from heaven the vail descends that wraps our heads in the fatall sentence. There is no age of man but it hath proper to it self some posterns and outlets for death, besides those infinite and open ports out of which myriads of men and women every day passe into the dark and the land of forgetfulnesse. *Infancie* hath life but *in effigie*, or like a spark dwelling in a pile of wood: the candle is so newly lighted, that every little shaking of the taper, and every ruder breath of air, puts it out, and it dies. . . .

In all the processe of our health we are running to our grave: we open our own sluces by vitiousness and unworthy actions; we powre in drink, and let out life; we increase diseases and know not how to bear them; we strangle our selves with our own intemperance; we suffer the feavers and the inflammations of lust, and we quench our soules with drunkennesse; we bury our understandings in loads of meat and surfets: and then we lie down upon our beds and roar with pain and disquietness of our soules: Nay, we kill one anothers souls and bodies with violence and folly, with the effects of pride and uncharitablenesse; we live and die like fools, and bring a *new mortality* upon our selves; wars and vexatious cares, and private duels, and publike disorders, and every thing that is unreasonable, and every thing that is violent: so that now we may adde this fourth gate to the grave: Besides *Nature* and *Chance*, and *the mistakes of art*, men die with their *own sins*, and then enter into the grave in haste and passion and pull the heavy stone of the monument upon their own heads. And thus we make our selves like water spilt on the ground: we throw away our lives as if they were unprofitable, (and indeed most men make them so) we let our years slip through our fingers like water; and nothing is to be seen, but like a showr of tears upon a spot of ground; there is a grave digged, and a solemn mourning and a great talk in the neighbourhood, and when the daies are finished, they shall be, and they shall be remembred, no more: And that 's like water too, when it is spilt, *it cannot be gathered up again*.

There is no redemption from the grave.

—— *inter se mortales mutua vivunt*
Et quasi cursores vitai lampada tradunt.

Men live in their course and by turns: their light burns a while, and then it burns blew and faint, and men go to converse with Spirits, and then they reach the taper to another; and as the hours of yesterday can never return again, so neither can the man whose hours they were, and who lived them over once, he shall never come to live them again, and live them better. . . .

The godly also come under the sense of these words. They descend into their graves, and shall no more be reckoned among the living; they have no concernment in all that is done under the sun. *Agamemnon* hath no more to do with the Turks armies invading and possessing that part of Greece where he reigned, then had the Hippocentaur, who never had a beeing: and *Cicero* hath no more interest in the present evils of Christendome, then we have to doe with his boasted discovery of *Catilines* conspiracie. What is it to me that Rome was taken by the Gaules? and what is it now to *Camillus* if different religions be tolerated amongst us? These things that now happen concern the living, and they are made the scenes of our duty or danger respectively: and when our wives are dead and sleep in charnel houses, they are not troubled when we laugh loudly at the songs sung at the next marriage feast; nor do they envy when another snatches away the gleanings of their husbands passion. . . .

But we are not yet passed the consideration of the sentence: This descending to the grave is the lot of all men, [*neither doth God respect the person of any man*] The rich is not protected for favour, nor the poor for pity, the old man is not reverenced for his age, nor the infant regarded for his tenderness; youth and beauty, learning and prudence, wit and strength lie down equally in the dishonours of the grave. All men, and all natures, and all persons resist the addresses and solennities of death, and strive to preserve a miserable and an unpleasant life; and yet they all sink down and die. For so have I seen the pillars of a building assisted with artificiall props bending under the pressure of a roof, and pertinaciously resisting the infallible and prepared ruine,

> *Donec certa dies omni compage solutâ*
> *Ipsum cum rebus subruat auxilium,*

till the determin'd day comes, and then the burden sunk upon the pillars, and disorder'd the aides and auxiliary rafters into a common ruine and a ruder grave: so are the desires and weak arts of man, with little aides and assistances of care and physick we strive to support our decaying bodies, and to put off the evil day; but quickly that day will come, and then neither Angels nor men can rescue us from our grave; but the roof sinks down upon the walls, and the walls descend to the foundation; and the beauty of the face, and the dishonours of the belly, the discerning head and the servile feet, the thinking heart and the working hand, the eyes and the guts together shall be crush'd into the confusion of a heap, and dwell with creatures of an equivocall production, with worms and serpents, the sons and daughters of our own bones, in a house of durt and darkness.

Funeral Sermon for Lady Carbery, 1650, pp. 3, 7, 11, 13

158. *The Reign of Death.*

A MAN is a Bubble (said the Greek Proverb); which Lucian represents with advantages and its proper circumstances, to this purpose; saying, that all the world is a storm, and Men rise up in their several generations like bubbles descending *à Jove pluvio*, from God, and the dew of Heaven, from a tear and drop of Man, from Nature and Providence: and some of these instantly sink into the deluge of their first parent, and are hidden in a sheet of Water, having had no other businesse in the world, but to be born that they might be able to die: others float up and down two or three turns, and suddenly disappear and give their place to others: and they that live longest upon the face of the waters are in perpetual motion, restlesse and uneasy, and being crushed with the great drop of a cloud sink into flatness and a froth; the change not being great, it being hardly possible it should be more a nothing then it was before. So is every man: He is born in vanity and sin; he comes into the world like morning Mushromes, soon thrusting up their heads into the air and conversing with their kinred of the same production, and as soon they turn into dust and forgetfulnesse; some of them without any other interest in the affairs of the world, but that they made their parents a little glad, and very sorrowful: others ride longer in the storm; it may be until seven yeers of Vanity be expired, and then peradventure the Sun shines hot upon their heads and they fall into the shades below, into the cover of death, and darknesse of the grave to hide them. But if the bubble stands the shock of a bigger drop, and outlives the chances of a childe, of a carelesse Nurse, of drowning in a pail of water, of being overlaid by a sleepy servant, or such little accidents, then the young man dances like a bubble, empty and gay, and shines like a Doves neck or the image of a rainbow, which hath no substance, and whose very imagery and colours are phantastical; and so he dances out the gayety of his youth, and is all the while in a storm, and endures, onely because he is not knocked on the head by a drop of bigger rain, or crushed by the pressure of a load of indigested meat, or quenched by the disorder of an ill placed humor: and to preserve a man alive in the midst of so many chances, and hostilities, is as great a miracle as to create him; to preserve him from rushing into nothing and at first to draw him up from nothing were equally the issues of an Almighty power. And therefore the wise men of the world have contended who shall best fit mans condition with words signifying his vanity and short abode. *Homer* cals a man *a leaf*, the smallest, the weakest piece of a short liv'd, unsteady plant. *Pindar* calls him *the dream of a shadow*: Another, *the dream of the shadow of smoak*. But S. *James* spake by a more excellent Spirit, saying, *Our life is but a vapor, viz.* drawn from the earth by a cœlestial influence; made of smoak, or the lighter parts of water, tossed with every winde, moved by the motion of a superiour body, without vertue in it self, lifted up on high, or left below, according as it pleases the Sun its Foster-father. But it is lighter yet. It is but *appearing*. A phantastic vapor, an apparition, nothing real; it is not so much as a mist, not the matter of a shower, nor substantial enough to make a cloud; but it is like *Cassiopeia's* chair, or *Pelops* shoulder, or the circles of Heaven, φαινόμενα, for which you cannot have a word that can signify a veryer nothing. And yet the expression is one degree more made diminutive: *A vapor*, and *phantastical*, or *a meer appearance*, and this but *for a little while* neither: the very dream, the phantasm disappears in a small time, *like the shadow that departeth*, or *like a tale that is told*, or *as a dream when one awaketh*: A man is so vain, so unfixed, so perishing a creature, that he cannot long last in the scene of fancy: a man goes off and is forgotten like the dream of a distracted person. The summe of all is this: *That thou art a man*, then whom there is not in the world any greater instance of heights and declensions, of lights and shadows, of misery and folly, of laughter and tears, of groans and death.

And because this consideration is of great usefulnesse and great necessity to many purposes of wisdom and the Spirit; all the succession of time, all the changes in nature, all the varieties of light and darknesse, the thousand thousands of accidents in the world, and every contingency to every man, and to every creature does preach our funeral sermon, and calls us to look, and see, how the old Sexton *Time* throws up the earth, and digs a Grave where we must lay our sins, or our sorrows, and sowe our bodies till they rise again in a fair, or in an intolerable eternity. Every revolution which the sun makes about the world, divides between life and death; and death possesses both those portions by the next morrow, and we are dead to all those moneths which we have already lived, and we shall never live them over again: and still God makes little periods of our age. First we change our world, when we come from the womb to feel the warmth of the sun: Then we sleep and enter into the image of death, in which state we are unconcerned in all the changes of the world; and if our Mothers, or our Nurses die, or a wilde boar destroy our vineyards, or our King be sick, we regard it not, but, during that state, are as disinterest, as if our eyes were closed with the clay that weeps in the bowels of the earth. At the end of seven years, our teeth fall and dye before us, representing a formal prologue to the Tragedie; and still every seven year it is oddes but we shall finish the last scene: and when Nature, or Chance, or Vice takes our body in pieces, weakening some parts, and loosing others, *we taste the grave* and the solennities of our own Funerals, first in those parts that ministred to Vice, and next in them that served for Ornament; and in a short time even they that served for necessity become uselesse, and intangled like the wheels of a broken clock. *Baldnesse* is but a dressing to our funerals, the proper ornament of mourning, and of a person entred very far into the regions and possession of Death: And we have many more of the same signification: Gray hairs, rotten teeth, dim eyes, trembling joynts, short breath, stiffe limbs, wrinkled skin, short memory, decayed appetite. Every dayes necessity calls for a reparation of that portion which death fed on all night when we lay in his lap, and slept in his outer chambers: The very spirits of a man prey upon the daily portion of bread and flesh, and every meal is a rescue from one death, and layes up for another; and while we think a thought, we die; and the clock strikes, and reckons on our portion of Eternity; we form our words with the breath of our nostrils, we have the lesse to live upon, for every word we speak.

Thus Nature calls us to meditate of death by those things which are the instruments of acting it; and God by all the variety of his Providence, makes us see death every where, in all variety of circumstances, and dressed up for all the fancies, and the expectation of every single person. Nature hath given us one harvest every year, but death hath two: and the Spring and the Autumn send throngs of Men and Women to charnel houses; and all the Summer long men are recovering from their evils of the Spring, till the dog dayes come, and then the Syrian star makes the summer deadly; And the fruits of Autumn are laid up for all the years provision, and the man that gathers them eats and surfets, and dies and needs them not, and himself is laid up for Eternity; and he that escapes till winter, only stayes for another opportunity, which the distempers of that quarter minister to him with great variety. Thus death reigns in all the portions of our time. The Autumn with its fruits provides disorders for us: and the Winters cold turns them into sharp diseases, and the Spring brings flowers to strew our herse, and the Summer gives green turfe and brambles to binde upon our graves. Calentures, and Surfet, Cold, and Agues, are the four quarters of the year, and all minister to Death; and you can go no whither, but you tread upon a dead mans bones.

The wilde fellow in *Petronius* that escaped upon a broken table from the furies of a shipwrack, as he was sunning himself upon the rocky shore espied a man rolled upon his floating bed of waves, ballasted with sand in the folds of his garment, and carried by his civil enemy the sea towards the shore to fine a grave; and it cast him into some sad thoughts: that peradventure this mans wife in some part of the Continent, safe and warme looks next moneth for the good mans return; or it may be his son knows nothing of the tempest; or his father thinks of that affectionate kiss which still is warm upon the good old mans cheek ever since he took a kinde farewel; and he weeps with joy to think how blessed he shall be when his beloved boy returns into the circle of his Fathers arms. These are the thoughts of mortals, this is the end and sum of all their designes: a dark night, and an ill Guide, a boysterous sea, and a broken Cable, a hard rock, and a rough winde dash'd in pieces the fortune of a whole family, and they that shall weep loudest for the accident, are not yet entred into the storm, and yet have suffered shipwrack. Then looking upon the carkasse, he knew it, and found it to be the Master of the ship, who the day before cast up the accounts of his patrimony and his trade, and named the day, when he thought to be at home: see how the man swims who was so angry two dayes since; his passions are becalm'd with the storm, his accounts cast up, his cares at an end, his voyage done, and his gains are the strange events of death, which whither they be good or evil, the men that are alive, seldom trouble themselves concerning the interest of the dead.

Holy Dying, 1651, p. 1

159. *Dying Daily.*

AND indeed since all our life we are dying, and this minute, in which I now write, death divides with me, and hath got the surer part, and more certain possession, it is but reasonable, that we should alwayes be doing the offices of preparation. If to day we were not dying and passing on to our grave, then we might with more safety defer our work till the morrow; but as fuel in a furnace in every degree of its heat, and reception of the flame is converting into fire and ashes, and the disposing it to the last mutation is the same work with the last instant of its change: so is the age of every day a beginning of death, and the night composing us to sleep bids us go to our lesser rest; because that night, which is the end of the preceding day is but a lesser death; and whereas now we have dyed so many dayes, the last day of our life is but the dying so many more, and when that last day of dying will come, we know not. There is nothing then added but the circumstance of sicknesse, which also happens many times before; onely men are pleased to call that, *death*, which is the end of dying, when we cease to dye any more: and therefore to put off our preparation till that which we call death, is to put off the work of all our life, till the time comes, in which it is to cease and determine. . . .

For since G O D hath not told us we shall not die suddenly, is it not certain he intended we should prepare for sudden death, as well as against death clothed in any other circumstances? *Fabius* sirnamed the Painter was choaked with a hair in a messe of milk, *Anacreon* with a raisin, Cardinall *Colonna* with figs crusted with ice, *Adrian* the fourth with a flye, *Drusus Pompeivs* with a peare, *Domitius*

Afer Quintilians Tutour with a full cuppe, *Casimire* the second, King of Polonia with a little draught of wine, *Amurath* with a full goblet, *Tarquinius Priscus* with a fish-bone. For as soon as a man is born, that which in nature onely remains to him, is to die, and if we differ in the way or time of our abode, or the manner of our exit, yet we are even at last, and since it is not determined by a naturall cause, which way we shall goe, or at what age; a wise man will suppose himself alwayes upon his death-bed; and such supposition is like making of his will, he is not the neerer death for doing it, but he is the readier for it when it comes.

S. *Jerome* said well; *He deserves not the name of a Christian, who will live in that state of life, in which he will not die.* And indeed it is a great venture to be in an evil state of life; because every minute of it hath a danger; and therefore a succession of actions, in every one of which he may as well perish as escape, is a boldnesse, that hath no mixture of wisdom or probable venture. How many persons have dyed in the midst of an act of sport, or at a merry meeting? *Grimoaldus* a Lombard King dyed with shooting of a Pigeon: *Thales* the Milesian in the Theatre; *Lucia* the sister of *Aurelius* the Emperour playing with her little son was wounded in her breast with a Needle and dyed: *Benno* Bishop of Adelburg, with great ceremony and joy consecrating S. *Michaels* Church, was crowded to death by the people; so was the Duke of Saxony at the inauguration of *Albert I.* The great Lawyer *Baldus* playing with a little Dog was bitten upon the lip, instantly grew mad and perished: *Charles* the eighth of France seeing certain Gentlemen playing at Teniscourt, swooned and recovered not. *Henry II.* was killed running at Tilt: *Ludovicus*

Borgia with riding the great Horse. And the old *Syracusan Archimedes* was slain by a rude Souldier, as he was making Diagrams in the sand, which was his greatest pleasure. How many Men have dyed laughing, or in the extasies of a great joy? *Philippides* the Comedian, and *Dionysius* the Tyrant of Sicily, died with joy at the news of a victory. *Diagoras* of Rhodes, and *Chilon* the Philosopher, expired in the embraces of their sons crowned with an Olympick Lawrel. *Polycrita Naxia* being saluted the Saviouresse of her countrey; *Marcus Juventius* when the Senate decreed him honours; the Emperour *Conrade* the second, when he triumphed after the conquest of Italy, had a joy bigger then their heart, and their phansie swell'd it, till they burst and dyed. Death can enter in at any door: *Philistion* of Nice dyed with excessive laughter, so did the Poet *Philemon*, being provoked to it onely by seeing an Asse eat figs.

The Great Exemplar, 1649, Pt. III, p. 141

160. *Death.*

IT is a thing that every one suffers, even persons of the lowest resolution, of the meanest vertue, of no breeding, of no discourse. Take away but the pomps of death, the disguises and solemn bug-bears, the tinsell, and the actings by candle-light, and proper and phantastic ceremonies, the minstrels and the noise-makers, the women and the weepers, the swoonings and the shrikings, the Nurses and the Physicians, the dark room and the Ministers, the Kin-red and the Watchers, and then to die is easie, ready and quitted from its troublesome circumstances. It is the same harmelesse thing, that a poor shepherd suffered yesterday, or a maid servant to day; and at the same time in which you die, in that very night, a thousand creatures die with you, some wise men, and many fools; and the wisdom of the first will not quit him, and the folly of the latter does not make him unable to die.

Holy Dying, 1651, p. 131

161. *The Death of a Good Man.*

FOR the death of the righteous is like the descending of ripe and wholesome fruits from a pleasant and florid tree; our senses intire, our limbs unbroken, without horrid tortures, after provision made for our children, with a blessing entail'd upon posterity, in the presence of our Friends, our deerest relative closing up our eyes, and binding our feet, leaving a good name behinde us. O let my soul dye such a death; for this, in whole or in part, according as GOD sees it good, is the manner that the righteous dye.

The Great Exemplar, 1649, Pt. III, p. 18

162. *Postponing Death.*

THERE is nothing which can make sicknesse unsancti-fied, but the same also will give us cause to fear death. If therefore we so order our affairs and spirits, that we do not fear death, our sickness may easily become our advantage, and we can then receive counsel, and consider, and do those acts of vertue, which are in that state the proper services of God: and such which men in bondage and fear are not capable of doing, or of advices how they should, when they come to the appointed dayes of mourning. And indeed if men would but place their designe of being happy in the noblenesse, courage and perfect resolutions of doing handsome things, and passing thorough our unavoidable

necessities; in the contempt and despite of the things of
this world, and in holy living, and the perfective desires
of our natures, the longings and pursuances after Heaven,
it is certain they could not be made miserable by chance
and change, by sicknesse and death. But we are so softned
and made effeminate with delicate thoughts and meditations of ease, and brutish satisfactions, that if our death
comes before we have seized upon a great-fortune, or enjoy
the promises of the fortune tellers, we esteem our selves
to be robbed of our goods, to be mocked, and miserable.
Hence it comes that men are impatient of the thoughts of
death; hence comes those arts of protraction and delaying
the significations of old age; thinking to deceive the world
men cosen themselves, and by representing themselves
youthfull, they certainly continue their vanity, till *Proserpina* pull the perruke from their heads. We cannot deceive
God and nature; for a coffin is a coffin, though it be
covered with a pompous veil; and the minutes of our time
strike on, and are counted by Angels, till the period comes
which must cause the passing bell to give warning to all
the neighbours that thou art dead, and they must be so:
and nothing can excuse or retard this: and if our death
could be put off a little longer, what advantage can it be
in thy accounts of nature or felicity? They that 3000 years
agone dyed unwillingly, and stopped death two dayes, or
staid it a week, what is their gain? *where is that week?* and
poor spirited men use arts of protraction, and make their
persons pitiable, but their condition contemptible; beeing
like the poor sinners at *Noahs* flood; the waters drove them
out of their lower rooms, then they crept up to the roof,
having lasted half a day longer: and then they knew not
how to get down: some crept upon the top branch of a

tree, and some climbed up to a mountain, and staid it may
be three dayes longer; but all that while they endured a
worse torment then death; they lived with amazement,
and were distracted with the ruines of mankinde, and the
horrour of an universal deluge.

Holy Dying, 1651, p. 125

163. *He Descended into Hell.*

BUT now it was that in the darke and undiscernd mansions, there was a scene of the greatest joy and the
greatest horrour represented, which yet was known since
the first falling of the morning starres. Those holy soules,
whom the Prophet *Zechary* calls, *prisoners of hope lying in
the lake where there is no water,* that is, no constant streame
of joy to refresh their present condition: but they were
supported with certain showres and gracious visitations
from GOD, and illuminations of their hope; and now that
they saw their Redeemer come to change their condition,
and to improve it into the neighbourhoods of glory and
cleerer revelations, must needs have the joy of intelligent
and beatified understandings of redeemed captives, of men
forgiven after the sentence of death, of men satisfied after
a tedious expectation, enjoying and seeing their LORD,
whom for so many ages they had expected. But the accursed spirits seeing the darknesse of their prison shine
with a new light, and their Empire invaded, and their
retirements of horror discovered, wondered how a man
durst venture thither, or if he were a GOD, how he should
come to dye.

The Great Exemplar, 1649, Pt. III, p. 174

164. *Life after Death.*

IF thou wilt be fearlesse of death, endeavour to be in love with the felicities of Saints and Angels: and be once perswaded to believe that there is a condition of living better then this; that there are creatures more noble then we; that above there is a countrey better then ours; that the inhabitants know more and know better; and are in places of rest and desire: and first learn to value it, and then learn to purchase it; and death cannot be a formidable thing, which lets us into so much joy & so much felicity. And indeed who would not think his condition mended if he passed from conversing with dull mortals, with ignorant and foolish persons, with Tyrants and enemies of learning, to converse with *Homer* and *Plato*, with *Socrates* and *Cicero*, with *Plutarch* and *Fabricius*? So the Heathens speculated: but we consider higher. The *dead that die in the Lord* shall converse with S. *Paul*, and all the Colledge of the Apostles, and all the Saints and Martyrs; with all the good men whose memory we preserve in honour: with excellent Kings and holy Bishops, and with *the great Shepherd and Bishop of our souls Jesus Christ*, and with God himself. For *Christ dyed for us, that whether we wake or sleep we might live together with him.* Then we shall be free from lust and envy, from fear and rage, from covetousnesse and sorrow, from tears and cowardice; and these indeed properly are the onely evils that are contrary to felicity and wisdom. Then we shall see strange things and know new propositions, and all things in another manner, and to higher purposes. *Cleombrotus* was so taken with this speculation, that having learned from *Plato's Phædon* the souls abode, he had not patience to stay natures dull leisure, but leapt from a wall to his portion of immortality. And when *Pomponius Atticus* resolved to die by famine, to ease the great pains of his gout, in the abstinence of two dayes found his foot at ease: But when he began to feel the pleasures of an approaching death, and the delicacies of that ease he was to inherit below, he would not withdraw his foot, but went on and finished his death; and so did *Cleanthes*; and every wise man will despise the little evils of that state, which indeed is *the daughter of fear*, but *the mother of rest*, and *peace*, and *felicity*.

If God should say to us, Cast thy self into the Sea (as Christ did to S. *Peter*, or as God concerning *Jonas*) I have provided for thee a Dolphin, or a Whale, or a Port, a safety or a deliverance, security or a reward, were we not incredulous and pusillanimous persons if we should tremble to put such a felicity into act, and our selves into possession? The very duty of resignation, and the love of our own interest are good antidotes against fear. In fourty or fifty years we finde evils enough, and arguments enough to make us weary of this life: And to a good man there are very many more reasons to be afraid of life then death, this having in it lesse of evil and more of advantage. And it was a rare wish of that Roman, that death might come onely to wise and excellent persons, and not to fools and cowards, that it might not be a sanctuary for the timerous, but the reward of the vertuous; and indeed they onely can make advantage of it.

Make no excuses to make thy desires of life seem reasonable; neither cover thy fear and pretences, but suppresse it rather, with arts of severity and ingenuity. Some are not willing to submit to Gods sentence and arrest of death, till they have finished such a designe, or made an end of the last paragraph of their book, or raised such portions for their children, or preached so many sermons, or built their house, or planted their orchard, or ordered their estate with such advantages; It is well for the modesty of these men that the excuse is ready; but if it were not, it is certain they would search one out: for an idle man is never ready to die, and is glad of any excuse; and a busied man hath alwayes something unfinished, and he is ready for every thing but death: and I remember that *Petronius* brings in *Eumolpus* composing verses in a desperate storm, and being called upon to shift for himself when the ship dashed upon the rock, cried out to let him alone till he had finished and trimmed his verse, which was lame in the hinder leg; the man either had too strong a desire to end his verse, or too great a desire not to end his life. But we must know Gods times are not to be measured by our circumstances; and what I value, God regards not, or if it be valuable in the accounts of men, yet God will supply it with other contingencies of his providence: and if *Epaphroditus* had died when he had his great sicknesse S. *Paul* speaks of, God would have secured the work of the Gospel without him, and he could have spared *Epaphroditus* as well as S. *Stephen*, and S. *Peter*, as well as S. *James*: Say no more, but when God calls, lay aside thy papers and first dresse thy soul, and then dresse thy hearse.

Blindnesse is odious, and widow-hood is sad, and destitution is without comfort, and persecution is full of trouble, and famine is intolerable, and tears are the sad ease of a sadder heart; but these are evils of our life, not of our death. For *the dead that die in the Lord* are so farre from

wanting the commodities of this life, that they do not
want life it self.

Holy Dying, 1651, p. 137

165. *Antepasts of Heaven.*

A MAN that hath tasted of Gods Spirit can instantly
discern the madnesse that is in rage, the folly and the
disease that is in envy, the anguish and tediousnesse that
is in lust, the dishonor that is in breaking our faith, and
telling a lie; and understands things truly as they are; that
is, that charity is the greatest noblenesse in the world;
that religion hath in it the greatest pleasures; that temperance is the best security of health; that humility is the
surest way to honour; and all these relishes are nothing
but antepasts of heaven, where the quintessence of all these
pleasures shall be swallowed for ever; where the chast shall
follow the Lamb, and the virgins sing there where the
Mother of God shall reign; and the zealous converters of
souls, and labourers in Gods vineyard shall worship eternally where S. Peter and S. Paul do wear their *crown of
righteousnesse*; and the patient persons shall be rewarded
with Job, and the meek persons with Christ and Moses,
and all with God; the very expectation of which proceeding from a hope begotten in us by *the spirit of mani-
festation*, and bred up and strengthened by *the spirit of
obsignation* is so delicious an entertainment of all our
reasonable appetites, that a spirituall man can no more be
removed, or intic'd from the love of God, and of religion,
then the Moon from her Orb, or a Mother from loving
the son of her joyes, and of her sorrows.

XXVIII Sermons, 1651, p. 8

166. *Christ's Kingdom.*

CHRISTS Kingdome being in order to the Kingdome of his Father, which shall be manifest at the day of Judgement, must therefore be spirituall, because then it is, that all things must become spirituall, not only by way of eminency, but by intire constitution and perfect change of natures. Men shall be like Angels, and Angels shall be comprehended in the lap of spirituall and eternall felicities; the soul shall not understand by materiall phantasmes, neither be served by the provisions of the body, but the body it self shall become spirituall, and the eye shall see intellectuall objects, and the mouth shall feed upon hymns and glorifications of God; the belly shall be then satisfied by the fulnesse of righteousnesse, and the tongue shall speak nothing but praises, and the propositions of a celestiall wisdome; the motion shall be the swiftnesse of an Angell; and it shall be cloathed with white as with a garment: Holinesse is the Sun, and righteousnesse is the Moon in that region; our society shall be Quires of singers, and our conversation wonder; contemplation shall be our food, and love shall be *the wine of elect souls*; and as to every naturall appetite there is now proportion'd an object, crasse, materiall, unsatisfying, and allayed with sorrow and uneasinesse: so there be new capacities and equall objects, the desires shall be fruition, and the appetite shall not suppose want, but a faculty of delight, and an unmeasureable complacency: the will and the understanding, love and wonder, joyes every day and the same forever; this shall be their state who shall be accounted worthy of the resurrection to this life; where the body shall be a partner, but no servant; where it shall have no work of its own, but it shall rejoyce with the soul; where the soul shall rule without resistance, or an enemy, and we shall be fitted to enjoy God who is the Lord and Father of spirits. In this world we see it is quite contrary: we long for perishing meat, and fill our stomachs with corruption; we look after white and red, and the weaker beauties of the night; we are passionate after rings and seals, and inraged at the breaking of a Crystall; we delight in the society of fools and weak persons; we laugh at sin, and contrive mischiefs; and the body rebels against the soul, and carries the cause against all its just pretences; and our soul it self is above half of it earth, and stone in its affections, and distempers; our hearts are hard, and inflexible to the softer whispers of mercy and compassion, having no loves for any thing but strange flesh, and heaps of money, and popular noises, for misery and folly; and therefore we are a huge way off from the Kingdome of God, whose excellencies, whose designs, whose ends, whose constitution is spirituall and holy, and separate, and sublime, and perfect.

XXV Sermons, 1653, p. 152

167. *An Abiding City.*

SINCE we stay not here, being people but of a dayes abode, and our age is like that of a flie, and contemporary with a gourd, we must look some where else for an abiding city, a place in another countrey to fix our house in, whose walls and foundation is God, where we must finde rest, or else be restlesse for ever. For whatsoever ease we can have or fancy here is shortly to be changed into sadnesse, or tediousnesse: it goes away too soon like the periods of our life; or stayes too long, like the sorrows of a sinner: its own wearinesse or a contrary disturbance is its load; or it is eased by its revolution into vanity & forgetfulness; and where either there is sorrow or an end of joy, there can be no true felicity: which because it must be had by some instrument, and in some period of our duration, we must carry up our affections to the mansions prepared for us above, where eternity is the measure, felicity is their state, Angels are the Company, the Lamb is the light, and God is the portion, and inheritance.

Holy Dying, 1651, p. 20

168. *Heaven.*

I BELIEVE that they who have their part in this Resurrection, shall meet the Lord in the Air, and when the blessed Sentence is pronounc'd upon them, they shall for ever be with the Lord in joys unspeakable and full of glory: God shall wipe all tears from their eyes; there shall be no fear or sorrow, no mourning or death, a friend shall never go away from thence, and an enemy shall never enter; there shall be fulness without want, light eternal brighter then the Sun; day, and no night; joy, and no weeping; difference in degree, and yet all full; there is *love without dissimulation*, excellency without envy, multitudes without confusion, musick without discord; there the Understandings are rich, the Will is satisfied, the Affections are all love, and all joy, and they shall reign with God and Christ for ever and ever.

The Golden Grove, 1655, p. 41

169. *The Sinner's Resurrection.*

AS for the recalling the wicked from their graves, it is no otherwise in the sense of the Spirit to be called a Resurrection, then taking a Criminal from the Prison to the Bar is a giving of liberty. When poor *Attilius Aviola* had been seized on by an Apoplexy, his friends supposing him dead carried him to his Funeral pile; but when the fire began to approach, and the heat to warm the body, he reviv'd, and seeing himself incircled with Funeral flames, call'd out aloud to his friends to rescue, not the dead, but *the living* Aviola *from that horrid burning. But it could not be. He onely was restor'd from his sickness to fall into death, and from his dull disease to a sharp and intolerable torment.* Just so shall the wicked live again; they shall receive their souls, that they may be a portion for Devils; they shall receive their bodies that they may feel the everlasting burning; they shall see Christ, that they may *look on him whom they have pierced*; and they shall hear the voice of God passing upon them the intolerable sentence; they shall come from their graves, that they may go into hell; and live again, that they may die for ever. So have we seen a poor condemned Criminal, the weight of whose sorrows sitting heavily upon his soul hath benummed him into a deep sleep, till he hath forgotten his grones, and laid aside his deep sighings; but on a sudden comes the messenger of death, and unbinds the Poppy garland, scatters the heavy cloud that incircled his miserable head, and makes him return to acts of life, that he may quickly descend into death and be no more. So is every sinner that lies down in shame, and makes his grave with the wicked; he shall indeed rise again, and be called upon by the voice of the Archangel, but then he shall descend into sorrows greater then the reason and the patience of a man, weeping and shrieking louder then the grones of the miserable children in the valley of *Hinnon.*

These indeed are sad stories, but true as the voice of

God and the Sermons of the holy Jesus. They are Gods words, and Gods decrees; and I wish that all who profess the belief of these, would consider sadly what they mean.

Sermon at the Funeral of the Archbishop of Armagh (*John Bramhall*),
3rd ed., 1663, p. 23

170. *To Lose one's Soul.*

THE pleasures of the world no man can have for a hundred yeers, and no man hath pleasure a hundred dayes together, but he hath some trouble intervening: or at least a wearinesse and a loathing of the pleasure; and therefore to endure insufferable calamities (suppose it be) for a hundred yeers, without any interruption, without so much comfort as the light of a small candle, or a drop of water amounts to in a fever, is a bargain to be made by no man that loves himself, or is not in love with infinite affliction.

If a man were condemned but to lie still, or to lie a bed in one posture without turning, for seven yeers together, would he not buy it off with the losse of all his estate? If a man were to be put upon the rack, for every day, three moneths together, (suppose him able to live so long) what would he do to be quit of his torture? Would any man curse the King to his face, if he were sure to have both his hands burnt off, and to be tormented with torments three yeers together? Would any man in his wits accept of a hundred pound a yeer for fourty yeers, if he were sure to be tormented in the fire for the next hundred yeers together without intermission? Think then what a thousand yeers signifie: Ten ages, the age of two Empires; but this account I must tell you is infinitely short, though I thus discourse to you, how great fools wicked men are, though this opinion should be true: A goodly comfort surely! that for two or three yeers sottish pleasure, a man shall be infinitely tormented but for *a thousand yeers*. But then when we cast up the minutes, and yeers, and ages of eternity, the consideration it self is a great hell to those persons who by their evil lives are consigned to such sad and miserable portions.

A thousand yeers is a long while to be in torment; we finde a fever of 21. dayes to be like an age in length: but when the duration of an intolerable misery is for ever in the height, and for ever beginning, and ten thousand yeers hath spent no part of its terme, but it makes a perpetual efflux, and is like the centre of a circle, which ever transmits lines to the circumference; this is a consideration so sad that the horrour of it and the reflexion upon its abode and duration, make a great part of the hell; for hell could not be hell without the despair of accursed souls; for any hope were a refreshment, and a drop of water, which would help to allay those flames, which as they burn intolerably, so they must burn for ever.

And I desire you to consider that although the Scripture uses the word [fire] to expresse the torments of accursed souls, yet fire can no more equal the pangs of hell then it can torment a material substance; the pains of perishing souls being as much more afflictive then the smart of fire, as the smart of fire is troublesome beyond the softnesse of Persian carpets, or the sensuality of the Asian Luxury: for the pains of hell; and the perishing or losing of the soul is to suffer the wrath of God, καὶ γὰρ ὁ Θεὸς ἡμῶν πῦρ καταναλίσκον *our God is a consuming fire*: that is the fire of hell, when God takes away all comfort from us, nothing to support our spirit is left us, when sorrow is our food and tears our drink; when it is eternal night without Sun or star, or lamp, or sleep; when we burn with fire without light, that is, are loaden with sadnesse, without remedy or hope or ease, and that this wrath is to be expressed, and to fall upon us, in spiritual, immateriall, but most accursed, most pungent and dolorous emanations, then we feel what it is to lose a soul.

XXVIII Sermons, 1651, p. 245

171. *Threatenings.*

Quest.

WHETHER it be lawful for a good end for Preachers to affright men with Panick terrors, and to create fears that have no ground; as to tell them if they be liars, their faces will be deformed; if they be perjur'd, the devil will haunt them in visible shapes; if they be sacrilegious, they shall have the leprosy; or any thing whereby weak and ignorant people can be most wrought upon?

I answer briefly:

There are terrors enough in the new Testament to affright any man from his sins, who can be wrought upon by fear: and if all that *Moses* and the Prophets say, and all that Christ and his Apostles published be not sufficient, then nothing can be. For I am sure, nothing can be a greater, or more formidable evil then hell; and no terrors can bring greater affrightment, then those which are the proper portion of the damned. But the measures of the permission and liberty that can be used, are these:

A Preacher or Governour may affright those that are under them, and deterre them from sin, by threatning them with any thing *which probably may happen*. So he may denounce a curse upon the estate of sacrilegious per-

T

sons, robbers of Churches, oppressors of Priests, and Widows, and Orphans; and particularly, whatsoever the Widow or Orphan in the bitterness of their souls doe pray, may happen upon such evil persons; or what the Church in the instruments of donation have expressed: as, to die childless; to be afflicted with the gout; to have an ambulatory life, the fortune of a penny, since for that he forsakes God and his religion; a distracted minde or fancy, or any thing of this nature. For since the curses of this life and of the other are indefinitely threatned to all sinners, and some particularly to certain sins, as want is to the deteiners of Tithes, a wandring fortune to Church-robbers; it is not unreasonable, and therefore it is lawful to make use of such particulars as are most likely to be effective upon the consciences of sinners.

It is lawful to affright men with the threatning of any thing that is *possible to happen in the ordinary effects of providence.* For every sin is against an infinite God, and his anger is sometimes the greatest, and can produce what evil he please; and he uses to arm all his creatures against sinners, and sometimes strikes a stroke with his own hand, and creates a prodigy of example to perpetuate a fear upon men to all ages.

But this is to be admitted with these Cautions:

It must be done so as to be limited within those ways which need not suppose a miracle to have them effected. Thus to threaten a sinner in *England*, that if he prophanes the holy Sacrament, a Tigre shall meet him in the Church-yard and tear him, is so improbable and unreasonable, that it is therefore not to be done, lest the authority, and the counsel, and the threatning become ridiculous: but we have warrant to threaten him with diseases, and sharp sicknesses, and temporal death; and the warrant is deriv'd from a precedent in Scripture, Gods dealing with the *Corinthian* Communicants.

He who thus intends to disswade, must in prudence be careful that he be not too decretory and determinate in the particular; but either wholly instance in general threatnings, or with exceptive and cautious terms in the particular; as, *Take heed lest such an evil happen:* or, *It is likely it may,* and *we have no security for a minute against it*; and *so God hath done to others.*

Let these be onely *threatnings*, not *prophesies*, lest the whole dispensation become contemptible; and therefore let all such threatnings be understood with a provision, that if such things doe not happen, the man hath not escaped Gods anger, but is reserv'd for worse. God walketh upon the face of the waters, and his footsteps are not seen; but however, evil is the portion of the sinner.

In all those threatnings which are according to the analogy of the Gospel, or the state of things and persons with which we have entercourse, we may take all that liberty that can by apt instruments concurre to the work of God; dressing them with circumstances of terror and affrightment, and representing spiritual events by metaphors, apologues and instances of nature. Thus our blessed Lord expressing the torments of hell, signifies the greatness of them by such things which in nature are most terrible; as *brimstone and fire, the worm of conscience, weeping and wailing, and gnashing of teeth.* But this I say must ever be kept within the limits of analogy to what is reveal'd, and must not make excursions to extraregular and ridiculous significations. Such as is the fancy of some Divines in the *Romane* Church, and particularly of *Cornelius à lapide*, that the souls of the damned shall be roll'd up in bundles like a heap and involv'd circles of snakes, and in hell shall sink down like a stone into the bottomeless pit, falling still downward for ever and ever. This is not well; but let the expressions be according to the proportions of what is reveal'd. The Divines in several ages have taken great liberty in this affair, which I know no reason to reprove, if some of their tragical expressions did not, or were not apt to pass into dogmatical affirmatives, and opinions of reality in such inventions.

Ductor Dubitantium, 1660, vol. i, p. 78

172. *Premonitions of Judgement.*

WE may guesse at the severity of the Judge by the lesser strokes of that Judgement which he is pleased to send upon sinners in this world, to make them afraid of the horrible pains of Doomsday : I mean the torments of an unquiet conscience, the amazement and confusions of some sins and some persons. For I have sometimes seen persons surpriz'd in a base action, and taken in the circumstances of crafty theft, and secret unjustices before their excuse was ready ; They have changed their colour, their speech hath faltered, their tongue stammer'd, their eyes did wander and fix no where, till shame made them sink into their hollow eye-pits to retreat from the images and circumstances of discovery ; their wits are lost, their reason uselesse, the whole order of their soul is discomposed, and they neither see, nor feel, nor think as they use to do, but they are broken into disorder by a stroke of damnation and a lesser stripe of hell ; but then if you come to observe a guilty and a base murtherer, a condemned traytor, and see him harrassed first by an evill conscience, and then

pull'd in pieces by the hangmans hooks, or broken upon
sorrows and the wheel, we may then guesse (as well as we
can in this life) what the pains of that day shall be to
accursed souls: But those we shall consider afterwards in
their proper scene; now only we are to estimate the
severity of our Judge by the intolerablenesse of an evill
conscience; if guilt will make a man despair, and despair
will make a man mad, confounded and dissolved in all the
regions of his senses and more noble faculties, that he shall
neither feel, nor hear, nor see any thing but spectres and
illusions, devils and frightfull dreams, and hear noises, and
shriek fearfully, and look pale and distracted like a hope-
lesse man from the horrors and confusions of a lost battell
upon which all his hopes did stand, then the wicked must
at the day of Judgement expect strange things and fearfull,
and such which now no language can expresse, and then
no patience can endure.

XXV Sermons, 1653, p. 20

173. *The Day of Judgement.*

THE persons who are to be judged: even you, and I,
and all the world: Kings and Priests, Nobles and
Learned, the Crafty and the Easie, the Wise and the
Foolish, the Rich and the Poor, the prevailing Tyrant and
the oppressed Party shall all appear to receive ther Symbol; and this is so farre from abating any thing of its terror
and our dear concernment, that it much increases it: for
although concerning Precepts and Discourses we are apt
to neglect in particular what is recommended in generall,
and in incidencies of Mortality and sad events the singularity of the chance heightens the apprehension of the
evill; yet it is so by accident, and only in regard of our

imperfection; it being an effect of self-love or some little creeping envie which adheres too often to the infortunate and miserable; or else because the sorrow is apt to increase by being apprehended to be a rare case and a singular unworthinesse in him who is afflicted, otherwise then is common to the sons of men, companions of his sin, and brethren of his nature, and partners of his usuall accidents; yet in finall and extreme events the multitude of sufferers does not lessen but increase the sufferings; and when *the first day of Judgement* happen'd, that (I mean) of the universall deluge of waters upon the old World, the calamity swell'd like the floud, and every man saw his friend perish, and the neighbours of his dwelling, and the relatives of his house, and the sharers of his joyes, and yesterdaies bride, and the new born heir, the Priest of the Family, and the honour of the Kindred, all dying or dead, drench'd in water and the divine vengeance; and then they had no place to flee unto, no man cared for their souls; they had none to goe unto for counsell, no sanctuary high enough to keep them from the vengeance that rain'd down from heaven: and so it shall be at the day of Judgement, when that world and this and all that shall be born hereafter, shall passe through the same Red sea, and be all baptized with the same fire, and be involv'd in the same cloud, in which shall be thundrings and terrors infinite; every Mans fear shall be increased by his neighbours shriekes, and the amazement that all the world shall be in, shall unite as the sparks of a raging furnace into a globe of fire, and roul upon its own principle, and increase by direct appearances, and intolerable reflexions. He that stands in a Church-yard in the time of a great plague, and hears the Passing-bell perpetually telling the sad stories of death, and sees crowds of infected bodies pressing to their Graves, and others sick and tremulous, and Death dress'd up in all the images of sorrow round about him, is not supported in his spirit by the variety of his sorrow: and at Dooms-day, when the terrors are universall, besides that it is in it self so much greater because it can affright the whole world, it is also made greater by communication and a sorrowfull influence; Grief being then strongly infectious: when there is no variety of state but an intire Kingdome of fear; and amazement is the King of all our passions, and all the world its subjects: and that shrieke must needs be terrible, when millions of Men and Women at the same instant shall fearfully cry out, and the noise shall mingle with the Trumpet of the Archangell, with the thunders of the dying and groaning heavens, and the crack of the dissolving world, when the whole fabrick of nature shall shake into dissolution and eternall ashes. . . .

We may consider that this infinite multitude of men and women, Angels and Devils, is not ineffective as a number in *Pythagoras* Tables, but must needs have influence upon every spirit that shall there appear. For the transactions of that court are not like Orations spoken by a *Grecian* Orator in the circles of his people, heard by them that croud nearest him, or that sound limited by the circles of aire, or the inclosure of a wall; but every thing is represented to every person, and then let it be considered, when thy shame and secret turpitude, thy midnight revels and secret hypocrisies, thy lustfull thoughts, and treacherous designes, thy falshood to God and startings from thy holy promises, thy follies and impieties shall be laid open before all the world, and that then shall be spoken by the trumpet of an Archangell upon the house top, the highest battle-

ments of Heaven, all those filthy words and lewd circumstances which thou didst act secretly, thou wilt find that
thou wilt have reason strangely to be ashamed. All the
wise men in the world shall know how vile thou hast been:
and then consider; with what confusion of face wouldst
thou stand in the presence of a good man and a severe, if
peradventure he should suddenly draw thy curtain, and
finde thee in the sins of shame and lust; it must be infinitely more, when God and all the Angels of heaven and
earth, all his holy myriads, and all his redeemed Saints
shall stare and wonder at thy impurities and follies. . . .

The Majesty of the Judge, and the terrors of the Judgement shall bee spoken aloud by the immediate forerunning
accidents, which shall bee so great violences to the old
constitutions of Nature, that it shall break her very bones,
and disorder her till shee be destroyed. St. *Hierom* relates
out of the *Jews* books, that their Doctors use to account
15 days of prodigie immediately before Christ's coming,
and to every day assigne a wonder, any one of which, if
wee should chance to see in the days of our flesh, it would
affright us into the like thoughts, which the old world had
when they saw the countreys round about them cover'd
with water, and the Divine vengeance; or as those poor
people neer *Adria*, and the *Mediterranean* sea, when their
houses and Cities are entring into graves, and the bowells
of the earth rent with convulsions and horrid tremblings.
The sea (say they) shall rise 15 cubits above the highest
Mountaines, and thence descend into hollownesse, and a
prodigious drought, and when they are reduc'd again to
their usuall proportions, then all the beasts and creeping
things, the monsters, and the usuall inhabitants of the sea
shall be gathered together, and make fearfull noyses to

distract Mankind: The birds shall mourne and change
their song into threnes and sad accents, rivers of fire shall
rise from East to West, and the stars shall be rent into
threds of light, and scatter like the beards of comets; Then
shall bee fearfull earthquakes, and the rocks shall rend in
pieces, the trees shall distill bloud, and the mountains and
fairest structures shall returne unto their primitive dust;
the wild beasts shall leave their dens and come into the
companies of men, so that you shall hardly tell how to call
them, *herds of Men* or *congregations of Beasts*; Then shall
the Graves open, and give up their dead, and those which
are alive in nature, and dead in fear, shall be forc'd from
the rocks, whither they went to hide them, and from
caverns of the earth, where they would fain have been
concealed; because their retirements are dismantled, and
their rocks are broken into wider ruptures, and admit a
strange light into their secret bowels; and the men being
forc'd abroad into the theatre of mighty horrors shall run
up and downe distracted and at their wits end; and then
some shall die, and some shall bee changed, and by this
time the Elect shall bee gathered together from the foure
quarters of the world, and Christ shall come along with
them to judgment.

XXV Sermons, 1653, pp. 3, 8, 11

174. *A Prayer for the Love of God.*

O HOLY and purest Jesus who wert pleased to espouse
every holy soul and joyn it to thee with a holy union,
and mysterious instruments of religious society and communications, O fill my soul with Religion and desires,
holy as the thoughts of Cherubim, passionate beyond the
love of women, that I may love thee as much as ever any

creature loved thee, even with all my soul, and all my faculties, and all the degrees of every faculty; let me know no loves but those of duty and charity, obedience and devotion, that I may for ever run after thee who art the King of Virgins, and with whom whole kingdoms are in love & for whose sake Queens have dyed; and at whose feet Kings with joy have laid their Crowns and Scepters: My soul is thine O dearest Jesu, thou art my Lord, and hast bound up my eyes and heart from all stranger affections; give me for my dowry purity and humility, modesty and devotion, charity and patience, & at last bring me into the Bride-chamber to partake of the felicities and to lye in the bosome of the Bridegroom to eternal ages, O holy and sweetest Saviour Jesus. *Amen.*

A prayer against sensuality.

O Eternal Father, thou that sittest in Heaven invested with essential Glories and Divine perfections, fill my soul with so deep a sence of the excellencies of spiritual and heavenly things, that my affections being weaned from the pleasures of the world and the false allurements of sin, I may, with great severity and the prudence of a holy discipline and strict desires, with clear resolutions and a free spirit, have my conversation in Heaven and heavenly imployments; that being in affections as in my condition a Pilgrim and a stranger here, I may covet after and labour for an abiding city, and at last may enter into and for ever dwell in the Cœlestial Jerusalem which is the mother of us all, through Jesus Christ our Lord. *Amen.*

Holy Living, 1650, pp. 175, 173

175. *A Prayer for Temporal Blessings.*

OPEN thy hand O God and fill us with thy loving kindnesse, that the Mower may fill his hand, and he that bindeth up the sheaves his bosome, that our garners may be full with all manner of store; that our sheep may bring forth thousands and ten thousands in our streets: That our oxen may be strong to labour, that there be no breaking in, or going out, that our hearts may be replenish'd with food and gladnesse, that there be no complaining in our streets. Give us sufficient for this life; food and raiment, the light of thy countenance, and contented spirits; and thy grace to seeke the Kingdom of heaven and the righteousnesse thereof in the first place, and then we are sure all these things shall be added unto us. Grant the desires and heare the prayer of thy servants for Jesus Christ his sake our Lord and onely saviour. Amen.

A Collection of Offices, 1658, Additionals

176. *A Prayer for Preservation.*

GIVE O Lord, to the Magistrates equity, sincerity, courage and prudence, that they may protect the good, defend religion, and punish the wrong doers: Give to the Nobility wisdom, valour, and loyalty: To Merchants justice and faithfulnesse: to all Artificers and Labourers truth and honesty: to our enemies forgivenesse and brotherly kindnesse.

Preserve to us the Heavens and the Ayre in healthful influence and disposition, the Earth in plenty, the kingdom in peace and good government, our marriages in peace, and sweetnesse and innocence of society, thy people from famine and pestilence, our houses from burning and robbery, our persons from being burnt alive, from banishment and prison, from Widowhood & destitution, from violence of pains and passions, from tempests and earth-quakes, from inundation of waters, from rebellion and invasion, from impatience and inordinate cares, from tediousness of spirit and despair, from murder, and all violent, accursed and unusual deaths, from the surprize of sudden and violent accidents, from passionate and unreasonable fears, from all thy wrath, and from all our sins, good Lord, deliver and preserve thy servants for ever. Amen.

Holy Living, 1650, p. 402

177. *A Prayer for Mercy.*

O MOST dreadful judge, I stand in amazement when I consider that the heavens are not pure in thine eyes: and if thou foundest perversenesse in thy Angels, and didst not spare them, what shall become of me? The stars fell from heaven, and what can I presume, who am but dust and ashes? They whose life hath seemed holy have fallen into an evil portion, and after they have eaten the bread of Angels, they have been delighted with Carobe nuts, with husks and draffe of Swine.

The Worthy Communicant, 1660, p. 190

178. *A Prayer for those in Affliction.*

BE a guide to the travellers, a star and a port to Mariners, the comfort and strength of Miners and Gallislaves. Pity good God, all Gentlemen that are fallen into poverty and sad misfortunes, strengthen and deliver all women that are in sharp and dangerous labour, all them that roar and groane with intolerable paines and noisome diseases: Have mercy and compassion upon all that are

afflicted with illusion of the night and frightfull appari-
tions, that are haunted or possessed with evill spirits, or
troubled with despairing or amazed consciences, with the
stone and with the gout, with violent colics and greivous
ulcers: give them pity and give them patience, a speedy
deliverance from their calamity, and a sanctified use of the
rod of God through Jesus Christ our Lord.

A Collection of Offices, 1658, Morning Prayer

179. *A Prayer for all Christian Kings, Princes and Governours.*

O KING of Kings, and Prince of all the Rulers of the
Earth, give thy grace and Spirit to all Christian
Princes, the spirit of wisdom and counsel, the spirit of
government and godly fear: Grant unto them to live in
peace and honour, that their people may love and feare
them, and they may love and fear God: speak good unto
their hearts concerning the Church, that they may be
nursing Fathers to it, Fathers of the Fatherlesse, Judges
and Avengers of the cause of Widowes, that they may be
compassionate to the wants of the poor, and the groans
of the oppressed, that they may not vex or kill the Lords
people with unjust or ambitious wars, but may feed the
flock of God, and may inquire after and do all things which
may promote peace, publick honesty and holy religion, so
administring things present, that they may not fail of the
everlasting glories of the world to come, where all thy
faithful people shall reign Kings for ever. *Amen.*

Holy Living, 1650, p. 397

180. *Holy, Holy.*

ALL Angels and Archangels, all Thrones and Dominions, all Principalities and Powers, the Cherubins with many eyes, and the Seraphins covered with wings from the terror and amazement of thy brightest glory: These and all the powers of Heaven do perpetually sing praises and never-ceasing Hymns, and eternal Anthems to the glory of the eternal God, the Almighty Father of Men and Angels.

Holy is our God: Holy is the Almighty: Holy is the Immortal: Holy, Holy, Holy, Lord God of Sabaoth, Heaven and Earth are full of the Majesty of thy glory. Amen. With these holy and blessed Spirits I also thy servant, O thou great lover of souls, though I be unworthy to offer praise to such a Majesty, yet out of my bounden duty humbly offer up my heart and voice to joyn in this blessed quire, and confesse the glories of the Lord. For thou art holy, and of thy greatnesse there is no end; and in thy justice and goodnesse thou hast measured out to us all thy works.

Thou madest man out of the earth and didst form him after thine own image: thou didst place him in a garden of pleasure, and gavest him laws of righteousnesse to be to him a seed of immortality.

O that men would therefore praise the Lord for his goodnesse: and declare the wonders that he hath done for the children of men.

Holy Living, 1650, p. 379

NOTES

p. **1**, l. 11. '*Delicata autem est*', etc. S. Bernard. *de praecept. de dispens.* xiii. [H.]

p. **3**, no. 2. '*To Lord Hatton*'. Christopher Hatton, first Baron Hatton (1605?–1670), a cousin of Lord Chancellor Hatton. After the death of Laud, Jeremy Taylor found a new patron in Lord Hatton, whose residence, Kirby Hall, was but a few miles from Taylor's living at Uppingham. Taylor also dedicated the first section of *The Great Exemplar* (1649), and his *Polemical and Moral Discourses* (1657), to Lord Hatton.

l. 17. 'a noble Enemy'. The identity of this 'noble Enemy' has much puzzled Taylor's biographers, but it was probably Lord Carbery, who though nominally a Royalist, was on such friendly terms with the Parliamentarians, that he might have been regarded as an enemy of Charles I.

l. 17. Οἱ γὰρ βάρβαροι. Acts xxviii. 2. [H.]

p. **4**, l. 9. '*ius trium liberorum*'. The privilege granted under the Empire to Romans with three legitimate children.

p. **5**, l. 8. 'Scripture'. 1 Cor. xiii. 9, 12. [H.]

l. 13. '*disputations*'. Rom. xiv. 1. [H.]

p. **7**, no. 5. '*To Lord Carbery*'. Richard Vaughan, second earl of Carbery (1600?–1686), inherited Golden Grove, and succeeded to the Irish earldom of his father in 1634. He was created Baron Vaughan in the English peerage in 1643. A Royalist Commander in Pembroke-shire in 1643, he was defeated in 1644 and fined as a delinquent, but was pardoned by Parliament in 1647, and afterwards remained neutral. (*D.N.B.*)

l. 23. '*undiq; totis*'. Virgil, *Ecl.* i. 11. [H.]

p. **9**, l. 9. 'I have a trade'. Jeremy Taylor had joined with two other clergymen, William Wyatt and William Nicholson (afterwards Bishop of Gloucester) in their school at Newton Hall, near Golden Grove.

no. 6. '*To Lady Carbery*'. Frances, daughter of Sir John Altham of Oxhey, and second wife of Lord Carbery, whom she married at a very early age. She died in 1650, after bearing ten children, eight of whom survived her. Lord Carbery married thirdly a daughter of the first Earl of Bridgewater, Lady Alice Egerton, who acted the part of the 'lady' when *Comus* was performed at Ludlow Castle in 1634. In the third edition of *The Great Exemplar* (1657) Jeremy Taylor added to part iii another dedication to the third Lady Carbery.

p. **12**, l. 15. 'a young Gentleman of Athens'. Plutarch, *de garrul.* [H.]

p. **19**, l. 8. '*Si gaudet, si flet*'. Martial, *Ep.* I. lxviii. [H.] The last lines of this quotation are correctly:

> Coenat, propinat, poscit, negat, innuit: una est
> Naevia.

p. **20**, l. 3. '*Solomon*', Prov. ii. 17. [H.]

p. **22**, l. 26. '*Bonum est*'. Lam. iii. 27. [H.]

p. **24**, l. 10. 'So have I seen a river'. In his *Essays in Criticism* Matthew Arnold quotes this sentence, adding 'that passage has been much admired, and, indeed, the genius in it is undeniable. I should say, for my part, that genius, the ruling divinity of poetry, had been too busy in it, and intelligence, the ruling divinity of prose, not busy enough.' *Essays in Criticism*, 3rd ed. (1875), p. 71.

p. **25**, l. 17. '*like one that bideth the winde*'. Prov. xxvii. 16. [H.]
l. 26. '*Magnifica verba*'. Sen. *Troad.*, Act III, sc. i. 575. [H.]

p. **26**, l. 5. '*Cato*'. Cicero, *Tusc. Quaest.*, lib. I, cap. 30. [H.]
l. 28. 'remonstrate'. This word was frequently used in the seventeenth century with the meaning of 'demonstrate'. (*O.E.D.*)

p. **27**, l. 32. '*Jucundum cum ætas*'. Catullus, lxviii. 16. [H.]

p. **29**, l. 15. '*Et cum supremos*'. Martial, *Ep.* I. lxxxviii. [H.]
l. 22. '*Nemo parum*', Cicero, *Tusc. Disp.* I. 45. 109.

p. **30**, l. 7. '*Mors illos consecrat*'. Seneca, *de Provid.* ii. [H.]

p. **33**, no. 12. From a letter printed in Heber's edition of Taylor's *Whole Works* (1861), vol. i, p. liii.

p. **34**, l. 8. 'the words of the Prophet'. Jer. xxx. 7. [H.]
l. 14. '*They shall serve*'. *Ibid.*, verse 9. [H.]
l. 23. 'persons condemn'd to metalls'. From the Latin phrase, *condemnare ad metalla*, to condemn to the mines.

p. **36**, l. 1. 'Godsips', god-sibbe, a godfather or godmother. [H.]
l. 29. 'A Bell'. See Dr. Reeves's *Eccles. Antiquities of Down, Connor, and Dromore* (Dublin, 1847), p. 369, and the same author's historical and illustrative description of 'The Bell of Patrick's Will'. (Belfast 1850). [H.]
l. 31. 'the late Rebellion'. The Irish rebellion of 1641.

p. **38**, l. 22. '*populus unius labii*'. Gen. xi. 1. [H.]

p. **39**, no. 16. John Bramhall (1594–1663), Bishop of Derry, 1634, Archbishop of Armagh, 1661. The text of this extract (as of nos. 17, 69, 169) is printed from the third edition of this sermon, as the text of the earlier editions is imperfect.

l. 4. *'In convertendo'*. Ps. cxxvi. 1.

p. **41**, l. 2. *'a worm and no Man'*. Ps. xxii. 6. [H.]

p. **42**, l. 20. 'But as when the Sun'. Coleridge knew this passage by heart, and repeated it, he tells us, before Michael Angelo's statue of Moses in Rome (*Biographia Literaria*, chap. xxi). It was reprinted by Hazlitt, who writes, 'This passage puts one in mind of the rising dawn and kindling skies in one of Claude's landscapes. Sir Thomas Brown has nothing of this rich finishing and exact gradation.' (*Lectures on the Dramatic Literature of the Age of Elizabeth*, 1820, p. 311.)

p. **45**, l. 22. 'wretchlesnesse', an obsolete form of 'retchlessness', which is an old variant of 'recklessness'.

p. **47**, no. 22, l. 1. *'Tostatus Abulensis'*. See his epitaph in Hakewill, *Apol*. III. vi. 1, p. 257. [H.]

p. **52**, no. 26, l. 6. 'sp[h]eare'. In the first edition 'speare', in the second 'spheare', and afterwards 'sphere'. [H.]

p. **55**, l. 8. 'as *Livius Drusus* said of himself'. Seneca, *de Brev. Vit.*, cap. vi. [H.]

p. **56**, l. 5. 'ascertain us', i.e. make us certain or secure.

p. **57**, l. 18. 'that saying of S. *Paul*'. Heb. xii. 14. [H.]

p. **58**, l. 17. *'Be not drunke with wine'*. Eph. v. 18. [H.]

p. **59**, no. 31, l. 1. *'Arianus'*. Arrian, *Epict.* i. 10. [H.]

l. 16. 'the *Wolfe* in the Fable', Odonis de Ceritona, *Fabulae* xxii, 'De Lupo qui voluit esse Monachus'.

p. **60**, l. 3. 'belike', i.e. 'like'; 'be like' in the first and subsequent editions.

l. 15. *'animal propter Convivia natum'*. Juvenal, i. 141. [H.]

l. 20. 'St. *Paul*'. Acts xxiv. 25. [H.]

p. **64**, l. 30. 'to make reflex acts'. The word 'reflex' was used, especially in the phrase 'reflex acts', before the word 'conscious' had acquired the modern meaning of 'directed upon the mind itself or its operations'. See p. 184 above, l. 17.

p. **72**, l. 17. 'The Collector'. Valerius Maximus, lib. VII, cap. i. [H.]

l. 28. '*the limit of our joy*'. Epicurus, *apud* Diog. Laert., lib. X, cap. 31. [H.]

p. **73**, l. 9. '*if we reckon them*'. Valerius Maximus, VI. ix. 14. [H.]

p. **76**, l. 7. 'univocal', i.e. confined to one kind or nature. (*O.E.D.*)

l. 24. 'Scævola'. Livy, ii. 12. [H.]

p. **77**, l. 29. 'Nazianzen'. *Carm.* xxxix. [H.]

p. **78**, no. 37, l. 1. '*No man is more miserable*'. Seneca, *de Prov.*, cap. iii. [H.]

p. **79**, l. 4. '*twice feel the cold*'. Virgil, *Georg.* i. 47 [H.]

p. **85**, l. 5. '*Cæsar* wondred'. Seneca, *Epistles*, 77, 18; but Taylor apparently was indebted to Florio's translation of Montaigne's *Essays* (I. xix) where the adjective 'crazed' occurs.

l. 25. 'Pompey', Cicero, *Tusc. Qu.* ii. 25. [H.]

p. **86**, l. 31. 'the rayes of the Sun'. Virgil, *Aen.* viii. 22. [H.]

p. **87**, l. 13. '*Massurius Sabinus*', ap. Macrob. *Saturn.* lib. I, cap. 10. [H.]

l. 24. 'S. *Eadsine*'. Eadsige, Eadsine, Edsie or Elsi (d. 1050), archbishop of Canterbury, 1038.

p. **89**, l. 16. '*Olympus*'. Olympia? [H.]

p. **94**, l. 23. '*Aristippus*'. Plutarch, *de An. Tranquill.* [H.]

p. **97**, no. 44, l. 2. '*in the sweat of our brows*'. Gen. iii. 19. [H.]

l. 4. '*salvation*'. Phil. ii. 12. [H.]

p. **98**, no. 45, l. 4. 'resentment'. Used here with the obsolete meaning of 'an appreciation or understanding *of* something'. (*O.E.D.*)

p. **99**, no. 46, l. 6. 'look babies', i.e. to see the small image of oneself reflected in the pupil of another's eye. (*O.E.D.*)

p. **102**, l. 26. 'who relates to my family', i.e. who is related to—a usage of 'relate' which is now obsolete with reference to persons or places. (*O.E.D.*)

p. **103**, l. 4. 'by evil men'. 'Cromwell's government must have been strong, to be able to permit, and to disregard, the pointed allusions to them which were continually proceeding from the pens of the royalist writers.' [H.]

p. **104**, l. 26. 'the *Grand Cyrus*'. *Artamène, ou le Grand Cyrus*, by Madaleine de Scudéry.

Notes. 291

l. 27. 'the *Countess of Exeter*'. Changed in the edition of 1678 to 'the *Infanta of Spain*, or any of the most perfect beauties and real excellencies of the world'. Jeremy Taylor was referring perhaps to the young and beautiful wife of the first Earl of Exeter, who, in 1618 was falsely accused of an attempt to poison Lady Roos, the wife of her husband's grandson and heir. (Gardiner, *History of England*, 1603–1642, vol. iii, p. 191.)

l. 28. 'abstracted friendships'; 'abstracted' with the obsolete meaning of 'ideal'. (*O.E.D.*)

p. **105**, l. 19. *Cassandre*, by Gauthier de Costes, seigneur de la Calprenède.

l. 19. '*Ibrahim Bassa*'. *Ibrahim, ou l'illustre Bassa*, by Madeleine de Scudéry.

l. 24. '*Amicitia*'. Cicero, *De Amicit.* xiv. [H.]

p. **106**, no. 50, l. 19. '*Confirmatur*'. *Ibid.* ix.

p. **108**, l. 7. '*Raphael*'. Tobit. v. [H.]

l. 21. 'throes'; 'throws' in first edition.

l. 22. '*she shall be saved*'. 1 Tim. ii. 15. [H.]

p. **110**, l. 25. '*Plutarch*'. *Praecept. Conjug.* [H.]

p. **113**, no. 57, l. 8. '*Nemo simul malus fit*'. Plutarch, *De Ser. Num. Vindict.* [H.]

p. **116**, l. 7. '*Pliny*'. *Hist. Nat.* lib. VII, proem. [H.]

l. 19. μετὰ γὰρ τὸν θάνατον. Chrysostom, *In Rom.* vi, hom. xi. 3. [H.]

p. **117**, l. 26. '*Dionysius* of *Athens*'. *Eccles. Hier.*, c. iii, part 3. [H.]

p. **118**, l. 1. '*Cicero*'. *In Hortens.* [H.]

p. **120**, no. 59, l. 8. '*Lucian*'. *Vit. Auct.* cap. xxvii. [H.]

l. 12. '*Varro*'. S. Aug., *De Civ. Dei*, lib. XIX, cap. 2. [H.]

p. **121**, no. 60. '*The Reynolds's*'. John Rainolds or Reynolds (1549–1607) President of Corpus Christi College, Oxford, and Dean of Lincoln, and his brother, William Rainolds (1544?–1594) Roman Catholic divine. Fuller (*Church History*, 1655, Book X, p. 47) tells the story of this disputation, representing John as, at the time, a zealous papist, and William as an earnest Protestant, but this story seems apocryphal. (*D.N.B.*)

p. **122**, no. 62, l. 11. '*Theocritus*'. Jeremy Taylor quotes from memory; the phrase in Theocritus is ἀνείλκυσα χρύσεον ἰχθῦν. (*Idyll* xxi. 52.)

p. **124,** l. 1. 'He that had an ill memory'. The allusion is to Montaigne; see his account of himself, *Essays*, i, 9. [H.]

p. **125,** no. 65, l. 2. '*Nebuchodonosor*'. Dan. iv. 30. [H.]

p. **127,** no. 67, l. 9. 'instances' is used here with the old meaning of 'details', 'circumstances'.

p. **129,** l. 8. '*Justice*'. Prov. xvii. 26. [H.]

p. **131,** l. 24. '*Combustusque senex*'. Dracontius, *hexam.—Magn. bibl. vett. patr.*, tom. vi, part i, p. 504 c. [H.]

p. **137,** l. 30. 'exauctoration'. 'Deprivation of office or authority'. (*O.E.D.*)

p. **139,** l. 17. '*Sozomen*'. Lib. VI, cap. 16. [H.]

l. 24. 'S. *Gregory*'. See Hooker, *Eccles. Pol.* v. 6. [H.]

l. 30. '*Apollinaris*'. *Ibid.* [H.]

p. **140,** no. 76, l. 13. '*Quem mea vix totum bibliotheca capit*'. Martial, xiv. 190 (for *vix*, read *non*). [H.]

p. **142,** l. 11. '*viam intelligentiæ*'. 'These words do not occur in the Vulgate'; *vias prudentiæ*, Prov. ix. 6; *via doctrinæ*, xxi. 16; both rendered in our version, 'way of understanding'. [H.]

no. 78, l. 1. '*Agricola*'. Heber says that this translation from Georgius Agricola, *De Animantibus Subterraneis*, was borrowed by Taylor from the *Golden Remains* of John Hales, p. 34 (ed. 1673). It is, however, more probably an independent translation.

no. 78, l. 16. '*Isidore*'. Isidore, *Orig.* lib. VI, cap. xiv. [H.]

p. **146,** l. 1. '*Quod volumus sanctum est*'. August. *contra epist. Parmen.* lib. II, cap. 13. [H.]

l. 3. '*Nemo suæ mentis*'. Prosper. *Epigr. de Cohibenda ira.* [H.]

p. **148,** l. 13. '*Davids* expression'. Ps. xl. 12. [H.]

p. **149,** no. 86, l. 10. '*Hic locus*'. Baptista Mantuanus. *Ecl.* I. 6, 7.

p. **152,** l. 13. 'the *Cynic*'. Vid. Diog. *ap.* Stobaeus, *Florilegium*, vi. 53. [H.]

p. **154,** l. 18. '*Non bene*'. Tibullus, III. vi. 35. [H.]

l. 27. '*Phalangia*'. Strabo, XI. iv. 7. [H.]

p. **155,** l. 3. '*immixto liventia*'. C. Valerii Flacci *Argonauticon*, i. 63. (For *immixto* read *hesterno*.) [H.]

no. 93, l. 15. 'upon another stock'—i.e. 'ground', or 'basis'. An obsolete use of the word 'stock' very frequent in Jeremy Taylor. (*O.E.D.*)

Notes.

p. **156**, no. 94, l. 2. *'Petronius'*, *Satyr.* cxi. Another version of this story, falsely ascribed to Jeremy Taylor, was published in 1659, under the title of 'The Ephesian Matron'. (See Bibliography below, no. 52.)

p. **159**, l. 14. 'impudent'. 'Imprudent' in the first edition; changed to 'impudent' in the second. [H.]

p. **160**, no. 97, l. 3. 'rending off'; 'renting' in the first edition.

p. **161**, l. 11. *'D'Avila'*. Davila, *Guerre Civili di Francia* (Paris, 1644), Lib. V, tom. i, p. 269. [H.]

p. **163**, l. 3. *'Plutarch'*. *De Curios.* [H.]

p. **168**, l. 11. *'Chrysippus'*. Juvenal, xiii. 184. [H.]

l. 20. 'the song of *Cyclops'*. 'Pascite vos herbas, sociis ego pascam Achivis.' Alciatus, *Emblem.* clxxii. [H.]

p. **169**, no. 104, l. 4. 'crueltie'. Dio Cassius, lib. LXVII. [H.]

p. **171**, l. 10. 'Apollodorus'. Plutarch, *de Ser. Num. Vind.* [H.]

p. **172**, l. 7. *'Auro bibitur venenum'*. Vid. Seneca, *Thyest.*, Act III. 453. [H.]

p. **177**, l. 5. *'Dionysius'*. Cicero, *Tusc.* v. 34. [H.]

p. **180**, no. 112, l. 6. 'dorter'. 'Dortour, dorter, a sleeping-room, bed-chamber, dormitory; *esp.* that of a monastery.' (*O.E.D.*)

p. **181**, no. 113, l. 2. 'The heathen gods'; cf. Pliny, *Nat. Hist.* xii. 1 (2) 3 *Arborum genera numinibus suis dicata perpetuo servantur, ut Iovi aesculus, Apollini laurus, Minervae olea, Veneri myrtus, Herculi populus.*

p. **182**, l. 1. *'Horatius Cocles'*. Livy, i. 26. [H.]

p. **185**, no. 117, l. 1. 'Madam'. Christiana, Dowager Countess of Devonshire (d. 1675), to whom the *Deus Justificatus* was written in the form of a letter.

p. **186**, no. 119, l. 1. *'If the righteous'*. 1 Pet. iv. 18.

p. **189**, no. 121, l. 17. 'a direct walking'. 'Direct' is used here with the obsolete meaning of 'positive', 'absolute'. (*O.E.D.*)

p. **195**, l. 7. *'Diomedon'*, Xenophon, *Hellen.* I. vii. 11. [H.]

l. 10. *'Chabrias'*. Diodorus Siculus, xv. 35. [H.]

l. 18. *'Erra pater'*. Erra Pater was formerly current as a name for an astrologer and also for an almanac. Nares, *Glossary* (1888), vol. i, p. 281.

l. 23. *'Aristodemus'*. Plutarch, *de Superst.* [H.]

l. 28. *'Nicias'*. Diodorus Siculus, xiii. 12. [H.]

p. **196**, no. 126, l. 2. '*Esto fidelis ad mortem*'. Rev. ii. 10. [H.]

p. **197**, l. 8. '*duplicis animi*'. James i. 8.

p. **199**, no. 130. This extract is from the funeral sermon of Sir George Dalston, which was preached in 1657, and first printed at the end of the 1674 edition of the *Worthy Communicant*.

p. **202**, l. 31. 'St. Paul'. 1 Cor. viii. 1. [H.]

p. **203**, l. 3. '*purifie your souls*'. 2 Cor. vii. 1. [H.]

p. **207**, l. 4. 'cognation', i.e. 'affinity', 'likeness'. Now rare or obsolete in this sense. (*O.E.D.*) See above, p. 225, l. 21.

p. **208**, l. 29. 'the Prophet'. Mal. i. 7. [H.]

p. **213**, l. 1. 'Madam'. Lady Devonshire, see *Ante*, no. 117.

l. 4. 'Nephews', i.e. grandsons. This use of nephew was common in the seventeenth century. (*O.E.D.*)

l. 17. 'Latimers', changed to 'London' in subsequent editions. Latimers was Lord Devonshire's seat in Buckinghamshire. [H.]

p. **221**, l. 18. '*Sion*'. Ps. cxxvi. 1. [H.]

p. **222**, l. 6. 'made accounts of', i.e. profited by. (*O.E.D.*)

p. **224**, l. 9. 'impropriate'. 'Appropriated to some particular person or persons. *? Obs.*' (*O.E.D.*)

p. **225**, l. 17. '*If you will obey*'. Isa. i. 19. [H.]

p. **226**, no. 144, l. 4. '*angelis*'. Ps. viii. 5. [H.]

p. **231**, l. 2. 'species', in the obsolete sense of 'reflections'. (*O.E.D.*)

l. 19. '*to laugh at*'. Ps. ii. 4. Prov. i. 26. [H.]

l. 23. '*the character*'. Heb. i. 3. [H.]

p. **232**, l. 25. '*eternall life*'. John vi. 68. [H.]

p. **238**, l. 17. 'S. *Paul*'. 1 Cor. xiii. 12. [H.]

p. **239**, l. 13. '*the fool hath said*'. Ps. xiv. 1; liii. 1.

p. **241**, l. 20. 'idle reputation'; 'idol' in the first edition.

p. **244**, l. 26. 'There is an acre sown with royal seed'. A paraphrase of Beaumont's lines,

> 'Here's an acre sown indeed
> With the richest, royall'st seed'. [H.]

p. **245**, l. 6. '*Athenæus*', i.e. Phoenix poeta Colophonius apud Athen., lib. XII. cap. 40. [H.]

p. **246**, l. 9. 'Chrysome childe'. 'A child in its chrisom-cloth; a child in its first month; an innocent babe'. (*O.E.D.*) So Falstaff died; 'A made a finer end, and went away and it had beene any Christome Child.' (*Hen. V*, ii. iii. 12.)

no. 157, l. 1. '*We are as water*'. 2 Sam. xiv. 14.

p. 247, l. 30. 'when *Lepidus*'. Pliny, *Nat. Hist.* vii. 53 (54), 181.

p. 248, l. 3. '*Quod quisque vitet*'. Horace, Od. II. xiii. 13. (For *Quod* read *Quid*.) [H.]

p. 249, l. 17. '*Et quasi cursores*'. Lucretius, ii. 77. [H.]

p. 250, l. 26. '*Donec certa dies*'. Maximian. (al. Corn. Gall.), Eleg. I. 173.

p. 251, no. 158, l. 2. '*Lucian*'. *In Charon.* c. xix. [H.]

p. 252, l. 29. '*Homer*'. *Il.* vi. 146. [H.]

l. 31. '*Pindar*'. *Pyth.* viii. 95. [H.]

l. 32. 'S. *James*'. Jam. iv. 14. [H.]

p. 256, l. 1. '*Petronius*'. *Satyr.* cxv. [H.]

p. 261, l. 15. '*Proserpina*'.
> Non omnes fallis; scit te Proserpina canum:
> Personam capiti detrahet illa tuo.

Martial, III. xliii. [H.]

p. 262, no. 163, l. 5. '*Zechary*'. Zech. ix. 11, 12. [H.]

p. 263, l. 21. '*Christ dyed for us*'. 1 Thess. v. 10. [H.]

l. 28. 'Cleombrotus'. Callim. *Ep.* xxiv. Cicero, *Tusc. Qu.* i. 34. [H.]

p. 264, l. 2. '*Pomponius Atticus*'. Cornelius Nepos, *In Vit. Pompon. Att.*, cap. 22. [H.]

l. 8. '*Cleanthes*'. Diogenes Laertius, VII. v. 7. [H.]

l. 24. 'that Roman'. Lucan, iv. 580. [H.]

p. 265, l. 10. '*Petronius*', *Satyr.* cxv. [H.]

l. 21. 'S. *Paul*'. Phil. ii. 27. [H.]

p. 270, l. 1. '*Attilius Aviola*'. Pliny, *Hist. Nat.* vii. 52. Valerius Maximus, I. viii. 2. [H.]

l. 14. '*pierced*'. Zech. xii. 10. [H.]

p. 272, l. 30. '*a consuming fire*'. Heb. xii. 29. [H.]

p. 275, l. 2. 'the *Corinthian* Communicants'. 1 Cor. xi. 30. [H.]

l. 32. '*Cornelius à lapide*'. In Apocal., vid. in cap. xiv, p. 240. [H.]

p. 280, l. 16. 'St. *Hierom*'. Apud Comestor. *Hist. Evang.*, cap. cxli.

A BIBLIOGRAPHY OF
JEREMY TAYLOR

HITHERTO the only bibliography of Jeremy Taylor has been in that useful but inaccurate book, Lowndes' 'Bibliographer's Manual'. Apart from mistakes the list often misleads by describing additions to earlier books as though they were separate publications, or by separating different parts of the same book. For instance 'The Essay on Friendship', and the 'Two Letters', are described as though they were different books (see No. 23); and the funeral sermon on Sir George Dalston (see No. 39) is also described as though it had been published separately.

The worst mistake is the attribution of 'The Martyrdom of King Charles' to Taylor. It was a sermon preached and printed at the Hague in 1649. The author was Henry Leslie, Taylor's predecessor as Bishop of Down and Connor.

Another puzzling entry is 'The Church of England Defended', 1674, folio. This is actually the third edition of 'Polemical Discourses', 'Wherein the Church of England is defended etc.'.

Jeremy Taylor's works were first collected in 1822, with a life by Heber. Charles Page Eden re-edited the Works and the Life; this edition, which is the best, was published 1847–51.

None of the first editions of Jeremy Taylor are common. 'The Worthy Communicant', 'The Liberty of Prophesying', 'Unum Necessarium', and 'The Great Exemplar' (with the longer imprint) are the easiest to come by. Many of the others are exceedingly rare, and some descriptions and collations have necessarily been made from single copies; there may therefore be variations in some books which I have not been able to discover. Some points, indeed, were added while the bibliography was in proof. There are no doubt others which will be discovered too late; but I hope the omission of them will be, in the words of Jeremy Taylor's publisher, 'no greater than an ordinary understanding may amend, and a little charity may forgive'.

R. G.-H.

AUTHENTIC BOOKS BY JEREMY TAYLOR

1. A / Sermon / Preached In / Saint Maries / Church in Oxford. / Vpon the Anniversary of the / Gunpowder-Treason. / (*Rule.*) / By Jeremy Taylor, Fellow of / *Allsoules Colledge in* Oxford. / (*Rule.*) / *Nolite tangere Christos meos.* / (*Square woodcut design of a clothed angel clutching a thistle.*) / Oxford, / Printed by Leonard Litchfield / Printer to the Vniversity. / M.DC.XXXVIII.

The title-page is enclosed in a double rule.

Quarto. A 1 (verso blank): title-page; A 2–B 1: dedication to Laud (pages unnumbered); B 2–F 2, G 1–L 2: text (pages 1–64).

The pagination is curious, viz. 1–34, 37–52, 45–64; the signatures, except for F being a half sheet, are normal.

Royston, in or before 1648, bought the unsold copies and bound them up in the composite volume 'Treatises', 1648 (see No. 6).

2. Of The / Sacred Order, / *And Offices of* / Episcopacy, / By Divine Institution, / Apostolicall Tradition, / *& Catholike practice.* / *Together* / With their titles of Honour, Secular / employment, manner of election, dele- / gation of their power, and other appen- / dant questions, asserted against the / *Aërians, and Acephali / new, and old.* / (*Rule.*) / By Ier. Taylor late Fellow of / *All-Soules* in *Oxon.* / (*Rule.*) / Published by His Maiesties Command. / (*Rule.*) / *There is no Power but of God. The powers that be are or-* / *dained of God.* Rom. 13. 1. / Council. Chalced. / (*Single-line Greek quotation.*) / (*Rule.*) / Oxford, / Printed by Leonard Litchfield, / *Printer to the Vniversity.* 1642.

The title-page is enclosed in a double rule.

Quarto. § 1 (verso blank): title-page; § 2–§ 4, ¶¶ 1–¶¶ 2 (verso blank): dedication to Sir Christopher Hatton (pages unnumbered); ¶¶ 3–¶¶ 4: Syllabus Paragraphorum (pages unnumbered); A 1–Ccc 1: text (pages 1–386); Ccc 2: blank.

There is a list of errata on ¶¶ 4 verso.

Some copies of this book were printed on large paper.

In 1647 Royston reissued the book, using the original sheets and printing a new title-page, the text of which, but for the imprint, is the same as that given. The setting is different, and the imprint reads: *London*, / Printed for Richard Royston, / at the Angel in Ivie-Lane. 1647.

Bibliography. 299

3. A / Discourse / *concerning* / Prayer *Ex tempore,* / or, / By pretence of the Spirit. / *Jn Justification of Authorized and* / *Set-formes of* Lyturgie. / (*Rule.*) / I. Cor. 14. 32. / (*Two-line Greek quotation and two-line translation.*) / (*Rule.*) / (*Woodcut ornaments.*) / (*Rule.*) / Printed in the Yeere, / CIƆ IƆC XLVI.

Quarto. A 1 (verso blank): title-page; A 2–E 4: text (pages 1–38). The absence of a printer's or publisher's name suggests that this tract was privately printed.

In 1647 Royston issued a second edition, with a title-page differing from the above only in small details and the imprint. It has 30 pages.

This book was republished in 1649, enlarged to about twice its original size, as 'An Apology, etc.' (see No. 7).

The woodcut ornaments on the title-page are the same as some used by Litchfield in 'The Psalter of David' (see No. 49). It is probable, therefore, that this book was printed at Oxford.

4. A new and easie / Institution / of / Grammar. / In / Which the Labour of many / yeares, usually spent in learning / the Latine Tongue, / is short- / ned and made easie. / In usum Juventutis Cambro-Britannicae. / (*Rule.*) / *Non obstant hæ Disciplinæ per illas eunti-* / *bus, sed circa illas hærentibus* Quint. / (*Rule.*) / (*Woodcut ornament.*) / (*Rule.*) / London, / Printed by *J. Young,* for *R. Royston,* and / are to be sold at the signe of the An- / gel in Ivie-Lane, 1647.

The title-page is enclosed in a border of fleur-de-lys.

Octavo. A 1 (recto blank): 'Explicatio Emblematis'; A 2 (verso blank): title-page; A 3–(a): Latin dedication to Christopher Lord Hatton by William Wyatt; (a 2)–(a 3): English dedication to Christopher, son of Lord Hatton, by Jeremy Taylor; (a 4): Latin verses to Jeremy Taylor by F. Gregory; B 1–H 7, recto: text (pages 1–109); H 7, verso: Latin verse; H 8: blank (?).

An engraved title-page is inserted between A 1 and A 2. It represents Apollo on a hill, holding a laurel wreath over two laurel-crowned figures, 'Philoponus' and 'Musaeus', who are holding up a sheet with the title engraved on it: A / New and Easy / Institution / of / Grammar. / *Expedire Grammatico* / *etiamsi quedam nesciat.* / *Quint.* Below are four schoolboys reading, two on each side of the arms of Oxford.

This book was the joint work of Taylor and Wyatt.

5. ΘΕΟΛΟΓΙΑ 'ΕΚΛΕΚΤΙΚΗ. / (*Rule.*) / A / Discourse / of / The Liberty of Prophesying. / *Shewing* / The Unreasonablenes / of prescribing to other mens Faith, and the / Iniquity of persecuting differing opinions. / (*Rule.*) / *By* Jer: Taylor, *D.D.* Chaplaine in / Ordinarie to His Majestie. / (*Rule.*) / (*Triangular woodcut design of a cherub.*) / (*Rule.*) / *London* / Printed for R. Royston, at the Angel / in Ivie-lane, 1647.

Quarto. Single unsigned sheet: engraved title-page, by Marshall, of the apostles at Pentecost; single unsigned sheet (verso blank): title-page; a 1–f 4: dedication to Christopher, Lord Hatton (pages 1–48); g 1–g 2: 'The Contents of the sections'; A 1–L l 2 (verso blank): text (pages 1–267).

There are two states of sheet a (the first four leaves of the dedication). In the first state pages 2, 3, 6, and 7 are unnumbered, in the second the omitted figures have been added.

Two errata leaves are sometimes found; they form no part of the book and are printed from different type. One contains a list of forty-one corrections, the other has a note 'The Printer to the Reader', and three corrections.

In 1657 the second, enlarged edition was printed, forming part of 'Polemical Discourses' (see No. 24).

There was added in this, after the chapter on the Anabaptists, a long refutation of their teaching, and a fable about Abraham as a new concluding paragraph to the last chapter.

6. Treatises / of / 1. *The Liberty of Prophesying.* / 2. *Prayer* Ex Tempore. / 3. *Episcopacie.* / Together with / *A Sermon preached at* Oxon. *on the Anni-versary of the 5 of* November. / (*Rule.*) / *By* Jer. Taylor, *D.D.* Chaplaine / in Ordinary to His Majesty. / (*Rule.*) / (*Woodcut design of the arms of Oxford.*) / *London,* / Printed for R. Royston, at the / Angel in *Ivie-lane.* 1648.

Quarto. A composite volume consisting of the title-page, the first edition of 'The Liberty of Prophesying', the second edition of 'Prayer Ex Tempore', the second issue of 'Episcopacy Asserted', and the first edition of the sermon. Like all such books it is liable to vary. I have seen a copy, untouched and in contemporary binding, with 'An Apology, etc., 1649' (see No. 7) instead of 'Prayer Ex Tempore'.

7. *An* / Apology / For / Authorised and Set Forms / *of* / Liturgie: / against / The Pretence / of / *The Spirit.* / 1. For *ex tempore* Prayer, /

And / 2. Formes of Private composition. / (*Rule.*) / Hierocl. in Pythag. / (*Four line Greek quotation.*) / (*Double rule.*) / *London,* / Printed for R. *Royston* in Ivie-lane, 1649.

The title-page is enclosed in a double rule.

Quarto. A 1: blank; A 2 (verso blank): title-page; A 3–A 4: dedication to Charles I; B–N 2: text (pages 1–92).

This is a very much enlarged edition of the anonymous 'Discourse on Prayer Ex Tempore', acknowledged, and dedicated to Charles I.

8. The / Great Exemplar / of / Sanctity and Holy Life / according to Christian Institution. / Described / In the History of the Life and Death / of the ever Blessed / Jesus Christ the Saviour of the World. / With / Considerations and Discourses / upon the several Parts of the Story, and Prayers / fitted to the several Mysteries. / (*Rule.*) / *In Three Parts.* / (*Rule.*) / By *Jer. Taylor*, D.D. Chaplain in Ordinary to His Majesty. / (*Engraved ornament with the sentence 'Qui sequitur me non ambulat in tenebris'.*) / London, / Printed by *R. N.* for *Francis Ash*, and are to be sold at the three Pigeons in / S. *Pauls* Church-yard. 1649.

Quarto. Unsigned blank leaf; unsigned leaf (verso blank): title-page; a 1–b 1: dedication to Christopher, Lord Hatton (pages unnumbered); A 1 (verso blank): title-page to Part I; A 2–L 3: text of Part I (pages 1–165); L 4: blank; Unsigned leaf (verso blank): title-page to Part II; Unsigned leaf: dedication to Mary, Countess of Northampton; A a 1–L l 4: text of Part II (pages 1–168); ¶ 1 (verso blank): title-page to Part III; ¶ 2: dedication to Frances, Countess of Carbery; Aaa–Mmm 3: text of part III (pages 1–182); Mmm 4: blank; Nnn 1–Ooo 4: 'The Table'.

The title-page is in red and black.

Dd 1 (page 49–50 of Part II) is sometimes cancelled. In the original state the word 'uningenuious' occurs in line 27 of page 49; in the cancelled state this reads 'uningenious'. The correction was not followed in subsequent editions.

There are two states of the title-page:

A, as described.

B, in which the imprint reads 'London, / Printed by *R. N.* for *Francis Ashe.* 1649.'

The word 'London' is red in A and black in B.

Francis Ashe was a Worcester bookseller, and the shorter imprint may have been for books sold by himself, in his own shop, the other being for those sold by his London agent.

Second edition. The title-page reads the same as in the first edition, except that:

(i) It is described as in three parts 'with many additionals'.

(ii) Jeremy Taylor is described as 'chaplaine . . . to his late Majesty'.

(iii) The imprint reads '*London*, Printed by *James Flesher*, for *Richard Royston*, at the signe of the / Angel in *Ivie-lane*, 1653'.

Folio. * 1: blank; * (verso blank): title-page; * 3–* 5: dedication; * 6–C 2: Preface (pages unnumbered); C 3–C 4 (verso blank): The Contents; D 1 (verso blank): title-page to part I; D 2–X 2 (verso blank): text of part I (pages 3–207); Unsigned leaf (verso blank): title-page to Part II; three unsigned leaves, y–Mm 5: dedication and text of part II (pages 211–382); Mm 6 (verso blank): title-page to Part III; Nn 1–Eee 2: dedication and text of Part III (pages 385–568); Eee 3–Fff 3: The Table; Fff 4 (verso blank): A Catalogue of some Books Printed for Richard Royston.

The verso of d 6 is blank.

The 'additionals' to this edition consist of the quatrains on the engravings of the evangelists, and two Discourses, 'Of Baptism' and 'Of Baptizing Infants', which had already been printed separately (see No. 14).

This book was illustrated with a portrait of Jeremy Taylor by Lombart, and the following eleven plates by Faithorne:—Engraved title-page, The Annunciation, St. Matthew, St. Mark, St. Luke, The Marriage in Cana, St. John, The Betrayal, The Last Supper, The Agony in the Garden, The Ascension.

Third edition. 1657. A dedication to Alice Countess of Carbery was added before Book III, following that to her predecessor, Frances.

Four plates, probably by Faithorne, were added to this edition:— The Massacre of the Innocents, The Flagellation, Christ crowned with Thorns, The Crucifixion.

The dates on the engravings of the Evangelists are altered from 1653 to 1657.

A Hebrew prayer and its translation and a note about it are added at the end of Part I. The prayer is supposed to have been spoken by Christ at his baptism.

Later editions were issued, in a single book with Dr. William Cave's 'Lives . . . of the Apostles', as 'Antiquates Christianae'.

9. *A* / Funerall Sermon, / *Preached* / At the Obsequies of the Right Honble / and most vertuous Lady, / The Lady / Frances, / Countesse of *Carbery*: / Who deceased *October* the 9th. 1650. / at her House Golden-Grove / in *Carmarthen-Shire.* / (*Rule.*) / By Jer. Taylor, D.D. / (*Rule.*) / (*Woodcut device of a pediment.*) / (*Rule.*) / London, / Printed by *J. F.* for *R. Royston* at the Angel in Ivie-lane. / (*Short rule.*) /. M.DC.L.

The title-page is enclosed in a double rule.

Quarto. A 1 (verso blank): title-page; A 2: dedication to Lord Carbery; A 3–E 4: text (pages 1–36).

10. The Rule / and / Exercises / of / Holy Living. / *In which are described* / The Means and Instruments / of obtaining every Vertue, and the / Remedies against every Vice, and / Considerations serving to the / resisting all temptations. / Together with / Prayers containing the whole duty of / A Christian, and the parts of Devotion / fitted to all Occasions, and furnish'd / for all Necessities. / (*Rule.*) / (*Woodcut ornament of a rose, in a border of fleurs de lys.*) / London / Printed for *Richard Royston* at the / Angel in *Ivie-Lane.* MDCL.

12mo. ¶: blank; ¶ 2 (verso blank): engraved title-page by Vaughan; ¶ 3 (verso blank): title-page; ¶ 4–¶ 10, recto: dedication to the Earl of Carbery (pages unnumbered); ¶ 10, verso–¶ 12: The Table; A 1–S 1: text (pages 1–410); S 2–S 3 (verso blank): The Appendix; S 4 (verso blank): imprint, 'London, Printed by *R. Norton.* MDCL'.

There is an alternative imprint on the title-page reading, London / Printed for *Francis Ash*, Book- / Seller in Worcester. / MDCL.

I have been able to examine only three copies of Holy Living, my own copy, that in the Bodleian Library, and that in the BritishMuseum.

My own copy, which was given to William Wyatt by the author, has the Worcester imprint; page 273 is misnumbered 173.

The Bodleian copy has the Worcester imprint, but differs from mine in having the words 'In which are described', in roman instead of italic; page 273 is correctly numbered.

The British Museum copy, London imprint, lacks the appendix, but has the last page with the printer's name; as the book has been rebound it is impossible to say if the appendix was ever there. Since it contains prayers for the king (presumably Charles II), it may have been removed for political reasons. Page 273 is correctly numbered.

It may be that there should be two blank leaves at the beginning, not one, and that the engraved title-page is printed on a separate leaf.

Second edition 1651. There are two varieties.

A. The title-page is similar to the first edition, except for the addition of the words '*The second Edition*', and the ornament which is a thistle. A line of text is omitted at the top of page 120 (misnumbered 220). Page 317 is misnumbered 371.

B. The title-page is similar to A, except that there is a rose instead of a thistle; there are three variations:

1. London imprint, without the words 'second Edition'. This edition has sometimes been mistaken for the first.
2. London imprint, with the words 'seeond edition' (sic) added.
3. Worcester imprint and 'seeond edition'.

Some copies of this issue have page 317 misnumbered; in some it has been corrected. Some have the misprint on page 120; in some this leaf has been replaced by a cancel. The collation of these two issues is the same. Since B sometimes corrects the errors of A it is probably later.

In both issues of the second edition the prayers from the Appendix to the first edition are incorporated in the text, the word 'Ruler' being substituted for 'King'. Charles II had been defeated at Worcester.

The fourth edition, 'corrected with Additionals' was published in 1654. The word 'King' is restored, but I can find no 'Additionals'. Cromwell had become Protector and either Taylor or Royston may have thought that he was no longer worthy of being prayed for.

A folding plate was added to this edition, representing Taylor pointing the way to heaven (represented by God enthroned) and the flowery way to hell (represented by a demon in a monster's flaming mouth). The likeness of Taylor was a bad one, and it was re-engraved for the fifth edition (1656). The date on the engraved title-page was altered in each case (to 1654 and 1657).

I have not seen a third edition, and it may be that the fourth was so numbered because of there being two printings of the second.

A figure of God enthroned similar to that in the folding plate was added to the frontispiece to 'The Golden Grove' in 'Polemical Discourses' (see No. 24).

11. The Rule / and / Excercises / of / Holy Dying. / *In which are described* / The Means and Instruments / of preparing our selves, and others / respectively, for a blessed Death: / and the remedies against the evils / and temptations proper to the state / of Sicknesse. / *Together with* / Prayers and Acts of Vertue to be used by / sick and dying persons, or by others / standing in their Attendance. / *To which are added.* / Rules for the visitation of the Sick, and offices pro- / per for that Ministry. / (*Three-line Greek quotation.*) *Isoc. ad Demonic.* / London, / Printed for *R. Royston*, and are to be sold / at the Angel in *Ivy-Lane.* / MDCLI.

12 mo. A 1: blank; A 2: title-page; A 3–A 6, a 1–a 5: The Epistle Dedicatory to the Earl of Carbery (pages unnumbered); a 6–a 8: The Table; B 1–Q 2 (verso blank): text (pages 1–339); Q 3: advertisement of books by Taylor and Royston's imprint; Q 4: blank.

There is an engraved title-page by Lombard between A 1 and A 2, and a folding plate, by the same artist, usually between A 8 and B 1.

There are three variations of the imprint, as follows:—London, / Printed for *R. R.* and are to be sold by /:

   (i) *William Ballard* in *Corn-street* / *Bristoll.* 1651
   (ii) *Johu Courtuey* Bookseller in / *Salisbury.* 1651
   (iii) *Francis Ash*, Bookseller in / *Worcester.* 1651

In some copies page 169 is unnumbered.

Second edition, 1652. The title-page has been reset, but except for the date, the words 'The Second Edition' and slight variations it is the same as in the first edition. The first two sheets are signed ¶ and A, instead of A and a; the dedication is addressed 'To the Right Honourable . . . Earl of Carbery, Knight of the Honourable Order of the Bath' instead of 'Earl of Carbery, Baron of Emlin and Molingar; Knight etc.'; it is signed 'Jer. Taylor' instead of 'Taylor'; otherwise the second edition is a page for page reprint of the first.

A Welsh translation of 'Holy Living' and 'Holy Dying', was published in 1701 in London. It is by E. Wynn, and the title-page reads 'Rheal buchedd sanctaidd yn dangos y moddion a'r arfeu i ynnil pôb grâs . . . Llundain, 1701'.

12. XXVIII / Sermons / Preached at Golden Grove; / Being for the Summer half-year, / *Beginning on Whitsunday,* / and ending on the XXV. Sunday after / *Trinity.* / *Together with* / A Discourse of the Divine Institution, Necessity, Sacredness, / and Separation of the Office Ministeriall. / (*Rule.*) / By *Jer. Taylor,* D.D. / (*Engraved ornament as in No. 8.*) / *London,* / Printed by *R. N.* for *Richard Royston* at the Angel / in Ivie-Lane. 1651.

Folio. ¶ 1 (verso blank): title-page; ¶ 2–¶ 4, * 1–* 4: dedication to the Earl of Carbery (pages unnumbered); * 4: Titles of the Sermons; A 1– Ii 3: text (pages 1–378); Ii 4: blank; A 1 (verso blank): title-page to 'Clerus Domini'; A 2–E 4, recto: text (pages 1–55); E 4, verso: note, The Printer to the Reader.

Though it has separate pagination and signatures, 'Clerus Domini' is an essential part of the book. This is shown by the note on E 4 asking the reader's indulgence for errors 'in the impression of these Sermons, and the Discourse annexed'.

There is sometimes a leaf of errata, with over 100 corrections.

Second edition. 1655. The date and the ornament are changed, and the setting is slightly different; otherwise the title-page reads as in the first edition.

Folio. ¶ 1–Gg 4: as in the first edition; Gg 5 (verso blank): Latin epitaph on the Countess of Carbery, arranged in the form of a pillar; Gg 6–Ii 4, A 1–E 4: remainder of text and 'Clerus Domini'.

The Latin epitaph on Lady Carbery was first printed in this volume. Except for some in Greek, the errors in the errata leaf of the first edition were corrected in this edition.

Third edition. 1668. This appears, with separate signatures and pagination, as part of the third edition of 'Eniautos' (see No. 17). The Funeral Sermon was printed in 'Ten Sermons' (see No. 37), and accordingly, being omitted from this part, the title became 'XXVII Sermons etc.'

Lowndes mentions an octavo edition of 'Clerus Domini', printed separately in 1651. I have never seen a copy and there probably never was such an edition. It may be an erroneous reference to the folio edition.

13. A short / Catechism / for / The institution of Young Persons / in the / Christian Religion. / To which is added, / An Explication / of the / Apostolical Creed, / (*Rule.*) / Easie and useful for these Times. / (*Rule.*) / Composed for the Use of the / Schools in *South-Wales*. / (*Rule.*) / (*Three-line Greek quotation.*) Plato de legibus. / (*Three-line translation.*) / (*Rule.*) / *London*, Printed by *J. Flesher* for *R. Royston*, at / the Angel in *Ivy-Lane*. / 1652.

The title-page is enclosed in a double rule.

12 mo. A 1: blank; A 2 (verso blank): title-page; A 3–C 5, recto: text (pages 5–57); C 5, verso–C 6, recto: a Catalogue of books; C 6,

verso: imprint, '*London*: / Printed for *Richard Royston*, and are to be / sold by *William Ballard* Bookseller in / *Corn-street* in *Bristol*. / 1652.'

William Ballard was one of the provincial booksellers for whom copies of 'Holy Dying' were printed.

This book was reprinted as part of 'The Golden Grove': the main text as 'Credenda', and two of the prayers at the end under 'Postulanda'. There is one prayer which was not reprinted.

14. *A* / Discourse / of / Baptisme, / Its Institution, / and Efficacy upon all Believers. / (*Rule.*) / *Together with* / A Consideration / of the Practise of the Church / In / Baptizing Infants / of Beleeving Parents: / And the Practise justified / (*Rule.*) / By Jer. Taylor D.D. / (*Rule.*) / (*Greek quotation.*) / *Suffer little children to come unto me, and forbid them not*, &c. / (*Rule.*) / London, / Printed by *J. Flesher* for *R. Royston*, at the *Angel* in *Ivy-Lane.* / (*Short rule.*) / *MDCLII*.

Quarto. A 1 (verso blank): title-page; A 2: 'To the Reader'; B 1– I 2: text (pages 1–60).

Except for the preface, this pamphlet was reprinted in the second edition of 'The Great Exemplar' (see No. 8).

15. Two / Discourses / 1. Of { Baptisme, / Its Institution, and Efficacy upon / all Believers. / 2. Of { Prayer *Ex tempore*, / or / By pretence of the Spirit. / (*Rule.*) / By Jer. Taylor D.D. / (*Rule.*) / 1 Cor. 14. 32. (*Three-line Greek quotation, and Three-line translation.*) / (*Double rule.*) / London, / Printed by *J. Flesher* for *R. Royston*, at the *Angel* in *Ivy-Lane.* / (*Short rule.*) / MDCLIII.

Quarto. Unsigned leaf: blank; unsigned leaf (verso blank): title-page; . . . A 2–D 4: Text of 'Prayer Ex Tempore' (pages 1–30).

The description is of an imperfect copy in the British Museum. 'The Discourse on Baptisme' is entirely lacking, and the title-page to 'Prayer Ex Tempore'. The title-pages may have been removed when this composite volume was made. It consisted, presumably, of the first edition of the 'Discourse of Baptisme', then being reprinted in the second edition of 'The Great Exemplar', and the second edition of 'Prayer Ex Tempore'.

16. XXV / Sermons / Preached At / Golden-Grove: / Being for the Winter half-year, / Beginning on / *Advent-Sunday*, / untill / *Whit-Sunday.* / (*Rule.*) / By *Jeremy Taylor*, D.D. / (*Rule.*) / *Væ mihi si non Evangelizavero.* / (*Rule.*) / (*Woodcut design of an open book.*) / (*Rule.*) /

London, / Printed by *E. Cotes,* for *Richard Royston* at the Angel / in *Ivie-Lane.* M.DC.LIII.

The title-page is enclosed in a double rule.

Folio. A 1 (verso blank): title-page; A 2–A 5 (verso blank): dedication to the Earl of Carbery (pages unnumbered); A 6: titles of Sermons; B 1–Ff 1: text (pages 1–334); Ff 2 (verso blank): Errata.

By an error of pagination page 109 immediately follows page 100.

Second (?) edition. XXV sermons ... The Third Edition Corrected ... Printed by *E. Tyler* for *Richard Royston* ... 1668.

This, with separate signatures and pagination, is part of the third edition of 'Eniautos'. It is probably the second edition, the printer having thought mistakenly that a second edition was used to make up the second edition of 'Eniautos' (see No. 17).

17. *ΕΝΙΑΥΤΟΣ* / (*Rule.*) / *A* / Course / of / Sermons / for / All the Sundaies / Of the Year; / Fitted to the great Necessities, and for the supplying / the Wants of *Preaching* in many parts / of this Nation. / (*Rule.*) / *Together with* / A Discourse of the Divine Institution, Necessity, Sacredness, / and Separation of the Office *Ministeriall.* / (*Rule.*) / By Jer. Taylor D.D. / (*Rule.*) / (*Two-line quotation from Pindar.*) / —*Commune periclum* / *Omnibus, Una salus*— / (*Double rule.*) / *London.* / Printed for *Richard Royston* at the Angel in Ivie-lane, 1653.

The title-page is enclosed in a double rule.

Folio. This is a composite book. It consists of the title-page, 'XXV Sermons' and 'XXVIII Sermons', the former being bound in first. A double leaf, signed F–F 2, 'A Table to both the Volumes of Sermons', is bound in at the end.

Second edition. 1655. The title-page is the same as in the first edition, except for the slight variations, the date, and the words '*The Second Edition Corrected*'.

Folio. Title-page; first edition of 'XXV Sermons'; second edition of 'XXVIII Sermons'.

The corrections are in the second edition of 'XXVIII Sermons'.

A double leaf, signed Kk–Kk 2, 'A brief Table to both Volumes of Sermons', is bound in at the end of 'XXVIII Sermons'.

The third edition. 1668.

Folio. Portrait by Lombart; A 1 (verso blank): title-page; A 2 (verso blank): title-page to the third (second?) edition of 'XXV Sermons'; A 3–A 5 (verso blank): dedication; A 6: 'Titles of the 25 Sermons';

A 7: 'Titles of the 27 Sermons'; A 8: 'Titles of the 10 Sermons'; B 1–Y 5: text of 'XXV Sermons'; XXVII Sermons; X Sermons.

'A Prayer before Sermon' and 'A Prayer after Sermon', are printed after 'Titles of the 10 Sermons'. They were first printed here.

The folio edition of Rust's Funeral Sermon on Jeremy Taylor (see No. 56) is sometimes bound in at the end of this edition of 'Eniautos'.

18. The / Real Presence / and / Spirituall / of / Christ / in the / Blessed Sacrament / Proved / Against the Doctrine of / *Transubstantia-tion.* / (*Rule.*) / By *Jer. Taylor*, D.D. / (*Rule.*) / (*Four-line Latin quotation.*) S. Cyril. in Joh. l. 4. c. 14. / (*Two-line Latin quotation.*) S. August. l. 3. de doct. Christ. / (*Rule.*) / London, / Printed by *James Flesher*, for *Richard Royston* at the / Angel in Ivie-lane. 1654.

The title-page is in red and black.

Octavo. A 1 (verso blank): title-page; A 2–A 7, recto: The Epistle Dedicatory to the Bishop of Rochester (pages unnumbered); A 7, verso–A 8: The Contents; B 1–Z 6, recto: text (pages 1–347); Z 6, verso–Z 8 (verso blank): advertisement.

19. The / *Golden Grove* / or, / A Manuall / of / Daily *Prayers* and *Letanies*, Fitted to the dayes of the Weeke. / Containing a short Summary of / *What is to be* {/ Believed, Practised, Desired. / (*Rule.*) / Also / Festival Hymns, / According to the manner of / *The Ancient Church.* / (*Rule.*) / Composed for the Use of the Devout, especially / of Younger Persons; the Author of / *The Great Exemplar.* / (*Rule.*) / London, Printed by *J. F.* for *R. Royston*, at the / Angel in *Ivie-Lane.* / 1655.

12 mo. Unsigned leaf (verso blank): half-title; A 1 (verso blank): title-page; A 2–A 8: 'To The Pious and Devout Reader (pages unnumbered); B 1–I 2: text (pages 1–171); I 3–I 4: advertisements.

The versos of B 1, C 11, E 6, E 7, G 12, H 1, and I 2 are blank.

There are some copies with 'Ivi-lane' in the imprint instead of 'Ivie', and 'especiall' for 'especially'.

A folding plate by Hollar should be bound in at the beginning of the book. This represents a view of Golden Grove and the valley of the Towy, with an angel and child in the foreground, the former carrying a cross, the latter a dove. The angel is inscribed 'Dux Viae', the cross 'Coronata tides', and the dove 'Prudens Simplicitas'. In the copies I have seen 'tides' has been altered in MS. to 'fides'. The plate does exist in an early state without any lettering.

A list of errata is printed on the verso of A 8.

A second issue appeared in the same year. It is printed from the same type, and up to page 73 the text corresponds, line for line. After page 73 the setting is compressed so as to save two pages, and page 83 becomes page 81. From page 82 to the end the text, but for slight variations, possibly due to mishaps in moving the setting, corresponds again. The list of errata is omitted and the errors have been corrected. The alterations seem to have been made to avoid the clumsy arrangement of beginning the book with a single odd leaf and ending with four leaves. The arrangement of sheets is, accordingly, altered, and the collation is as follows:

A 1 (verso blank): half-title; A 2 (verso blank): title-page; A 3–A 9: To the . . . reader; A 10–H 10: text (pages 1–169); H 11–H 12: advertisements.

The British Museum has both issues, bound in a single volume, the first lacking the half-title, and the second, the folding plate. In each the date has been altered in a contemporary hand to 1654.

In the fourth edition, 1659, a fourth Hymn for Christmas Day was added, beginning 'Awake my soul and come away'.

20. (*Rule.*) / *Unum Necessarium* / (*Rule.*) / or, / The Doctrine and Practice / of / Repentance. / *Describing* / The Necessities and Measures of a / Strict, a Holy, and a Christian Life. / And / *Rescued from Popular Errors.* / (*Rule.*) / By *Jer. Taylor* D.D. / (*Rule.*) / (*Two-line Latin quotation.*) Tertullian de Pœnit. / (*Latin quotation.*) / (*Rule.*) / *London,* / Printed by *James Flesher* for *R. Royston*, at the Angel / in *Ivy-Lane.* 1655.

Octavo. A 1 (verso blank): engraved title-page by Lombart, representing the Good Shepherd; A 2 (verso blank): title-page; A 3– A 6: dedication to the Earl of Carbery (pages unnumbered); A 7– C 4: Preface (pages unnumbered); C 5–C 8: The Contents; D 1– Aaa 1: text (pages 1–690); Aaa 2–Aaa 4: The Table.

K 2, verso (page 100) is blank.

There is a list of errata on Aaa 1, verso (page 690).

There is a folding plate by Lombart of St. Peter and Mary Magdalen clutching a bleeding heart. This is usually inserted between C 8 and D 1.

The Bishop of Rochester objected so strongly to parts of this work when he read an early copy of it, that Taylor defended himself in a pamphlet 'A further Explication of The Doctrine of Original Sin' (see No. 21). This is usually bound up between pages 448 and 449, but I have seen copies of 'Unum Necessarium', untouched and in contemporary binding, without these extra leaves.

21. *A further* / Explication / of / The Doctrine / of / Original Sin, / (*Rule.*) / By *Jer. Taylor* D.D. / (*Double rule.*) / *London*, / Printed by *James Flesher* for *R. Royston*, at the Angel / in *Ivy-lane*, / 1656.

Octavo. [*hh* 1] (verso blank): title-page; [*hh* 2]–[*hh* 4]: dedication to the Bishop of Rochester (pages unnumbered); [hh 5]–[Ll 8]: text (pages [449]–[504]).

Page 504 is misnumbered 404.

At the foot of page 504 is a short list of errata.

This is hardly a separate book, but having been printed a year later than 'Unum Necessarium' it may exist separately in contemporary binding. Separate copies were probably sent to scandalized friends.

22. *Deus Justificatus.* / (*Rule.*) / Two / Discourses / of / *Original Sin,* / Contained in two Letters / To / Persons of Honour, / Wherein the question is rightly / stated, several objections answe- / red, and the truth further cleared / and proved by many arguments / newly added or explain'd. / (*Rule.*) / By *Jer. Taylor.* D.D. / (*Rule.*) / *London*, / Printed for *Richard Royston* 1656.

The title-page is enclosed in a double rule.

12mo. General title-page (verso blank); A 1 (verso blank): title-page, *Deus Justificatus,* / (*Rule.*) / Or, / A Vindication of the / glory of the Divine / Attributes in the / Question of / Original Sin. / Against the Presbyterian way of / Understanding it. / (*Rule.*) / By Jer. Taylor, D.D. / (*Rule.*) / *Lucretius.* / (*Two-line Latin quotation.*) / (*Rule.*) / *London*, / Printed by *R. N.* for *R. Royston* at the / Angel in *Ivie-Lane.* 1656.; A 2 (verso blank): Dedication to the Countess of Devonshire; A 3–A 7: Prefatory letter (pages 1–7); A 8–G 1, recto: text (pages 11–143); G 1, verso–G 2, recto: Author's postscript; G 2, verso–G 5: The Stationer's postscript; G 6, recto: advertisement; G 6, verso: errata; A 1 (verso blank): signed leaf A; A 2 (verso blank): title-page—An Answer to a Letter / Written by the R. R. / The Ld Bp of *Rochester.* / Concerning / The Chapter of *Original Sin,* / In the / *Unum Necessarium.* / (*Rule.*) / By Jer. Taylor D.D. / (*Rule.*) / (*Woodcut ornament.*) / *London*, Printed by *E. Cotes* for *R. Royston* / at the Angel in *Ivie-Lane,* 1656.; B 1–D 8: An Answer etc. (pages 1–64); D 8–D 12; The Bp of

Rochester's Letter (pages 65–72); E 1–F 8, recto: An Answer, etc. (pages 73–111); F 8, verso: An Advertisement to the Reader; F 9– F 10 (verso blank): Advertisement.

These tracts have different printers, and were probably issued separately. The first was reprinted in 'Polemical Discourses' (see No. 24), but not the second. The dedication was not reprinted, and, since it is sometimes lacking in the first edition, it may be that it was suppressed, the Countess of Devonshire not liking to have her name associated with an apparently heretical tract.

23. A / Discourse of the Nature, / Offices and Measures of / Friend- ship, / with / Rules of conducting it. / Written in answer to a Letter from / the most ingenious and vertuous / *M. K. P.* / (*Rule.*) / *By* J. T. D.D. / (*Rule.*) / (*Two-line Greek quotation.*) / Dion. orat. 1. de regno. / (*Rule.*) / *London,* / Printed for *R. Royston* at the Angel / in *Ivie-lane.* 1657.

The title-page is enclosed in a single rule.

Second title-page. To which are added / Two Letters written to per- / sons newly changed in their / Religion. / The first to a Gentle- woman sedu- / ced to the Roman Church, / The other to a person returning to the Church of *England.* / (*Rule.*) / *By* J. T. D.D. / Volo *solidum Perenne.*

The second title-page is enclosed in a single rule.

12 mo. Unsigned leaf (verso blank): first title-page; unsigned leaf (verso blank): second title-page; B 1–F 3, recto: text of 'Friendship' (pages 1–101); F 3, verso–F 4: Postscript; F 5–H 9: First Letter (pages 105–62); H 10–I 4: Second Letter (pages 163–76).

It may be that the two title-pages are printed on I 5 and I 6, and folded round.

M. K. P. is Mrs. Katharine Phillips, 'The Matchless Orinda'.

A second edition was published in 1657, called 'The Measures and Offices of Friendship' etc. The third edition was published in 1662.

In 1678 this book was reprinted with additions as 'B. Taylor's Opuscula' (see No. 40). The first letter was reprinted separately in London in 1687. It takes up one complete 12 mo sheet.

24. *ΣΥΜΒΟΛΟΝ ΗΘΙΚΟΠΟΛΕΜΙΚΟΝ.* / (*Rule.*) / Or A / Col- lection of Polemical / and / Moral Discourses. / (*Rule.*) / *By* Jer. Taylor *D.D.* Chaplain in Ordinary / to his late Majesty. / (*Rule.*) / S.

Bibliography. 313

Bartholomæus / (*Greek quotation.*) / (*Engraving by Lombart.*) / Ecce agnus
Dei qui tollit peccata Mundi / London / Printed for R. Royston 1657.

The last three lines are from the engraving, which had been
already used for the title-page to 'Unum Necessarium'. It has been
cut down, and the date has been altered.

Folio. A 1: engraved portrait by Lombart (or blank?); A 2 (verso
blank): title-page; A 3–A 6–a 1: dedication to Lord Hatton (pages
unnumbered); a 2–a 4 (verso blank): 'The Names of the several Books';
B 1–G 3: 'The Golden Grove'; Unsigned leaf—G 4–L 4: 'An Apology
for . . . Liturgy'; L 5–Bb 6: Episcopacy Asserted; Cc 1–Oo 4: 'The
Real Presence'; Oo 5–Kkk 1: 'The Liberty of Prophesying'; Kkk 2–
Nnn 3: 'Deus Justificatus'; Nnn 4–Ppp 3: 'A Discourse . . . of Friendship'; Ppp 4–Sss 4: 'Sermon on the Gunpowder-Treason'; Sss 6–Ttt 6:
'Two letters to Persons changed in their Religion'; unsigned leaf of
advertisements.

The pagination is continuous throughout the book, but the title-
pages and the preliminary matter to each part are not counted.

Hollar's plate is printed on the half-title of 'The Golden Grove'.
The words 'The Golden Grove', have been added above the representation of a castle, and the figure of God in heaven, copied from the folding plate in the 4th edition of 'Holy Living', has been added in the top
right-hand corner, apparently by another engraver.

Marshall's engraved title-page is printed as a frontispiece to 'The
Liberty of Prophesying'. It is re-engraved, a Greek text has been added,
and, at the foot of the plate, the words 'The second Edition enlarged.
1657'.

The matter printed for the first time in this book consists of the
dedication, and the extra matter in 'The Liberty of Prophesying', that
is, the refutation of the anabaptists and the concluding paragraph
(see No. 5).

25. A / Collection of offices / or / Forms of Prayer / in / Cases Ordinary
and Extraordinary. / *Taken out of the Scriptures and the ancient Litur-* /
gies of several Churches, especially / *the* Greek. / (*Rule.*) / *Together with* /
The Psalter or Psalms of *David*, according to / the Kings Translations; with Argu- / ments to the same. / (*Rule.*) / *S. Ignatius.* / (*Two-
line Greek quotation.*) / (*Rule.*) / *London*, / Printed by *J. Flesher* for *R.
Royston*, at the sign of / the Angel in *Ivy-lane*. 1658.

The title-page is in red and black.

Octavo. A 1, recto: half-title; A 1, verso: engraved frontispiece of Christ praying; A 2 (verso blank): title-page; A 3–C 6: The Preface; d 1–e 5: almanack etc. (similar to the Book of Common Prayer); e 6–e 7, recto: a table: 'A Table'; e 7, verso–e 8, recto: 'An Advertisement,' etc.; e 8, verso: note; B 1–x 8: text (pages unnumbered); A 1 (verso blank): title-page, as follows;—The Psalter: or Psalms of David, / After the King's Translation. / With Arguments to every Psalm. / (*Engraving of David.*) / *Te decet Hymnus.*; A 2–O 2: Text of the Psalms (pages unnumbered).

A 7 in the preface is a cancel in all copies that I have examined.

It is said that Jeremy Taylor was imprisoned in the Tower because the frontispiece has a representation of Christ praying. But since 'The Great Exemplar' of 1653 and 1657 had pictures of Christ in every sort of attitude it is probable that he had given some other offence. Possibly the close and indiscreet resemblance of this book to the prohibited Prayer Book was a cause of the trouble. As with many representations of Christ in books of this period the frontispiece is very often missing.

It is sometimes said that this is an enlargement of 'The Psalter of David' of 1644 (see No. 49). This is not so. The two books are entirely different.

26. The Worthy / Communicant / or / A Discourse of the Nature, Effects, and / Blessings consequent to the worthy / receiving of the / Lords Supper / And of all the duties required in order to / a worthy preparation: / Together / With the *Cases of Conscience* occuring in / the duty of him that *Ministers* and of him / that *Communicates*. / To which are added / Devotions fitted to every part of the / Ministration. / (*Rule.*) / By *Jeremy Taylor* D.D. *and Bishop Elect* of / *Down* and *Connor*. / (*Rule.*) / *London*, / Printed by *R. Norton* for *John Martin*, / *James Allestry*, and *Thomas Dicas* at the / *Bell* in *St. Pauls Churchyard*, 1660.

The title-page is enclosed in a double rule.

Octavo. Unsigned leaf (recto blank): engraved frontispiece; A 1 (verso blank): title-page; A 2–A 4: dedication to Marie, Princess of Great Britain, Dowager of Orange; A 5–A 8 (verso blank): the contents; B 1–Oo 8: text (pages 1–576).

Owing to a printer's error there is no sheet Dd, and page 417 immediately follows page 400.

There are two states of sheet Ee. In the earlier all the pages on one side of the unfolded sheet are misnumbered so that the pagination is as follows: 417, 394, 395, 420, &c. In the later state the pagination has been corrected and is normal.

In some copies page 380 is misnumbered 80.

In the following year there was an issue consisting of the original sheets and a new title-page dated 1661. I have seen a copy with a 1661 title-page and sheet Ee uncorrected.

The engraved frontispiece is by Hertochs and represents a church, with two angels kneeling before an altar, on which is the Sacrament. It is repeated in later editions of the book.

In 1674 and subsequently a previously unpublished sermon was printed with 'The Worthy Communicant' (see No. 39).

In 1642 Jeremy Dyke, a puritan divine, had published a book in London called 'A Worthy Communicant: or a Treatise shewing the Due Order of receiving the Sacrament of the Lords Supper'. The plagiary, if the similarity was not accidental, ended with the title-page; the two books have no more in common than can be accounted for by the subject. In 1683 another variation of the title appeared in 'The Unworthy Non-Communicant' by William Smythier, 'the Morning Lecturer at Saint Michael Cornhil'.

27. *Ductor Dubitantium,* / or / The Rule / of / Conscience / In all her general measures; / Serving as a great Instrument for the determination of / Cases of Conscience. / In Four Books. / By Jeremy Taylor, D.D. / Prov. 14. 8. / (*Greek quotation.*) / *London,* / Printed by *James Flesher,* for *Richard Royston* at the Angel / in Ivy-lane, 1660.

Folio, two volumes.

Vol. I. A 1: blank; A 2 (verso blank): title-page; A 3–A 4: dedication to Charles II; a–b 5 (verso blank): Preface (pages i–xxi); b 6–d 4: Table (pages xxiii–xl); B–Bbb 4 (verso blank): text (pages 1–559).

An engraved frontispiece is inserted between A 1 and A 2; it represents a hand writing on a heart above a book, called Liber Conscientiae.

There is an engraved portrait by Lombart, inserted as a frontispiece, or between d 4 and B.

Vol. II. *Ductor Dubitantium....* Cases of Conscience (*as in Vol. I*). / The Second Volume, / By Jeremy Taylor, D.D. / (*Rule.*) / Romans 13. 5. / (*Greek quotation.*) / (*Engraving with text as in 'Polemical Discourses' and 'Unum Necessarium'.*) / *London* printed for R. Roiston at yᵉ *Angell* / in Ivy lane. 1660.

The imprint is engraved.

Unsigned leaf (verso blank): title-page; A 1 (verso blank): title-page to the Third Book: A 2–Oo (verso blank): text of Book III (pages 3–433); OO 2 (verso blank): title-page to the Fourth Book; Oo 3–Xx 6 (verso blank): text of Book IV (pages 437–527); Yy–Aaa 3: The Table (pages 529–58); Aaa 4 (verso blank): list of errata and advertisement.

A small strip of additional errata, not part of the book, is sometimes pasted on Aaa 4. As in other books of the period it may be the printed matter cut off an entire page.

28. A Sermon / Preached at the *Consecration* of two / *Archbishops* and ten *Bishops*, / in the / Cathedral Church of S. *Patrick* in Dublin, / *January* 27. 1660. / (*Rule*.) / By *Jeremie Taylor* D.D. L^d. Bishop / of *Downe* and *Connor*. / (*Rule*.) / *Sal liquifit, ut condiat.* / (*Rule*.) / (*Rule*.) / *Dublin*, / Printed by *W. Bladen* for *John North* / Bookseller in Castle-street, / *Anno Dom.* 1661.

The title-page is enclosed in a border of ornaments.

Quarto. A 1: blank; A 2 (verso blank): title-page; A 3–A 4: 'To the Christian Reader'; B 1–G 4 (verso blank): text (pages 1–47).

There is a list of errata at the foot of A 4 verso.

A second edition was published in London by Royston in 1663.

29. A / Sermon / Preached / At the opening of the Parliament / of Ireland, / *May* 8. 1661. / Before the right Honourable / the Lords Justices, and the Lords / Spiritual and Temporal and / the Commons. / (*Rule*.) / By Jeremy Lord Bishop of / *Down* and *Connor*. / (*Rule*.) / *Salus in multitudine consulentium.* / (*Rule*.) / *London*, / Printed by *J. F.* for *R. Royston*, Bookseller to his / most Sacred Majesty, 1661.

The title-page is enclosed in a double rule.

Quarto. A 1 (recto blank): order to print; A 2 (verso blank): title-page; A 3–A 4–a 1–a 4: To the . . . Lords Spiritual and Temporal etc.; B 1–G 3 (verso blank): text (pages 1–45); G 4 (verso blank): advertisement.

30. Rules / and / Advices / To the / Clergy / Of the / Diocesse / of / *Down* and *Connor*: / For their Deportment in their Personal / and Publick Capacities. / *Given by the Bishop at the Visitation,* / *at* Lisne-garvey. / (*Rule*.) / *Dublin*, Printed by *John Crook*, Prin- / ter to the King's most Excellent Maje- / sty; and are to be sold by *John North*, / Book-seller in *Castle-Street*. 1661.

The title-page is enclosed in a double rule.

Octavo. A 1 (verso blank): title-page; A 2–C 8: text (pages 1–46).

Another edition of this book was printed in the same year; it is impossible to say which of the two is earlier. The other form is as follows:—

Rules . . . capacities (*as above, except that Connor is spelt Conner*). / (*Rule.*) / Given by Jer. Taylor, Bishop of / that Diocess, at the Visitation at *Lisne-* / *garvey.* / (*Rule.*) / *Dublin*, Printed by *John Crooke*, Printer / to the King's Most Excellent Maje- / sty, 1661.

The title-page is enclosed in a double rule.

Octavo. Collation as above.

The two books are printed from different settings. One is not a page for page reprint of the other, but in each the seven main headings appear on the same pages.

In 1663 a so-called second edition, in quarto, actually the third, was printed in London for Royston.

31. Via Intelligentiæ. / A / Sermom / Preached to the / University / of / Dublin: / Shewing by what means the Scho- / lars shall become most Learned and / most Usefull. / *Published at their desire.* / By the R. R. Father in God, Jeremy, Lord Bi- / shop of *Downe*, &c. and Vice-chancellour of / that University. / (*Rule.*) / *Ad majorem Dei gloriam.* / (*Rule.*) / *London*: / Printed for *R. Royston* Bookseller to the Kings most / Excellent Majesty, 1662.

The title is enclosed in a double rule.

Quarto. A 1: blank; A 2 (verso blank): Title-page; A 3–A 4, recto: 'To the reader'; A 4, verso: advertisement; B 1– I 4: text (pages 1–64).

32. A / Sermon / Preached in / Christ-Church, / *Dublin*: / at the Funeral / of / The most Reverend Father in God, / John, / Late Lord Arch-bishop of *Armagh*, / and / Primate of all *Ireland*: / with / *A succinct Narrative of his whole Life.* / (*Rule.*) / By / The Right Reverend Father in God, / Jeremy, / Lord Bishop of *Down* and *Connor.* / (*Rule.*) / *Dublin*, Printed by *John Crooke*, Printer to the / Kings Most Excellent Majesty, and are to be sold by / *Samuel Dancer* in *Castle-Street*, 1663.

Quarto. Unsigned leaf (verso blank): title-page; A–F 2: text (pages 1–44).

An edition was published in London in the same year. Since it was issued for the Irish bookseller who published several of Taylor's Dublin editions it may be that the two issues were simultaneous. The title-page and collation are as follows:

Title-page: as above except that the author is named in full 'Dr. Jeremy Taylor' etc., and the imprint reads, '*London*, / Printed for *John Crooke*, at the Sign of the / Ship in St *Paul's* Church-Yard. 1663.'

Quarto. A 1 (recto blank): Imprimatur; A 2 (verso blank): title-page; A 3–F 4: text (pages 1–44).

A 'Third Edition, Enlarged' was printed for Royston in the same year. The title-page reads, with slight variations, as in the first edition, except for Royston's imprint, and the words 'The third Edition, enlarged'. It is in quarto, and the collation is as follows:

A 1 (recto blank): imprimatur; A 2 (verso blank): title-page; A 3–I 3: text (pages 1–66); 14: blank.

A passage, from 'Everything', five lines from the bottom of page 12, to 'dead', page 14, line one, was first printed in this edition.

The 'Imprimatur' of Crooke's edition is dated Aug. 21. Royston's is dated Sept. 21.

33. The / Righteousness Evangelical / *Describ'd.* / The / Christians Conquest / Over the Body of Sin. / *Fides Formata,* / or / Faith working by Love. / (*Rule.*) / In Three / Sermons / preached at / Christ-Church, / *Dublin.* / (*Rule.*) / By the Right Reverend Father in God / *Jeremiah,* / Lord Bishop of *Down* and *Connor.* / (*Rule.*) / *The second Edition.* / (*Rule.*) / *London,* Printed for *R. Royston*, Book-seller to the / Kings most Excellent Majesty, 1663.

The title-page is enclosed in a double rule.

Quarto. A 1, recto: title-page; A 1, verso: Imprimatur; A 2: dedication to the Duchess of Ormonde; B 1–S 4: text (pages 1–136).

According to Lowndes the first edition was a 12mo printed at Dublin in 1663. I have not seen a copy, and have accordingly described this, the first London edition.

34. '*ΕΒΔΟΜᾺΣ* '*ΕΜΒΟΛΙΜΑῖΟΣ,* / A Supplement / to the / *ΕΝΙΑΥΤΟΣ,* / Or Course of Sermons for the whole year: / Being / Seven Sermons / Explaining the Nature of Faith, and Obedience; / in relation to God, and Ecclesiastical and Secular / Powers respectively. / (*Rule.*) / All that have been Preached and Published / (since the Restauration) / *By the Right Reverend Father in God,* / Jeremy, / *Lord Bishop of* Down *and* Connor. / *To which is adjoyned,* / His Advice to the Clergy of his Diocese. / (*Rule.*) / *London*: / Printed for *Richard Royston*, Bookseller to the Kings / most Sacred Majesty, 1663.

The title-page is enclosed in a double rule.

Quarto. This is a composite book.

Unsigned leaf (verso blank): general title-page; Three Sermons, second edition; Sermon preached at the Consecration, etc., first edition; Sermon preached at the opening of Parliament, first edition; Via Intelligentiae, first edition; Funeral sermon on the Archbishop of Armagh, third edition; Rules and Advices, 'second' (really third) edition.

A general index to the whole book is inserted after the dedication of 'Three Sermons'. This was printed on a single sheet with the title-page.

A second issued was published in 1664. But for the date, the general title-page and list of contents are a line for line resetting of those in the 1663 issue.

This book naturally varies and the description given will not necessarily apply to all copies. The British Museum copy for instance, which lacks 'Rules and Advices', has the second edition of the Sermon preached at the opening of Parliament. Sometimes the collection is found without a general title-page. An engraving of the royal arms may be bound in as a frontispiece. This, with another engraving of Charles II in his robes, was freely used at this period for sermons preached on state occasions, and the latter may sometimes be bound in with this book. Neither would be in any way an essential part of the book.

35. *ΧΡΙΣΙΣ ΤΕΛΕΙΩΤΙΚΗ.* / A / Discourse / of / Confirmation. / (*Rule.*) / By / Jeremy *Lord Bishop of* Down. / (*Rule.*) / Acts 19. 2. / (*Greek quotation.*) / (*Rule.*) / *London*, / Printed for *Richard Royston*, Book-seller / to His most Sacred Majesty. / (*Short rule.*) / M DC LXIV.

Octavo. A (recto blank): engraved portrait; A 2 (verso blank): title-page; A 3–A 8–a 1–a 3 (verso blank): dedication to the Duke of Ormonde; a 4: The Contents; B–L 4 (verso blank): text (pages 1–151).

36. A / Dissuasive / from / Popery / To the People of / Ireland. / (*Rule.*) / By the Right Reverend Father in God / *Jeremy Taylor*, D.D. / Lord Bishop of *Down* and *Connor*. / (*Rule.*) / Printed at *Dublin* by *John Crook*, Printer to the / Kings most Excellent Majesty: / And Reprinted at *London* for *Tho. Johnson*, at / the *Key* in St. *Pauls* Church-Yard, 1664.

The title-page is enclosed in a double rule.

Quarto. A 1 (recto blank): imprimatur; A 2 (verso blank): title-page; A 3–A 4–a 1–a 4 (verso blank): Preface; B 1–Z 4 (verso blank): text (pages 1–173).

I have not been able to find a copy of the Dublin edition.

37. *ΔΕΚᾺΣ 'ΕΜΒΟΛΙΜΑῖΟΣ,*/ A / Supplement / to the /*'ΕΝΙΑΥΤΟΣ* Or Course of Sermons for the whole Year: / Being / Ten Sermons / Explaining the Nature of Faith, and Obedience, / in relation to God, and the Ecclesiastical and / Secular Powers respectively. / *(Rule.)* / All that have been Preached and Published / (since the Restauration) / By the Right Reverend Father in God / *Jeremy* Lord Bishop of *Down* and *Connor.* / With / His Advice to the Clergy of his Diocess. / *(Rule.)* / *London,* / Printed for *R. Royston* Book-seller to the Kings Most Ex- / cellent Majesty. 1667.

The title-page is enclosed in a double rule.

Folio. A 1: title-page; A 2–E 5: preliminary matter (pages unnumbered) and text of 'Three Sermons, 1667' (pages 1–45); E 6–G 5, recto: Consecration sermon, 1666 (pages 47–69); G 5, verso: order to print; G 6–I 5: Sermon at the Opening of Parliament, 1666 (pages 70–93); I 6–M 1: Via Intelligentiae, 1666 (pages 95–121); M 2–O 2: Funeral Sermon on the Archbishop of Armagh, 1666 (pages 123–47); O 3–Q 2: Funeral Sermon on Lady Carbery, 1666 (pages 149–72); Q 3–T 1: The Whole Duty of the Clergy, 1666 (pages 171–206): T 2–U 2: Rules and Advices, 1667 (pages 207–19).

The versos of the following leaves are blank:—A 1, A 2, C 2, E 5, F 2, G 6, I 5, I 6, M 1, M 2, O 2, O 3, O 5, and U 2.

Each part has a separate title-page, and the dates of these vary between 1666 and 1667 as shown.

Sermons IX and X, 'The Whole Duty of the Clergy', were first printed here. The separate title-page is as follows:—

The / Whole Duty / of the / Clergy / in / Life, Belief, / and / Doctrine: / Described, and pressed effectually upon their Con- / sciences in Two Sermons on *Tit.* 2. 7, 8. / Preached in so many several / Visitations. / *(Rule.)* / By the Right Reverend Father in God / *Jeremy* Lord Bishop of *Down* and *Connor.* / *(Double rule.)* / *London,* / Printed for *R. Royston* Bookseller to the Kings Most Ex- / cellent Majesty. 1666.

The title-page is enclosed in a double rule and is signed Q 3.

Since Taylor is not described on the title-page as 'Late lord bishop etc.', this book was presumably printed, if not published, while he was alive, and precedes the 'Second Part of the Dissuasive from Popery'.

38. The Second Part / of the / Dissuasive / from / Popery: / In Vindication of / The First Part, / And further / Reproof and Conviction / of the / Roman Errors. / (*Rule.*) / By *Jer. Taylor* Chaplain in Ordinary to King *Charles* / the First, and late Lord Bishop of *Downe* and *Conner*. / (*Rule.*) / *Curavimus Babylonem & non est Sanata.* / (*Rule.*) / *London*, / Printed for *R. Royston*, Bookseller to the Kings most / Excellent Majesty, at the Angel in S. *Bartholomew's* / Hospital, MDCLXVII.

The title-page is enclosed in a double rule.

Quarto. Unsigned leaf (verso blank): title-page; Unsigned leaf: recto, 'A Table of the Sections', verso, imprimatur; A 1–K 2 (verso blank): The Introduction (pages unnumbered); A 1–Oo 4 (verso blank): text of Book I (pages 1–295); A 1–U 4 (verso blank): text of Book II (pages 1–159).

The two preliminary unsigned leaves, and K 1 and K 2 of the introduction are a single sheet folded round the rest of the introductory matter.

39. The worthy Communicant . . . Ministration (*but for slight variations, as in No. 26*) / To which is added a Sermon, never Printed / with the Folio Volume of Sermons. / (*Rule.*) / By / *Jeremy Taylor*, D.D. / and late Lord Bishop of *Down* and *Connor*. / (*Rule.*) / *London*, / Printed by *T. N.* for *John Martyn*, at the *Bell* / in St. *Pauls* Church yard, 1674.

The title-page is enclosed in a double rule.

Octavo. A 1 (verso blank): engraved title-page as in No. 26; A 2 (verso blank): title-page; A 3–Dd 7: The Worthy Communicant (12 unnumbered pages, and pages 1–414); Dd 8: blank; Ee 1–Gg 8: *A Sermon Preached at the Funeral of that Worthy Knight Sir* George Dalston *of* Dalston *in* Cumberland, September 28. 1657 (pages 415–62).

'The Worthy Communicant' in this form was reprinted several times during the seventeenth century.

40. B. Taylor's / *Opuscula.* / (*Rule.*) / The / Measures of Friendship. / With / Additional Tracts. / *To which is now Added,* / His *Moral Demonstration*, proving that / the Religion of *Jesus Christ* is from *God.* / Never before Printed in this Volume. / (*Engraved ornament of two angels among clouds holding an open book, with a hand above writing.*) /

London, Printed for *Rich. Royston*, / Bookseller to His most Sacred Majesty, 1678.

12mo. A 1 (recto blank): engraved portrait; A 2 (verso blank): title-page; A 3: advertisement; A 4: the contents; B 1–E 1: Text of 'Friendship' (pages 1–74); E 2 (verso blank); Title, 'Five / Letters / More, To / Persons / Changed, and Tempted to a Change / *in their* / *Religion.*' / (*Rule.*) / By the same Author. / (*Rule.*) / E 3–H 2 (verso blank): text of the five letters (pages 77–147); H 3 (verso blank): Title to 'A Discourse Proving that the Christian Religion is from God'; H 4: preface by 'A. B.' addressed to Royston; H 5–K 8 (verso blank): text of the 'Discourse' (pages 153–207).

This book is a reprint, with additions, of 'The Offices and Measures of Friendship'. Letters III, IV, and V were first printed here. The 'Moral Demonstration' is reprinted from 'Ductor Dubitantium'.

41. Christ's Yoke / an / Easy Yoke, / And yet, / *The Gate to Heaven a Strait Gate.* / In two excellent / Sermons, / well worthy the serious perusal of / the strictest Professors. / (*Rule.*) / By a Learned and Re- / verend Divine. / (*Rule.*) / Heb. 11. 4. / *Who being dead, yet speaketh.* / (*Rule.*) / *London*: / Printed for *F. Smith*, at the Elephant and Castle / near the Royal Exchange in *Cornhil*. 1675.

Octavo. A 1 (recto blank): portrait; A 2 (verso blank): title-page; A 3–A 4, recto: To the Reader; A 4, verso: advertisement; B 1–D 6 (verso blank): Text of 'Christ's Yoke etc.' (pages 1–43); D 7– G 4, recto: Text of 'The Gate to Heaven etc.' (pages 45–87); G 4, verso, two unsigned leaves: 'A Table of the Contents'.

These are apparently two early sermons of Jeremy Taylor. The text of them, but in a different form, had been already published in 'The Great Exemplar'.

42. On / The Reverence / Due to the Altar, / By / Jeremy Taylor, D.D., / Formerly Bishop of Down and Connor. / Now first printed from the original manuscript in the library of / Queen's College, Oxford. / Edited by the / Rev. John Barrow, M.A., / Fellow of Queen's College. / Oxford, / John Henry Parker; / and 377, Strand, London. / M DCCC XLVIII.

The title-page is enclosed in a single rule.

Quarto. A 1 (verso blank): half-title; A 2: title-page, with imprint on verso; A 3–B 4 (verso blank): Preface (pages v–xv); B 1–H 3 (verso blank): text (pages 1–53); H 4–I 4 (verso blank): Appendix (pages 55–63); single leaf: facsimile of a page of the MS.

The book was issued cut, in cloth, with the title stamped in gilt on the front cover.

43. Miscellanies / of / The Fuller Worthies' Library. / (*Short Rule.*) / The / Poems / and / Verse-Translations / of the / Right Rev. Jeremy Taylor, D.D. / Lord Bishop of Down, Connor, and Dromore. / For the / First Time Collected and Edited / after the author's own text: / with / Introduction. / By the / Rev. Alexander B. Grosart, / St. George's, Blackburn, Lancashire. / Printed For Private Circulation. / 1870. / 156 copies only.

Foolscap 8vo. Unsigned leaf: title-page; Unsigned leaf: Contents; A 1–D 1: introduction, text, notes (pages 5–66).

The book was issued in blue printed wrappers. Being intended to make a single book with other pamphlets under the title of 'Miscellanies' there is separate pagination, 61–122, at the foot of each page.

FIRST EDITIONS OF BOOKS TO WHICH JEREMY TAYLOR CONTRIBUTED

44. Choice Forms of Prayer, by severall Reverend and Godly Divines, used by them both before and after Sermon. 1651.

Heber mentions this book, and reprints two prayers used, and presumably composed, by Jeremy Taylor. I have not been able to find a copy.

45. ΘΑΝΑΤΑΛΟΓΙΑ, / seu / De Morte / Dissertatio; / In quâ, / Mortis Natura, Causæ, Mobili- / tas, Remoræ & Remedia pro- / ponuntur; ac variæ de Cadavere / & Animâ seperatâ contro- / versiæ enodantur. / (*Rule.*) / *Authore* / Johanne Stearne, Medicinæ Doctore / & Professore Publico in Universitate / Dubliniensi. / (*Rule.*) / *Quotidiè morior*. 1. Corinth. 15. 31. / (*Rule.*) / Dublinii, / Typis *Gulielmi Bladen*, & prostat ve- / nalis apud *Georgium Sawbridg*, sub / signo Bibliorum, justa *Fleetbridg*, / Londini, MDCLIX.

The title-page is enclosed in a border of ornaments.

Octavo. (a 1)–(a 6) recto: title-page and preliminary matter; (a 6) verso–(a 7) recto: Latin letter from Jeremy Taylor; (a 7)–(a 8): remainder of preliminary matter; A 1–S 8: text (pages 1–288); T 1–T 4: Index.

46. A Discourse of / Praying / with the / Spirit, / And with the / Understanding. / Where / of {Extemporary / Premeditate / Set Forms of} Prayer. / Preached in two Sermons at Hillsborough / *Anno* 1659. / (*Rule.*) / By *Henry Leslie* (maugre all Antichristian oppo- / sition) Bishop of *Down* and *Conner*. / (*Rule.*) / And now published for the Redresse of the great abuse of / Prayer in that Diocesse, / whereof he had, / and ought to have a Charge. / *Whereunto is annexed* / A Letter of Jer. Taylor, D.D. / Concerning the same Subject. / Eccles. 5. 2. / (*Three-line English quotation.*) / (*Rule.*) / London, / Printed for *John Crooke*, and are to be sold at / the Ship in St. *Pauls* Church-Yard. 1660.

Quarto. a 1 (verso blank): title-page; a 2–a 4: Letter by Jeremy Taylor (pages unnumbered); A 1–E 4: text (pages 1–36).

47. A / Second Part / of / *The Mixture* / of / Scholasticall Divinity, / with / Practical, / in several / Tractates: / Wherein some of the most difficult Knots in Divinity / are untyed, many dark places of Scripture clear- / ed, Sundry Heresies and Errors refuted. / (*Rule.*) / By *Henry Jeanes*, Minister of Gods Word at *Chedzoy* in *Somersetshire*. / (*Rule.*) / Whereunto are annexed, / Several Letters of the same Author, and Dr. / *Jeremy Taylor*, / concerning Original Sin. / Together with / A Reply / unto Dr. *Hammonds* Vindication of his / grounds of *Uniformity* from / *1 Cor.* 14. 40 / (*Rule.*) / *Oxford*, Printed by *H. Hall*, Printer to the University, / for *Thomas Robinson*. 1660.

The title-page is enclosed in a double rule.

Quarto. a 1–b 4: title-page and preliminary matter; B 1–Ccc 2: separate title-page (Oxford, 1659) and text etc. of 'A Treatise concerning the Indifference of Human Action'; Ccc 3, recto: separate title-page of 'Certaine Letters of Henry Jeanes . . . and Dr. Jeremy Taylor, Oxford, 1660': Ccc 3, verso; quotation from Jeremy Taylor; Ccc 4 (recto blank): 'To the unprejudiced reader'; Ddd 1–Hhh 4: 'Letters of the Author and Dr. Jeremy Taylor To Mr. C. T.' (pages 1–48); A 1–M 2: separate title-page and text etc. of 'Uniformity . . . A Reply unto Dr. Hammond's Vindication, Oxford. 1660.'

Two letters of Jeremy Taylor were published in this book.

48. *Miscellanea Sacra*: / or, / Poems / on / Divine & Moral / sub- jects. / (*Rule.*) / Vol. I. / (*Rule.*) / Collected by *N. Tate*, Servant to His / Majesty. / (*Rule.*) / *'Tis not that which* First *we love,* / *But what*

Bibliography.

Dying we approve. / *Mr.* Waller. / *(Rule.)* / *London*: / Printed for *Hen.*
Playford in the *Temple-Change*, / in *Fleetstreet*. MCDXCVI.

The title-page is enclosed in a double rule.

Octavo. Unsigned leaf: frontispiece by Gribelin; A 1 (verso blank):
title-page; A 2–A 4 (verso blank): dedication; A 5–A 8: preface;
B 1–K 6: text (pages 1–140); K 7–K 8: The Contents.

On page 11 is 'Job's Curse', and on page 29 'The Penitent', both by
Jeremy Taylor. 'Job's Curse' had never been printed before; 'The
Penitent' is from 'The Golden Grove'.

In most copies pages 58–9 have been cancelled, a Hymn by 'H. W.'
being substituted for 'A Paraphrase of the Third Psalm, by Mr
Wright'.

There was no second volume, and in 1698 the sheets of the first
edition were reissued with a new title-page as 'The Second Edition,
with Additions of Several Poems and Meditations in Prose'.

The poems were added on a half sheet between the preface and the
text. 'The Meditations' were printed on a single sheet, added at the
end; it consists of a title-page, six meditations, and a blank page.

BOOKS OF DOUBTFUL AUTHORSHIP WHICH HAVE BEEN ATTRIBUTED TO JEREMY TAYLOR

49. *The* / Psalter / of / David / with / Titles and Collects accor- / ding
to the matter of each / Psalme. / *(Woodcut ornaments.)* / Oxford, /
Printed by *Leonard Litchfield*, Printer to / *the University*. 1644.

The title-page is enclosed in a double rule.

Octavo. Unsigned leaf: engraved frontispiece by Vaughan; * 1
(verso blank): title-page; * 2–** 2: The Preface (pages unnumbered);
A–Bb 4: text (pages 1–392).

There is a summary before and a prayer after each psalm. See
No. 50.

50. Devotions / for the / Helpe and assistance / Of All / *Christian*
People: / In all occasions and necessities. / *(Rule.)* / *(Woodcut ornament.)* /
(Rule.) / Printed in the Yeare, / 1644.

The title-page is enclosed in a double rule.

A 1 (verso blank): title-page; A 2–D 8 (verso blank): text (pages
1–63). In the copy examined the title-page is a cancel.

In 1646 this and 'The Psalter of David', were printed in London, in one volume with a single title-page. The book was advertised as by 'The Right Honourable Chr. Hatton', until, in 1672, Royston published the 8th edition with Taylor's name, as author, on the title-page. Antony Wood, who is an exceedingly unreliable authority, attributed the book to Taylor. Heber accepted it and Eden rejected it 'with an understood probability that Taylor gave large assistance towards it'. The internal evidence, of style, thought and piety, is strongly in favour of Taylor. The plan was probably Hatton's, but I believe the book to have been written almost entirely by Taylor.

51. A / Discourse / of / Auxiliary Beauty. / Or / Artificiall Hansomenesse. / In point of / Conscience / *Between* / Two *Ladies.* / (*Engraved ornament, as in the first edition of 'The Great Exemplar'.*) / Printed for *R: Royston,* at the Angel in *Ivie-* / *Lane,* 1656.

Octavo. A 1 (verso blank): title-page; A 2–A 4, recto: 'The Publishers to the Ingenious Reader'; A 4, verso: 'The Objections contained in this Book'; B 1–O 4: text (pages 1–200).

There should be an errata slip (possibly an entire page which has usually been cut down).

The book was reprinted in 1662 as 'A Discourse of Artificial Beauty ... with some Satyrical Censures on the Vulgar Errors of these Times'. This edition has a frontispiece of the ladies discoursing. 'Satyrical Censures' is an imitation of Sir Thomas Browne; it was first published in 1659. A third edition of 'Auxiliary Beauty' was published in 1692.

Antony Wood attributed this book to Taylor. According to Heber the 1662 and 1692 editions were published as by 'J. T. D.D.', and he is slightly puzzled that an edition should have been apparently assigned to Taylor during his life. But the copies of these later editions which I have seen are anonymous; Heber may have been speaking by hearsay of a copy in which the initials were added in MS. Both Heber and Eden rejected this book. The style, neither of preface nor of text, suggests that Taylor is the author of any part of it.

In the British Museum copy of the 1692 edition a contemporary MS. note assigns 'The following Frothy Metaforical Book' to Gauden.

52. The / Ephesian / Matron / (*Rule.*) / (*Two-line Latin quotation.*) / Juvenal. Satyr. 6. / (*Rule.*) / (*Ornaments.*) / (*Rule.*) / *London,* / Printed for *Henry Herringman* at th / *Anchor* in the Lower Walke in / the New Exchange. 1659.

12mo. A 1 (verso blank): title-page; A 2–A 9 (verso blank): A Letter concerning the Ephesian Matron; To a person of Honour; A 10–F 10: text (pages 1–124); F 11–F 12: blank.

Antony Wood's copy is in the Bodleian Library. It is bound up with the second edition of 'Friendship', and another book. He made an index in which he wrote '1. The Ephesian Matron—, by Dr Jer. Taylor. 2. The Measures & Offices of Friendship by the same hand—'.

The book is a short romance expanded from the story in Petronius. Any one at all familiar with Taylor's work can see at once that he was not the author. He had used the story in 'Holy Dying', and Wood may have imagined that this was a reprint.

53. *Christian Consolations* / Taught from / Five Heads / In / Religion / i. *Faith.*} {iii. *The Holy Spirit.* / ii. *Hope*} {iv. *Prayer.* / v. *The Sacraments.* / (*Rule.*) / Written by a Learned Prelate. / (*Rule.*) / Isaiah 40. 1, 2. / (*Six-line quotation.*) / (*Rule.*) / *London*, / Printed for *R. Royston*, Bookseller to his / most Excellent Majesty, 1671.

The title-page is enclosed in a double rule.

12mo. A 1 (verso blank): title-page; A 2–A 5, recto: 'To the Reader'; A 5, verso–A 6: The Contents of the Chapters; B 1–B 3 (verso blank): The Introduction; B 4–L 5, recto: text (pages 1–219); L 5, verso–L 6 (verso blank): advertisement.

This was accepted by Heber and rejected by Eden.

54. Contemplations / of the / State of Man / in this / Life, / and in / That which is to come. / (*Rule.*) / (*Latin quotation.*) / By *Jeremy Taylor*, D.D. and / late Lord Bishop of *Down* and *Connor*. / (*Rule.*) / *London:* / Printed for *John Kidgell* at the *Golden-Ball*, near / *Grays-Inn-Gate*, in *Holborn*. 1684.

The title-page is enclosed in a double rule.

Octavo. Unsigned leaf: engraved portrait; unsigned leaf (verso blank): title-page; A 1–A 2, recto: 'To the Reader', Signed B. Hale; A 2, verso: 'To the Reader', signed Robert Harris; A 3–A 4 (verso blank): The Contents; B 1–R 4 (verso blank): text (pages 1–247).

Pages 241–7 (R 1–R 4) are misnumbered 297–303. Of these, pages 297–300 (R 1–R 2) are printed in smaller type to that in the rest of the book.

In 1740 a Welsh translation was published. The title is 'Ystyriaethau o Gyflwr Dyn yn y Bywyd Hwn'. Another Welsh translation was published in 1825.

In 1848 Archdeacon Churton printed a tract showing that this book was a compilation of extracts from 'Diferencia de lo Temporal y Eterno', by Eusebius Nieremberg, a Spanish Jesuit. A translation of this by Sir Vivian Mullineux was published in 1672 as 'A Treatise of the Difference betwixt the Temporal and Eternal'. Churton affirms that 'Contemplations' was compiled from this translation; but the parallel passages which he quotes have no more resemblance than a common origin might account for. He also says that Taylor can have had nothing to do with it, for he knew no Spanish; but Latin and Italian translations were in print during his lifetime.

My own opinion is that the book, which is said in the preface to have been found among his papers, was a collection of select passages translated by Taylor from a foreign translation.

OBITUARY PAMPHLETS

55. A / Pandarique Elegie / Upon the death of the R. R. Father in God / Jeremy, / Late Lord Bishop of *Doune*, / *Connor, and Dromore*. / (*Rule*.) / *By Le* Mathews *A. M. à sacr. domest*. / (*Rule*.) / (*Woodcut ornaments*.) / (*Rule*.) / *Dublin*, Printed by *John Crook*, Printer to the Kings / most Excellent Majesty, and are to be sold by *Samuel* / *Dancer*, Bookseller in *Castlestreet*, 1667.

Quarto. The description is from the British Museum copy. The collation seems peculiar.

A 1 (verso blank): title-page; A 2–A 3, B 1–B 3: text (pages 5–14).

A 2 is numbered as pages 5–6. Probably there should be a blank leaf before the title-page, and one after B 3, the signatures being inaccurate.

56. A / Funeral / Sermon, / Preached at the / Obsequies / Of the / Right Reverend Father in God, / Jeremy / Lord Bishop of Down; / Who deceased at Lysburne, / *August* 13th 1667. / (*Rule*.) / By Dr. *George Rust*, / Dean of *Connor*. / (*Rule*.) / *London*, / Printed by *E. Tyler* for *Richard Royston* Book-seller to / the King's most Excellent Majesty, 1668.

The title-page is enclosed in a double rule.

Quarto. A 1, recto: title-page; A 1, verso: Imprimatur; A 2–F 2, recto: text (pages 1–41); F 2, verso: advertisement.

A folio edition was published by Royston in the same year. It has no 'Imprimatur', and may have been intended only to be bound up with the third, 1668, edition of Eniautos.

CONTROVERSIAL ANSWERS TO JEREMY TAYLOR

Lowndes mentions a folio broadside 'Toleration Tolerated, or Bp. Taylor's Opinion concerning Toleration of Religion, with some Observations thereon. London'. I have never seen a copy of this, which must refer to 'The Liberty of Prophesying'. The Chapter on Anabaptists in 'The Liberty of Prophesying', which Taylor answered himself in the second edition, was attacked in 'Anabaptism Routed . . . together with a particular answer to all that is alledged in favour of the Anabaptists by D^r. Jer. Taylor, in ..! The Liberty of Prophesying . . . by John Reading B.D. . . . London, 1655'. It is printed in quarto.

'The Liberty of Prophesying' was attacked, as a plea for toleration, in 'A Free Disputation against Pretended Liberty of Conscience, Tending to Resolve Doubts Moved by . . . Dr. Jer. Taylor . . . by Samuel Rutherfurd . . . London, 1649'. It was this book which Milton attacked in his poem 'On the new forcers of Conscience under the Long Parliament', in the words 'a classic hierarchy Taught ye by meer A. S. and Rotherford'.

Jeremy Taylor's opinions on original sin were attacked by Henry Jeanes (see No. 47) and in a book, published in quarto in London in 1658, called 'Vindiciae Fundamenti', by Nathaniel Stephens, Minister of Fenny Drayton in Leicestershire.

'The Dissuasive from Popery' was answered in 'Diaphanta, or Three Attendants on Fiat Lux . . . 1665'. The sheets of this were reissued in 1671, with a new title-page, as 'Three Letters declaring the strange odd Proceedings of Protestant Divines . . . by J. V. C.'

In the 'Second Part of the Dissuasive from Popery' Jeremy Taylor answers 'The fourth Appendix to J. S. his Sure Footing; intended against the general way of procedure in the Dissuasive from Popery'. I do not know what book he refers to.

PRIVATE LETTERS OF JEREMY TAYLOR

There are three important books in which letters from Jeremy Taylor were published.

(1) Evelyn's Diary, 1818, and subsequent editions in which his correspondence with Evelyn was published. It was not published complete in the first edition.

(2) Heber's Life. This, which prefaced the collected edition of 1822 and appeared separately in 1823, contains the correspondence with Evelyn and a number of other letters.

(3) Heber's Life, a new edition, edited by Charles Page Eden. 1851. Many important letters were published by Eden in the form of footnotes to the 'Life'.

BIOGRAPHIES OF JEREMY TAYLOR

Taylor is mentioned in 'Sadducismus Triumphatus', 1681, by Joseph Glanvill, as advising a man how to speak to a ghost. A short account of him is given in Daniel Lloyds 'Memoirs of the Loyalists', 1668, and in Clement Barksdale's 'Remembrances of Excellent Men', 1670. Rust's Funeral Sermon contains a short life of Taylor (see No. 56). Later Biographies of Taylor are as follows:—Wheeldon, 1793; Bonney, 1815; Heber, 1822; Wilmott, 1847; Eden's edition of Heber, 1851; Duychinck, New York ,1860; Barry, 1877; Worley, 1904; Gosse, 1904.

Of these, though Gosse is valuable, Eden's edition of Heber remains the best.

PRINTED IN GREAT BRITAIN AT THE UNIVERSITY PRESS, OXFORD
BY JOHN JOHNSON, PRINTER TO THE UNIVERSITY